NEWSLETTERS FROM THE ARCHPRESBYTERATE OF GEORGE BIRKHEAD

NEWSLETTERS FROM THE ARCHPRESBYTERATE OF GEORGE BIRKHEAD

edited by

MICHAEL C. QUESTIER

CAMDEN FIFTH SERIES
Volume 12

CAMBRIDGE
UNIVERSITY PRESS

FOR THE ROYAL HISTORICAL SOCIETY
University College London, Gower Street, London WC1E 6BT
1998

Published by the Press Syndicate of the University of Cambridge
The Edinburgh Building, Cambridge CB2 2RU, United Kingdom
40 West 20th Street, New York, NY 10011–4211, USA
10 Stamford Road, Oakleigh, Melbourne 3166, Australia

© Royal Historical Society 1998

First published 1998

A catalogue record for this book is available from the British Library

Library of Congress cataloguing in publication data

ISBN 0 521 65260 x hardback

SUBSCRIPTIONS. The serial publications of the Royal Historical Society, *Royal Historical Society Transactions* (ISSN 0080–4401), Camden Fifth Series (ISSN 0960–1163) volumes and volumes of the Guides and Handbooks (ISSN 0080–4398) may be purchased together on annual subscription. The 1998 subscription price (which includes postage but not VAT) is £50 (US$80 in the USA, Canada and Mexico) and includes Camden Fifth Series, volumes 11 and 12 (published in July and December) and Transactions Sixth Series, volume 8 (published in December). Japanese prices are available from Kinokuniya Company Ltd, P.O. Box 55, Chitose, Tokyo 156, Japan. EU subscribers (outside the UK) who are not registered for VAT should add VAT at their country's rate. VAT registered subscribers should provide their VAT registration number. Prices include delivery by air.

Subscription orders, which must be accompanied by payment, may be sent to a bookseller, subscription agent or direct to the publisher: Cambridge University Press, The Edinburgh Building, Shaftesbury Road, Cambridge CB2 2RU, UK; or in the USA, Canada and Mexico: Cambridge University Press, 40 West 20th Street, New York, NY 10011–4211, USA.

SINGLE VOLUMES AND BACK VOLUMES. A list of Royal Historical Society volumes available from Cambridge University Press may be obtained from the Humanities Marketing Department at the address above.

Printed and bound in the United Kingdom by Butler & Tanner Ltd, Frome and London

CONTENTS

viii CONTENTS

ACKNOWLEDGEMENTS

The newsletters printed in this book are bound in volumes VIII to XIII of the 'Series A', an important section of the records of the English Catholic secular clergy kept in the archives of Westminster Cathedral. I am very grateful to several people who assisted me with this project. First I would like to thank the Reverend Ian Dickie, the custodian of the archives, who gave me greater access to this collection than that enjoyed by any previous researcher. Without his help, the task would never have been undertaken. Kenneth Fincham, who used this material so profitably in his research on Archbishop George Abbot, first directed me to this source and persuaded me that a printed edition of some of the newsletters would be useful to researchers. Timothy McCann's and Christopher Whittick's formidable command of local history has helped make sense of the letters which deal with events in Hampshire and Sussex. The Reverend Thomas McCoog SJ was very generous in his comments and criticism and made available to me the resources of the Farm Street Library and Archive as well as his unrivalled knowledge of the English province of the Society of Jesus. Several people helped me by reading through parts of the text, especially Andrew Foster and Andrew Pettegree. I am grateful also to Richard Johnson of Johnson Electronics for considerable technical assistance. Many people sorted out specific references for me, particularly Simon Adams, Joan Barham, Joseph Bergin, Caroline Bowden, Brian Causton, Edward Chaney, David Como, Pauline Croft, Thomas Freeman, Simon Healy, Peter Lake, Patrick Little, the Reverend Albert Loomie SJ, Anthony Milton, Martin Murphy, Helen Payne, Linda Levy Peck, Conrad Russell, William Sheils and Andrew Thrush.

And, secondly, my thanks to a former researcher – Mr Edwin Chadwick who worked in the 1940s as an assistant to the Reverend Leo Hicks SJ at the Farm Street archive. Chadwick, whose assistance Hicks acknowledged in his introduction to his volume on the correspondence of Thomas Fitzherbert,[1] produced draft transcripts which Hicks required from volumes IX to XII in the Westminster Series A. Considering that Chadwick had no special knowledge of the people whose names appear in these letters, his powers of transcription were, by the time of his death in 1947, extremely good. (Some of these manuscripts were rapidly becoming almost illegible owing to an inadequate method of conservation adopted in the late nineteenth century when they were bound in their present form. In addition, the hands of

[1] CRS 41, 4.

some of the correspondents were nearly indecipherable even to those to whom the letters were addressed).[2] Working to Hicks's instructions, not every letter was transcribed and, of course, for this edition all the material had to be checked against the originals and then edited in accordance with modern practice. But it would be true to say that without Mr Chadwick's preliminary work this project would have taken so many years as to be impracticable.

I had much hoped to profit from the assistance of Mr Antony Allison. His recent death took away a scholar whose work on Catholic ecclesiastical politics in the 1620s and 1630s made considerable use of the Westminster papers. I am very grateful to his wife Marion for making available to me some of his notes and transcripts.

[2] Robert Pett had to apologise to Thomas More at the beginning of September 1612 that 'I never wrote to yo*w* of the duke of Medina but of the duke of Regio and Modina wher yo*w* toke an o for an e and soe made yt Medina. yo*w* must pardon my bad scriblinge but yet as I remember I wrot that he was an Italian duke by w*h*ich yo*w* might have conceaved that yt could not be the duke of Medina', AAW A XI, no. 142 (p. 393). See also **Letters 35, 44**.

NOTE ON THE TEXT

The manuscripts published here are reproduced in their entirety, with both routine openings and terminations, and endorsements and annotations. The original spellings have been preserved, except that modern usage is employed for *u* and *v*. Most abbreviations have been extended. The original punctuation has been retained (though I have supplied additional punctuation in square brackets to aid the sense where this is required), as has the writers' use of italics and paragraphing. Indentation has been used to create a new paragraph where unfilled space towards the end of a line suggests that the writer intended it. Original capitalisation has also been retained though the majuscule and minuscule forms of some letters have often been extremely difficult to ascertain and a certain amount of discretion has had to be employed. Interlineations have been incorporated silently unless the positioning of the interlineation is not certain and then it is included at the end of the sentence or section to which it refers. Words and letters which have been accidentally left out are supplied in the text in square brackets. Obliterations, deletions and lacunae are noted, also in square brackets. All references are to page number unless otherwise indicated. Cross-references to letters in the volume are made by citing in bold type the number of the letter, *e.g.* '**Letter 23**'. I have indicated where particular words or passages of text have been underlined in the body of the text itself though I have not included vertical lines drawn in the margin.

The letters are printed in chronological sequence. I have assumed that letters which were written on the Continent were dated according to the New Style and those written in England were dated Old Style, though, with Old Style dates, I take the year as beginning on 1 January and not 25 March. (Letters dated according to the New Style are marked 'NS'.) Unless otherwise indicated the place of publication of all printed works is London.

ABBREVIATIONS

AAW A	Archives of the Archdiocese of Westminster, A Series
ABSI	Archivum Britannicum Societatis Iesu
Adams	S. Adams, 'The Protestant Cause: Religious Alliance with the West European Calvinist Communities as a Political Issue in England, 1585–1630' (unpubl. D. Phil. thesis, Oxford, 1973)
Allison, 'Later Life'	A.F. Allison, 'The Later Life and Writings of Joseph Creswell, S.J. (1556–1623)', *RH* 15 (1979), 79–144
Allison, 'Richard Smith'	A.F. Allison, 'Richard Smith, Richelieu and the French Marriage. The political context of Smith's appointment as bishop for England in 1624', *RH* 7 (1964), 148–211
Ancaster	S.C. Lomas (ed.), *Report on the Manuscripts of the Earl of Ancaster* (1907)
Anstr.	G. Anstruther, *The Seminary Priests* (4 vols, Ware and Great Wakering, 1968–1977)
APC	J.R. Dasent *et al.* (eds), *Acts of the Privy Council of England (1542–1628)*, (32 vols, 1890–1907)
ARCR	A.F. Allison and D.M. Rogers, *The Contemporary Printed Literature of the English Counter-Reformation between 1558 and 1640* (2 vols, Aldershot, 1989–1994)
ARSI	Archivum Romanum Societatis Iesu
Belvederi	R. Belvederi (ed.), *Guido Bentivoglio Diplomatico* (2 vols in one, np, 1947), II
BL	British Library
Cokayne	G.E. Cokayne, *The Complete Peerage* (13 vols, London, 1910–59)
Conway *AH* 23	D. Conway, 'Guide to Documents of Irish and British Interest in Fondo Borghese, Series I', *Archivium Hibernicum* 23 (1960), 1–147
Conway *AH* 24	D. Conway, 'Guide to Documents of Irish and British Interest in Fondo Borghese, Series II–IV', *Archivium Hibernicum* 24 (1961), 31–102
CRS	Catholic Record Society
CRS 1	*Miscellanea I* (CRS 1, 1905)
CRS 7	*Miscellanea VI* (CRS 7, 1909)
CRS 10–11	E.H. Burton and T.L. Williams (eds), *The Douay College Diaries* (CRS 10–11, 1911)
CRS 18	M.M.C. Calthrop (ed.), *Recusant Roll No. 1., 1592–3* (CRS 18, 1916)
CRS 34	H. Bowler (ed.), *London Sessions Records 1605–1685* (CRS 34, 1934)
CRS 41	L. Hicks (ed.), *Letters of Thomas Fitzherbert 1608–1610* (CRS 41, 1948)

CRS 51	P. Renold (ed.), *The Wisbech Stirs (1595–1598)* (CRS 51, 1958)
CRS 53	C. Talbot (ed.), *Miscellanea* (CRS 53, 1961)
CRS 54–5	A. Kenny (ed.), *The Responsa Scholarum of the English College, Rome* (2 vols, CRS 54–5, 1962–3)
CRS 57	H. Bowler (ed.), *Recusant Roll No. 2 (1593–1594)* (CRS 57, 1965)
CRS 58	P. Renold (ed.), *Letters of William Allen and Richard Barret 1572–1598* (CRS 58, 1965)
CRS 60	A.G. Petti (ed.), *Recusant Documents from the Ellesmere Manuscripts* (CRS 60, 1968)
CRS 64/68	A.J. Loomie (ed.), *Spain and the Jacobean Catholics* (2 vols, CRS 64, 68, 1973, 1978)
CRS 69	T.G. Holt (ed.), *St. Omers and Bruges Colleges, 1593–1773: A Biographical Dictionary* (CRS 69, 1979)
CRS 71	H. Bowler and T.J. McCann (eds), *Recusants in the Exchequer Pipe Rolls 1581–1592* (CRS 71, 1986)
CRS 74–5	T.M. McCoog (ed.), *English and Welsh Jesuits 1555–1650* (2 vols, CRS 74–5, 1994–5)
CSPD	R. Lemon and M.A.E. Green (eds), *Calendar of State Papers, Domestic Series* (12 vols for 1547–1625), (1856–72)
CSPV	H.F. Brown and A.B. Hinds (eds), *Calendar of State Papers, Venetian Series* (11 vols for 1581–1625), (1894–1912)
Davidson	A. Davidson, 'Roman Catholicism in Oxfordshire from the Late Elizabethan Period to the Civil War *c.* 1580–1640' (unpubl. Ph. D. thesis, Bristol, 1970).
DNB	*Dictionary of National Biography*
Downshire MSS	E.K. Purnell *et al.* (eds), *Report on the Manuscripts of the Marquess of Downshire*, (5 vols, HMC, 1924–8)
ESRO	East Sussex Record Office
Foley	H. Foley, *Records of the English Province of the Society of Jesus* (7 vols, 1875–83)
Harris, 'Reports'	P.R. Harris, 'The Reports of William Udall, Informer, 1605–1612', part I, *RH* 8 (1965), 192–284
Hasler	P.W. Hasler (ed.), *The House of Commons 1558–1603* (3 vols, 1981)
HMC	Historical Manuscripts Commission
Larkin & Hughes	J.F. Larkin and P.L. Hughes (eds), *Stuart Royal Proclamations of King James I 1603–1625* (Oxford, 1973)
Law	T.G. Law, *The Archpriest Controversy* (2 vols, Camden Society, second series, 56, 58, 1896, 1898)
Lunn, *EB*	D. Lunn, *The English Benedictines, 1540–1688* (1980)
Lunn, 'English Cassinese'	D. Lunn, 'The English Cassinese (1611–50)', *RH* 13 (1975), 62–9

McClure	N. McClure (ed.), *The Letters of John Chamberlain* (2 vols, Philadelphia, 1939), I
McCoog	T.M. McCoog, 'The Society of Jesus in England, 1623–1688: An Institutional Study' (unpubl. Ph. D. thesis, Warwick, 1984).
Milward I	P. Milward, *Religious Controversies of the Elizabethan Age* (1977).
Milward II	P. Milward, *Religious Controversies of the Jacobean Age* (1978)
Mott	A. Mott, 'A Dictionary of Hampshire Recusants: Tempo Eliz' (typescript at ABSI)
np	no place [of publication]
OED	Oxford English Dictionary
OFM	Order of Friars Minor
OP	Order of Preachers
OSB	Order of St Benedict
PRO	Public Record Office
RH	*Recusant History*
Salisbury MSS	M.S. Giuseppi *et al.* (eds), *Calendar of the Manuscripts of the Most Honourable the Marquess of Salisbury*, (24 vols, HMC, 1888–1976)
SJ	Society of Jesus
Smith, *Life*	L.P. Smith, *The Life and Letters of Sir Henry Wotton* (2 vols, Oxford, 1907)
STC	A.W. Pollard and G.R. Redgrave, *A Short Title Catalogue of Books Printed in England, Scotland and Ireland and of English Books Printed Abroad, 1475–1640*, second edition revised by W.A. Jackson, F.S Ferguson and K.F. Pantzer (3 vols, 1976–91).
TD	M.A. Tierney, *Dodd's Church History of England* (5 vols, 1839–43)
WSRO	West Sussex Record Office

INTRODUCTION

The Newsletters and their Historical Context

In his book on the Catholic recusants of the West Riding of Yorkshire, the perceptive John Aveling noted that although some of the holdings of the archive of the archdiocese of Westminster had been published the archive itself was 'not yet plumbed'.[1] Of course, several scholars have used the papers which are bound in the volumes of the Westminster archive's well known 'Series A'. Charles Dodd (*vere* Hugh Tootell), whose influential *Church History of England* still governs the way we think about English Catholicism, used them extensively. Canon Mark Tierney, who produced an edition of Dodd's work, printed many of these papers as appendices to sections of Dodd's text. More recently, Antony Allison mined them for his work on Joseph Creswell SJ and Richard Smith. David Lunn employed them for his history of the Benedictines in England, and Alan Davidson used them for his work on post-Reformation Oxfordshire Catholicism.[2] But, as Davidson remarks, the Series A volumes' largely uncatalogued state has discouraged researchers.[3] This book is supposed to go some way towards remedying that situation. It contains edited transcripts of a selection of the newsletters written by the Catholic secular priests in England, France and Belgium to their agents in Rome between 1609 and 1614.

In 1609, the second of the English archpriests, George Birkhead (appointed by Pope Paul V in 1608 to replace the recently deposed George Blackwell as superior of the English secular clergy), started to petition the pope and various members of the Roman curia to implement a programme of ecclesiastical reform among English Catholics. The two representatives whom he sent to Rome first to assist and then to replace the agent appointed by Blackwell, Thomas Fitzherbert, were the leading secular priests Richard Smith and Thomas More. (Smith acted as Birkhead's agent in Rome during 1609 and 1610, and, on his departure for Paris, More succeeded to his office.) They were supplied

---

[1] J.C.H. Aveling, *The Catholic Recusants of the West Riding of Yorkshire 1558–1790* (Proceedings of the Leeds Philosophical and Literary Society, Literary and Historical Section, X, pt 6, Leeds, 1963), 304.

[2] TD; Allison, 'Richard Smith'; Allison, 'Later Life'; *idem*, 'Richard Smith's Gallican Backers and Jesuit Opponents: some of the issues raised by Kellison's *Treatise of the Hierarchie* 1629', part I, *RH* 18 (1987), 329–401; Lunn, *EB*; Davidson.

[3] Davidson, 12.

with information by a network of clerics. They used it to write the
memoranda which they placed before the cardinals who were responsible for English Catholics' spiritual well-being. The agents' papers, the
contents of their daily in-tray, constitute a great deal of the surviving
material for the secular clergy in this period. Except for a few copy
letters, almost all the letters which Smith and More wrote back to
their friends are lost, as are almost all the letters which the agents'
correspondents simultaneously wrote to each other, though often such
letters simply enclosed material to be passed on to the agent. The
surviving letters and papers, preserved first at Rome and then at the
seminary college at Douai in Flanders, were brought back to England
at the end of the eighteenth century. In the nineteenth century they
were extracted out of their original files, recatalogued and bound in
their present form. When the Oratorian priest Thomas Rant was
writing instructions for a new agent in Rome in 1625 he advised him
to 'reade over all M^r. Mores, and M^r. Bennetts[4] memorialls and writings,
they will give yow a greate deale of light of paste matters'. He advised
the new agent also to read 'yf yow have leisure the letters writt to M^r.
More, from the Archpreiste annis 1612, 1613, &c to 1616. many excellent
good things in them'.[5]

In some ways, the often plaintive letters received in Rome by the
agents do look rather petty and insignificant. The priestly writers of
these letters seem to have spent much of their day penning accounts
of their various woes – how they were persecuted in England by the
Protestant authorities, how they lacked sufficient funds, and how
unchristian some other Catholic clergymen were. Long gone, apparently, were the days of heroism and youthful self-sacrifice which had
characterised the early seminarist movement. The requests which these
priests made to the Roman curial officials to correct the abuses which
they perceived in English Catholicism were seemingly minor. Their
concerns have become the province of a few scholars who have
specialised in the largely defunct area known as 'recusant history'.

Yet, as I hope to show in the rest of this introduction, the issues with
which the priests concerned themselves in their letters to their agents
in Rome were not as petty as they seem. And those things which have
long been treated as the priests' minor administrative concerns were
not, in fact, detached from all other contemporary ecclesiastical and
political issues. An understanding of them in the light cast on them
by these clerical newsletters may recast our concepts of what early
seventeenth-century English Catholicism was and show how our nar-

----

[4] John Bennett, secular priest, who in 1621 went to Rome as agent for the secular
clergy, Anstr. I, 32.
[5] AAW A XIX, no. 83 (p. 252).

ratives of it can be integrated into the broader political narratives of the period. I wish now to offer a brief account of the agency and its petitioning programme between 1609 and 1614. It provides an essential context for the events narrated in the newsletters printed in this volume. It is also an interpretative key to the themes which run through these letters.

The Archpriest and his Agents

When George Birkhead, the second of the three archpriests appointed between 1598 and 1621 to rule over the English Catholic secular clergy, sent his representatives, Richard Smith and Thomas More, to Rome in 1609, these priests had several different issues which they wanted the papal curia to address. Many of these issues were inherited directly from the time of the famous 'Appellant' dispute when some of the secular clergy had appealed to Rome against the appointment of Birkhead's predecessor, the archpriest George Blackwell. As is well known, the root cause of the appeal was the perceived irregular influence of the English Jesuits over the secular clergy. After the formal settlement of the controversy by papal breve in late 1602[6] it became clear that the ecclesiastical grievances of that complex and vitriolic quarrel were not settled at all.[7] Blackwell was still seen as the leader of a pro-Spanish faction among the priests. Matthew Sutcliffe, Dean of Exeter, wrote in 1604 'he is very ignorant that knoweth not, how the arch-priestes faction hath long time stood for the Infantaes title. yet now forsoth that the King is quietly possessed of the Crowne, their heartes are all "replenished with ioy", to see it. They may beeleve it that list, wee cannot'.[8]

Several of the priests who had been appointed as 'assistants' to Blackwell were notoriously pro-Jesuit.[9] (With the new regime of George Birkhead they would be levered out of their assistantships.)[10] What were

---

[6] By a breve of 5 October 1602 (NS) Clement VIII had tried to settle the secular priests' main grievance (that the English Jesuits were surreptitiously asserting an uncanonical authority over them) by ordering Blackwell not to consult with SJ about the secular clergy's affairs in England.

[7] For the best narrative of the controversy, see J.H. Pollen, *The Institution of the Archpriest Blackwell* (1916).

[8] Matthew Sutcliffe, *The Supplication of Certaine Masse-Priests falsely called Catholikes* (1604), sig. Q2v.

[9] The archpriest had twelve assistants. They were an integral part of the archpriest's regime, but, as John Bossy describes them, they were also 'an oligarchy of powerful individuals whose prestige often exceeded that of the archpriest himself', J. Bossy, *The English Catholic Community 1570–1850* (1975), 208, 210.

[10] See **Letter 1**.

the most frequently expressed complaints of the anti-Jesuit secular priests? First came the administration of the seminaries. Douai College, with its chronic indebtedness, cried out for reform.[11] The anti-Jesuit priests hated Thomas Worthington, the president of the college, who was regarded, with some justice, as an instrument of the infamous though ageing Jesuit Robert Persons.[12] They were irritated by the way in which, academically, the secular clergy were forced to play second fiddle to the religious who enjoyed in their own novitiates an education which could not so easily be had in the seminary. They disliked the papal breve of 1597 which restricted the progress of the secular priests towards higher degrees in continental universities.[13] They were infuriated by the constant refusal of their requests that the more senior secular priests should be allowed to reside and study at Douai. Furthermore, they said, the inadequate education of the young sem-inarists meant that those who were sent to England (far too many of them in any case[14]) were generally ill equipped for their missionary tasks. They did not measure up to the standard which the English Catholic gentry expected,[15] and this led to many other evils – immorality, the defection of some priests to the Church of England, and the laity's increasing refusal to shelter priests who were incompetent in their function. The collapse of the secular clergy's educational system threat-ened to asphyxiate English Catholicism, at least in the form in which these secular clergy activists imagined it.

How, then, did these seculars think that reform would be accom-plished? Primarily through the establishment of a fledgling, immature but nevertheless self-sufficient system of church government in England which would both propagate Catholicism and yet not be seen as a dangerous political challenge to the authority of the State. Ultimately all the projects which the secular priests pursued stood or fell by how their request, their 'principal suit' as they called it, that one of their number should be appointed as a bishop over the English Catholics, proceeded at Rome. The archpresbyterate, they said, was an inadequate

---

[11] Peter Guilday suggests that Douai's debts were contracted primarily by the college's move back from Rheims to Douai in 1593, P. Guilday, *The English Catholic Refugees on the Continent, 1558–1795* (1914), 106–7. For previous strife over the running of the seminary at Douai and Rheims, and the college in Rome, see CRS 58, pp. xvi-xvii, xxi-ii, and *passim*; M.E. Williams, *The Venerable English College, Rome* (1979), ch. 1.

[12] Guilday, *English Catholic Refugees*, 114.

[13] CRS 41, 52–3; CRS 58, 146; CRS 51, 294, 301; **Letter 19**.

[14] CRS 41, 53–4.

[15] The priest Thomas Martin wrote in June 1611 that he had 'seene a catholick gentilwoman...by her very iudgment to determyne an ordinary dowbt in lerning, when a preist notably' erred and 'persisted in his error'. 'Two years in Positive Divinity & cases of conscience' did not make priests 'compleate men & able warriers for god Almighties band', AAW A X, no. 68 (p. 181).

vehicle for the government of priests and Catholic laity in England.[16] The source of the Appellant controversy itself had been not just that Blackwell was too weak to stand up to the Society of Jesus but that his letters of appointment gave him such limited authority. As John Bossy has put it, summarising the Appellants' line in 1598, the 'archpriest's office was without precedence in the English Church; he did not exercise his functions within the framework of canon law...; he had a kind of propulsive power, but no real jurisdiction, over the seminary clergy, and none whatever over the regulars or the laity'.[17] By influencing him, the Jesuits, who enjoyed their own system of self-regulation, could rule the secular priests as well. This was not fully rectified by the papal breve of October 1602 which supposedly settled the Appellant controversy.

In June 1607 Blackwell was arrested. Under intense pressure from the authorities he took the Jacobean oath of allegiance, an oath which the Jesuits said was the ideological equivalent of the oath of supremacy and which had been swiftly condemned by Paul V when it was issued in 1606. Blackwell also advised other Catholics to take it. Rome swiftly deposed him. In February 1608 George Birkhead was appointed in his place. Though the anti-Jesuits among the secular priests initially had doubts about Birkhead, he at least was not a Jesuit stooge. But the jurisdictional inadequacy of his position was still, some of his priests thought, a glaring anomaly. In Bossy's words, 'it was always', for the Appellants, 'a sham and a monstrosity'.[18] It was outrageous that the laity had no spiritual head, lacked the sacrament of confirmation, and the clerical body in England remained rent by quarrels through the absence of a single authority. The natural course and order of the church, government through bishop, dean and chapter, was still withheld from English Catholics.[19] William Bishop summarised the seculars' case, that 'wher all things be in good order, and are come to their full perfection' in the Church then all is well, 'but in our case, who have nothing almost in order, or in so good order, as cannot be amended' the Church cannot do without its natural forms of regulation and government.[20] These secular priests' Catholic enemies simply retorted that those who petitioned most vigorously for the appointment of a bishop with authority over English Catholics intended first and foremost

---

[16] TD V, 8–9.

[17] Bossy, *English Catholic Community*, 46.

[18] Bossy, *English Catholic Community*, 48.

[19] For an authoritative introduction to the issues involved in the controversy over whether a bishop should be appointed for English Catholics, see Allison, 'Richard Smith', 148–61.

[20] AAW A XI, no. 149 (p. 409).

to use that authority against their opponents among the regular clergy[21] and to wrest from them the substantial patronage of the Catholic gentry which they had accumulated.[22] Unjustly they would overthrow the natural friendship between secular and regular priests. They would jeopardise the spread of the gospel in the English mission.

With Birkhead's appointment it was at last possible to commence a serious petitioning campaign to get what the leading anti-Jesuit secular clergy wanted.[23] Initially, Birkhead was conciliatory as he laid his reform proposals before the curia. But the messages which came back via Robert Persons and Thomas Fitzherbert (formerly Blackwell's agent who still retained his position in Rome as agent for the archpriest) were far from encouraging. Not only was it thought in Rome that there was a significant weight of Catholic opinion in England against the appointment of a bishop. It was even advised that Birkhead should not send procurators to Rome to pursue the matter.[24] Slowly Birkhead's mood in his letters became more impatient. As Charles Dodd's narrative has it, Birkhead, out of weakness, at first entered into a friendly correspondence with the duplicitous Robert Persons about the secular clergy's proposed measures. Only when he found that he was being cruelly manipulated did he come to see that a more aggressive course and a greater rapport with people such as the leading anti-Jesuit secular priests Anthony Champney, William Bishop and Richard Smith were necessary.[25] The decision was taken to send Richard Smith as agent to Rome. He was to be accompanied by Thomas More. They had both been chaplains to the recently deceased Magdalen Browne (née Dacres), dowager Viscountess Montague, at Battle in Sussex, step-grandmother of the second viscount, Anthony Maria Browne. This peer was now the principal aristocratic patron on whom these priests relied.

Dodd's narrative then recounts how Robert Persons and his friend Thomas Fitzherbert sought to obstruct the agency's programme. Owing to Persons's machinations, Rome had already stipulated that there must be unanimity among the secular clergy about both the project for appointing a bishop and who should be accorded the honour.[26] To the

---

[21] Edward Bennett reminded Richard Smith in 1608 that the Jesuits had no right to meddle with the seculars, but that 'it is the superiors of the seculer [who] reforme and visitt the religious, and of this we have daylye presidentes in all Catholicke Countreys about us', AAW A VIII, no. 72 (p. 385).

[22] See **Letter 5**. In a petition to Pope Paul V of August 1611 Birkhead suggested that both religious and seculars should be bound to the pope under pain of excommunication to account to the archpriest and his assistants for the alms received by them, AAW A X, no. 107.

[23] TD V, 12–13; Bossy, *English Catholic Community*, 48.

[24] AAW A VIII, no. 69 (printed in CRS 41, 33–7).

[25] TD V, 14–16; Allison, 'Richard Smith', 166–7.

[26] Allison, 'Richard Smith', 166–7. Birkhead wrote to Smith on 11 October 1609 that

supporters of the measure, who knew how difficult unanimity would be to obtain, this was clearly designed to prevent the project entirely.[27] There were some pro-Jesuit secular priests who would vigorously oppose it. Other priests would not dare to put their names to a proposal which would excite the wrath of the Jacobean regime. In consequence the suit for bishops was temporarily laid aside by Birkhead, and petitions to remedy other 'abuses' were considered instead.[28]

Smith and More left for Rome in early March 1609 and arrived there in May.[29] The two priests made contact with Persons at the English College and then appeared before Pope Paul V on 24 May. They presented the secular clergy's programme for reform. Birkhead's commission instructed Smith to ask first that Paul V should confirm the breve of 1602 issued by Pope Clement VIII separating the administration of the Jesuits and seculars in England. This the pope did. Smith then presented six other petitions for the better regulation of the secular clergy, principally for their maintenance and education, for removal of all obstructions hindering the secular priests from proceeding to higher academic degrees, and for provision of facilities for some of them to study and write works of polemical theology.[30]

Relations between Persons and Smith, however, were already frosty. Persons expressed quite clearly his reservations about Smith in the letters which he continued to write to Birkhead. Thomas Fitzherbert, who was technically joined with Smith in Birkhead's agency commission, was soon left in no doubt as to Smith's and More's opinion of him.[31] During June 1609 Smith still maintained contact with Persons, trying to get him to agree to the seculars' subsidiary demands – particularly concerning the foundation of a college or house of studies for the seculars, and the matter of higher academic degrees.[32] These other petitions were presented to the vice-protector Cardinal Lawrence Bianchetti on 26 June, but they were not granted in the form which

Persons 'writeth to me that the lords of the inquisition have resolved *nihil innovandum esse*, in the things that I have proposed', *i.e.* without universal consent among the English secular clergy, TD V, p. lxxxii.

[27] TD V, 18–20.

[28] TD V, p. lvi. Of course it was still being actively considered how the petition for a bishop might be successfully presented, AAW A VIII, nos 120, 161.

[29] As late as 15 February 1609 Birkhead reported that travel passes for Smith and More had not yet been obtained. Viscount Montague was trying to procure them, AAW A VIII, no. 92. More's pass was obtained from the privy council (signed by, among others, Archbishop Richard Bancroft) on 4 March 1609, AAW A VIII, no. 94. In May 1609 Richard Holtby SJ was already informing Persons that Bancroft 'looketh dailie for newes of R.S. [Richard Smith] his negotiations', AAW A VIII, no. 105 (p. 498).

[30] TD V, p. lvi.

[31] F. Edwards, *Robert Persons* (St Louis, Missouri, 1996), 376–7.

[32] Edwards, *Robert Persons*, 378.

the seculars desired, though the Inquisition on 23 July did allow a modification of the rules governing degrees, and, later on, gave permission for a writers' college in Paris.[33] Thomas More now returned to England to start collecting (or extracting) signatures for the petition for a grant of ordinary jurisdiction.[34]

Dodd's narrative and Mark Tierney's annotations on that narrative then catalogue a series of scandalous slanders, formulated by Persons in Rome and Jesuits such as Richard Holtby in England who wanted to defame Smith and all the leading supporters of the suit for the appointment of a bishop.[35] Smith's detractors had plenty of ammunition. Smith had unwisely been defending the priests gaoled in London's Clink prison who would not accept the absolute denunciation of the Jacobean oath of allegiance contained in Paul V's breves against it.[36] A polemical tract which Smith had written in 1605, *An Answer to Thomas Bels late Challeng*, which deliberately omitted to refute the former secular priest Thomas Bell's attack on the papal deposing power, was delated to the Inquisition.[37] Birkhead became increasingly cold towards Persons. Their secret correspondence (which had continued alongside their 'official' correspondence) broke down.[38] But, although Birkhead now deprived Thomas Fitzherbert of his commission to act as agent for the archpriest,[39] these secular priests' opponents were apparently obstructing the presentation of subsequent petitions. In fact, virtually everything seemed to militate against the seculars' plans: Persons's power in Rome and the natural reluctance of the curia to take their side; the slowness and uncertainty of their letters' carriage to Rome; their difficulties in

---

[33] Edwards, *Robert Persons*, 378–9; A.C.F. Beales, *Education under Penalty* (1963), 139; CRS 41, 51–2. The modification of the rules about higher degrees did not satisfy priests like John Jackson, **Letter 52**. For the role of the cardinal protector and cardinal vice-protector in regulating English Catholicism, see McCoog, 62 n. 25. For the founding of the writers' college, with the assistance of the Benedictine Abbey of St Vaast at Arras, see A.F. Allison, 'Richard Smith's Gallican Backers and Jesuit Opponents', part II, *RH* 19 (1989), 234–85, at pp. 255–8.

[34] AAW A VIII, no. 179. The priest Benjamin Norton had recently done a tour to visit the archpriest's assistants and elicit their opinion on the matter, **Letter 5**. For More's account of his journey from Rome, see AAW A VIII, no. 154; for his newsletters from England, see AAW A VIII, no. 164, **Letters 6, 7**. When he crossed to England, he 'hardlie escaped' at his 'comming in' because of 'dyvers advertisments' of his 'being upon the way', AAW A VIII, no. 164 (p. 649).

[35] TD V, 24–6.

[36] Edwards, *Robert Persons*, 378–9. See AAW A IX, no. 72, a memorandum by Smith in 1610 to Paul V advising him (on the basis of information supplied by Birkhead) against depriving the oath-favourers of their faculties as missionary priests.

[37] CRS 41, 122–3. The accuser was almost certainly Robert Persons, Allison, 'Richard Smith', 167; Edwards, *Robert Persons*, 382. The case was quite soon allowed to drop.

[38] Edwards, *Robert Persons*, 383.

[39] Cardinal Bianchetti sharply admonished Birkhead for dismissing Fitzherbert as his agent, AAW A IX, no. 88.

financing the agency; the geographical dispersal of the priests in England; and the disadvantage that several of the promoters of the agency (none of whom was very young), particularly Birkhead, suffered from serious ill health.[40] And in September 1610 Smith resigned his commission as Birkhead's agent. More, who had returned to Rome in early 1610, took his place. Smith returned to Paris.[41] It seems likely that Smith, already a morose and difficult character, had been driven close to a nervous breakdown by the undeniably vigorous way in which Persons treated those whom he considered to be his enemies.[42]

Of course by then Robert Persons was dead.[43] Many of the seculars believed that he had been the principal obstacle to their plans and all would now proceed smoothly.[44] It was encouraging that Persons's replacement as rector of the English College in Rome, Thomas Owen SJ, was related to some of the secular priests who were promoting the agency.[45] But the opposition which the seculars had experienced did not evaporate as they had expected. According to Dodd this was because the malevolent 'spirit, which he [Persons] had created', lingered on after his death.[46] Actually, the curial officials who dealt with the English had real doubts about the wisdom of allowing the secular clergy's demands. The risk, from Rome's perspective, was that if a bishop was appointed for England he might be arrested. If he, like the first of the archpriests, George Blackwell, then took the Jacobean oath of allegiance and ordered other Catholics to do the same there would

[40] In July 1612 Thomas Heath reported to Rome that Birkhead had fallen sick 'of a burning feaver & [was] so consumed that his legges seemed as little as a mans wrest [*i.e.* wrist]'. He was 'made so weake that being uphoulden by two, he could scarce set one legg before the other', AAW A XI, no. 115 (p. 316).

[41] See **Letter 11**.

[42] John (Augustine) Bradshaw OSB, a friend of the seculars, wrote to Smith on 28 March 1610 (NS) that he should 'procure a testimony from the inquisition what passed with you for your booke [Smith's *Answer to Thomas Bels late Challeng*] for it is reported here that you were meette weeping coming out of the inquisition', AAW A IX, no. 29 (p. 73). When Smith came back to Paris in August 1611 from a short stay in England, Champney reported to More that Smith had just recovered from 'some malencholie att his furst arrivall', AAW A X, no. 109 (p. 319).

[43] Persons died in April 1610. In September 1611 we find Smith taking satisfaction in the providential injuries and sudden deaths which had befallen those who opposed the agency: 'perhaps if they looke abowt them they may find that God hath a stroke in our defence' and 'what meaneth it that amongst so many priests as are on this side of the sea both elder and weaker none are dead since this last opposition was made against the Archpr: demands but F. Persons and his three principal instruments in the opposition', AAW A X, no. 126 (p. 363).

[44] Birkhead reported to Smith on 2 July 1610 that their brethren were animated following Persons's death: 'there heades be full of new petitions', AAW A IX, no. 49 (p. 131).

[45] See **Letter 14**.

[46] TD V, 28.

then be a danger of a schism in England as perhaps the majority of
English Catholics might, with their new bishop, take the State for their
protector and openly reject important aspects of papal authority.

This continuing opposition to their plans goaded the more aggressive
of the secular priests into pressing forward the petition for the appointment of a bishop.[47] Birkhead tried to procrastinate, claiming that he
did not want to risk failure.[48] (They could, after all, ask only once, and
refusal by Rome would mean the end of their dreams.) In May 1611
Birkhead was still reiterating that he would not do what he knew would
be impeded or censured in Rome. But priests such as John Jackson
seemed to be threatening now that they would not tolerate being
ignored by Rome.[49] (Indeed, in December 1613, we find Jackson
reporting that some English Catholics were fed up with Paul V, who,
they said, was indiscreet and 'vayne, in cutting his beard one white
spade & an other white pike...also in the maner of his attire & in
wearing of points & I know not what'. Jackson said he did his best to
'discredit the reports' but added 'they also say he spendeth all eyther
in building or upon his kinred'.[50]) Jackson and others constantly warned
that the current scandals in English Catholicism, apostasy among the
clergy and laxity over the oath of allegiance, would multiply if the
seculars' programme was not implemented.[51]

These secular priests wanted to persuade the curia that matters in
England were balanced on a knife edge. The right decisions taken at
Rome would safeguard the English Catholic inheritance; the wrong
ones would waste it entirely. It was vital for the priests to preserve the
appearance of precarious balance so as not to lose Rome's attention.
In some ways the seculars achieved far more than the gloominess of
the newsletters might lead us to believe. Thomas Sackville, fourth son
of Thomas Sackville, first earl of Dorset, now appeared in France with
the necessary funding to put into effect their cherished project of a
writers' college.[52] William Bishop was arrested in May 1611 as he was
about to leave for France. He refused to take the oath and, after a
well-reported shouting match with Archbishop George Abbot about
the oath, he was banished. This strengthened his and the seculars'
credit.[53] In mid-August 1611 Birkhead finally summoned up enough
courage to do as he had been ordered by Rome and take away the

---

[47] See *e.g.* **Letter 16**.
[48] **Letter 10**.
[49] AAW A X, nos 50, 64 (printed in TD IV, pp. clxxiii-xxv).
[50] AAW A XII, no. 218 (p. 486). In 1615 Jackson still fumed that the 'court of R[ome]
was the cause of continuance of all our miseries', AAW A XIV, no. 6 (p. 15).
[51] **Letters 1, 22, 23, 25, 27, 31, 44, 46**.
[52] **Letter 11**.
[53] **Letters 16, 25**.

missionary faculties of the secular priests who publicly affirmed the Jacobean oath of allegiance.[54] The Benedictines had started to break ranks very visibly over the question of the oath. Among the Cassinese congregation, some of whom opposed the seculars' 'principal suit' for ordinary jurisdiction, Roland (Thomas) Preston, publishing under the name of the Northumberland squire Roger Widdrington, turned out tracts which underwrote the regime's demands over the matter of allegiance. Preston's books may have caused difficulties for the seculars when they tried to persuade their own lay adherents that the oath had to be refused at all costs. Yet it was all grist to the seculars' mill. It was an object lesson for Rome about how lacking the religious were in their self-government. It showed that a bishop must be appointed to exert control over all the clergy. The seculars' contempt for the Society of Jesus could be vindicated by pointing, for example, to the Jesuit John Salkeld who had deserted his Spanish university, landed in Cornwall and started to work as a propagandist for the regime.[55]

Furthermore, despite the rejection of the first petition for reform of Douai,[56] and the appointment of the pro-Jesuit secular priests William Singleton and John Knatchbull to official posts in the seminary,[57] Worthington was prepared, now that Persons had died, to make peace with those who had been his bitterest enemies, and even to assist them. Through the mediation of the Benedictine John (Augustine) Bradshaw and Thomas Sackville, a conference was organised at Douai in May 1612 in order to present a show of unity to the curia in the pursuit of the seculars' aims. Thomas Harley, provost of Cambrai, Matthew Kellison and Henry Holland went on Worthington's behalf; Bishop, Smith and Champney went on Birkhead's. This conference agreed that certain reforms should take place in the seminary, notably that the confessor at Douai should be a secular priest, not a Jesuit; and that the archpriest should assert his control over the college.[58]

Initially Champney and Kellison let slip the opportunity for a real truce with Worthington,[59] and the new petitions sent to Rome for the cardinal protector's agreement were not approved.[60] A struggle ensued between Worthington and the pro-Jesuit faction in the college, principally William Singleton and John Knatchbull.[61] A visitation of the

[54] **Letter 21.**
[55] **Letter 29**.
[56] TD V, 27–8; AAW A VIII, no. 162.
[57] **Letter 11.**
[58] For the conference at Douai, see TD V, 53–4; AAW A XI, no. 85; Belvederi, 214.
[59] AAW A XI, no. 183.
[60] AAW A XI, nos 138, 141. Cardinal Scipio [Caffarelli] Borghese, the papal secretary of state, had little confidence in the May conference's proceedings and distrusted William Bishop, Conway *AH* 23, 109–10, 112; *cf.* Belvederi, 243.
[61] TD V, 32–4.

college now followed. (Tierney implies that the Jesuits, or rather
Knatchbull and Singleton, solicited it.)[62] It affirmed the position of
Singleton and Knatchbull, condemned those who resisted, and dismissed
student petitions for change, particularly in the matter of the Jesuit
confessor. Douai's indebtedness was then used, allegedly, as a pretext
for dismissing malcontents.[63]

But the seculars did secure a review of the visitors' decisions about
the rules by which the seminary was administered.[64] And then a seizure
of power, as peaceful as it was unexpected, took place. At the end of
April 1613 Worthington left Douai for Brussels in order to be interviewed
by the nuncio there.[65] Thence he departed for Rome.[66] Matthew
Kellison took over the running of Douai.[67] Kellison had the reputation
of a moderate and one so wily that he could govern there without
arousing opposition.[68] Worthington started to behave somewhat errat-
ically, and this caused the Society's opponents to decide that he must
not return. Kellison made it absolutely clear that if Worthington came
back he would leave.[69] Kellison became president of the college finally
on 11 November 1613 (NS). On 5 November 1613 (NS) William Bishop
had written to More that the confessor at Douai, Michael Walpole SJ,
'is retired thence, fearing belike to be thrust out'.[70]

Yet these very real successes accomplished by what was, for all its
self-deprecation and self-pity, really quite a powerful faction among the
English Catholic clergy, could not alter the fact that it was still not
winning the more fundamental struggle for influence. Even the task of
collecting signatures in favour of the suit for a bishop's appointment
was far from easy. Many of Birkhead's letters in 1610 and 1611 mention

[62] It was carried out by Caesar Clement and Robert Chambers, two clerics reckoned
by some as hostile to the seculars' cause. Their report was devastating in its condemnation
of the Douai establishment, and of the incompetence of Worthington, TD V, 34–44.
Worthington was led to believe that the visitation was Jesuit-inspired, Belvederi, 271. For
a different reading of the origins of the visitation, see Beales, *Education*, 140.

[63] After the imposition of the rules laid down by the visitors in November 1612,
Worthington seemed to gravitate back to SJ and the secular clergy's opponents, AAW A
XII, no. 1, *cf.* nos 106, 179; Belvederi, 309.

[64] For William Bishop's, Richard Smith's and Anthony Champney's petitions against
the visitation, addressed to Cardinal Millini and Cardinal Borghese, see AAW A XII,
no. 10 (pp. 24–5) (15 January 1613 (NS)). For the favourable response from Borghese over
the college's rules, see AAW A XII, no. 73.

[65] AAW A XII, no. 93.

[66] Belvederi, 291.

[67] TD V, 45; Guilday, *English Catholic Refugees*, 117–19.

[68] Allison, 'Later Life', 103.

[69] AAW A XII, no. 180.

[70] William Bishop noted, however, that Walpole's busy-headed young Jesuit replacement, Thomas Rand, was suborning John Knatchbull to get Kellison's assurances that
Kellison would cease collaborating with the anti-Jesuit secular priests, AAW A XII, no.
198 (p. 441).

the difficulty of fulfilling papal decree in this respect. As we have already noted, not all seculars were in favour of the suit. Some priests, such as John Bavant, thought the episcopal project would needlessly antagonise the regime by violating the laws relating to praemunire and bringing foreign jurisdiction into the kingdom. It would reduce the prospects for toleration of Catholicism.[71]

Birkhead delayed for months before finally despatching to Rome, at some point in later 1611, packets containing the names of those who were in favour of the appointment of a bishop over English Catholics. He also sent instructions for further delay until the result of the conference at Douai was known.[72] In March 1612 Birkhead, though he still urged extreme caution, gave his agent permission to 'beginne the suit when yo*w* shall see it convenient'.[73] There was now a concerted effort to lobby the leading cardinals in the curia who were concerned with English affairs, notably Aldobrandini, Sfondrata and Bellarmine.[74] In addition the seculars' stern critic Cardinal Bianchetti had died and been replaced as vice-protector by Cardinal Millini.[75] But More's letters from Rome in July and August told his correspondents that the suit, which had evidently in some manner been presented, was not likely to take effect as they desired, and the pope looked with disfavour on their demands.[76] John Jackson was reduced to suggesting that merely cosmetic adjustments be made to Birkhead's status: More should consult in Rome about Birkhead's 'habit, as the wearing of such a purple habit as those of his place doe in R.[ome] and also a Rochet'.[77] Edward Bennett urged they should cut their losses and 'if bb be not granted a

---

[71] **Letters 4, 7**. Birkhead himself conceded in April 1611 that some people thought that so long as the king were 'secured from all practises' by Catholics he would not care 'though 200 masses were said upon a day in London', AAW A X, no. 31 (p. 73). For John Bavant, see Bossy, *English Catholic Community*, 206, 208n; P. Caraman (ed.), *John Gerard* (1951), 23.

[72] See **Letter 17**. The petition and lists of signatures were sent in separate packets, AAW A X, nos 128, 136, 142; TD V, 51–2. Even though Birkhead claimed in July that he and Smith had sent a list of 100 names, AAW A X, no. 93 (a letter which More noted was received with the 'great pacquet' only on 27 December 1611 (NS)), in August he was saying that he still retained 'one or two packettes...about the suit' and dared not send them 'unles I have securitie', AAW A X, no. 99 (pp. 277-8). Champney was still forwarding lists of names from Paris during December, TD V, 51–2.

[73] AAW A XI, nos 46 (p. 123), 74. On 15 July 1612, however, Birkhead remarked to More that 'yt comforteth me exceedinge much that yo*w* have but insinuated our suite' to the pope, AAW A XI, no. 119 (p. 325).

[74] The seculars also had the support of the nuncio in Paris, Robert Ubaldini, AAW A XI, no. 148.

[75] **Letter 31**. In fact Millini consistently advised against the appointment of a bishop. The seculars soon realised he was as unsympathetic to them as Bianchetti had been, Allison, 'Richard Smith', 160–1; AAW A XI, no. 183.

[76] AAW A XI, nos 144, 175.

[77] AAW A XI, no. 185 (p. 537).

vicegerente with ordinary episcopall autoritye would helpe well'.[78]

For a short time in the second half of 1612 there seemed to be some reason for hope, especially since the Jesuit Cardinal Robert Bellarmine seemed sympathetic towards them. Birkhead wrote to More on 10 November 1612 that More's letters of mid-September greatly reassured him. Birkhead had received a 'courteouse Letter' from Bellarmine who 'wisheth that some way may be found out, to hasten our suit for bb'; and 'it is rumored in the Low countries that our suit for bb is like to be h[e]ard'.[79] But, in fact, by early 1613 it was clear that their suit was definitely failing. In January Birkhead suggested to More that 'yf our suite will take no place for bb, I wold to god we could have any ordinarie iurisdiction under some other title, to witt, of suffragane, ordinarie, vicar, etc*etera*. for many of our brethren wold be content therewith, and think it less odious to the state'.[80] Obstruction in Rome was proving too strong.[81] Robert Pett wrote to More on 21 April 1613 (NS) from Brussels that he had often observed 'that in all thes businesses w*h*ich yo*w* have negotiated noe directe answer is or hath ben retorned to your selfe of any one petition w*h*ich yo*w* have exhibited but that allwayes by indirecte meanes [yo*w*] are shifted of wherby may be perceaved how little our cause or our selves are favored or affected'.[82] More and Bishop had schemed even to have bishops created for England 'by the helpe of our neighbour bb', a plan which Birkhead forbade on the grounds that it was worthless without papal confirmation.[83] During mid-1613, however, Birkhead continued to bombard Cardinals Millini and Borghese with petitions that a bishop should be appointed.[84] In June and July 1613 Champney and Bishop were also looking to get the suit renewed and were seeking the help of French clerics, especially of Cardinal Joyeuse and Cardinal Du Perron, in lobbying the pope and the curia.[85] But further letters and memorials to Borghese and the pope produced no effect. The cardinal protector, Edward Farnese, and others were advising Birkhead to petition for some authority less than absolute ordinary jurisdiction, though Birkhead told More to continue with the original project for as long as he could.[86]

[78] AAW A XI, no. 192 (p. 555).

[79] AAW A XI, no. 201 (p. 577). For Birkhead's reply to Bellarmine, AAW A XI, no. 212 (not sent until January 1613, AAW A XII, no. 4).

[80] AAW A XII, no. 4 (p. 9).

[81] Rome was also acting on advice from other observers of the English scene, for example the Minim friar, Bartholomew Teles, who recommended against the appointment of a bishop for England, **Letter 40**.

[82] AAW A XII, no. 80 (p. 171).

[83] AAW A XII, no. 201.

[84] AAW A XII, no. 151, *cf.* XIII, no. 8; TD V, p. clviii-ix.

[85] AAW A XII, nos 121, 157.

[86] AAW A XII, no. 132.

Temporarily the Douai seminary was a more pressing matter. In late November 1613 Edward Bennett urged More that Birkhead was willing 'that the sute of BB should not be muche' promoted 'while...the colledge of doway be better setled', *i.e.* while Kellison tried to force through the necessary changes there.[87].

The high hopes which had attended Birkhead's appointment in 1608 had, therefore, not been fully realised. In Dodd's narrative, Birkhead's labours laid him open to anxiety attacks and made him feel that he was inadequate for his task. This led to a worsening of his health and an agonising though pious death in early April 1614, though not before he had made provision for an attempt to influence the appointment of a successor to himself who would be a favourer of the secular clergy's projects.[88]

The Place of Birkhead's Agency in Catholic Historiography

Such in brief is a narrative of the struggle between the Catholic clerical factions in the mid-Jacobean period. In general this story has been told polemically. The predominant narrative remains that of Charles Dodd. Here the vast majority of the English clergy suffered from a seriously defective missionary structure. They were no match for the wiliness of their Jesuit adversaries. The Jesuits were motivated by vainglory and a self-interested determination to maintain their hold on the principal sources of patronage available to the Catholic clergy in England, especially the seigneurial chaplaincies on which most Catholic clerics were forced to rely.

Dodd's narrative and Tierney's annotations of that narrative in Tierney's own edition of Dodd's work, *Dodd's Church History of England* (frequently treated as a simple source book for the history of the Catholic clergy in this period) replicate much of the secular priests' polemic. The only reply, equally polemical, which made extensive use of the same sources, came from the pen of Leo Hicks SJ – his *Letters of Thomas Fitzherbert 1608–1610*. In this book Hicks printed some of Fitzherbert's letters, and annotated them extensively by referring to the letters in the Westminster Cathedral archive. Hicks contended that Tierney's presentation of the material in the appendices of his volumes of Dodd's *Church History* 'though passable, it may be, for his time, leaves much to be desired according to modern standards'.[89] Hicks objected

---

[87] AAW A XII, no. 213 (p. 475).
[88] Birkhead was succeeded, after some delay, by William Harrison, AAW A XIV, nos 127, 132, 139, 164, 181.
[89] CRS 41, 1.

to Tierney's habitual 'muddle-headedness' but condemned mainly his pernicious attack on the Society of Jesus and his serious mis-representation of the state of the English Catholic Church.[90]

Hicks used his sources to try to vindicate the contemporary Jesuit line that the persecution was too violent in England during these years to risk the appointment of a bishop. In Hicks's view, the Jesuits' reservations about such an appointment were wilfully misinterpreted by Dodd and Tierney as selfish obstruction of the measure at all costs in the Society's own interests. The correspondence of leading members of the curia in Rome showed that they were definitely not being hoodwinked by the likes of Persons.[91] Furthermore, the evidence of serious persecution in England was proof enough that the continual financial difficulties of the secular clergy, mentioned so frequently in the Westminster papers, were the result of the government's dep-redations, not the Jesuits' greed. Also, the Jesuits had been genuinely unsure how far Clement VIII's breve forbade the two clerical bodies, Jesuits and seculars, from communicating with one another.[92] Hicks, echoing Persons, argued that those who supported the secular priests' agency to Rome were really only a small faction among the seculars. So the agency of 1609 was a continuation by similar means of the earlier scandalous excesses of the appellant priests. He illustrated this from passages in the seculars' own correspondence where they seemed to admit the smallness of the number who actively campaigned for their objectives.[93] And so Hicks proceeded on the presupposition, evident in all the contemporary writings of the English Jesuits, that the Society was essential for the maintenance of the Catholic faith in England. Dodd and Tierney, pointing to an opposed contemporary tradition, had assumed exactly the opposite.

All of these documents in the Westminster archive can, indeed, be read in two, directly opposite, ways, either according to the rhetoric of Dodd and Tierney, or that of Hicks. But the priests' battles were not as straightforward as these conflicting rhetorics often imply. It is clear that while the leaders of the secular clergy could count on a substantial

---

[90] The annotation of Hicks's volume often takes the form of polemical mini-essays about Tierney's failings as a historian. Hicks expressed his thoughts further in the margins of his own transcripts (at ABSI) of Robert Persons's letters: for example on one of 26 November 1608 (NS) – 'If I acted as T[ierney] has done I should consider myself dishonest. – and that was the adjective Bishop [John Henry] King [of Portsmouth] used when I read the original to him whilst he checked from Tierney's printed edition'. On the transcript of one of Matthew Kellison's letters to Thomas More (AAW A XII, no. 137) the transcriber, Edwin Chadwick, noted 'This seems a really sensible letter' and Hicks added underneath 'one of the few'.

[91] CRS 41, 4, 14–16, 53–4, 70–1.

[92] CRS 41, 48–9.

[93] CRS 41, 9–10, 75–101.

show of support for the main elements of their programme, principally
the appointment of a bishop over English Catholics, the bitter divisions
between clergy which these letters record cannot simply be put down
to the rival interests of two clearly separate clerical bodies. As Thomas
Fitzherbert wrote, 'some will make all to be Jesuits, that will not be
enemyes to Jesuits'.[94] This was the crux of the matter. Those who had
an inclination to join the Society, or were simply sympathetic towards
it, were not necessarily following all the directives of Jesuit activists
such as Robert Persons. Yet enough people who seemed to be opposed
to the aims of the secular clergy grouped around Birkhead did eventually
enter the Society, notably Thomas Fitzherbert himself and John Knatchbull. Others who did not, and yet opposed some of the secular
agency programme, such as John Bavant, objected to some aspects of
the Society's presence in England, and yet not to others.[95] Other priests,
such as the northerners Cuthbert Trollop and Cuthbert Crayford,
hated the Cassinese Benedictines (nearly as objectionable in some ways
as Jesuits) yet it was not clear how far this committed them to working
for the archpriest's objectives.[96] The newsletters printed here cast light
on the complexity of the internal politics of the Catholic clergy in
England during this period.

It has often been assumed that the priests were very narrow in their
outlook. For Catholicism was the religion of a tiny introspective minority
entirely absorbed with its own rather marginal concerns and petty
clerical squabbles. Yet the clergy's newsletters report substantial quan-
tities of English politico-ecclesiastical news and they comment on it
quite extensively. They closely observed what went on at the Jacobean
court and in James's privy council. Nor was this just idle gossip. Their
speculations in their newsletters about current political affairs and what
might happen in the future show that they thought they could exploit
fluctuations in Jacobean policy-making, particularly concerning the
Church in England and James's contacts with continental Catholic
powers.

*The English Political Context for Birkhead's Archpresbyterate and the Agency in
Rome*

How did the secular priests think that the Jacobean regime regarded
them, and how did they believe that they could improve their standing
with the king? In the period immediately after the Gunpowder Plot

[94] CRS 41, 59.
[95] **Letter 17**.
[96] **Letters 18, 21**.

King James explicitly announced that he did not regard all Catholics as treasonous king-killers. He said that the new statutory oath of allegiance of 1606 was designed merely to show who was loyal and who was not.[97] Initially it was far from clear that Catholics would be prohibited by Rome from taking the Jacobean oath. Also, the English Jesuits had clearly suffered a considerable public relations setback after the trial and execution of their superior Henry Garnet. Some of the secular priests had good reason for thinking that Rome might allow them to compromise over the oath and score a public relations victory at the expense of the Society by posturing as loyalists. Yet Paul V soon unequivocally condemned the oath of allegiance and, as we have noted, Birkhead was ordered to deprive any overtly oath-favouring priest of his missionary faculties.

All of this made life difficult for those like Birkhead who not only wanted to assure Rome that they could be relied on to support the pope's prerogatives but also desperately wanted to convince the Jacobean regime that moderate Catholicism represented no political threat to it. The seculars watched for any sign which might indicate how the regime construed their attitude to the oath. Detailed reports were sent to Rome of James's speech in the 1610 Parliament about Catholicism and recusancy. The signals were contradictory. The king seemed to be saying that in some sense Catholicism was tolerable yet he demanded that the laws against papists be enforced in full.[98] In May 1610 the assassination of Henri IV provoked a much more thorough and widespread enforcement of the oath. A proclamation of June 1610 ordered the oath to be ministered 'to all such persons, and in all such cases, as by the Lawe' could be summoned to take it.[99] Yet James's public statements (including the text of this proclamation) continued to distinguish between acceptable and unacceptable Catholicism. This implied that all avenues of approach to the regime and to some degree of favour were not closed.

But, as Birkhead pointed out to Richard Smith in July 1610, this need to have an eye to both the English and the Roman courts posed a real dilemma. The Jesuits were constantly upstaging the seculars by posing as papalists who were ready to die in defence of the pope's prerogatives. In order to keep up with the Jesuits, the seculars, who had no real wish to die in defence of the theory of the papal deposing power, had to claim that they were equally loyal to Rome, and that they persuaded those who came to them for the sacrament of confession

---

[97] See M. Questier, 'Religion, Loyalism and State Power in Early Modern England: English Romanists and the Jacobean Oath of Allegiance', *Historical Journal* 40 (1997), 311–29, at p. 314.

[98] **Letter 10**.

[99] Larkin and Hughes, 249.

not to take the oath of allegiance. But a very sizeable proportion of the English Catholic laity were even less keen than the average secular priest to challenge the regime on this score. As Birkhead wrote in early July 1610, now that 'this new oath is so pressed by the Kinge', 'it causeth many to stagger, yea even such of the laitie as much disliked it before'. The laity were trying to distinguish between their loyalty to James and to Rome by tacking a protestation onto the oath that they take it only as far as it affects their temporal loyalty to the king. Birkhead insisted, however, that he had made it clear the papal breves against the oath allowed for no such thing. He vainly claimed to believe that most of his clergy would stand firm. Nevertheless, he said, the Jesuit superior Robert Jones 'hath advertised me that it is supposed that the gravest and most lerned of the [secular] Clergie seame to incline therunto'.[100] As Birkhead knew well, the secular clergy were, potentially, vulnerable to accusations that they were weak in opposing the oath. Birkhead had written to Smith in April 1610 that 'some make me beleve that more honour is don to my predecessor [George Blackwell, who allowed the oath] then to me'. Some influential secular clergy, including even Thomas More, refused to break correspondence with Blackwell.[101]

There was, in fact, a distinct gallican element among the seculars. Priests such as Anthony Champney and William Bishop were not willing to be dragooned into a Jesuitical papalist refutation of the oath, and were open, therefore, to criticism.[102] There were certainly hints that, although Viscount Montague made a point of standing out against the oath,[103] other of the seculars' lay patrons, the Roper and More

---

[100] AAW A IX, no. 49 (p. 131) [part printed in TD IV, p. clxv]. The English Jesuits claimed to be the principal Catholic opponents of the oath, and 'sole maintainers and defenders of the deposing power', Foley VII, 1059.

[101] AAW A IX, no. 31 (p. 78) [part printed in TD IV, p. clxxx]; Questier, 'Loyalty', 316.

[102] Anthony Champney wrote to Thomas More on 31 July 1612 (NS) that he and William Bishop had been told by Robert Ubaldini, the nuncio in Paris, that accusations were made against them to Paul V that they favoured the oath, though Champney could allege that he had always counselled Catholics against it, and had two brothers who had been condemned in praemunire for refusing it and who had died in prison, AAW A XI, no. 128; E. Peacock (ed.), *A List of the Roman Catholics in the County of York in 1604* (1872), 2–4.

[103] Montague paid a fine of £6000, imposed in Star Chamber, for refusal of the oath (on condition, however, that it would not be offered again), **Letter 15**. Smith said Montague would have willingly lost all had he not been threatened with his son and heir being taken from him and drawn into heresy. Still, there was speculation that Montague had paid the fine in return for complete immunity from prosecution and that he had revealed information about the priests, AAW A X, nos 126, 142. In early 1612 Birkhead assured More that Montague's fine 'protecteth him nothinge for receyving of preistes. in so much that the other day comminge to London, [William] atkinson and another

families in particular, were in sympathy with the loyalist monk Roland (Thomas) Preston.[104] Birkhead was put in a quandary when *Controversia Anglicana*, a treatise by the Jesuit theologian Martinus Becanus, was censured by Rome and the Sorbonne in 1613: 'I wrote by chaunce to a frend that I marveled becanus his book was forbidden and not m[r] widderingtons [Preston's], and with all that Card. bellar[mine's] booke against him was not published: one of my owne brethren hath given it out to my disgrace, that I affirmed his hol [Pope Paul V] to have Censured Card. bell. which is false and never so much as dreamed of by me. but this I write to lett yow see, how redie those that should assist me, are to make men waver, and to colour it by lainge that imputation upon me'.[105]

The secular priests strove therefore to weigh up the consequences of every slight fluctuation in opinion and every new political development not just among the curial cardinals in Rome but also within the Jacobean regime in London. This is clearly reflected in the shape and content of their newsletters at this time. The controversy over the oath, mentioned in almost every single letter after mid-1610, was the backdrop to all their own political activity. It caused them horrendous difficulties. But the fact that King James had started a high-profile debate about what constituted loyalty to the regime, and where the division between public duty and private conscience should be fixed, did allow them the opportunity to negotiate a way into royal favour and make a pitch for toleration.

At first glance, the period immediately after Smith abandoned his agency in 1610 and returned to Paris was not, politically, a particularly auspicious one for the priests in England. Archbishop Bancroft died in November 1610 and, though the seculars thought briefly that his replacement would be either Lancelot Andrewes or Thomas Bilson,[106] it turned out to be the vehemently anti-Catholic bishop of London, George Abbot (in March 1611). In late 1610 executions of priests for treason began again after a period of more than a year when there were none: of Roger Cadwallader and George Napper in August and November 1610; of Thomas Somers and the seculars' friend John Roberts OSB in December 1610.

But even though the regime issued another proclamation (in 1611) enforcing the oath,[107] and more executions followed in 1612 (three

---

pursivant tooke a man of his one Iohn bennett from his heeles for suspicion of being a preist', AAW A XI, no. 13 (p. 36).

[104] See *e.g.* **Letter 55**.
[105] AAW A XII, no. 86 (p. 187). See **Letter 40**.
[106] AAW A IX, no. 88, X, nos 9, 10.
[107] Larkin and Hughes, no. 118.

priests and a layman), all was not lost.[108] There were still rumours of a proposed toleration. After the execution of Richard Newport and William (Maurus) Scott OSB, the layman Roger Widdrington was reported to have spread the news at Douai that James 'was displeased att the executione of the two prestes when he hearde howe they dyed with so great affectione to his service in all dutefull alleadgeance. He added further that there ys hope of more meeke courses in tyme'.[109] Even in December 1611 Edward Bennett had thought that James was likely to offer Catholics freedom from all penal statutes relating to recusancy in return for an annual composition of £20,000.[110] The death in 1612 of the lord treasurer, Robert Cecil, Earl of Salisbury, could not but be seen by many Catholics as promising a release from the enforcement of the penal statutes.[111] And the determination of the mid-Jacobean fiscal authorities to raise more revenue for the crown without resort to parliament meant that the officials of the exchequer had a vested interest in doing deals with Catholic recusants in order to derive some revenue from them rather than see them driven into conformity.[112]

The priests were very aware that the religious complexion of the court and of court politics was not a fixed quantity. They had even taken comfort in 1609 from James's 'Premonition'[113] (defending his published defence of the oath of allegiance) where he, as William Bishop said, 'in the end' adds 'this remarkable clause. that he is and ever wilbe of that faith and religion that [was] taught & received for

---

[108] In addition, the clergy were learning how to put these trials to good polemical use in Rome. They represented their martyrs as dying exclusively for refusing to take the oath. And when Cornelius O'Devany, Bishop of Down and Connor (also refusing the oath of allegiance) was executed for treason in Dublin at the beginning of 1612, **Letter 24**, this was represented as typical of the courage which a newly appointed *English* bishop might show if he came into conflict with the State: Champney wrote to More on 5 May 1612 (NS) that the execution had been attended by various miracles and 'the good bishope hadd his life offered him yf he would goe once to churche[.] what glorie would be to *our* countrie yf the lyke hadd happened there but alas we are farr from that happiness. I hope this will forwarde and facilitate *your* suite [for the appointment of a bishop]. the sufferinge of one Bishope dothe exceede the deathe of manie prestes for lustre and edificatione', AAW A XI, no. 73 (p. 211). (The enemies of the English secular clergy tended to use Ireland as an instance of a Protestant-dominated country where the papal policy of continuing to appoint bishops had been counter-productive, Conway *AH* 24, 41.)

[109] AAW A XI, no. 121 (p. 329).

[110] See **Letter 23**.

[111] **Letter 33**. *Cf.*, however, P. Croft, 'Robert Cecil, Catholics and the Creation of the Baronets of 1611', in P. Lake and M. Questier (eds), *Conformity and Orthodoxy in the English Church, c. 1560–1660* (forthcoming).

[112] See M. Questier, 'Sir Henry Spiller, Recusancy and the Efficiency of the Jacobean Exchequer', *Historical Research* 66 (1993), 251–66, at p. 262; AAW A XI, nos 1, 19.

[113] James I, *An Apologie for the Oath of Allegiance. ... Together with a Premonition of his Maiesties, to all most Mightie Monarches, Kings, free Princes and States of Christendome* (1609).

the first four or five hu[n]dreth yeres after Christ. he acknowledgeth his holines to be one of the first four patriarkes of the church, and is willing to grace him with the first place of those fower, because he is patriarck of the west church whereof his is a member'. Bishop did not pretend to understand how this could be reconciled 'with another principle of his, that the pope is Antichrist'. Nevertheless the pope should 'request the king of france', James's 'next neighbour, and much respected Ally' to notice 'the former part of his profession, that he imbraceth the faith' of the early church, 'and desire to ioyne Issue with him in a publicke Conference of some half dosen of ech of their subiectes, to try whether religion florished in the first five hyndreth yeres'.[114] In the period after 1610 entertainment was provided at the Jacobean court for people such as the sonneteer and former seminarist William Alabaster and the continental scholar Isaac Casaubon.[115] They were very anti-Jesuit but clearly not Calvinist and they were acceptable to, even favoured by, James. This reinforced other strong hints that the regime might realign ecclesiastically as it tried to play off various European powers against each other for foreign policy reasons. James constantly reworked his pose as a defender of orthodoxy, for example, as the priests carefully noted, in his reported pronouncements against writers such as Richard Field,[116] his campaign against Conradus Vorstius,[117] and the prosecution of the English Arians Bartholomew Legate and Edward Wightman.[118] In James's polemical reply to Cardinal Du Perron's open letter to Casaubon, the secular priest William Rayner noted 'yt is penned as from his maiesties mouth soom gesse by my lord of Canterburie others by the dean of Paules'. 'You would wonder to see how neer he cometh in manie points to the catholik fayth', in matters such as the Real Presence, prayer for the dead, and the Blessed Virgin. Also, 'divers other such lik speeches of other matters concerning religion and manie touching his...desier (for so he calleth it) of concorde, arr ther sett downe wherbie here is soom good hope conceaved of soom overture to furder good liklie to ensu'. Despite James's railing against Bellarmine he concluded courteously to Du Perron, whom the seculars

---

[114] AAW A VIII, no. 138 (pp. 577–8); Milward II, 92.

[115] **Letter 19**; AAW A XI, no. 49; **Letter 27**.

[116] **Letter 9**.

[117] **Letters 22, 23**. Simon Adams shows that the Vorstius controversy was used by English diplomats like Sir Ralph Winwood as a way of reasserting Protestant Calvinist links between England and the United Provinces against the presumed dangers from Johan van Oldenbarnevelt's pro-French and anti-Calvinist tendencies, Adams, 195–9. But the English Catholic commentators concentrated primarily on James's own announcement that his concern was to uphold religious orthodoxy (which did not have to be seen as simply a Protestant orthodoxy). See also F. Shriver, 'Orthodoxy and Diplomacy: James I and the Vorstius Affair', *English Historical Review* 85 (1970), 449–74.

[118] **Letters 24, 25, 26**.

regarded as one of their patrons.[119] There was, it seemed to the more optimistic priests, the chance that James's rage for orthodoxy might at some point become combined with a more moderate attitude towards Rome and Catholicism.

The main political issues for the priests were the marriage of the heir to the throne and, hence, the succession. The sudden union of Arabella Stuart and William Seymour in 1611 looked very like a bid for the succession.[120] In addition, as Simon Adams has shown, hostility between the Bourbons and the Habsburgs had, until 1610, allowed James to stay independent of them. After the assassination of Henri IV this Habsburg-Bourbon hostility was suspended. The negotiation in 1611 of the double match between France and Spain threatened the revival of a Catholic league. Something had to be done. It was a matter of urgency for the regime to make some definite provision for the succession. Although one possibility was alliance with German Protestant princes, a match at some stage with a continental Catholic power would almost certainly be necessary.[121] Successful negotiations were, indeed, concluded in late 1612 for a match between Princess Elizabeth and the Protestant Frederick V, Elector Palatine. But what mattered far more was the match to be arranged for the Stuart male heir.

A central component of all the marriage treaty negotiations on behalf of Prince Henry and then Prince Charles between the Protestant English Court and Catholic continental powers was a complex array of feints and gambits concerned with religion. The ceremonial observances to be followed by the prince's spouse, the number of her chaplains and the religious education of the children were crucially important. These domestic arrangements for religious observance could not be kept separate from the European power politics which informed the complexion of each marriage which was discussed. Inevitably, also, the religious provisions of the treaty would have an impact on the balance of power at the English court and the relationship between English Catholics and the State.

Florentine, Spanish, Savoyard and French brides were all suggested for Prince Henry. As Roy Strong has shown, the Medici family persisted in their strenuous efforts to conclude this dynastic treaty with the House of Stuart, but at every turn the match was obstructed, partly because of critics at the Stuart court, and partly because Rome could not be persuaded to sanction it.[122] The secular priests were far more optimistic

---

[119] AAW A XI, nos 48 (p. 127), 49; Milward II, 34–5.

[120] **Letter 15**.

[121] Adams, 192.

[122] For the Florentine marriage project, see R. Strong, 'England and Italy: The Marriage of Henry Prince of Wales', in R. Ollard and P. Tudor-Craig (eds), *For Veronica Wedgwood These* (1986), 59–87, at pp. 63–75.

about the prospects for a Savoyard match. Charles Emmanuel, Duke
of Savoy, who was politically isolated in Europe after the assassination
of Henri IV,[123] offered a double marriage, a daughter, Mary, for Prince
Henry and his eldest son, Victor Amadeus, for Princess Elizabeth. In
January 1611 the ambassador Sir Henry Wotton embarked on the
preliminary stages of negotiation for this alliance and thereafter pursued
it consistently. Initially the project ran into the opposition of the earl
of Salisbury, and the embassy of the Savoyard ambassador, the Count
of Cartignana, who brought the formal offer, met with refusal. But
when in November 1611 Cartignana returned with an offer of a match
just for Princess Elizabeth he met with James's interest in reviving the
proposal for Prince Henry to take a Savoyard bride. (Briefly James had
considered that Prince Henry might marry a Spanish infanta, but he
discovered in September 1611 the Spaniards were not serious about
their offer.[124]) The Savoyard diplomatic representatives remained in
England during 1611–1612 and the prospects for the marriage looked
good. The earl of Salisbury's death silenced his objections to it. It
seemed this was the way to settle the succession and, via the dowry,
the crown's mounting debts. Considerable diplomatic difficulties were
overcome by the Italians, in particular concerning the religious observance to be followed by the bride, to make the match a serious
proposition.[125]

But the French court, which in April 1612 had offered Princess
Christine, the second daughter of France, as a bride for Prince
Henry, now responded with a much improved dowry offer. James was
persuaded to look towards France.[126] Prince Henry, after a short illness,
died in early November 1612.[127] Birkhead told More in mid-December
1612 that 'all your fantasies of mariages were but dreames'. A London
preacher had said that Prince Henry had consulted, not long before
his death, 'x or xii of the best lerned ministers' who all advised against
a Catholic match, and so he proclaimed 'he wold never marrie with
any such'. But, in any case, the seculars themselves started to lose
interest when they learned that Savoy was making concessions about

[123] Smith, *Life*, I, 113, 467–8, 484, 487; R. Strong, *Henry, Prince of Wales and England's
Lost Renaissance* (1986), 81.

[124] Smith, *Life*, I, 119–20, II, 1; Strong, *Henry, Prince of Wales*, 80–3.

[125] Andrew Thrush, following Roy Strong, has argued that the Stuart regime was
taking seriously the Savoyard match for Prince Henry up until the prince's death, 'The
French Marriage and the Origins of the 1614 Parliament'. I am grateful to Andrew
Thrush for showing me a draft of this forthcoming article. See also Strong, *Henry, Prince
of Wales*, 82–3.

[126] Thrush, 'French Marriage'.

[127] A new Savoyard proposal offering another infanta, Catherine, for Prince Charles
never made much progress, despite James's initial willingness to negotiate, *CSPV 1610–
13*, 456.

the arrangements for the princess's religious observance. It seemed she would attend the liturgy of the established Church as well as having Mass said privately for herself.[128]

But soon James was considering a new offer from France – Princess Christine as a bride for Prince Charles. The principal go-between was the Huguenot Henri de la Tour, Duke of Bouillon.[129] Bouillon had led an embassy to England in April 1612. His purpose was technically to reassure the English court that the current Franco-Spanish double marriage treaty was not a sign of hostility towards England and to encourage (with Marie de Médicis's blessing) the Palatine marriage. But he had been authorised to negotiate the French dynastic marriage treaty with England which was first formally proposed at that time. For the English this represented both a defence against a Habsburg-Bourbon compact and a way of establishing some measure of influence in the French court. It would, as Simon Adams points out, have underwritten also an English involvement in the European 'Protestant cause'.[130]

Nevertheless, certain elements of this dynastic policy which might favour English Catholicism caught the priests' attention as they observed the arrivals and departures of ambassadors at James's court. Dynastic alliance with France could never have the same 'Catholic' overtones as a match with Spain. Yet, politically, any match with France would be informed by the character of the French Church, where the Jesuits often seemed to have far from an easy time.[131] Such a match could, the priests thought, with the rise to power of Robert Ker and the Howard ascendancy which detached Ker from his Protestant friends and brought

---

[128] AAW A XI, no. 228 (p. 657); cf. CSPV 1610–13, p. xi; AAW A XI, nos 195, 201, XII, no. 103. Cf. Smith, Life, I, 123–5; Adams, 214; Strong, Henry, Prince of Wales, 82–4; AAW A XI, nos 116, 192; **Letter 37**.

[129] Adams, 188–9.

[130] Adams, ch. 6. Bouillon had as early as spring 1611 proposed a French match for Prince Henry, which, as Adams describes it, would have been a '"protestant" French marriage', allowing for the extension of English influence into France rather than vice-versa, Adams, 191. As Richard Smith informed Thomas More from Paris in early February 1613, 'D. Bullion told a principal Gentleman who told it me that our late Prince was to have maried the second daughter of France and that he concluded that mariage at his last being in England. And that he assureth him self he shall returne thither to make the same mach with this new Prince. Here is saied that if our Prince had lived he wold have bene Captaine of the Hugenots in France and have made warr in thes partes', AAW A XII, no. 30 (p. 69). For Bouillon there was the possibility even of breaking the French-Spanish double match by this means (or at least of protecting French Huguenots from the potential effects of it) and bringing off a coup d'état in the French court by removing the leading minister Villeroi, Adams, 203, 211–12.

[131] In September 1612 the seculars were encouraged by attempts in the University of Paris to ensure the continued exclusion of SJ from it. Champney proudly reported that 'the advocate of the universitie' had argued against SJ by citing the facts of the Appellant controversy, AAW A XI, no. 148 (p. 405).

him under the influence of Henry Howard, Earl of Northampton,[132] instigate a fundamental change in English domestic religious politics, the sort from which self-professed moderates such as the clerical underwriters of the agency to Rome could hope to benefit.[133] As Ker gravitated towards the Howards (and towards marriage with Frances Howard) and away from Sir Thomas Overbury, Sir Ralph Winwood and Sir Henry Neville, James's own interest in Protestant politics abroad was seen to decline.[134] Robert Pett wrote to Thomas More on 10 November 1612 (NS) that Thomas Sackville, the sponsor of the secular clergy's writers' college in Paris, had told him of the rise of the Howards and of Ker who had 'the eare and purs of' Prince Henry. Sackville conceived he would now be able to exert some influence in the court on the Catholics' behalf.[135] John Jackson reported, through Pett, that, even before Prince Henry's death, Ker ruled 'all in scotland as absolutely' as James's favourite, George Home, Earl of Dunbar ever did; 'yt is thought he shalbe secretarye and the Erle of Northampton Tresorer'. They were now lined up against George Abbot, William Herbert, third Earl of Pembroke and Edward Lord Zouch. A recent spate of anti-Catholic rumours, mostly spread about by Abbot, had been exposed for their falsehood and Abbot 'is sayed to have had the foyle in 3 or 4 of this nature'.[136]

It seemed that the often repeated Catholic toleration polemic about Elizabethan Catholics having done no more than support the rightful Stuart heir was finally making sense. Robert Pett passed on John Jackson's account of the reinterment of Mary Stuart's remains in Westminster Abbey in 1612: she was brought 'one thursday the 8th of October past at 7 of the Clock in the night from St: James...to Westminster: accompanied with torch Light and some 8 coches wherin were the Lord Chancelour the Erle of Northampt. the Archb: and some others and ther was ringing all that night, and I remember beinge a boy that I heard the bels ringe all night for Ioy of the cuttinge of, of her hed, soe that yow sea what chang of tymes doth work and how

---

[132] Adams, 216–17.

[133] The secular clergy watched the rise of Ker with interest. Admittedly in June 1611 Champney thought it 'badd tydinges' that Ker 'whoe ys alreadie knight of the garter and as some say Earle of Devonshire and expecteth or hopethe to be Duke of Buckinghame' was rumoured to 'have begged my lord montacute' [*i.e.* Viscount Montague's forfeiture for refusing the oath of allegiance], but he noted that it displeased the 'haeretikes' as well, AAW A X, no. 63 (p. 171). And, in fact, Ker told Northampton that he refused to accept Montague's forfeiture, *CSPD 1611–18*, 151. In September 1613 the Spanish ambassador was reported to have informed the Spanish court that Ker was 'no persecutor' of English Catholics, *CSPD 1611–18*, 199.

[134] Adams, 236.

[135] AAW A XI, no. 208 (p. 597).

[136] AAW A XI, no. 215 (p. 615).

trew that vers of Claudian is; Mobile mutatur semper cum principe vulgus'. Pett noted encouragingly that 'some mutteringe alsoe we heare of some breach and fallinge out betwene the Erle of Northamp: and the Archb: and that ther hath hard words passed betwixt them'.[137] The Calvinist court party which had stood for a Protestant strategy in Europe took the wrong side in the divorce proceedings when Frances Howard separated from the earl of Essex in order to marry Ker.[138]

Naturally, there was a certain illogicality in the priests' hope that a French marriage project would come out of these alterations in the balance of power at the court of James I. Very few privy councillors were in favour of the French marriage.[139] The new, though temporary, dominance of a loosely-allied 'Spanish' faction, centred on the Howards and assisted by the Spanish ambassador, Diego Sarmiento de Acuña (the future Count of Gondomar), would hardly further it! Northampton actually incorporated the French marriage project as one of the targets of his anti-Scots campaign in 1613-1614.[140] The Howards were soon set on a Spanish match for Prince Charles.

But for the secular clergy the prospects of a French dynastic match seemed, while they lasted, to tie in well with their own petitioning campaign in Rome and their hopes for the amelioration of their conditions in England. In February 1613 William Bishop wrote to More that 'the best meanes that I can now think of is by the way of france'. And if Marie de Médicis 'be not to hasty after the match, but do stand as in Christian honour she is bound, to have good conditions for the intertaineing of her daughter in the Catholike faith as to have a Chapple allowed i[n] England, & three or fower chaplinges & fre accesse to her chapple, then will she bee a great countenance to other Catholike Ladyes, & may be in tyme a speciall good meanes with her husband for the bearing with all Catholikes'. More should lobby the pope and curia to ensure that any advantage which might come to Catholics through the marriage should not be lost.[141]

Promising signs were to be found in the conversion to Catholicism of such as the royal chaplain Benjamin Carier. In mid-to late 1613 he pitched an appeal for the king's attention with a diatribe against the evils of Calvinism. He was a sworn enemy of George Abbot. He was refreshingly moderate when it came to the difficult question of the oath

[137] AAW A XI, no. 226 (p. 653). See J. Woodward, *The Theatre of Death* (Woodbridge, Suffolk, 1997), 139–40.

[138] Adams, 241.

[139] Thrush, 'French Marriage'.

[140] Adams, 243. Thrush shows that Thomas Howard, Earl of Suffolk, urged the calling of parliament in 1614, rather than making a dynastic treaty with the French, as a solution to the crown's debt problems, Thrush, 'French Marriage'.

[141] AAW A XII, no. 35 (p. 78).

of allegiance. For some reason he seemed attracted to the Jesuits, but, before his unfortunate early death in 1614, he tried to make contact with the secular clergy in Paris. The poet Henry Constable, the seculars' lay associate, was instructed to recruit him for their Paris writers' institute, the Collège d'Arras.[142] It seemed significant that Carier, a founding member of Chelsea College, the Protestant writers' academy which enjoyed a royal financial subsidy, might cross over to its Catholic opposite in Paris. It was suggested also that he might return to England in the train of the French princess if the dynastic match arrangements with France were successfully completed.[143]

Meanwhile, in London, the secular clergy watched for every sign that the regime's policy of stifling Catholicism was becoming destabilised. The Spanish noblewoman Luisa de Carvajal y Mendoza was resident in London at this time, and was often mentioned in the secular clergy's letters. She was, with her utter disregard for the regime's policy towards Catholics, a sort of running test case to see if the regime had the nerve to maintain its normal hard line towards the capital's Catholics while at the same time negotiating with foreign ambassadors over proposed Catholic dynastic marriages for Prince Charles.[144]

Yet the French match failed. As we have already noted, there was considerable opposition to it among James's privy councillors. The duke of Bouillon whose services were essential to the pursuit of the project lost his former influence at the French court and he was soon to be driven into open defiance to Marie de Médicis. This breakdown in French politics made the further pursuit of the marriage proposal impossible. James turned to a Spanish marriage instead.[145] Spain was almost always more active in representing and promoting the interests of English Catholics than the French were. And William Bishop was finally appointed Bishop of Chalcedon with authority over English Catholics in mid-1623 when it looked as if the Spanish match would succeed. But this was almost ten years in the future. The seculars would not be able to exploit fully their French contacts again until the failure of the Spanish marriage project and the choice of Henrietta Maria as a bride for Prince Charles, an event which was intimately connected with the appointment of Richard Smith as second bishop of Chalcedon, in succession to William Bishop.[146]

In the end, then, the dislocation of mid-Jacobean foreign policy coincided with and confirmed the breakdown of the secular priests'

[142] G. Wickes, 'Henry Constable, Poet and Courtier, 1562-1613', *Biographical Studies* 2 (1953–4), 272–300, at p. 293.
[143] Questier, 'Crypto-Catholicism', 49.
[144] **Letter 48**.
[145] There was a brief attempt to revive the French project in 1616.
[146] Adams, 256, 261–72; Allison, 'Richard Smith'.

own ecclesiastical programme for reform. They had achieved only a limited measure of success. They would now have to wait. The newsletters from the English seculars to the agent in Rome continued, but the pace and urgency which characterised the 1609–1614 period were not seen again until the early 1620s.

The Agency Newsletters and the Reporting of News

The news reported by the secular clergy to their agent was a crucial weapon for him to do battle with in the struggle against his adversaries in Rome. Even the most trifling bits of news were carefully composed and inflected. These clerical newsletters were never merely lists of interesting facts which just happened to be reported by English Catholic priests to a more than usually inquisitive correspondent in Italy. All of these letters carry a set of clearly identifiable glosses produced by an acute political sense of how Catholicism fitted into early seventeenth-century English political culture. Even if the significance of some of the information is not always immediately clear, the very fact of the expensive postal rates[147] ensured that the things reported by the writers were never random. The agent summarised and translated them, and placed them in front of the eyes of the curial cardinals on whom the priests were relying for favour. Many such summaries by Thomas More survive in copy in the Westminster papers.[148]

What seem like incidental pieces of gossip were usually not idle chatter. For example, when John Bennett reported from the South West on 19 October 1610 that an ex-secular priest, Peter Chambers, who had joined the Church of England, found a patron in Matthew Sutcliffe, and, having obtained a post in Exeter Cathedral, had then been hanged for sodomising choir boys,[149] this was not mere tittle-tattle but a case study of what happened when secular priests were sent into England without adequate seminary formation, were then deprived of funds and adequate Catholic patronage, and were not subject to proper regulation. And these were all things which could be blamed on the seculars' enemies, the Jesuits, who maladministered the seminaries under their control, kept Douai short of funds, collared gentry patronage

---

[147] The priests sometimes ripped covers off books in order to reduce their weight and thus save money when sending the books around Europe, AAW A XI, no. 116.

[148] See *e.g.* AAW A X, no. 110 (Latin summary of aspects of the persecution of English Catholics in letters of July and August 1611); AAW A XI, no. 229 (summary in Latin of some of Birkhead's newsletters, incorporating *inter alia* the story about George Abbot, the goldsmiths' company and St Dunstan, for which see M. Questier, *Conversion, Politics and Religion in England, 1580–1625* (Cambridge, 1996), 24n).

[149] AAW A VIII, no. 167 (pp. 657–8).

in England and prevented the appointment of a bishop.

The reports retailed by the seculars about the famous convert Benjamin Carier served several functions and operated on several different planes. On one level it was simply heartening that this moderate Protestant should decide, at an opportune moment, to cross the seas in search of a new spiritual home. Yet Carier figures in the newsletters because he could be used to express so much of the seculars' propaganda. He showed that a faction within the Church of England which valued hierarchy and order above misguided puritan zeal was sympathetic towards Rome. Crucially, it seemed that even after converting to Catholicism he retained some influence within the English Church. Anthony Champney noted that Carier was 'recalled into England with great promises'. Carier was, therefore, proof that the seculars' claims that their kind of churchmanship was the right one for England and this time, and would not be offensive to the increasingly influential more moderate Church-of-England clergymen or to the crown. If Carier's conversion were, however, not to prove permanent, this would simply show how 'yt ys much to be lamented that the heretikes are so readie to entertayne our runegates and that we are so could to receave suche as seeke the harboure of godes churche'. This would be simply more evidence that the lack of institutional supports for the English secular clergy was holding back the conversion of England.[150]

These newsletters were also a primary source for the construction of martyrology. Narratives of the sufferings of the most recent martyr were often embedded in or enclosed with them when they were sent to Rome.[151] In part these accounts tried to contest the regime's assertions that priests convicted in the royal courts under the 1585 statute ('An Act against Jesuits, seminary priests and such other disobedient persons', 27 Eliz. I, c. 2) were guilty of treason. Each martyr story stressed that the priest could have saved his life by taking the Jacobean oath of allegiance, which the Roman authorities had condemned as a Protestant religious, not a political, test. Hence the priest suffered for his religion alone.[152] This was a much more complex task than might be imagined from the easy phrasing of these narratives as they have come down to

[150] AAW A XII, no. 190. See also **Letters 45, 49, 52, 53.**

[151] After the executions of priests such as Roger Cadwallader, George Napper, William (Maurus) Scott OSB and Richard Newport, a flurry of accounts of how they died were directed towards Rome. Anthony Champney replied to More's letter to him of 8 August 1612 (NS), 'wherein you wishe a more particuler and ample narratione of our brethrens sufferances', by saying that he had 'a letter writen by a frenche gentleman out of Ingland to his frend here in parise contayninge almost the whole manner of the deathes of the two last martyrs [Newport and Scott] which beinge writen by a stranger will beare more credit'. He would send it as soon as he could, though he understood there was already an Italian version of it doing the rounds in Rome, AAW A XI, no. 141 (p. 391).

us in the pages of Bishop Challoner's *Memoirs of Missionary Priests*. It was necessary for the secular clergy martyrologists to gloss over the fact that the Jacobean regime was quite consistent about those whom it brought to the gallows. The priests who were executed in this period all had an air of extremism about them. For example, Roger Cadwallader, put to death in August 1610, had been involved in the disturbances in Herefordshire in 1605 when the regime first learnt the dangers of its new spirit of toleration.[153] He had been a good friend of the priest Robert Drury, executed in February 1607. Drury had behaved outrageously in the court room during his trial, deliberately mocking the Elizabethan statute against reconciling to Rome.[154] Drury and the Benedictine John Roberts were both seen with Powder plotters days before the treason came to light.[155] And John Almond, who was executed in December 1612, had apparently played down the evil of tyrannicide.[156] So the secular priests' narratives of the trials and punishment of priests often needed to perform an elaborate redescription of such cases in order to make them serviceable. This was one of the newsletters' most important and taxing functions.

The martyrological accounts of the secular priests served another important polemical purpose. Their claims that their executed priests had, in fact, been loyal became a way of stressing to the Jacobean regime that the secular clergy and the laity whose patronage they enjoyed ought to be granted some form of toleration whereas the Jesuits, because of their political extremism, ought not. Equally they were designed to show the authorities in Rome that it was the secular priests (together with a few Benedictines) who primarily suffered the wrath of the authorities and thus irrigated the faith in England with their blood.[157] The seculars wanted to disabuse those in Rome who thought that the Jesuits in England were the ones who principally suffered for the faith. Edward Bennett wrote to Thomas More in November 1612 that as for the recently arrested Jesuits John Percy and

---

[152] For an account of John Almond's execution which shows how the tradition around a martyr was constructed, see **Letter 38**.

[153] Anstr. I, 237; **Letter 12**.

[154] *A True Report of the Araignment, Tryall, Conviction and Condemnation of...Robert Drewrie* (1607), sig. B4r-v.

[155] AAW A VIII, no. 85 (pp. 432–3); J.H. Pollen (ed.), *Acts of English Martyrs* (1891), 149.

[156] See **Letter 38**.

[157] The fact that both John Roberts OSB and William (Maurus) Scott OSB were executed with a secular priest was a visible symbol of the perfect accord and union which ought to and could exist between the secular clergy and the best intentioned of the religious. (Roberts and Scott were both Benedictines of the Spanish congregation which supported the secular clergy's petitions for ordinary jurisdiction, whereas the Cassinese congregation of OSB generally did not.)

Nicholas Hart,[158] the rumour that they had been martyred was utterly
false: 'it is soe farr from it, that by this as I heere they are at liberty in
flawnders'; they had merely been banished 'as the report goeth; soe
that you see how sore they be persecuted'.[159] As Birkhead noted in mid-
December 1612, 'no men are so bitterly spoken of as the Iesuites, yett
be they never soe odiouse, they escape farre better then preistes'.[160]
And the witness of the martyr could be turned into an argument for
the aims of the agency. Some of the martyrs of the 1610–1612 period
are reported as affirming just before their deaths that they think the
English Catholics are in dire need of a secular clergyman with episcopal
authority in order to govern them![161]

Yet, in their reports of the severity of the persecution (one of the
principal arguments which Jesuits such as Robert Persons used to show
that a grant of ordinary jurisdiction to English secular clergy could not
be risked because it would further enrage the Protestant regime and it
would thus be impossible for the bishop to exercise his functions
properly), these newsletter writers draw back to some degree. In other
words, though the persecution is bad, it is not so bad that Rome cannot
appoint a bishop for England. This is one explanation for the martyr
stories' frequent references to the malice of high-ranking Protestant
clergy whereas they make far fewer references to the intolerance of the
secular authorities. In December 1609 Birkhead wrote that the bishops
'bend ther indignation against us', but 'the civil magistrate is somewhat
more mild'.[162] The death of Roger Cadwallader in 1610 was blamed
on the animosity of Robert Bennett, Bishop of Hereford.[163] Archbishop
George Abbot was said to be especially malevolent. After his promotion
to the see of Canterbury the priests tended to load the blame for the
persecution almost entirely on him. The martyr John Roberts, in his
'last dying speech' at the gallows, was recorded as saying, 'neither is it
the King that causes us to die, he is a clement king; it is heresy, it is
heresy that does this'. This account stressed that George Abbot was
'Father Roberts his chief adversary, and had stood with greatest
vehemency against him at his trial, animating the Judge against him'.[164]

Admittedly Abbot was furiously anti-Catholic, but the structure of
these narratives of persecution was undoubtedly designed to make

[158] See **Letter 20**.

[159] AAW A XI, no. 192 (p. 555).

[160] AAW A XI, no. 228 (p. 657).

[161] See e.g. AAW A IX, no. 88 (p.293) (Birkhead's note of 15 November 1610 that
George Napper, the day before his execution, sent his 'voice for bb under his owne
hand' and his nomination of those he thought 'fitt for such a dignitie'). See also AAW A
XI, no. 164.

[162] AAW A VIII, no. 188 (p. 705).

[163] **Letter 12**.

[164] Richard Challoner, ed. J.H. Pollen, *Memoirs of Missionary Priests* (1924), 320–1.

curial officials in Rome think that the Jacobean regime's secular officials were fundamentally tolerant. So the maverick archbishop, so encouragingly unlike some other members of the episcopal bench (particularly Andrewes[165] and Bilson), and the busybodies employed as high commission pursuivants were more or less the sole cause of the Catholics' difficulties. And, perhaps, despite Catholics' suffering, the English situation was on the verge of alteration. The evidence was there in Abbot's apparently increasing political isolation. Champney noted with enthusiasm that Abbot had been overzealous in abusing the Irish deputies who were summoned to England in late 1613 over matters of religion. King James gave him 'a sharpe reprimande...telling him he hadd caused him to have the name of a tyranicall and bloodie kinge abroad amongst his neyghboure princes'. When Abbot was 'bould to expostulate' with Ferdinand Boischat, Archduke Albert's ambassador in England, about his master's support for English Jesuits and seminary priests and for allowing the printing of seditious pamphlets, which, Abbot claimed, breached the peace treaty between their two countries, Boischat treated him with disdainful contempt. Others said that Abbot was 'in disgrace for the ladie Elsabethe her mariage as a thinge solicited by him and nowe turninge to the dishonoure of the kingedome and the smale contentment of the ladie in whome lyethe the greatest hope of posteritie the prince [Charles] beinge verie weake'.[166] Abbot also suffered a reverse over the divorce of the earl of Essex and Frances Howard which Abbot opposed. Champney noted in mid-December 1613 that 'Bilson. b. of winchester [who supported the divorce] ys like to be of the councell by the Howardes meanes and Carres [Ker's] together in despit of Canterburie'. And he added that Thomas Harley 'wrote unto me that he harde the kinge was about to reforme the oathe but I knowe not what truthe there ys in that'.[167]

But, at the same time, the circulation of martyrological narratives prevented people from playing down the persecution. It guarded, therefore, against the danger that, if a dynastic match were arranged for one of the royal children with a Catholic power, the possibility of securing some form of legal toleration for Catholics would be lost because the regime's treatment of them could be safely ignored by the negotiators. The secular priests hated the scholar Isaac Casaubon who came to England to enjoy King James's patronage, for, as Thomas

[165] The secular priests continued to enthuse about Andrewes because of his offensiveness to Calvinists and moderate puritans. In December 1621 William Bishop reported that King James 'did countenance' Andrewes 'seeming to say masse' and that the chapel royal should be decorated 'after thold maner' and a 'crucifix of gold...sett in it', AAW A XVI, no. 72 (p. 248).

[166] AAW A XII, no. 179 (p. 395); **Letter 47**.

[167] AAW A XII, no. 224 (p. 501); K.C. Fincham, *Prelate as Pastor* (Oxford, 1990), 44–5.

Heath wrote to More in July 1612, 'Monsieur Casabon...so much excuseth our state, to the Christian world abroad, saying that none are punished for Catholick Religion'. This, Heath insisted, was a scandal in view of the miseries which prominent Catholics were now suffering.[168] William Bishop wrote to More in February 1613 that it would be a good idea to petition Paul V to instruct the nuncio in Paris 'to call upon the preachers...to speake freely of the greate persecution in England, which do dayly increase. for it might be a speciall good meanes to make our king to stopp those cruell courses, yf he heard' that 'the neighbours countryes did ring of them'.[169]

The writers' sources of information were generally good, even if the priests frequently complained about the difficulty of sending letters. Some who lived outside London, such as Benjamin Norton, marooned in the Midhurst area in Sussex, did think themselves rather isolated. Norton complained that 'wee can have noe certaintye of newes (unlesse it bee of thinges donne under owr nose) but from London & by that tyme wee have from thence & sende it thither againe & from thence to yow wee thinke it will be stale & therefore wee sende it not att all'.[170] Yet Norton's letters provide unique detail of what was happening in and around the main centres of Catholicism in Sussex and Hampshire. They are also a source for studying how fast and effectively news was transmitted and how national news networks interacted with local ones.

These priests' newsletters do not always add substantially to our knowledge of current affairs, but, in their accounts of, for example, the execution of Lord Sanquhair, the death of Sir Edward Hoby's son, the conversion of Protestant clerics such as Theophilus Higgons, Humphrey Leech and Benjamin Carier, the burnings of the Arians Legate and Wightman, events in parliament and at the court of James I, and so on, one obtains a Catholic gloss on items of news which tells one a great deal about the clerical network which was generating these letters and how English Catholicism worked politically.

The Newsletters and the Structure of English Catholicism

It is normal and correct in historical accounts of the post-Reformation English Catholic community to stress that clerical Catholicism in England relied heavily on a structure of closely interrelated families, usually of gentry status and above. But far less often have historians delved into these gentry networks. Did these associations of families

[168] AAW A XI, no. 115 (p. 315).
[169] AAW A XII, no. 43 (p. 93).
[170] AAW A X, no. 29 (p. 67).

come into being after the Reformation or did they exist before it? What was it that brought certain priests to particular gentry houses and not others? These are hard questions to answer. But these newsletters are one source which enables the historian to start addressing them.

Neither this introduction nor the annotation of these letters make any pretence to have fully unravelled the network around which these letters were passed. But it is clear that these letters with their constant reference to lay and clerical friends, contacts and enemies do demonstrate, to a greater degree than can be gleaned from any other source, who knew, trusted, and hated whom among the promoters of Birkhead's agency. They tell us something about how the coalition which promoted that agency came into existence, how it saw itself, and how it was maintained.

On one level, the newsletter writers were simply the archpriest Birkhead's assistants and confidants who wrote to Rome in order to support the archpriest's agent. Yet to describe them either as representatives of the entire secular clergy, as Tierney and Dodd imply,[171] or as a small and unrepresentative faction, as Hicks suggests,[172] is partly to miss the point. Not the least significant aspect of this collected correspondence is that it is a record of a clientage network based primarily on the Browne family at Cowdray. The priests' interests were heavily sponsored by Anthony Maria Browne, second Viscount Montague. Birkhead and several other priests moved regularly between Viscount Montague's houses in Sussex and London. As noted above, Smith and More had also been chaplains at Battle in Sussex to Magdalen, dowager Viscountess Montague. One of the families with which the Brownes had important marital alliances was the Dormer family of Wing in Buckinghamshire. Edward Bennett, one of the newsletter writers, was chaplain to Lady Elizabeth Dormer (daughter of Anthony Browne, first Viscount Montague). Another secular priest, Cuthbert Johnson, served Margaret Constable (née Dormer) as a chaplain in Yorkshire. In 1606 Johnson was temporarily resident with the Tyrwhit family in Lincolnshire. (The first viscount's second son, Sir George Browne, married a Tyrwhit;[173] and so would the second viscount's daughter Catherine.) Henry Shaw, one of Blackwell's assistants who seems to have been acceptable to the Birkhead regime, was resident in 1606 with Sir Francis Lacon. Lacon's father had married the first Viscount Montague's daughter Jane.[174]

[171] TD V, 22, 29.
[172] CRS 41, 9–10.
[173] See W.H. Rylands (ed.), *The Four Visitations of Berkshire* (2 vols, 1907–8), I, 76. *Cf.* W. Page, P.H. Ditchfield and J.H. Cope, *The Victoria County History of Berkshire* IV (1924), 239.
[174] PRO, SP 14/19/111; W. Bruce Bannerman (ed.), *The Visitations of the County of Sussex* (1905), 84; **Letter 53**.

There has been a tendency to ignore the political potential of this sort of patronage. Christopher Haigh, for example, argues that the activities and correspondence of these priests shows that Catholicism had retreated into a quiet seigneurial existence. Priests such as Birkhead were trying to monopolise the plum chaplaincies in the Catholic gentry's houses. 'From a missionary point of view', says Haigh, 'the placing of three chaplains' with Lady Montague at Battle was 'indefensible'. Presumably he means they should have been more evenly distributed around the Sussex countryside, ministering to rural Catholics of lowly status, but were too lazy to exert themselves thus. Yet since Richard Smith and Thomas More were two of those chaplains, and these priests were using their seigneurial residences to spearhead their programme to reform Catholicism in England, we cannot think about them, their influence and contacts, and the clientage network they inhabited simply on the basis of whether they performed quasi-parochial duties for the benefit of the populace or stubbornly stuck to the gentry instead.[175]

It seems clear that Birkhead's closeness to Montague must have influenced his appointment as archpriest in succession to Blackwell.[176] He had, of course, been a coordinator of the seminary priests from at least the early 1590s,[177] and evidently he was acceptable to Rome because he was sufficiently distanced from the disgraced Blackwell, was not rampantly pro-Jesuit and yet had not been an Appellant. But we know that Anthony Lambton,[178] Birkhead's sister's brother-in-law, had a son, Richard, who, disappointed of his inheritance in the North, made his way to Midhurst in Sussex where he became a gentleman retainer of Viscount Montague. This undoubtedly facilitated Birkhead's residence with Montague. Birkhead was living at Cowdray from at least 1605, probably earlier.[179]

Thomas More, the clergy agent, was actually related by marriage to the Browne family as a result of the union between Lucy Browne, the first Viscount Montague's sister, and Thomas Roper of Eltham (the son of William Roper and Margaret More). The More and Roper families helped to sponsor and support these priests who came to coalesce around the second Viscount Montague. William Bishop, the leading secular clergyman who became, at an advanced age, the first Bishop of Chalcedon in England, had at the very start of his priestly career in early 1582 been put in charge of a house belonging to the Mores in or

[175] C. Haigh, 'From Monopoly to Minority: Catholicism in Early Modern England', *Transactions of the Royal Historical Society*, fifth series, 31 (1981), 129–47, at p. 142.

[176] Rather unconvincingly Robert Persons assured Birkhead that his appointment was essentially fortuitous, TD V, pp. xxxii-iii.

[177] PRO, SP 12/240/144.

[178] Also written 'Lambe'.

[179] PRO, SP 14/19/111; *Salisbury MSS* XVII, 500.

near London, possibly the one at Low Leyton in Essex.[180] John Colleton, another of More's correspondents, lived during his last years in the Ropers' house at Eltham where he died in October 1637.[181] Seemingly minor clergy who crop up in the seculars' correspondence seem to merit their stray mentions because they were part of the More-Roper network. For example, George Tias, arrested at Bentley in 1612, was one of the Tias family who were tenants of the Mores at Barnburgh in Yorkshire.[182] Thomas Doughty[183] the Carmelite, an occasional correspondent of the seculars, had been, for a time, a servant of the Ropers.[184] John Redman, another priest who was regularly mentioned as a reliable source of help with funding the agency to Rome, and also with printing Richard Smith's books, was the son of Robert Redman and Bridget Clement, and thus a grandson of Margaret Giggs, Sir Thomas More's adopted daughter.[185] Edward Bentley, who visited Robert Pett in Brussels in mid-1613, was one of More's cousins.[186] John and Thomas Roper, sons of Sir William Roper and cousins of More, were active promoters of the agency. In late 1613 Champney asked More to give his regards to Thomas Roper, currently in Rome. Champney hoped that he would become a 'churche man', and also that God would 'one daye' make him 'fitt to doe *our* countrie manie good offices'.[187] (The words 'countrie' and 'the secular clergy' appear to have been interchangeable in Champney's letters!)

The Montague clerical network extended throughout the Catholic families of Sussex and Hampshire. For instance, Geoffrey Pole, son of the prominent Sussex Catholics Geoffrey and Katherine Pole, and a great nephew of Cardinal Reginald Pole, was a close associate of the secular priests, and had himself at one time been in the English College in Rome. When Smith and More were sent to Rome in 1609, Pole soon followed. He took up residence in the household of Edward Farnese, Cardinal Protector of the English nation, formerly his 'grand patron', in order to influence his judgment about English matters.[188] The priest and newsletter writer Benjamin Norton was related to most of the Sussex and Hampshire families mentioned in these letters,

---

[180] AAW A X, no. 115; Anstr. I, 37.

[181] Anstr. I, 84.

[182] **Letter 31**; Anstr. I, 357–8.

[183] alias or *vere* Dawson. His name in religion was Simon Stock.

[184] Anstr. II, 83.

[185] Anstr. I, 287; AAW A VIII, nos 102, 183, IX, no. 3.

[186] AAW A XII, nos 109, 147; D. Shanahan, 'The Family of St. Thomas More in Essex 1581–1640', *Essex Recusant* 7 (1966), 105-14, at p. 107; A.J. Loomie, 'A Grandniece of Thomas More: Catherine Bentley *ca.* 1565-*ca.* 1625', *Moreana* 8 (1971) 13–15; T.J. McCann, 'Catherine Bentley, Great Grand-Daughter of St. Thomas More, and her Catholic Connections in Sussex', *Moreana* 11 (1974), 41–5.

[187] AAW A XII, no. 205 (p. 460).

including the Poles to whom he was very closely attached. So were the Heath brothers, one of whom, Thomas, was Richard Smith's servant.[189] So also was the secular priest John Copley, whose 'apostasy' and betrayal of the 'principal suit' [for the appointment of a bishop] to Archbishop Abbot so amazed the clergy.[190]

The Irish dimension of these newsletters clearly has something to do with the Brownes' Irish relations, the FitzGerald family, earls of Kildare.[191] The appellant priest Francis Barnaby went to serve as chaplain to Mabel, the elder countess of Kildare who was one of the sisters of the first Viscount Montague.[192] The Irish Catholics' complex but flexible relationship with the English crown, and their credible assertions of loyalty to James, impressed these secular priests. The Irish Catholicism described in these newsletters, particularly since it incorporated episcopacy, was evidently included in order to be used in Thomas More's petitions to the curia in Rome.[193]

It seems possible, tentatively, to suggest therefore that after the death in 1592 of the conformist first Viscount Montague, his grandson, Anthony Maria Browne, who succeeded to the title as the second viscount, changed the religious complexion of the Montague household. Relying on the Brownes' virtually clear political record and reputation for loyalism, he decided to assist, and perhaps also profit from the rhetoric of, the secular clergy's continuing struggle against the Society of Jesus in England. Though he is represented in these letters as a meek and persecuted figure, it is clear that if the agency's schemes for extending the priests' authority in England came to fruition, Montague would to some considerable degree be influencing what the Catholic Church in England was like and what it did. This web of clerical relationships, sketched only in outline here, suggests that these news-letters, and other material like them, constitute a source for constructing a very different history of both clerical and lay Catholicism in England during this period. They illuminate the opinions and aspirations which this network of families had. They take us beyond saying just that these families invested a great deal in a separated English Roman Catholicism, a statement which itself simply begs a great many questions about them and their religion.

---

[188] **Letter 6**. In 1613 Benjamin Norton was discussing the possibility of a marriage between Katherine Pole (Geoffrey's sister) and Thomas More's brother, AAW A XII, no 126; **Letter 46**.

[189] **Letters 1, 6**.

[190] **Letter 22**.

[191] **Letters 12, 24**.

[192] **Letter 12**. Francis Barnaby came from the same Yorkshire parish, Cawthorne, as Anthony Champney.

[193] See *e.g.* **Letter 54**.

The Source

In my annotation of this material I have tried to indicate the identity, where I am certain of it, of all of the individuals cited. (I have generally identified individuals when they first appear in the text, and then again in each letter when there is any doubt about their identity, as for example when their names are not given sufficiently in full or aliases are used.) I have also added material from other letters in the Westminster Series A. I have done this, rather than simply print more letters, partly because of the constraints on length in modern publishing, and also because, inevitably, the letters are repetitive. Five or six writers were writing regularly to the same recipient. Frequently they were recording and commenting on the same events as well as urging similar courses of action. Some letters contain only one substantial point of information. Thus, while the printing of all, or even most, of the extant letters could not really be justified, it is hoped that the annotation which I have incorporated, pointing briefly to significant material in other letters, will make the letters which are printed here that much more useful and open up these volumes of the Westminster papers to researchers. However, partly to save space and partly because it is not really necessary, I have omitted to annotate fully the episodes and occurrences the basic details of which can easily be ascertained from other sources. Likewise I have not provided full annotation for the agency of Richard Smith in Rome (1609–1610) because much of it was dealt with by Hicks in his volume of Thomas Fitzherbert's letters. Again, I have not attempted to add standard biographical information as a matter of course about, for example, each of the priests whose names occur in these letters. The basic facts of their ordination and career can usually be elicited from the standard works – such as Anstruther's biographical dictionary of seminary priests, Foley's records of the English province of the Society of Jesus, and other well-known Catholic sources. I have provided biographical detail about them only where it is necessary for the interpretation of the text, particularly where the material from the Westminster papers about them is not recorded in any other source.

THE NEWSLETTERS

1 *Benjamin Norton to Richard Smith and [in Smith's absence] Thomas More (8 May 1609)   (AAW A VIII, no. 106, pp. 499–500. Holograph)*

My very good frendes I deferred my wrightinge soe long that I feared mee yow woulde thinke I had forgotten yow for wante of matter to wright of, and meanes to sende. but nowe I have to to muche matter unlesse yt weare better. Wee weare verry lyke to have loste M.ʳ Wilson[1] whoe abought the latter ende of Aprill fell daingerouslye sicke, abought which tyme hee wrought unto yow, but hee was lyke to have beene in his grave beefore the letters wente owte of the howse. and albeeit hee stande a hylene (as children saye) yett is it generallye thought thatt hee is soe wasted, and spente with the sicknes, that hee will scareslye bee able to goe to them which some tymes sende for him. to whome hee had now gone had not his sicknes hindred him. but thankes bee to god he wente not. for when that side [?] hathe him amongst [word illegible] them [?] whatt maye they not doe with him? Accowmpte of him as noe longe liver & provide againste suche a sede vacante whatt is best ['bee' deleted] to bee donne. Mʳ Dorme[2] is well but to to busye in alteringe of Roomes in his howse. for whome yow might doe well (as Mʳ Brough[3] adviseth mee to wright) to begg a vestmente & tunic of his holynes. for yt woulde bee taken kindelye in the highest degree. All thinges goe well in ouer partes & there are some 3 or 4 of the Ministerye abought us that are willinge to ryse, & as manye moe not far of woulde doe the lyke, yf there weare some good order taken for them when

---

[1] George Birkhead.

[2] Elsewhere (*e.g.* AAW A X, no. 126) references which Richard Smith makes to 'Mr Dorme' clearly indicate Anthony Maria Browne, second Viscount Montague. However, Sir Robert Dormer, of Wing in Buckinghamshire, who married Elizabeth Browne, daughter of Anthony Browne, first Viscount Montague, was also a host to the secular clergy.

[3] Richard Broughton, secular priest.

theye came to our side. M.ʳ Mʳ [sic] Parker⁴ & Draton⁵ have resigned there offices as Mʳ Brough telleth mee whoe sawe owne of theire letters abought it; butt none are chosen in theire places. M.ʳ Rich. Carye⁶ hathe beene beetrayed, searched, & apprehended, & Mʳ Marshall⁷ with him, and well nigh 15ᶜˡ taken from him, which moneye they woulde macke us beeleave pertained to the Archepriest.⁸ but yf it did, it was moore then hee knewe, & I thinke. for butt a weeke beefore (as M.ʳ Archepriest. tolde mee him selfe) M.ʳ Carye complained of wante & sente unto him for money and had xˡ sente him. the Lorde of Salesb:⁹sayed that it pertained to Rich¹⁰ a riche Iesuitt & therefore lett them looke (or bee lookt unto) howe they gather suche somes when many bothe preests & poore Catholiques bee in great wante. For there is continnuall [?] begginge of Recusantes both riche & poore, & Claud [or 'Cland'] the blacksmithe of our parishe skapeth not Free [?]. There

⁴ Richard Parker, secular priest, became an assistant to the archpriest George Blackwell and went to Rome in 1602 with Giles Archer to represent Blackwell against the appellants, Anstr. I, 269. He entered SJ in 1608, CRS 75, 261. He died at the end of April 1609, AAW A VIII, no. 123. Birkhead was unaware in May 1609 that Parker had become a Jesuit, AAW A VIII, no. 110. Cuthbert Trollop was appointed in Parker's place in May 1610, **Letter 10**.

⁵ William Hanse, secular priest, who resided mainly with the East Anglian pro-Jesuit families of Drury and Rookwood, Anstr. I, 147–8. He became one of George Blackwell's assistants in 1598. In December 1609 we find him, with the priests John Bavant and Ralph Stamford, refusing to sign the secular clergy's letters to the cardinal protector, AAW A VIII, nos 187, 188.

⁶ The recusant Richard Carey, CRS 76, 19, 41, 66, 80. Cf. CSPD 1603–10, 310, 403, 503; ARSI, Anglia 37, fos 105v–6r.

⁷ Birkhead reported Carey's arrest on 22 March 1609, and said that Marshall, a footman (apparently in Viscount Montague's service), was imprisoned in the Gatehouse because he 'shuffled off' the oath of allegiance when it was tendered to him, AAW A VIII, no. 96 (p. 471). The informer William Udall effected the arrest. Marshall was thought to be a priest, possibly Hugh Philips alias Evans, ordained in 1602, since Marshall's own alias was Phillips. Richard Blount SJ noted that Marshall was arrested at Carey's house in a secret hiding place, ARSI, Anglia 37, fo. 104r.

⁸ Birkhead said the sum of money was £1100, AAW A VIII, no. 96; Richard Blount said it was £1300 'and bonds for some 3000ˡⁱ more', ARSI, Anglia 37, fo. 106r. Cf. CRS 76, 66; Harris, 'Reports', 242. Some of this money belonged to the deceased recusant Thomas Hoord (who had a sister in the service of the Browne, Dormer and subsequently Sackville families, Davidson, 257). Both Carey and Hoord seem to have been trustees of funds for the maintenance of the Catholic clergy, PRO, SP 14/20/21, 31/26. According to Blount, the seizure was made at Carey's brother's house in Holborn. Thomas Ravis, Bishop of London, intended to retain Carey's property but 'the Treasurer hath seased all for the King', ARSI, Anglia 37, fos 104r, 106r.

⁹ Robert Cecil, first Earl of Salisbury.

¹⁰ This may be Edward Walpole SJ whose alias was Rich. But Edward's brother, Michael, also a Jesuit, used the same alias. See **Letter 9**.

hath beene greate searchinge in hampeshire at one M[r] Cuffolds[11] by
Rowse.[12] Cross.[13] Bonneragg[14] & Braye[15]. & one M.[r] Finche[16] hathe
latelye ioyned him selfe with Cross. & came downe to his sisters by
Battell & gott x[l] from her. Theare was found drowned in a ponde not
far from thense at a place called chintinge[17] one Robert a Cooke, whoe
was some tymes fellowe servaunt with my Cosin Tho: heathe.[18] This

[11] Alexander Cuffauld, the son of William Cuffauld and Mary the daughter of Sir
Geoffrey Pole of Lordington (fourth son of Sir Richard Pole by Margaret Pole, Countess
of Salisbury). Constance Cuffauld, one of William Cuffauld's daughters, married Richard
Lambe of Sussex. During this period Benjamin Norton usually resided with the Lambe
family. Constance was formerly a gentlewoman of Magdalen, Viscountess Montague,
second wife of Anthony Browne, first Viscount Montague, *CSPD 1591–4*, 381. The Lambes
lived in Midhurst, **Letter 42**, although the family also had property in Tillington,
WSRO, Ep. I/17/11, fo. 37r; J. Cockburn (ed.), *Calendar of Assize Records: Sussex Indictments:
James I* (1975), 17.
[12] Anthony Rouse, secular priest. He was banished in mid-1606, returned to England
and renounced his Catholic clerical orders. See Anstr. I, 295–6; A. Jessopp, *Letters of Fa.
Henry Walpole, S.J.* (Norwich, 1873), 39–40.
[13] Humphrey Cross, a messenger of the chamber who was employed also as a high
commission pursuivant.
[14] John Wragge, high commission pursuivant, who had arrested George Blackwell in
June 1607.
[15] Richard Bray (or Bracy), messenger of the chamber and high commission pursuivant;
cf. Salisbury MSS XXI, 63–4. The secular priest Edward Bennett wrote on 26 December
1611 that, four days before, on 22 December, as George Gage was being escorted to
appear before Archbishop George Abbot by Wragge, Rouse, Bray and John Griffin, a
struggle took place in Milford Lane between the pursuivants and Sir William Price, one
of Price's brothers, and a Lieutenant Frost. Gage escaped. Griffin and Wragge were
wounded. Rouse was thrown into the Thames. Wragge killed someone who came out of
a tavern to intervene. Wragge was arrested and taken to Newgate, but was released,
AAW A X, no. 166; *cf. Downshire MSS* III, 181. On 31 January 1612 (NS) Anthony
Champney reported that 'the newe commission given to the pour[s]ivantes…extendethe
to the seasinge of all money and goodes which by probable coniecture are ordayned to
the mayntenance of prestes but they cannot execute this without the assistance of a
constable which…will excuse on m[r]. Gage who ys sayd to have killed a pursuivant who
chalenged him or his man for a preest', AAW A XI, no. 11 (p. 25). (Earlier, on 20
November 1611, Bennett, too optimistically, had written that, on 17 November, Wragge
had been so badly injured by a gentleman, who defended a priest whom Wragge tried
to arrest, that Wragge was likely to die, AAW A X, no. 148.)
[16] Thomas Finch, a secular priest who had turned renegade. He was a cousin of the
Shelley family at West Mapledurham, Buriton, Hampshire, Mott, fo. 364v. On 23
September 1609 (NS) however, Thomas More, in Paris, wrote to Richard Smith that
Finch had now come to Paris 'poor and needie [r]epenting him selfe of his former
courses', AAW A VIII, no. 154 (p. 625). Later, in March 1611, Norton noted that Finch
had left the Benedictines whom he had temporarily joined in Louvain and had returned
to England with Sir Henry Wotton, AAW A X, no. 29.
[17] Chyngton in Seaford parish, East Sussex.
[18] Thomas Heath, son of Jerome Heath, at whose house in Winchester in 1592 Norton
had narrowly escaped arrest, Anstr. I, 257. See **Letter 17**.

laste weeke a servingman of on S.ʳ Io: Carrells[19] in fervencye & zeele desired hee might dye a protestaunte. Yt hapned that hee fell drunke in the lorde, & fell downe a paier of stares, & brused him selfe soe that hee died the nexte morning [sic] & beefore dinner hee stuncke untollerablye. those of the Clinke[20] doe Clincke [?] still. onelye Mʳ Charnocke[21] is at libertye & confined to a place.[22] yt is sayed the prisoners shall bee remooved to Frammingam[23] but it is not done, & it is rather feared thatt they shall starve elswhere in prison. Wee have gathered noe multitude of voyces[24] in our partes, butt wee meete with none butt beeinge [?] asked graunted theire consents. soe thatt there is noe doubte of thatt matter. Theare was (as Mʳ Wood[25] tellethe mee) an insurrection of iiiᶜ woomen in Glostershere in defence of theire wood & common.[26] Theare is nowe a greate some of money to bee leavied uppon the Cuntry towards the knightinge of the prince.[27] the Kinges booke is come owte &c & recauled by proclamation, & some saye come owte againe[.][28] wee muste not saye whatt is in it. butt beeinge dedicated principallye to the Emperour & other Christian princes I doubt not butt yow shall knowe by theire ledger ambassaters[.] D. Westons booke is printed againe & hath a newe name I knowe not what.[29] There is a booke come owte of an xxviiiˢ price in defence of the prerogative of princes againste the pope.[30] I speake but by hearesaye. The beeginninge

---

[19] Either Sir John Caryll of Warnham, who died in 1613, or his son Sir John Caryll of Harting, though probably the former.

[20] Norton means the priests in the Clink prison in London who favoured the 1606 oath of allegiance.

[21] Robert Charnock, secular priest.

[22] Birkhead reported on 2 May 1609 that other prisoners might also enjoy liberty on the same conditions as Robert Charnock, 'namely to reside with some man no recusant and to returne when the…state calleth for them upon a moneths warninge', AAW A VIII, no. 102 (p. 489).

[23] Framlingham Castle in Suffolk.

[24] i.e. for the suit for the appointment of a bishop over the English Catholics. Birkhead had recently ordered his assistants to collect the signatures of all the secular priests assenting to the suit.

[25] Identity uncertain.

[26] Richard Holtby SJ informed Robert Persons SJ that '3. or 400' women resisted 'the kings officers about cutting downe the wood of the forest of Dean', though they were 'suppressed' by Sir Edward Winter and the sheriff; but 'manie men of wealth are called in question for it and some [are] in prison', AAW A VIII, no. 105 (p. 498); cf. Hasler III, 675.

[27] Prince Henry. See CSPD 1603–10, 494.

[28] James I, An Apologie for the Oath of Allegiance (1609); STC 14401, 14402. The revised edition was issued on 8 April 1609 after the first edition was called in on 7 April, Larkin and Hughes, 211.

[29] Edward Weston, De Triplici Hominis Officio (Antwerp, 1602), reissued twice in 1609. See ARCR I, nos 1359–61 (for the different titles).

[30] William Barclay, De Potestate Papae (1609).

of Maye is extraordinarye hott, & therefore wee feare wee shall have
fatt Churchyardes. The sicknes increasethe and is despersed [?] in the
Cuntrye. Mr Poore^{31} taketh but smaule Comforte, & the rather for that
your cuntryman hath gotten the starte of him. hee telleth mee of a
spitefull answere that is come foorthe against them that doe nothinge.
I woulde yow did knowe howe I pittye him. Well. farewell my good
frends & assure your selfe thatt wee your poore bretheren will not bee
unmindefull of yow. & I hope yow will sometymes thinke of us. yf yow
wright to mee yow shall the oftener heere from me. yf not then will I
not wright untill some urgente occasion offer it selfe for feare leaste I
bee to bolde with my frends. Commende mee to my frends with yow
especially Mr Beech^{32} by whose meanes I hope yow shall receeve theese
letters which are writtne in haste this 8th of Maye. My Nedd^{33} hath a
younge Nedd. I keepe the ringe on my finger which yow putt mee in
truste to keepe untill your returne by which token yow may [word
illegible] mee.
(On p. 500)
Addressed: Al Illustre et molto Reverendo Sigr Ricardo Smitheo Inglese,

---

^{31} Not certainly identified. For the recusant family of Poure of Bletchingdon, Oxfordshire, see Davidson, 148–50.
^{32} Robert (Anselm) Beech, ordained in 1594 and professed OSB at St Justina, Padua
in 1596, Anstr. I, 28. Henry Bird's anti-Jesuit account of the troubles in the English
College in Rome during the 1590s alleged that the Jesuits called Beech 'miserable and
perfidious' after he left for OSB, because 'for the sixe fyrst yeares which he stayd in the
Colleedge, he was a vowed Iesuit', AAW A V, no. 112 (p. 407); Lunn, *EB*, 18. In late
1607 Beech had arrived in Rome in order to resist SJ's efforts to have the Benedictines'
English mission suppressed. Under the terms of the settlement of December 1608 imposed
on SJ and OSB by the Inquisition, Beech was ordered not to return to England, Lunn,
EB, 78, 82.
^{33} The identity of this individual is uncertain. In Norton's letters, 'Nedd' seems to
indicate his brother-in-law, the husband of a sister named Sybil/Isabel. Internal evidence
in the newsletters suggests that 'Nedd' may be the leading Kentish recusant Edward
Wyborne of Hawkwell. In a letter to More of September 1613, Norton wrote that the
letters which he had most recently written to Rome were full of 'Irishe matters' because
he had been in a place where he heard Irish rather than English news. At the same
place he had heard that an 'earle', whom he describes as 'neighbour' to 'my Nedd', was
'not like to be sente into his one [= own] cuntrye in haste', AAW A XII, no. 164 (p.
365). This may refer to Richard Bourke, fourth Earl of Clanricard, who had property at
Tonbridge, close to Pembury where Edward Wyborne of Hawkwell lived. Edward and
his wife were presented as recusants at Battle in East Sussex during this period, as well
as at Pembury in March 1613 with the earl of Clanricard himself. In the Sussex
presentments Edward's wife's name is given as Sybil, J. Cockburn, *Calendar of Assize
Records: Kent Indictments: James I* (1980), no. 761; **Letter 39**. (Norton mentions Wyborne
by his surname in his account of the seizure of recusants' property at Battle in October
1610, **Letter 12**.) However, genealogical and other evidence fails to support this. There
is a consensus that Wyborne's first wife was Susan, daughter of Richard Warnford, but
no consensus about his second wife's identity. So the question of identification here
remains unsettled.

sacerdote et Doctor della sacra Theologia, et in sua absentia
al Signore Tomaso moro sacerdote Inglese[.]   Roma
Endorsed: (1) [word illegible] May. 8: 609 [sic]
        (2) Archpr sicknesse; Kings book

2 *George Salvin (Birkhead) to Richard Smith (9 July 1609)*   (AAW A VIII,
no. 127, pp. 549–50. Holograph)

my verie Good S^r, I cannot expresse the ioy which we all have had
from your letters which I received last from M^r swinnerton[34] of the 23
of may and 6 of Iune.[35] we much Congratulate your good beginninges
hopinge greatly that yow shall make an happie end. I am glad yow
have so well spedd in the first point, and also that both fa Rob[36] and
m^r Swin agreed so well with yow therin.[37] my whole desire is that yow
keepe frendshipe with them, and that yow first Conferre and treat of
matters before yow propose them to our superiours, both because I
had no other intention in settinge downe the articles,[38] and also for
that yf yow canne conclude amongst your selves yt will beare greater
shew of love and peace, and I dowbt not but that his hol will soonest
yeld unto that wherin yow shall unitely agree. Againe I wold desire
yow (as I have written unto yow in another of the 6 of Iuly[39]) that for
so much as I have in my declaration conioyned yow and m^r Swin to
deale in our matters, and have signified so much to his hol Card

---

[34] Thomas Fitzherbert, the secular clergy agent in Rome appointed by George
Blackwell.

[35] The first of these letters has not survived. That of 6 June is AAW A VIII, no. 116,
in which Smith relates his favourable reception at Rome.

[36] Robert Persons SJ. Thomas Fitzherbert's letter to Birkhead of 23 May 1609 (NS)
(TD V, p. lviii; CRS 41, 48) stated that Persons had already met with Smith and promised
cooperation in the clarification of the status of the breve of Clement VIII of 5 October
1602 (NS) which ordered the archpriest not to consult with SJ about the government of
the secular clergy. For the breve, see CRS 41, 11 n. 5. Birkhead had been appointed
archpriest without a specific reference to the relevant clause in the breve, the meaning
of which was, in any case, disputed, TD V, p. xxxix; CRS 41, 48 n. 3, 119 n. 12.

[37] Persons had written to Birkhead on 14 February 1609 (NS) that he would assist
Smith, as long as Smith came to Rome well-intentioned, in a private capacity, and was
willing to cooperate with Fitzherbert, TD V, p. lvii. Persons notified Birkhead on 6 June
1609 (NS) that, at Smith's request, he had assented to the agency's first object, that
Birkhead should, like Blackwell, be 'bound' not to deal with SJ 'in matters of your
government', TD V, pp. lxii–iii. Persons's private letters to Birkhead were soon expressing
criticism of Smith, TD V, pp. lxvi–viii, lxxii–iii.

[38] The articles carried by Smith as agent for Birkhead.

[39] AAW A VIII, no. 125.

farnesius,[40] and to the Generall,[41] in my Letters unto them, yow wilbe
verie carefull in usinge <u>the said m^r Swin confidently</u> in our affaires,
who hath promised me to be serviceable, and most redie to helpe yow
in what he can.[42] your other Letter of the 16 of may I heare not of as
yet, and therfor have not the Copie of your Supplica, which I could
have wished to have seen for diverse respectes. this letter shall come
unto yow by a new waie which I hope wilbe secure. the way by Paris
is the most unsure of all the rest, and therfor I have no list to use yt. I
will omitt no opportunitie, to lett yow heare often from yow [sic for
'me']. assure your selfe that seinge yt hath pleased his hol to make this
interpretation of Clem his breve, I wilbe verie carefull to observe yt,
and yett to keepe frendshippe also with our foresaid frendes, because
the thinges wherin we may communicate with them will minister cause
sufficient of the Continuance thereof.[43] I have written also unto yow to
putt up a memorial for a pensione for me, use I pray yow <u>m^r fitz</u> helpe
about the same, I am the more willinge to aske yt because yt may be
a good helpe for your charges there, and I shall take as much heare of
the comon, yf yow impart unto me what the pension is.[44] I beleve yow
shall find much difficultie about dowaie,[45] but I have don what I can
to dispose m^r Rob and m^r Swin to concurre with yow therein. we have
no extraordinarie occurrences, the <u>b of</u> London[46] <u>braggeth that we all
are not</u> able to answere m^r blackwels bookes,[47] yf we were, yt wold

---

[40] The cardinal protector of the English nation, Edward Farnese (son of Alexander
Farnese, Prince of Parma). No copy of Birkhead's letter is in AAW.

[41] A copy of Birkhead's letter (taken to Rome by Smith) of 17 February 1609 to the
Jesuit general Claudio Acquaviva is AAW A VIII, no. 93.

[42] Persons was soon reporting to Birkhead that Smith and More were bypassing
Fitzherbert in their efforts to secure an audience with the pope, TD V, p. lxxi.

[43] See CRS 41, 48 n. 3. In his letter to Smith of 6 July Birkhead noted that Paul V
confirmed Birkhead was 'not to impart any thinge to the fathers concerninge the regiment
of our Clergie but to deale onely with them in dubiis theologicis, in casibus conscientiae et
in rebus spiritualibus, which I trust we shall strictly observe', AAW A VIII, no. 125 (p. 543).

[44] In a letter to Smith of 9 August 1609 Birkhead acknowledged that both Smith and
Persons were trying to secure the sum (150 crowns) which would be retained in Rome, and
an equivalent sum given to Birkhead by Smith's 'frendes' in England, AAW A VIII, no. 140
(p. 583). The attempts to secure the pension were, apparently, unsuccessful, CRS 41, 62, 67.

[45] For the English College at Douai, see CRS 41, 58 n. 5. Birkhead acknowledged that
Fitzherbert resolutely opposed the secular clergy's proposed reforms of the college, but
wanted Smith 'to keepe his frendshippe still' because he might help in other ways, AAW
A VIII, no. 130 (p. 555). (Fitzherbert reminded Birkhead that 'your charge is limited only
to the government of priests within England, and Scotland...the matters of Doway or of
the other seminaries, or priests abroad, doe not belong any way unto you', CRS 41, 73.)

[46] Thomas Ravis (though perhaps Birkhead was thinking of Richard Bancroft, Arch-
ishop of Canterbury).

[47] *Mr. George Blackwel ... his Answeres* (1607); *A Large examination ... of M. George Blakwell*
(1607), translated as *In Georgium Blackvellum Angliae Archipresbyterum ... Quaestio Bipartita*
(1609).

have ben answered by this. the bookes of m^r Higgons[48] and m^r leach[49] are to excedinge good purpose and have don much good. m^r Higgons is answered by s^r Edward Hobie,[50] but he will gaine no great commendacion for it. D Andrewes b of Chichester hath sett a Latine booke against Tortus,[51] I have not yet seen yt, but they say it is most eloquent with little substance. and so beseechinge almightie God to blesse yow in your proceedinges to the increase of our wished peace with hartie Commendacions from all your frendes, I leave yow to his most holy protection. this 9 of Iuly. 1609.

yours alwaies assured

Geo Salvine[52]

(On p. 550)

Addressed: To his verie good frend M^r D Smith give these at Rome

Endorsed: 9: Iuly: 609 [sic]

3 *Christopher Bagshaw to Thomas More (4 August 1609 (NS))*   *(AAW A VIII, no. 137, pp. 573–6. Holograph)*

Good m^r More.

I reaceved only one letter from yow by m^r Champneys[53] pacquett & he no more as he will signifye. What will ensue Bianchetto[54] his letters[55] theffect will showe. Many conceyve smalle hope from an Antihierarchicall Archpriest[56] of any good & that conceypte fortyfyed by delegation to m^r Thomas fitzherbert a man of good partes & my freinde in particular but against whome some suppose inefragable exseptions. This very day was signifyed to me by reporte (& letters they

[48] Theophilus Higgons, *The First Motive of T.H. Maister of Arts, and lately Minister, to suspect the Integrity of his Religion* (Douai, 1609); *idem, The Apology of Theophilus Higgons lately Minister, now Catholique* (Rouen, 1609).

[49] Humphrey Leech, *A Triumph of Truth* (Douai, 1609).

[50] Sir Edward Hoby, *A Letter to Mr. T. H. Late Minister* (1609).

[51] Lancelot Andrewes, *Tortura Torti: Sive, ad Matthaei Torti Librum Responsio* (1609), replying to Cardinal Robert Bellarmine SJ, *Responsio Matthaei Torti Presbyteri, & Theologi Papiensis, ad Librum Inscriptum, Triplici Nodo, triplex cuneus* (Cologne, 1608).

[52] Birkhead started to sign his surname as 'Birkhead' but then changed it to 'Salvine'.

[53] Anthony Champney, secular priest.

[54] Cardinal Lawrence Bianchetti, Vice-Protector of the English nation, generally regarded by the secular clergy as unfavourable to their interests. He had been a chamberlain to Gregory XIII. He had supported the scholars in the English College in Rome in 1579 when they campaigned for the Jesuits to be installed there, J.H. Pollen, *The English Catholics in the Reign of Elizabeth I* (1920), 280. He represented SJ's case to the pope during the conflict between SJ and the students at the college in the 1590s. Bianchetti was enlisted by SJ in their struggles against OSB in 1607–8, Lunn, *EB*, 78.

[55] See **Letter 8**.

[56] Birkhead was aware that Bagshaw did not trust him, AAW A VIII, no. 92.

say) from Rome that the Pope meaneth to make Byshopps for Englande. I have tolde the Nuntio[57] heere that some will not mislike if f Parsons be made a Byshoppe (the Pope in his conscience thinckinge him able, wherof others dowbte) so that he will goe into Englande from whence he ranne awaye[58] & there defende that Oathe wherof he talketh & writeth beinge out of gunshott.[59] The Kinge hath turned him over to the halter & one Barloe who termeth him selfe of Lincolne hathe bestowed more Epithetes of him than will be conteyned in a sheete of Paper.[60] d Andrewes calleth him Person[ ] Histrio & what further I shall see in the processe of the booke. If leasure had served I had sent yow his portraycte[.] Ante omnia spoliat*us* e*st* restituend*us* saythe the lawe.[61] Our college in Rome due to our cleargy is nowe to be gotten wher so many i[n] banisheme*n*t of the Cleargy ar ready to starte. [p. 574] The*d*ucation of yowths in hope to have them of the Cleargye is a good thinge uppon a fundation destined to that ende under the governieme*n*t of the Cleargye & in suche a forme as is sutable for our cawse & cowntrye. W*i*th these reiglement[s] [?] things prospered under

---

[57] Robert Ubaldini, Bishop of Montepulciano, papal nuncio in France. In June 1609 he tried half-heartedly to obstruct Richard Smith's journey to Rome (or at least to moderate Smith's impetuosity), AAW A VIII, no. 115; Conway *AH* 23, 133. But in 1612 he advised Rome that on balance a bishop should be appointed for English Catholics in spite of Jesuit objections, Allison, 'Richard Smith's Gallican Backers', part I, 341. The leading secular priest William Bishop, however, still did not trust him, AAW A XII, no. 35, although Ubaldini in June and August 1612 had assured the papal secretary of state, Cardinal Borghese, that Bishop was firmly opposed to the 1606 oath of allegiance, Conway *AH* 23, 98–9.

[58] For Bagshaw's antagonism towards Robert Persons at Balliol College, Oxford in the 1570s, and ever since, see A. Kenny, 'Reform and Reaction in Elizabethan Balliol, 1559–1588', in J. Prest (ed.), *Balliol Studies* (1982), 17–51.

[59] Bagshaw refers to Persons's most recent work against the oath of allegiance of 1606, *The Iudgment of a Catholicke English-Man* (St Omer, 1608).

[60] William Barlow, Bishop of Lincoln, attacked Persons in *An Answer to a Catholike English-Man* (1609). Richard Holtby SJ reminded Persons in a letter of 6 May 1609 that Barlow 'was my Lo. of Essex his Confessor at his death' and 'published al that the poor Lo. had told him in secrett for the discharge of his conscience, as this minister then pe*r*suaded him'. Holtby noted that Barlow's book would shortly appear, and that Barlow was concerned at James's words in the first edition of his *Apologie for the Oath of Allegiance* that he would leave Persons to the 'hangman'. Barlow thought it might remind the public of his role in justifying (at Paul's Cross) the condemnation and execution of Robert Devereux, second Earl of Essex in 1601. Seeing that the king's 'booke was called in to be in some thinges corrected, he wold be pleased, that those wordes (the hangman) might be leaft out', 'for otherwise persons wold in his reply play upon him, and call him by his ma*ie*sties warrant Hangman, for answering his booke' and so 'in the next edition he wished instead of the (Hangman) the (Rope) might be put in', AAW A VIII, no. 105 (p. 498). Barlow noted in his *Answer*, sig. Ar, that James 'vouchsafed not the Conflict with such a Rake-shame, but adiudged a Rope the fittest answer for him'. See James I, *An Apologie for the Oath of Allegiance…Together with a Premonition* (second edition, 1609), sig. (c)r; Milward II, 110–11.

[61] 'out of Barloes booke' written above.

d Allen.[62] The defectes since his time yow see what troobles & scandals they have browght & lytle else. Pope <u>Gregorye the thirtenth so liberall & Apostolicall towardes owr cowntrye might dispose of many thinges</u> before banishement of priestes was practized which he <u>woulde not doe nowe</u> if he were alive. Doway is nowe termed a place for fooles. Besides Rome & dowaye we have nowhere a library without which it will be harde to answeare suche bookes as dayly come out against us.[63] S[r] Edwarde Hoby hath written against m[r] Higgins a late converted minister[64] & it is thowght they will drawe lay men to be writers to have a party more stronge against us. further they nowe erect a college neere london[65] for twelve or more to write in controversyes who shall be passing well furnished of all thinges.[66] Urge yow the like for Catholiqus[.][67] Hic Rhodus, hic saltus.

My fellowe Parsons his writinges ar so odiouse that as they have pictured the divell eatinge souldiors & excrementinge Iesuites (with your reverence) so some say his bookes will serve for paper to make all cleane & ar for litle better use. [p. 575]

The complementes of that place ar not to preiudice godes churche in our cowntrye which is nowe almost browghte into ruine. I have talked with m[r] d Stephens[68] whome I would yow had saluted. He liveth where many holde yt not only Apostoli[c] but also <u>Seniores ar videre [word illegible] verbo hoc that</u> is of businesses concerninge the churche & that iure Divino. He knoweth him selfe to be one of the aunciest [sic for 'auncientest' ?] of our Cleargye & others of the woorthyest. Suche men ar not to be neglected.

In respect of your owne person & coastly travayle in our affayres I wishe yow all good & dayly (I assure yow) remember yow at the altar

[62] Cardinal William Allen.

[63] Bagshaw and John Cecil were distrusted by secular priests like William Bishop because they had ruined a project for a college in the University of Paris for the secular clergy, AAW A XI, no. 172; PRO, SP 12/269/27, fo. 44r; CRS 41, 51–2.

[64] Hoby, A Letter. For Theophilus Higgons's conversions to and from the Church of Rome, see Questier, 'Crypto-Catholicism', 60.

[65] Chelsea College.

[66] Anthony Champney noted on 14 August 1609 (NS) that Archbishop Richard Bancroft 'gevethe a librarie of 3000[li] [Matthew] Sutcliff [Dean of Exeter] 800[li]' and King James had promised financial assistance, AAW A VIII, no. 142 (p. 589).

[67] A college in Paris was desired by the secular clergy in which they could respond to Protestant polemicists and also pursue higher degrees at the Sorbonne. The college was set up in October 1611, housed and financed by the generosity of Thomas Sackville, fourth son of the first earl of Dorset. In 1613 it moved into the recently refurbished Collège d'Arras, a fourteenth-century foundation belonging to the Benedictine Abbey of St Vaast at Arras, Allison, 'Richard Smith's Gallican Backers', part II, 255–8; idem, 'The Origins of St. Gregory's, Paris', RH 21 (1992), 11–25, at pp. 12–13; CRS 41, 51–2.

[68] Richard Stevens, formerly a secretary to Bishop John Jewel of Salisbury, Anstr. I, 334.

that god may make your labowres well to succede yett I finde some willinge to propose nothinge to the Pope. Thinges be so farre out of square, time & opportunyty so neglected that they thincke (& some have tolde me) the Iesuites woulde poppe us in the mouthe with some formalle nothinge & therfore that yt is best to leave the[m] to theyre owne contrition & infaelicytye. The learnedest of all the Iesuites[69] in fraunce tolde me within these fewe dayes that to [g]rante Byshopps in Englande was against all au[tho]rytye [&] religion. your grandfather St Sr Thomas[70] iesteth [(y]ow Knowe) at him who woulde have beene byshoppe of Utopia & commendeth him non obstante lege ambitus.[71] The inference I referre to yow & comend me humbly to yowr holy devotions. Saluto ex corde d doctore Smithe. Parisiis E Collegio Ave-mariano[72] August 4°: 1609.

Yours in all sinceryty

   Christofer Bagshaw

(On p. 576)

Addressed: To his very Worshipfull & good frende m^r Thomas More
        Preist in [?] Rome

Endorsed: (1) Aug. 4. 609 [sic]
        (2) Hagshaw [sic] 4 Aug.

4 *George Salvin (Birkhead) to Richard Baker (Smith) (17 September
   1609)   (AAW A VIII, no. 152, pp. 617–20. Holograph)*

my Good S^r I have received yours of the 7 and 29 of Aug and 7 of 7^b, and am verie glad yow have received all myne. I am sorie yow have so soone promoted the suit for dowaie,[73] because upon your last letters that yow wold first heare from me, I supposed yow wold not begin that suit so speedily. and therfor I was of mind to have sent one of purpose to the president,[74] who now staggereth, thinkinge to draw him to concurre with us.[75] but now I am affeard he will take the matter ill and be verie hardly drawen. but yow must do as well as yow may, yet my desire is that yow wold not prosecute the matter hotely until I send yow word what I have don with the said partie. I have conferred this

[69] Probably a reference to Pierre Coton SJ.
[70] Sir Thomas More, *great*-grandfather of Thomas More the clergy agent.
[71] *Cf.* Sir Thomas More, *Utopia*, ed. E. Surtz and J.H. Hexter (Yale Edition of the Complete Works of St. Thomas More, vol. 4, New Haven, 1965), 43.
[72] Founded in the fourteenth century. See C. Le Maire, *Paris Ancien et Nouveau* (3 vols, Paris, 1685), II, 473.
[73] See CRS 41, 146–50; Edwards, *Robert Persons*, 385.
[74] Thomas Worthington, secular priest, President of Douai College.
[75] See Edwards, *Robert Persons*, 381–2.

sommer with some of our brethren, and neither they nor I can tell
how to releive the said Colledge. and for us to beginne a thinge w*h*ich
we are not able to performe, wilbe deamed somewhat temerariu*m*. I
have spoken with D Bavan[76] who liketh well of this new autoritie given
to me, and of the pointes that I willed yo*w* to propose, and marvaleth
that any reasonable man should mislike of the moderation of sendinge
in so many workmen.[77] yo*w* say well, lett us prosecute our owne suites
in charitie, and sheift as well as we can for our selves. yf we be crossed,
lett us beare it with patience. yo*w* shall do good service in getting yo*ur*
selfe some stoare of frendes, though yo*w* speed not in yo*ur* suites. and
hereafter God will send us better successe. the thinges we desire are
expedient, but yet though we do not obteine them, I hope we shall not
be undon[.] because yo*w* give me notice in secret of our backward
freindes, I take no <u>exceptions against them</u>, but passe all thinges over
with affable speeches as though all went well but when yo*w* shall thinke
it meet I shalbe redie to assist yo*w* as well as I can, and am fully
determined to send yo*w* shortly a letter, wherin I meane in good termes
to remove m^r swin.[78] and to com*m*itt the whole charge to yo*ur* selfe, yf
yo*w* shall thinke it expedient for me to take that course. now at this
pr*e*sent I had don it but that I have no tyme for the calumniations that
yo*w* in yo*ur* former letters [three words deleted] do mention in secret,
<u>that some of yo*ur*</u> frendes here do deale with <u>the Counsell</u>, <u>I hope they
shall</u> not be <u>proved</u>. but yf <u>my old</u> frend[79] persist <u>in that course</u> I dowbt
not but to gett m^r Coll.[80] m. D. bush.[81] and m^r mushe[82] to come to
purge them selfes, yf yo*w* thinke it necessarie. Leeke[83] male audit, and

---

[76] John Bavant was a Marian priest, and formerly tutor and close friend of Edmund
Campion. He had been one of the arbitrators appointed in the mid-1590s to resolve the
quarrels among the Catholic clergy imprisoned in Wisbech Castle, CRS 51, *passim*. See
CRS 41, 75–101; **Letter 5**.

[77] One of the principal aims of the secular priests who promoted the agency was to
limit the number of newly ordained seminary priests who were being sent to England
each year, CRS 41, 145.

[78] Thomas Fitzherbert.

[79] Robert Persons SJ.

[80] John Colleton, secular priest. For Colleton's ambiguous relationship with the regime,
see P. Renold, 'The Wisbech Stirs, 1595–1598' (unpubl. M.A. thesis, London, 1959), 72–
86.

[81] William Bishop, secular priest. Robert Persons had written to Birkhead in May 1608
alleging that both Bishop and Colleton allowed the taking of the oath of allegiance, TD
V, p. xxx.

[82] John Mush, secular priest.

[83] Thomas Leek, secular priest. Richard Blount SJ regarded Leek as a favourer of the
Jacobean oath of allegiance, AAW A VIII, no. 186. William Bishop wrote on 1 May 1610
'that m^r leake with whom we were uniustly slandered, being taken before Christmas
last & put the oath did constantly refused [sic] it', AAW A IX, no. 38 (p. 102). He was
allowed into exile in July 1610. Birkhead noted his departure for Rome with Thomas
Wright: 'in some sense their iorney may be to good purpose', because they might 'purge

I know not how to helpe it. the crime obiected of dealinge with the counsell, I meane shortly to have examined; The good old doctor bavan, though he like of my [p. 618] articles, yett is he most unwillinge to have us use any rough dealinge especially against d worth.[84] and therfor I promised him that yow wold not commence this suit, and that I wold deale with the said doctor worth: and he said that yf he will not agree with us, he wilbe as redie to prosecute that matter as wee. so that I trust my old frend will not have so many letters from myne as he hopeth for. I see the thinge is ment which yow signifie, but yf my frendes tell me true, they shall do no good, and so I have longe since in Generall signified to my old frend, by whose letters I gessed at some such thinge.

one m[r] Pratt[85] a preist was taken of late, the oth was offered unto him, but refused by him, and he sent to the Clink, where he craveth a remove, in regard of the molestation he findeth from the Clinkers. Father Chrisostome a scottish Cappucin who had don much good in scotland fled hither of late upon iust occasion and is now taken and set in the towre, I know not why as yett.[86] my newes of graves end were verie true, for the two parties them selves in there submissive letters to me, signified the whole accident as yt fell out.[87] I have often written to my old frend that his enformations are false, but I perceive, [two words deleted] my wordes are of no moment with him. I feare not much his contradictions but that in tyme he will ioyne with us. all my fellowes wold be upon him rather then there lives, yf I wold lett them. but yt is best to proceed peacably for so we shall have moe to ioyne with us. by this tyme I hope yow know my mind how to deale

themselves of reportes given out, yf they be obiected unto them', AAW A IX, no. 53 (p. 149); cf. Foley VII, 1019. Leek, however, returned, was arrested again (**Letter 19**) and by December 1612 was in consultation with the leading Catholic defenders of the regime's stance on allegiance – Roger Widdrington, Roland (Thomas) Preston OSB and William Barrett (the former opponent of the Calvinists in Cambridge in the 1590s), AAW A XI, no. 220.

[84] Thomas Worthington.

[85] Henry Pratt, secular priest. See Anstr. II, 255.

[86] According to Anthony Champney, the Capuchin John Chrysostom Campbell was betrayed by someone who knew him in France, AAW A VIII, no. 165. The Capuchins were regarded as allies by the seculars. William Singleton had noted in April 1609 that as Smith and More were travelling to Rome through France, one who was travelling with them, presumably Thomas Heath (see **Letters 1, 6**), diverted to Rouen to see the Capuchin William Fitch (Benet of Canfield) 'to draw him to their bend', AAW A VIII, no. 100 (p. 483); cf. VIII, no. 164; TD V, p. lviii. In December 1609 and March 1610 Champney was sending letters to Smith in Rome via the Capuchins in Paris, AAW A VIII, no. 189, IX, no. 26.

[87] On 25 June 1609 Birkhead had noted that two priests, coming from Dunkirk, had been taken, with their breviaries, faculties and various letters, but the earl of Salisbury ordered their release, AAW A VIII, no. 121. They had probably taken the oath of allegiance.

with m^r Swin yf he will not Concurre with yo*w*. I have sett yo*w* at Libertie, and shall do more hearafter as I have said. I sent yo*w* also one letter to his hol, and another to Bianch.[88] send me word how they speed. m^r Brian[89] com*m*endeth him to yo*w*, and wilbe secretarie hearafter for yo*u*r of that [sic] sent yo*w* the lattine Letter. All his and our frendes salute yo*w*, and wish yo*w* most happie successe in Christ, to whose holy grace I com*m*itt yo*w*. this 17 of 7^b 1609.

yours ever assured [three words deleted]

　　George Salvine[90] [p. 619]

I thank yo*w* for the picture of the persian ambassadour,[91] but one worde Sr Rob shurleyes man hath ben heare to provide waie for his m^{rs} returne home, and is dismissed with most courteouse wordes. so that the persian Ladie is expected to dwell in England.[92]

I have divers Letters to send yo*w* from m^r far.[93] and D bush. but I have no meanes to do it as yet. nothinge greeveth more then the waunt of good meanes to send my letters. this way is good, but I may not be to urgent, for feare I chardge my selfe with to great an obligation for there frendship.[94]

(On p. 620)

Addressed: To his worshipfull frend m^r Richard baker give these at
　　　　　Rome.

　　Sept.17. 1609

Endorsed: (1) Sept. 17. 609 [sic]
　　　　　(2) Archpr*i*est 17 sept.

[88] These letters were sent enclosed with Birkhead's letter to Smith of 30 July 1609, AAW A VIII, no. 133. No copies survive in AAW.

[89] Francis Brian. In a letter of December 1611 Smith noted Brian's death, AAW A X, no. 162.

[90] Birkhead signed using his own name, then crossed it out and substituted 'George Salvine'.

[91] Robert Shirley, see *DNB*, *sub* Shirley.

[92] Before 1607 Shirley married Teresia, daughter of Ismael Khan. He left Persia with his wife on 12 February 1608 (NS), was received in Prague in June 1609, where he left her, and proceeded via Florence to Rome (entering the city on 27 September 1609 (NS)), *DNB*, *sub* Shirley; Conway *AH* 23, 85, 138. In late September 1611 Birkhead informed More that Shirley and his 'persian wife are heare in England and Conforme themselves wholly to the tyme, goinge to the Church as freely as any other', AAW A X, no. 128 (p. 368).

[93] Edward Bennett.

[94] The seculars relied on OSB (both the Cassinese and Spanish congregations) for the carriage of their letters, Lunn, *EB*, 99.

5 *George Salvin (Birkhead) to Richard Baker (Smith) (9 October 1609) (AAW A VIII, no. 160, pp. 637–40. Holograph)*

my lovinge Sir, three Letters I have received now together, one of the 16 and another of the Last of Aug by m^r moore, and the third a little before of the 22 of Aug. by all w*hi*ch I well conceive what difficulties yo*w* fynd. I Like well of yo*u*r course in sendinge m^r moore, who is safely arrived, but at the writinge hereof not come unto us.[95] yt pleaseth me also that yo*w* fynd frendes who advise yo*w* not to deale by way of opposition on our partes, but unitedly and constantly to seeke our owne. a thinge w*hi*ch yo*w* know I have alwaies liked. m^r moore shall have at my handes what favour I canne shewe: to make him one of my Assistantes I could easily incline, but that m^r parkers place w*hi*ch is void, is so farre from those partes, where he is like to remaine. howbeit herein I meane to follow the advise of my other frendes. m^r mush is earnest with me for another. I never dowbted but that it wold Cost yo*w* much the first yeare, w*hi*ch hath made me often presse yo*u*r frendes with there promise. I have now at the Last gotten xxxv^{li}, w*hi*ch I have directed to London to be made over unto yo*w*. our frend m^r I.G.[96] will make it to bruxels, and from thenc m^r Colford[97] will make yt over to yo*w*. Let us know how yo*w* speed by this waie, for I know no other as

---

[95] From Rome Thomas More travelled via Milan, Cambrai and Lyons, and arrived in Paris about 18 September 1609 (NS), AAW A VIII, no. 154 (p. 625). Via St Omer (where he met Richard Holtby SJ who was peace-making among the English in Flanders, *Downshire MSS* II, 173) More arrived in England by 15 October 1609, AAW A VIII, no. 164. He had Birkhead's authority (according to Edward Bennett) 'to visitt all England over'. 'The som*me* of his commission' was to give good reports of the agency's progress, to exhort to peace and unity, and, riding with the assistant in each circuit, to enquire 'if any disorders' were comitted 'by any of o*u*r brethern & to call them to accownt for it in every division as the assistant of the place & hym self seeth cause…soe that by godes grace it will in tyme apeare to his holl that the clergy w*i*thowt f par [Robert Persons SJ] direction' can 'govern it self'. In addition, 'as he goeth a longe' he was to elicit support for the appointment of a bishop for England, AAW A VIII, no. 179 (p. 685); **Letter 6**. John Bavant's hostile account, written to Persons in March 1610, said that More had confessed that for all this he had received 'no commission from our Archpriest', CRS 41, 98–9.

[96] Identity uncertain.

[97] Gabriel Colford, a friend of the intelligencer Richard Verstegan, CRS 64, 142, was resident in Brussels, *Downshire MSS* II, 79. He acted as a conveyer of letters and money for the priests, though he also associated with the English diplomat William Trumbull, *Downshire MSS* II, 129–30, III, *passim*. (However, by January 1610, Colford was making it known that he was too busy with his commercial projects 'to receave and derect the Archepriests lettres', AAW A IX, no. 3 (p. 7).) His daughter Martha was professed in the English Benedictine convent at Brussels with Elizabeth Digby and Elizabeth (Lucy) Knatchbull (the sister of John Knatchbull) in January 1611, AAW A X, no. 7. Later a commercial dispute arose between Colford and the secular priest Robert Pett, **Letter 35.**

yet, and then I trust that God will send yo*w* more supplie. I know well enough, yo*w* shall have but Little helpe there. do not marvell that the Nuntio[98] at paris, reported that of yo*w*, for here came no other report from him then w*h*ich I could shew yo*w* out of his owne Letter. I easily beleve that my old frend[99] liketh nothinge of that w*h*ich I have proposed, for yet I never received any signe from him thereof. but he may do as he list; for my part I still remaine of opinion, that yf he had concurred with me in such indifferent pointes, he might have gotten much love amongst us. but now he taketh the direct waie for <u>new combustions</u>, unlesse we use the foresaid patience yo*w* speake of. have not I often told yo*w*, that it <u>wold be obiected</u>, yt was the faction of a few that pressed me to send? but seinge it is begonne, and not disliked by his hol, I meane to proceede w*i*thout any termes of exasperation. yea not so much as to take notice of there opposite dealinge unles yo*w* thinke it requisite. m^r washington[100] I trust shall fynde verie few to assist him. yt seameth mens whole delyte is in factions. I much marvell that yo*u*r reasons will not suffice when as I am redie to ratefie them. but it seameth, they meane to wearie me out. yo*w* shall shortly heare of Letters to the parties yo*w* nominate, from all my Assistantes.[101] I have alredie directed Ben. Nor.[102] to gett all there handes unto them.[103] my old [p. 638] frend shall never have any thinge proposed againe by me. I hope God will open the eares and hartes of our Superiours. yf three or foure have pressed me by faction, I wold they might be called thither to answere for themselves. and pittie it is but they should, yf any do chardge them with dealinge, to our pr*ei*udice, with the co*m*mon enemie. procure it yf yo*w* can. yt might do much good to rippe matters to the bottom, yf so be our superiours will please to admitt yt. I must confesse I was much pressed, but yt was don with some reasons w*h*ich I could not answere; Let them be called to shew the same reasons in place where iustice may be had. I send yo*w* together with this, certen instructions whereby yo*w* may perceive, how farre I have by advise of our frendes delt with m^r D. worthington.[104] yf yt take no place, then

[98] Robert Ubaldini.

[99] Robert Persons SJ.

[100] This is probably the priest Paul Green alias Washington who had arrived in Rome in May 1609 (having been in England since June 1603), Anstr. I, 137. Birkhead implies here that Green was interfering in the agency petitioning counter to the archpriest's party's interest, although on 14 March 1609 (NS) Persons had written to Birkhead that he was 'very willing to doe any thinge I can for Mr Washington whom you recommend hither', Milton House MSS (transcript at ABSI).

[101] Among these letters was one from Birkhead's assistants to Cardinal Lawrence Bianchetti of 21 September 1609, AAW A VIII, no. 153.

[102] Benjamin Norton.

[103] See **Letter 6**.

[104] See TD V, p. ciii.

must we have patience to lett the Colledge goe, as it shall please god to dispose. for we canne do no more, and I feare we are not able to doe so much. moe workmen[105] do daly come over, and thinke much they have not releife from me, which I assure yow they should yf I had yt, but exceedinge little commeth to my handes. the great Gobbetes Goe where the distributers please, who are all for our opposites. for I have as yet small favour amongst them. I beleve it is don to wearie me, which they may eas[e]ly do, for I have ben wearie long since. my old Ass. D Bavan told me that he sendinge to the places of there residences within his circuit, he received no other answere about the collections then that he shold make none there, att all, because they ment to bestow there almes onely upon the fa.[106] which answere did somewhat move the good old man. many other signes of crosse dealinge I could recite, but it wold make to longe a discourse, and I love not to rippe up disgustes. my endevour shalbe to keepe peace as much as lieth in me, howsoever they [word deleted] meddle and toile about our affaires. I am commanded not to use there labors in our Goverment, and yet they will needes be doinge: yow write that a letter is come unto me from Bianch. about the Clinkers, but I heare not of yt as yet.[107] I desire to have had no more doinges in that kynd, but they care not how many thornes they thurst [sic] into other mens heeles, beinge out of gonneshot themselves.[108] howbeit when it cometh I trust in God to

---

[105] *i.e.* priests.

[106] *i.e.* upon the Jesuits. Birkhead complained to Smith in April 1610 of 'votive brethren' who 'though they beare shew of secular people yet I finde them wholly directed by them to whome they have made there vowes', and 'so by consequent the almes commeth verie sparingly to us'. He had instructed his own 'Assistantes...to make Collections, but yow wold marvell to see how even some of my owne, are sent abroad to declare against that course'. The deposed archpriest Blackwell was still in higher repute than Birkhead, Birkhead judged, because 'a Catholique lately deceased hath bequeathed him 40li yearly for his lyfe. but no such gobbetes falleth to me', AAW A IX, no. 31 (pp. 77–8) [part printed in TD IV, p. clxxx in note]. In October 1609 Birkhead had listed 'those that have the great summes to distribute' as 'Mr Roger manners, my Lord Lumley, mᵣ Hord, and my Lord of dorset [Richard Sackville, third earl of Dorset]', AAW A VIII, no. 168 (p. 661). In May 1612 John Mush complained that Catholics such as Manners, Lumley, Hoord and Jane Shelley had given many thousands of pounds for the aid of the clergy and yet SJ had appropriated all of it, AAW A XI, no. 70. *Cf.* McCoog, 194 (showing how the Lumley, Manners and Sackville families came within SJ's mission), 252. Nevertheless Birkhead acknowledged in 1613 that 'I fynd no falt with them that have the common almes. for they are honest, and distribute the almes better then my selfe can do'. The problem was his own impecuniosity and consequently very limited powers of patronage, AAW A XII, no. 233 (p. 519).

[107] See **Letter 8.**

[108] Birkhead did not want to use his own authority to deprive the oath-favouring priests in the Clink prison of their faculties since he feared they would retaliate by denouncing him to the authorities. The breve of Paul V appointing Birkhead specified that he should

do my deutie therin. yt is a great hindrance to me that I have not often conference with my brethren. I cannot therfor returne yow so spedie answeres as perhaps yow require. what can be don, I will not omitt so farre at [sic for 'as'] lieth in me. the men [p. 639] of the Clinke resort daily to the b of London[109] in most bold and familiar sort to the scandal of many. I dowbt that any hard procedinge against them, will do them no good notwithstandinge. when I had written thus much came m[r] more our frend, whom I was to see. he telleth me nothinge, but which your letters made me to conceive before. be yow still of good couradge, and yow shall have the best information that we can give yow. yf yow thinke it meet, I could gett a general letter from all our brethren in approvance of the pointes I proposed. this pursivantes [sic] are so greedie of money, that no man dare looke out of the doores. All your frendes are in health, and wish yow most happie successe, and I also wishinge the same do commend me to your praiers, and your selfe to the protection of our saviour. this 9 of octob. 1609.

yours ever

George Salvine

(On p. 640)

Addressed: To his verie lovinge frend mr Richard Baker give these.

Endorsed: (1) Oct 9: 609 [sic]

   (2) Archpriest 9 Oct.

admonish those priests who took the Jacobean oath of allegiance or taught it was licit, and, if they did not reform themselves, they should be deprived of their priestly faculties, CRS 41, 13 n.2; for the partial success of the admonition, CRS 41, 85–6. His admonition to these priests was issued on 2 May 1608. In July 1609 Birkhead wrote to Smith that Blackwell 'holdeth his opinion still verie strongly for the oath. because nothinge is don against' the oath-favourers 'many catholiques begin to imagin' Blackwell's 'fault is not so heynous as it was thought to be'; the oath-favouring priests should undoubtedly be censured by 'declaringe the losse of there faculties, but not to be executed by me', AAW A VIII, no. 133 (p. 561). As late as 3 August 1611 Birkhead wrote to thank More for his efforts to obstruct any order to proceed formally with the oath-favourers' deprivation, which 'may hurt me and my best frendes exceedinge much'; 'those that are wise' think 'that an excommunication' from Rome 'wold serve' better, AAW A X, no. 97 (p. 273). A compromise was reached when Birkhead received a precept from the pope that he should send out private letters to his assistants depriving the oath-favourers (AAW A X, nos 101, 114) 'so as they [the assistants] shall give it out to there frendes both of the Clergie and laitie in there circuites I was once of mynd to have admonished the parties them selves, but that living under the protection of the state, they are like to contemme my admonition to my great perill', AAW A X, no. 112 (p. 329). William Bishop opposed Birkhead's action, adding to the general suspicion that he was unreliable about the oath, AAW A X, no. 115.

[109] Thomas Ravis. Perhaps Birkhead meant Archbishop Bancroft.

6 *Thomas More to Richard Baker (Smith) (31 October 1609)   (AAW A*
VIII, no. 169, pp. 663–6. Holograph)

Good S.ʳ since my return I have skantlie stirred from your dearest
frend,[110] wher, I take it, I find the kindlier welcome for your sake, he
remayning stil extraordinarilie affected to the common cause, and you
in particuler, for which both you & we al are too too much endebted,
discharg it as we may. your poor mʳ is quite cassierd, and gone, I pray
god it be not imputed to you, but the worst, you know is, what was
meant you from the first: who succeedeth him is a Licentiat of the
Lawes, and Divinitie, a sufficient man, as it seemeth, and wel practized
in these our causes, as having in former times occasion to trie his wits.
He seemeth staied, suerlie settled, sincerlie affected, and of a verie good
iudgment in matters of government. he lyved latelie if you can remember
him with D. Kell.[111] I doubt not but he wil do good service, to god,
and the common cause. I have awaited almost a month to hear
somthing from you, and yet nothing is come, and now am I almost
past hope to hear anie thing, because I intend shortlie to ride in
visitation of al my breethren, for which purpose I am furnished with
my Superiors[112] commendatorie letters. I trust herbie to be able to give
you true advertisment of the estate of our poor afflicted Church.
Complaints of want, and extremities ring dailie in our Superiors ears,
who good man not having to releeve them is even hart sick to hear
them, and protesteth often that such letters more troble him, then al
the crosses he receaveth from these parts. we al are much bownd unto
him, and wel I perceave that he is wholie bent to benefit his poor
Cleargie, for whose good he spareth no pains, and wil adventure what
disfavor soever. Smal almes commeth to his hands to distribute, and
manie crie to him for releif, as if he had a fowntein of al abondance.
He is fain to excuse him self, and give fair words, and inwardlie feeleth
the smart, that such poor suters have impressed in his hart. It is no
smal grief to him, that his old frends passe over the wants of our
cowntrie soe slightlie, and provide therfore so slenderlie, as if they were
mockeries, but indeed they are far of, and it little toucheth them, what
is laid upon us, and soe their senses can not exercise their functions
because the obiect is not in dew distance, or coniunction. wel I see, he
seeth, and wil not easelie be deceaved, reports he wil not sone beleeve,
nor condemne one in absence before his cause be examined, which
how important a point it is you know. His confidence is in you, your
credit he wil not neglect, others he relyeth not upon, but assureth me

---

[110] Presumably Anthony Maria Browne, second Viscount Montague.
[111] Matthew Kellison, secular priest.
[112] *i.e.* George Birkhead's.

he hath discharged from dealing as his Agents in anie matter concerning us. Desirous he is to uphold his Cleargie, and satisfie his Hol. order in the strictest manner for the manteinance of peace. He hath dealt with manie verie effectuallie about his sending to Rome, and sundrie that misliked it, as misconceaving of matters by his substantial information he hath brought to like verie wel therof, others not soe wel conceated therof in respect of the charg, he hath meerlie [or 'meetlie'] wel pacifyed, so that in al probabilitie howsoever the action be censured none wil oppose against their Superiors proceedings. Your old Cosen[113] hath given of late some disgust to his and your especial Patron[114] in sending his seelie censure about the matter of Bishops, to wit, that he deemeth them not convenient for our times, because of the new stirrs, and trobles that he dreameth wold be occasioned therbie to Catholiks, and the hazard of our disagreements, and wranglings in having them. In a word he reiecteth them as preiudicial to our peace, and quiet, both amongst our selves, and with the state. I wish you cold write unto him, or I speak with him of the matter. I doubt not but he wold be ruled by reason, and give better satisfaction. Shortlie at the return of Mr Beni.[115] who hath fetcht a rownd about most of this land, you shal see the minds of our Assistants, and at my return (for I mind also to visit) you shal understand how our breethren generallie stand affected. your frends ther cease not to undermine you here with your best frends, but al in vaine, and to the same passe, I hope, wil come al ther informations from hence. Some of them merily cast forth that your credit is not much ther, and whie think you? because forsooth you may not read the kings book[116] ther. soe your poor m^r to your assured freind. I signifyed here how C. Pinello[117] shewed us the points censured by the Inquisition, that the book was in answering, and what advise you gave C. Bell.[118] therabout. I have not yet spoken with m^r Farrington[119] because I see noe necessitie of hast, especiallie seeing that althings stand in soe good tearms, as they do, and that monie is alreadie sent to serve your turn for a time. I will be ernest therabout, that wants may not preiudice our cause. I am now this good time to visit your yong frend,[120] a ioylie boy he is, and it wold do your hart good to see him. Pray with

---

[113] In a note on the transcript of this letter at ABSI, L.J. Hicks suggested that this refers to John Bavant.

[114] Anthony Maria Browne, second Viscount Montague.

[115] Benjamin Norton.

[116] James I, *An Apologie for the Oath of Allegiance*.

[117] Cardinal Dominic Pinelli, Bishop of Fermo (who died in August 1611). In 1602, during the second Appeal, he censured the courses of the appellant priests, but promised to do what he could for them, Law II, 16.

[118] Cardinal Robert Bellarmine SJ.

[119] Edward Bennett.

[120] Identity uncertain.

us that he may be a comfort to his Parents as they are Patrons of our cause. Tit my Ladies gentlewoman[121] is his Nurse, at her owne house she tendeth him, and is not a little prowd, and charie of soe rare a iewel. your little frend[122] on that side the water together with her two Coosens I visited, they have not forgotten you, and desire you not to forget them. your God-daughter[123] remembreth her dutie to you. she hath (as I think you know) receaved extraordinary courtesies at your friends hands for your sake. you must not be unmindful to take notice therof. She was never so wel in health, as she hath bene since her comming into these quarters.[124] I think content of mind manteineth the good disposition of her bodie. I wish her stil to be wise, and beware that through her owne default she be not defeated of soe rare favors. I have written to Ubald.[125] in excuse of our negligence in not writing unto him. I have signifyed unto him the extreamities of poor distressed Catholiks, partlie by the roaming about of pursuivants, that cease not to molest everie good house, apprehending Priests, ransacking everie corner, and carying away books, and churchstuffe. Now they make their cooler as if they had commission to search for two very odious books to the State, and extreame dangerous to Catholiks, the one is ['intitul' deleted] in French entituled Maister Iaque,[126] the other is called Quaeres.[127] Neither of them have I ever seen, and therfore can not give my iudgment of them, onlie generallie I hear them both misliked.[128]

---

[121] Not identified.

[122] Identity uncertain.

[123] Elizabeth Dacres, daughter of Francis Dacres, the brother of Magdalen, dowager Viscountess Montague.

[124] Birkhead had sent Smith a letter from her on 20 July 1609 and remarked that she 'remaineth with us to her comfort', AAW A VIII, no. 130 (p. 555).

[125] Robert Ubaldini.

[126] CSPV 1607–10, 319.

[127] i.e. Prurit-anus, vel nec omne, nec ex omni, published under the pseudonym Horatius Dolabella. See ARCR I, nos 304–6. The reissue of Prurit-anus contained an appendix ridiculing James I's 'Praefatio Monitoria' in his Apologia pro Iuramento Fidelitatis (1609); STC 14405; CSPV 1607–10, 288, 300, 307, 313–14, 322; Salisbury MSS XXI, 100; Harris, 'Reports', 203. Information from William Udall led to searches for it at the Venetian ambassador's house where the ambassador's chaplain was storing this and other Catholic books, Harris, 'Reports', 203, 245–7. It attacked not just puritan errors but also, in personal terms, Henry VIII, Elizabeth and James. It was explicitly anti-Scottish, CSPV 1607–10, 322–3. Sir Henry Wotton reported that the chaplain was an English subject, a pupil of the Jesuits at Douai, and formerly resident in the archduke's ambassador's house in London, CSPV 1607–10, 323. He was William Law (or Low), a son of Thomas Law, the bursar of Douai College. He was taken to Dover to be banished before 18 October 1609, Anstr. II, 203–4. On 29 August 1609 Birkhead recorded the recent incineration in St Paul's churchyard of 700 copies of the book, on which occasion there were two sermons preached, AAW A VIII, no. 144; CSPV 1607–10, 319. See also Lewis Owen, The Running Register (1623), sig. C3v; STC 6991.5.

[128] Birkhead, on 3 October 1609, wrote to Smith of 'the book of queres and another in french (as they say) worse then it'. Birkhead thought the creation of xx bb [bishops]

[p. 664] The later most men <u>deam to have bene made, and published by the societie</u>, though now they disavow the same.[129] I saw a letter of one of the companies, that fel into the hand of searchers wherin mention was made of a letter from the Nuncio in Flanders[130] to our Superior wishing him to forbid them al Catholiks in this land, which letter is said to be in the L. Tresurers hands. I wish you might see one of these books that we might hear the Inquisitions censure therof. surelie manie are scandalized therbie, because they see smal profit, and great inconvenience by such kind of books, and [word deleted] manie are like to smart therfore. These continual searches have driven such an impression of fear into manie houskeapers, that they skantlie dare harbor anie Priest, and manie grow soe politick, that they soe provide that one Priest shal serve fortie of them, which wil grow to a further inconvenience if some order be not taken therin. The king of late hath granted to a Scott[131] the somm of 24000 crowns to be leavied in yorkshire from the Nihils.[132] soe are they termed that are soe poor Recusants, that upon enquirie made of their estats ther is nothing fownd for the King.[133] upon this occasion our Cowntrie is harried, and not long since a poor widow, mother to the two Brughes,[134] though she had by a deed of gift passed al her goods unto one of her sonns, by whom she was manteined, had al her houshold stuff seased on, and her featherbeds tombled forth into the streets, ther to be set to sale. In Scotland is expected great persecution, and nothing inferior to ours, our penal statuts against priests and recusants being alsoe admitted ther, yea and sundrie of their Catholik gentlemen being put latelie to

wold not vex them so much', AAW A VIII, no. 166 (p. 654). Like More, he attributed the recent activity of the pursuivants against Catholics to the appearance of these works.

[129] Both Tobie Mathew and Thomas Worthington were also rumoured to be the author, *Salisbury MSS* XXI, 100; Belvederi, 146. William Udall, the informer, at first attributed authorship in part to William Wright SJ and later claimed that the authors were Wright and his ex-Jesuit brother Thomas. Udall said that the book was 'performed' at Sir Francis Lacon's house at Kinlet, Shropshire, where Thomas Wright had his residence, Harris, 'Reports', 203–4, 255.

[130] Guido Bentivoglio, Archbishop of Rhodes.

[131] John Livingstone, Master of Livingstone, son of the first earl of Linlithgow.

[132] For the grant, see J. Morris, *The Troubles of our Catholic Forefathers* (3 vols, 1872–7), III, 460. *Cf.* PRO, SP 14/56/27A, fo. 53r, for Thomas Felton's allegation that, in the recent grant 'of Nichilled Recusantes in all Yorkshire, Northumberland, Cumberland and the Bishoppricke' to the 'L of Livingston', the exchequer clerk Henry Spiller committed 'all the whole execucon of that service' to two Catholics who compounded with the listed recusants for very small sums.

[133] For 'nichilled' debts in the exchequer, see BL, Lansdowne MS 156, no. 110.

[134] On 15 October 1609 More wrote to Smith that 'Mr Brugh and his brother' were following Smith's progress in Rome, AAW A VIII, no. 164 (p. 650). It is possible that 'Brugh', elsewhere written also as 'Brough' (AAW A XI, no. 184), indicates 'Broughton', *i.e.* suggesting perhaps that the 'two Brughes' are the secular priest Richard Broughton and his brother.

death, but how true this is I know not assuredlie.[135] This is certain that
F. Chrisostome,[136] a Scottish Capuchine, and a seculer Priest of the
same nation are in hold in the towr of London. In Newgate ther live
five catholik Priests in great distres by reason that noe resort is permitted
thither, as in former times. Two or three others of the Cleargie are
taken in the North,[137] and stil the knaves prowle about for their pray,
and take monie wher they can gett it. One the[y] ransomed twise or
thrise and at the length cast him into prison, wher he now remayneth.
Of an other they got as good as fiftie pownd, and soe let him goe.[138]
Thus poor Priests, and Catholicks are fleeced that manie be in extream
wants. yet to tel half a wonder, an ancient Schismatick,[139] a man of
good worship, and great wealth, my L. Peters brother in law, comming
to die, and indeed dying a Catholick neglecting our distressed estate
leaft 8000¹ sterling, and fowr hundred pounds land a year towards the
building, and fowndation of a new Colledg in Oxford.[140] Somthing is
said to have bene bestowed upon good uses, but to whose disposal it
is committed god knoweth. If the Religious finger it, the poor seculers
shal finde smal releif therbie. If such a somme had bene wel employed
to the benefit of the common cause, it might have suted to verie good
purpose, but you may conceave by your owne Unckle how far above
reason affection prevaileth in manie, and pittie our case, because you
know it, that is so little pittyed, because it is not known.[141] Mʳ Geffrey[142]
commendeth him self most kindlie to you, and by you most dutifullie
to his grand Patron,[143] whom he purposeth to visit out of hand by

[135] *Cf.* AAW A VIII no. 145 (Benjamin Norton's account in August 1609 of statutes recently passed in Scotland).

[136] John Chrysostom Campbell.

[137] See **Letter 7**.

[138] *Cf.* Harris, 'Reports', 239, for William Udall's list (17 November 1608) of priests released for money. Corrupt high commission officials were prosecuted in Star Chamber in July 1610, PRO, STAC 8/15/8.

[139] Nicholas Wadham, who had married Dorothy, the daughter of Sir William Petre.

[140] Wadham College; *cf.* Foley II, 397–8; N. Briggs, 'The Foundation of Wadham College, Oxford', *Oxoniensia* 21 (1956), 61–81; Davidson, 640–1; T.M. McCoog, 'Apostasy and Knavery in Restoration England: The Checkered Career of John Travers', *Catholic Historical Review* 78 (1992), 395–412, at p. 402. On 9 April 1611 (NS) Francis Hore wrote to More that Wadham had left £17,000 'in monie to buy lands' for the college, 'and his widow gives 7 thousand pounds more', AAW A X, no. 32 (pp. 77–8); *cf. Downshire MSS* II, 275.

[141] Anthony à Wood related an unlikely story that Nicholas and Dorothy Wadham had first decided to found a seminary in Venice, Davidson, 639.

[142] Geoffrey Pole.

[143] Cardinal Edward Farnese. Arthur, son and heir of Geoffrey Pole (snr) of Lordington, Sussex, was taken to Rome aged seven and placed with Farnese. Geoffrey Pole, Arthur's younger brother, subsequently entered Farnese's household as well, BL, Harleian MS 7042, fo. 166v; *Salisbury MSS* XVII, 67, XIX, 221.

letter, and follow sone after in parson, the winter being passed.[144] He seemeth a man of very good parts, gentlemanlike in discorse, and cariage. He hath good testimonie of al that know him, and is able to relate our case sufficientlie, and much deceaveth me if anie wil be wanting to further our cause. yesterday he was amongst us here, and gave good satisfaction to al parties. He hath not bene so kindlie dealt withal here by some persons, that professed great frend ship unto him in words, and underhand labored his discredit with a very honorable parsonage his especiall frend, and kindred, but they prevailed not. you know who in al probabilitie failed not to pursue the like courses against him ther,[145] how wrongfullie his owne testimonie hereafter wil prove.[146] Prepare his way in the best manner you may, and I doubt not but he wil prove a comfort to you, and us al. Al your frends, and acquaintance in these parts as they reioyced much to here of your good health, soe they desire ernestlie to be remembred unto you; Ther names I forbear because you can not imagine of more then ['desire' deleted] wish to be commended unto you. Commend, and excuse me for not writing to my most especial good Frends M[r] D. Thornhil,[147] M[r] Nich.[148] M[r] D. Perce,[149] M[r] Bruerton,[150] and the rest, and forget me not in al kindnes

[144] Birkhead noted in mid-December 1609 that Geoffrey Pole wrote that Farnese 'wilbe our assured frend, yf we be confident with him' but both Farnese and Bianchetti, the vice-protector, were 'greived' because Smith had already 'sought for helpe at the handes of so many other Card. besides', AAW A VIII, no. 191 (p. 715).

[145] i.e. in Rome.

[146] In the 1590s Geoffrey Pole was one of the seminarists at the English College in Rome who was supposedly accused of sexual deviance by Edmund Harwood SJ, AAW A V, no. 112.

[147] For Edmund Thornell, a canon at Vicenza, see Anstr. I, 352–3; CRS 51, 277; CRS 41, 72–3; PRO, SP 14/17/102 (an undated discourse by him in Italian against SJ's dangerous politics). Thornell was regularly cited as a friend of the anti-Jesuit secular priests, particularly by Benjamin Norton, e.g. AAW A XI, no. 170, though he was less well regarded by some of them, e.g. Edward Bennett, AAW A XI, no. 69; see also **Letter 10**. Thornell was Thomas More's confessor, D. Shanahan, 'Thomas More IV Secular Priest 1565–1625', Essex Recusant 7 (1966), 105–14, at p. 106.

[148] Nicholas Fitzherbert, first cousin of Thomas Fitzherbert.

[149] William Percy, a doctor of the Sorbonne, Anstr. I, 272. He was an opponent of Robert Persons SJ, AAW A VI, nos 19–20, but was antagonistic in 1603 towards the appellants John Mush, Anthony Champney and John Cecil while they were in Rome, Law II, 4, 5, 26, 235–42; cf. Robert Persons, A Briefe Apologie (Antwerp, 1601), fo. 126r. In 1595 Percy, with Worthington, had written a memorial to the protector, Henry Caietan, praising the Jesuit administration of the English College in Rome, A. Kenny, 'The Inglorious Revolution 1594–1597', Venerabile XVI (1957), 240–58, XVII (1958), 7–25, 77–94, 136–55, XX (1961), 208–23, at vol. XVII, pp. 77–8. In December 1596 Percy signed an attestation in favour of William Holt SJ during the agitation against him in Flanders, AAW A V, no. 99.

[150] Identity uncertain. In 1591 Robert Weston, an informer, reported that a priest whom he called 'Bruarton' had stayed at the Gages' residence at Bentley, Sussex in early December 1590, Foley I, 382.

to Thomas,[151] and Augstine [sic].[152] I have dealt with two or three of myne owne coat about m^r Isams soon,[153] who promise me to give him notice of his Fathers desire. Noe more but Christ Iesus have you in his keaping. From my lodging this last of October
your assured loving Frend
    Tho. More:
(On p. 666)
Addressed: To my assured, and especial good Frend Mr R. Baker give these:
Endorsed: (1) Octob: 31 1609
        (2) M. Th. More

7 *George West (Thomas More)*[154] *to Richard Baker (Smith) (No date)*   *(AAW A IX, no. 78, pp. 265–8. Holograph)*

Though endorsed 11 October 1609, this letter is dated 2 October 1610 in the AAW catalogue but (from internal evidence) was written at some time after 7 January 1610 but before More's arrival in Rome on 20 March 1610 (NS) (see **Letter 9**). The reference to Coeffeteau's book may indicate that the letter was written in Paris.

My singuler good S.^{r}
    Much do I admire, and highlie prize th*e* great love, and affection you bear me testifyed by so manie letters, even when you might iustlie deem me extream negligent in never writing unto you. yet now I p*e*rceave one or two of my *lette*rs are come to your hands, and I hope the other likwise you have er this wherin I have written unto you the

---

[151] Thomas Heath. He had travelled to Rome with Smith and More and acted as Smith's servant, AAW A IX, no. 16.

[152] By 'Augustine' the secular priests generally indicated John (Augustine) Bradshaw OSB alias White (for whom see Lunn, *EB*, *passim*), though the Cassinese Edmund (Augustine) Smith OSB was involved in trying to set up a convent in Paris which some of Geoffrey Pole's sisters intended to enter, Lunn, 'English Cassinese', 63–4. Possibly here More meant to write 'Anselm', *i.e.* Robert (Anselm) Beech OSB who was in Rome; neither Bradshaw nor Edmund Smith were.

[153] Christopher Isham was the father of Francis and William, students respectively at Rome and Valladolid. Christopher had been refused admission as a convictor at the English College in Rome by its Jesuit administrators. He had been a member of Cardinal Allen's household, Kenny, 'Inglorious Revolution', XVII, 18, 141; Foley VI, 19f; Anstr. I, 184. The Ishams were relations of the priest Richard Newport, executed at Tyburn in 1612, AAW A XI, no. 113, and were in regular contact with the secular priest Robert Pett. William Isham was dissatisfied with his lot. Pett implies that he was not really inclined to take the secular clergy's part in the current ecclesiastical disputes in England, AAW A XII, no. 158.

[154] For More's alias, see J.C.H. Aveling, 'The More Family and Yorkshire', in R.S. Sylvester and G.P. Marc'hadour, *Essential Articles for the Study of Thomas More* (Hamden, Connecticut, 1977), 26–48, at p. 31.

copie of the leafe you soe much desire under good attestation. you wil not think how much it greevethe me that you are driven to these exigents for default of a new supplie, it being one of the principal matters I undertook to deal in, yea and which I dare say I have not failed to urge to the uttermost of my powr. but the 35^l being disposed of before hand, and I assured that it wold not fail to be sent unto you I had little to prosecute in *particu*ler for the time.[155] onlie I have bene ernest with some, and have bene put in good hopes th*a*t order shold be taken as behooved soe important a busines. wel assure y*ou*r self I will travel al I may and in me ther shal be noe default. I trust that the cheif Authors of th*e* mission knowing wel the necessitie of y*ou*r abode ther wil be better advised then through default of manteinance to let slip soe goodlie an occasion to raise th*e* ruyns of o*u*r decaied Cleargie. One great hinderance to us is Mr Farr[s][156] extreme sicknes, who ever since Christmas hath bene more liklie to die then to live. yet now is he somwhat recovered though far from p*er*fect health. he saluteth you exceeding kindlie as alsoe his hostesse[157] and desireth to be excused for not writing being skantly able to hold pen in hand or to write his owne name. Mr Mush hath hurt his leg that he can not travel. Mr Collington was taken about the 10 of December [sic for 'November'], and remayneth in the Clink,[158] and the pursuivantes so ranged the contries th*a*t none durst adventure to keap ther houses. On the first of December was Mr M. walpole taken immediatlie after masse th*a*t he had skantlie leasure to unvest him self:[159] Mr Cuthb. Ihonson[160] and Mr Hutton[161] a

---

[155] In October 1609 Birkhead tried to forward this sum to Smith via Gabriel Colford at Brussels; Colford refused to forward it. Via bills of exchange directed to Nicholas Fitzherbert, this money, with at least one further sum of £65, eventually reached Smith partly by Thomas More's and partly by OSB's means, AAW A VIII, nos 161, 166, 168, 180, 187, 191, IX, nos 42, 43, 49, 53. It was clearly difficult and expensive to arrange bills of exchange but the reasons for the chronic underfunding of Smith and More in Rome are still something of a puzzle.

[156] Edward Bennett.

[157] Elizabeth, wife of Sir Robert Dormer, and daughter of Anthony Browne, first Viscount Montague.

[158] According to Edward Bennett's letter to Smith of 12 November 1609, John Colleton was arrested on 11 November and was sent by Archbishop Richard Bancroft to Newgate, AAW A VIII, no. 179. Colleton had, just previously, been arrested and released on payment of a bribe, Foley VII, 1005; AAW A VIII, no. 186. The Jesuits said that he was imprisoned first in the Gatehouse and then transferred to the more commodious Clink prison because he only 'appeared' to refuse the oath of allegiance when required by Bancroft to take it, Foley VII, 1005.

[159] Michael Walpole SJ's arrest, according to Birkhead, was on 30 November, AAW A VIII, no. 191. See **Letter 9**.

[160] Cuthbert Johnson, secular priest. Johnson was sent into exile after this arrest but returned to become chaplain to Margaret Dormer, the wife of Sir Henry Constable of Burton Constable, Anstr. I, 190.

[161] John (Thomas) Hutton OSB. See Lunn, *EB*, 155.

spanish Benedictin were taken at Mr Cholmleies,[162] wherupon his goods & lands <u>were begd</u> and now is constreined to compownd for life and lands for well nighe 1000^l.[163] This gentle. married my L. Br: sister.[164] Others were taken but escaped upon considerateons as D. Norrice[165] (of whom I wold no words were made because he requested me to conceal it soe much as might be for fear of preiudice to some persons)[.] Mr Battie[166] alsoe was taken upon the high way. yea it may be proved that the knaves have gotten by sale of preist[s] <u>within this two year about thirteen hundred pownds.</u>[167] Ihon Birrington[168] and an other preist was sought for by special commission but the one cold not be found, and Birr. fownd means to get a certifycate of his being a soldier, and by Mr Skidmors[169] good word upon his personal apparance before Canterburie[170] had his discharg and protection. Mr Button[171] being taken

[162] Richard Cholmeley of Brandsby; Morris, *Troubles*, III, 464–5.

[163] Birkhead wrote to Smith on 14 December 1609 that Johnson and Hutton were arrested on 1 November 1609, AAW A VIII, no. 191. On 28 March 1610 Richard Cholmeley and his wife were called to the assizes, and the minister of the parish and Thomas Masterman, one of Cholmeley's servants, were bound to give evidence against them, John Hutton and 'Pearcye als Dorrell' [i.e. Cuthbert Johnson]. On 29 March Cholmeley and his wife 'pleaded our pardons' (obtained in December 1609, *CSPD 1603–10*, 570) before Sir James Altham, the exchequer baron, Richard Cholmeley, 'The Memorandum Book of Richard Cholmeley of Brandsby 1602–1623', *North Yorkshire County Record Office Publications* 44 (1988), 29.

[164] Richard Cholmeley married Mary Hungate of Saxton, whose sister Elizabeth married first Sir Marmaduke Grimston who died in 1604, and then Sir Henry Browne of Kiddington, a younger son of Anthony Browne, first Viscount Montague, 'The Memorandum Book of Richard Cholmeley of Brandsby', 358. For the confusion over the genealogy, see Davidson, 92.

[165] Sylvester Norris SJ.

[166] Reginald Bates, secular priest. On 29 May 1611 William Bishop recorded Bates's release from Newgate, AAW A X, no. 48.

[167] *Cf.* Harris, 'Reports', 239, 266–7.

[168] John Berington, secular priest.

[169] John Scudamore, renegade secular priest, was resident in the household of Archbishop Richard Bancroft. For Scudamore, see Questier, *Conversion, Politics and Religion*, 47, 52, 53, 118, 119, 160.

[170] Archbishop Richard Bancroft.

[171] Richard Button, a Staffordshire secular priest, had been expelled from the English College in Rome in 1596. He then travelled to England with Sylvester Norris, Anstr. I, 60. On 6 July 1609 Birkhead had reported that Button 'was staied' by Bancroft's order while he was visiting the priest William Warmington in the Clink prison, AAW A VIII, no. 125 (pp. 543–4). Birkhead thought Button, the future renegade priest Edward Collier and even the priest John Jackson were unreliable on the question of the oath of allegiance because they all had the privilege of a 'protection' to go out of the Clink prison at their pleasure. Birkhead thought Bancroft and George Abbot were using them to divide the secular clergy, AAW A VIII, no. 132 (p. 559).

by fair entreatie I know not how got to be confyned in Staffordshire & is to return to prison upon 30 daies warning. Mr Fennel[172] is likewise confined about London, I know not upon what tearms, and Mr Collington expected the like favour, but the report is now that if he refuse as others did to take the oath he shal be brought to his answere. I have bene visiting the cowntrie abroad especiallie D. Bavans circuit wher I find him self with the other with him stif against BB. or the manteining of an Agent ther. with whom I guesse that Mr Broughton[173] concurreth, Mr Drayton,[174] & I know not who els, but in my iudgment ther number is but few[.] The Doct is not to be drawn from anie opinion he holdeth as is apparent by his conceipt of the kings Maiestie whom in noe case he wil have thought to persecute us otherwise then in pollicie, as minding in time to doe us good, a[n]d set up cath religion we know [two words obliterated: 'not how' ?] soone. this is soe settled in his head that al the art one can use is not able to dispossesse his brains therof. I fear much that he is egged forward by some that wold not have unitie amongst us, & work what may be underhand to hinder our Archp. proceedings in his clergies behalf. He is might, and maine for D. worth.[175] whom he wold not have reprooved for anie thing, esteeming him to have dealt for the common cause soe much as he was possiblie able. and what defect was in the Colledg was not by any oversight, or default of his but mere penurie that drive him to such courses, or rather our Protectors[176] command. One word from our Protector wold stop ther mouths, and dash ther designes for ever, they being as it seemeth born in hand that he is wholie for them, & their proceedings esteeming them peaceable, and ours contentious, and ful of debate. Al things he wold have contynue as they were, & our informations to be sent by Mr D. Worth, whom he saith his hol appointed Assistant to our Archpr, for the same purpose. Trulie he seemeth to work wholie for others noe way tendring the good of his owne bodie, but casting beyond the moon as if whatsoever were intended the upshot wold be the expelling of the F.[177] out of England. [p. 266] Mr Banks[178] his man is become a persecutor, and most treacherouslie haith sought to overthrow such places where his m^r and others of that companie haunted, but god wonderfullie hath delivered some without anie notorious preiudice thowgh [?] troble, and searches he hath procured, and more mischeif be dailie expected from him. Not

---

[172] Simon Fennell, secular priest.
[173] *Cf.* **Letter 49**.
[174] William Hanse.
[175] Thomas Worthington.
[176] Cardinal Edward Farnese.
[177] Jesuits.
[178] Richard Banks SJ.

long before, an other that belonged to them plaied the like pranks, but with like successe, for being discovered after one treacherous trick his malice can noe more prevail. One Owen[179] likwise is become a spie, and a worker of much mischeif. he was the occasion of m^r Collingt[ons] apprehension, and some others, and having procured a commission to search wormeth [?] about in London, & useth extreame dealing with sundrie poor Catholiks. Herbie may you gather in what pittiful plight we live, and what need we have to crie and cal for helpe to those parts, that order being here settled we may ether better prevent mischeifs, & more patiently bear them being laid upon us. In my peregrination in those [or 'these'] parts I forgot not to make diligent enquirie for the Author of the letter you mention <u>wherby our informations were discredited</u>, and our motions crossed. Much wonder ther was that anie such letter cold be written especiallie as our case standeth. yet <u>comming into worcestershire my report</u> concurred with certein speeches of a good soul[180] that frequented those parts, wherby not onlie my self but diverse others presentlie conceaved that if anie such thing were reallie done none seemed in simplicitie more subiect to such an error then was that partie. wherupon comming in place wher he was, I failed not to laie it in good <u>tearms</u> to his charg, req<u>uesting him that if he cold tel</u> <u>what pro</u>vision might be made for anie of us, he wold not conceal it from those whom it concerned. The good man presentlie acknowledged that such a letter <u>indeed he had written to Mr Rob.</u>[181] but protested withal that he never meant therbie <u>to preiudice our</u> proceedinges, or diminishe the credit of <u>our</u> propositions. onlie manie <u>poor souls</u> he said (and I know it to be true) ther were in those parts <u>whoe [or 'whom']</u> <u>in charitie we were not to leave</u> comfortles. But being demanded wher he cold provide for anie one priest there ether of residence were it never soe mean, or of manteinance never soe simple he protested that he cold doe nether, onlie such as were of abilitie to mantein them selves yea and had superabondant to releeve others were for these parts. He him self had spent some years ther having his residence not far of, & had taken great pains, yea and not spared his owne purse among the poor creaturs, and now <u>made suit to Mr Rob for</u> an other of his owne companie to assist him in so charitable an action, <u>but so little he</u> <u>pre</u>vailed that nether was ther anie other sent, nor he permitted to continue ther, but is called away to be disposed of in some other cowntrie. This good simple man is called <u>Cornford al</u>ias Kilton, one of <u>the</u> <u>societie, and</u> the onlie man of [sic] I know of them <u>that footeth it</u>

[179] Lewis Owen, high commission pursuivant. Owen compiled a list in July 1610 of the seven priests he had arrested since he came to England in May 1609, AAW A IX, no. 52 (p. 146).

[180] Thomas Cornforth SJ. See Foley IV, 583–9.

[181] Robert Persons SJ.

up, and downe, & by his zeal procureth more credit to his Order then manie a one by ther deep reach, and pollicie. I enquired of the good man that now is imployed about the same busines, being one of ours how the state of the cowntrie standeth for the poorer sort, & he protesteth that the number is very great yea and dailie encreaseth soe that work ther is for three persons, and soe manie he saith are in the same circuit, but soe poor the people are that above a meals meat is not to be expected, yea he having some manteinance out of other parts findeth it not sufficient to releeve the wante of the poorer sort, and the worst inconvenience of al is that ther is skant anie place wher he can soe much as get his cloaths washt but if he or anie of the other shold fal sick they know not wher to bestow them selves, or how to make provision ether of house or means to recover them selves. This is the place, and the means for such workmen as be desired, and onlie obiected to gain time that they might find out more fetches at further leasure. But surlie our poor breethren grudge wonderfullie that ther extremities are noe better considered of, nor provision made accord-inglie. Things if they cold appear as they are wold move pittie, and pittie enforce our Sup. to settle our goverment in better order. The preists I conferred withal like exceeding wel of our Archp^r. care and providence (onlie I except Mr D. Bavan, and m^r Vaghan[182]) and wil concur in anie sort to the redresse of soe manie inconveniences as dailie grow upon us, and wil more and more pester us to the remediles ruyne of our poor clergie if speedie redresse be not procured. Trulie never was Clergie in soe poor estate as ours is, being soe manie soe insufficient, so void of means to help them selves, and dailie more and more growing upon us, soe that the wisest head may be far short in seeing to what issue it is like to grow. Your book[183] is now finished at last but great difficultie is made for the transporting. our host is stept in and brought fowr of them[184] with him to be delivered according to your direction to foure of your [p. 267] especiall frends, they [sic] print wil stand you in wel nighe lxxx^l before the books be distributed, great hinderance it was that none cold tel what was become of the articles drawne between you and the printer. Some wold have bargained for the whole print but they soon fel of again, and wold onlie meddle with 200 copies, wherto it was not agreed for fear of choaking the sale of the rest. I will cal for your clapper & order it according to your mind at

---

[182] Not certainly identified, but this may refer to either one of the priests George or Richard Grisold, one of whom may have used the alias 'Vaughan', AAW A X, no. 3. The Welsh priest Lewis Vaughan (not in Anstr.) was a supporter of the agency's aims, AAW A XI, no. 140.

[183] Richard Smith, *The Prudentiall Ballance of Religion* (St Omer, 1609); ARCR II, no. 709.

[184] For the four copies, see **Letter 8**. See also AAW A VIII, no. 183.

my comming which is intended out of hand that you may be encoraged
what may be, and have the companion when you desire[.] I have taken
order for the transporting of some monie[.] I trust other wil be sent in
time. you shal hear of it by the means you appointed in your letter. I
think you have herd of the renewing of the Indulg of a chappel, and
changing the place, it is much desired to be gotten with al convenient
speed, the place being such as is now almost readie but may not be
used until you have obteined the suit. It wil be much more bewtiful, &
convenient, It is desired that wheras in the old grant ther be these or
the like words quod habeat in domo sua quoddam cappellum in
honorem vener. sacr. et deiparae virg. etcetera, that these words may be
added or the like. quod quidem cappellum vener. sacr. et deiparae
virg. ab omnibus haberi volumus et apostolica nostra authoritate esse
declaramus. etcetera. the meaning is to have it ratifyed, and made soe
de novo. and further grant to be made that within the Octave of corpus
Christi noe feast be served within the house but those principal feasts
of S. Ihon Bapt. and SS. Peter, and Paul. your best frend respecteth
you greatlie and for your sake useth your goddaughter[185] (who remembreth her dutie to you) exceeding kindlie. onlie wishing that if anie
breach shold chanc upon anie occasion you wold not take it il, or
impute it as want of affection unto you. Card. Bel. book[186] was in the
K hands before Christmas, and seemeth not much displeasing to him,
but I can not hear that it hath bene seen of anie cath in the land.
Diverse reports according to the diversitie of affections, al agreeing that
it seemeth more complemental then solid. It is given to D. Andrews B.
of Elie to answer,[187] who affirmed to a frend of his not il affected that
in praise or dispraise therof he wold say nothing, onlie he wold assure
him that he missed of his aime if we for our parts wold brag much
therof.[188] Such care ther was at the first arrival therof that being to be
bownd up in Pauls churchyerd one of his Maiesties privie chamber was
appointed to oversee the book binder, and stand by him al the whil, &
strictlie charging him not soe much as to looke upon the title of the
book. Other two bookes ther are of the same argument in french here
one published by the K ordinarie preacher,[189] the auther of the other

[185] Elizabeth Dacres.

[186] Cardinal Bellarmine's reply to Lancelot Andrewes's *Tortura Torti* and to James's
'Praefatio Monitoria' in his *Apologia pro Iuramento Fidelitatis* was issued at Rome in late
autumun 1609, Cardinal Robert Bellarmine SJ, *Apologia Roberti S.R.E. Cardinalis Bellarmini,
pro Responsione sua ad librum Iacobi Magnae Britanniae Regis* (Rome, 1609); ARCR I, no. 1491;
J. Brodrick, *The Life and Work of Blessed Robert Francis Cardinal Bellarmine, S.J. 1542–1621* (2
vols, 1928), II, 217.

[187] Andrewes replied with *Responsio ad Apologiam Cardinalis Bellarmini* (1610).

[188] For Andrewes's reported low opinion of Bellarmine's book, see McClure, 295.

[189] Nicolas Coeffeteau OP, Bishop of Marseilles, *Responce à l'Advertissement, addressé par le
Serenissime Roy de la Grande Bretagne, Iacques I. à tous les Princes & Potentats de la Chrestienté*

I now remember not, of al which the last mentioned is said to be the most sufficient. I wil not omit to relate unto you how upon ['the' deleted] our 7. of Ianuarie this present year 1610. a gossip of wellingboro[190] being a widdow wooman called goodwife Orper being hired for xx[s] to tend some visited with the plague as was supposed then and indeed proved [word illegible] after sent to the officers of the towne, being constables or church wardens for a manchet and a quart of muscaden. they not willing to stand upon points with her in that case as they denyed nothing was demanded soe they provided her of that she asked wherwith she provided together with the rest enclosed with her being likwise woomen to celebrate the lords supper, and she as excelling in spirit with bible clearklik, and book of common prayer performed the ministers office receaved and administred to the rest, song the psalme in conclusion and soe departed. This fact was diverslie censured and the minister a fortnight after made a sermon wherin he affirmed that he approved not her fact. yet her zeal seemed excusable to manie. Now is she dead of the plague, and rid of al obiections.[191] Noe more but Christ Iesus have you in his keaping together with al our good frends to whom I pray you commend me D. Th.[192] D. Ans.[193] D. Const.[194] M. Nic.[195] M[r] Per.[196]

yours ever most assuredlie
    G. West.
(On p. 268)
Addressed: To the worshipfull my assured good Frend m[r] R. Baker give
        these
Endorsed: (1) October ii. [= 11] 609 [sic]
        (2) Geo: West ie ['perhaps' deleted] m. Th. Moor ii [= 11]
        Oct.

(Paris, 1609). The Jesuits said that apparently James I did 'not dislike' this book because of its 'moderation', Foley VII, 1006, but John Chamberlain wrote that James took it in no 'better part then yf…he shold have bid a T. in his teeth and then crie sir reverence', McClure, 294.

[190] Wellingborough, Northamptonshire.

[191] Elizabeth Orper, a widow, was buried on 14 January 1610, Parish register of All Hallows, Wellingborough (microfiche copy, Society of Genealogists, reference NH/Reg/7967A). Unfortunately the ecclesiastical court records for the southern division of the Northampton deanery are lacking for this period so these events cannot be checked, E.J.I. Allen, 'The State of the Church in the Diocese of Peterborough, 1601–1642' (unpubl. B. Litt. thesis, Oxford, 1972), 163–4.

[192] Edmund Thornell.

[193] Robert (Anselm) Beech OSB.

[194] Not identified.

[195] Nicholas Fitzherbert.

[196] William Percy.

8 *George Salvin (Birkhead) to Richard Baker (Smith) (11 April 1610)   (AAW*
A IX, no. 33, pp. 85–8. Holograph. Dated 12 April in AAW A catalogue)

my Good S[r], I have in effect alredie answered both yo*u*r letters of the
29 of Ianuarie and of the 20 of feb. and have adventured to send it by
my old frend[197] unto yo*w*, with the inclosed copie of Cardinal bianch.
Letter to me.[198] I was the bolder to do it because it conteineth nothinge
but what I care not yf he see. for sith that paul hath made this
resolution,[199] and that both yo*w* and I are willinge to obey it, I write
not any thinge therin, but wh*i*ch may insinuate so much, and I hope
albeit my said frend should see it, he could take no great exceptions
therat. and it may be a furtherance to increase frendship betwene him
and yo*w* wh*i*ch I am not much against, the case standinge with us as
it doth. we must have patience and be content with the first clause of
not beinge bound to deale with the fathers in our Goverment. As in
that letter I sent yo*w* a coppie of bianch. letter to me, so in this I send
yo*w* another copie of my answere to him,[200] that yo*w* may see how I
proceed. I trust yo*w* will learne whether any thinge in this doinge be
surreptitiu*m* or no, of wh*i*ch surely I make no doubt, but I feare that
some of our brethren wilbe redie enough to do it. Concerninge yo*u*r
com*m*inge awaie, in my forsaid Letter I have told yo*w* my minde and
therfor will say no more of that. my said Letter beareth the same date
that this doth. I send yo*w* also heareinclosed a letter to farnese our
protector,[201] I praie deliver it after yo*w* have sealed it up, and gett m[r]
Geffrey[202] to helpe yo*w*. it is to the same effect with my letter to bianch.
though it conteine not so much. what that werall,[203] or mallet[204] are I

[197] Robert Persons SJ. The letter is AAW A IX, no. 32.

[198] This letter is AAW A IX, no. 22, dated 26 February 1610 (NS). It instructs Birkhead
that he must send the names of those who defend the oath of allegiance so that they
may be proceeded against canonically. Secondly, he is to keep strictly to the breves and
faculties accorded to his predecessor. The third section of the letter, while dealing with
Smith's presentation of petitions, exhorts matters in England to be conducted in peace
and charity. The cardinal says that this letter is written in place of a letter to Birkhead
the previous summer which he thought had miscarried. (For Hicks's clarification of the
dating of these letters, CRS 41, 68.)

[199] The confirmation by Paul V of Clement VIII's breve of 5 October 1602 (NS)
forbidding the involvement of SJ in secular clergy affairs in England.

[200] This letter of 23 February 1610 is AAW A IX, no. 20, printed in TD V, pp. xciii–
vi.

[201] A copy of this letter is AAW A IX, no. 21 (23 February 1610, printed in TD V, pp.
xcii–iii).

[202] Geoffrey Pole.

[203] Not identified.

[204] Probably the secular priest John Muttlebury alias Mallet who was ordained in 1601.
After banishment in 1607 he returned to England in April 1608 and entered OSB in
1609 or 1610, Anstr. I, 242. However, a layman called Mallet was a substantial financial
donor to SJ between 1607 and 1609, McCoog, 251.

know not, but some telleth me that mallet is a simple fellow. Lett me see yf either he or the other can give yo*w* such a beed roull against bb, as I send yo*w* hereinclosed.[205] Iohn Bennet procured the same in a iorney thither into wales. And yo*w* shall see that m[r] mush will procure many moe. In deed yf yo*w* and I had ben backed by tyme, perhaps we should have had another end. the pursuivantes were never so busie, w*h*ich maketh us to lurke in corners more then ever we did. Doctor Worthington hath sent a bible to m[r] Blackwell for a token.[206] and yet must I be forced to deale with those men[207] as with heretiques. I am glad for my part to have nothinge to do with dowaie. Lett them runne [p. 86] on there course, and yo*w* shall see before it be longe what brave youthes we shall have sent into England. here be heretiques newly risen that may be called separistes. because they say all Consisteth in prainge alone. for sith that diverse men do ordinarily praie for diverse thin[ges] they account it a babilonicall confusion to praie to gether. one Smith a preacher is ther leader, and both he and his followers are driven into holland.[208] none of our brethren are yet come unto me, but I now expect them daly. they must be quiet, as I hope they will, and yt seameth to me that we shall therby please his hol. better. I will therfor persuade them to expect for a tyme some better opportunitie. our state is now much busied and perturbed, and yf we beginne to enter also into new broiles, we may much hurt our selves and do [word deleted] no good. his hol. resolution must needes be knowen to yo*w* before yow saw m[r] more, and therfor I iudge that all my Letters sent by him did come to Late. I praie yo*w* keepe my old frendes and m[r] fitz[209] letter verie secrete. I [thi]nk they will not be now to any great use. for I perceive we must be frendes and give no mutuall disgust. when my brethren and I have talked, yo*w* shall heare what we have don. I have sent the vi pound to m[r] heath accordinge as yo*w* requested. I shall paie my selfe againe by one meane [word deleted] or other. of late were bookes to the valew of five hunderd pound [taken ?], and many were burnt at Paules churchyard. foure of yo*u*rs[210] I have received and one of yo*u*r La lyfe.[211] they be all distributed as yo*w*

[205] AAW A IX, no. 23, dated 3 March 1610 (a list of names of twenty priests, mostly in South Wales, who favour the appointment of a bishop).

[206] On 3 April 1610 Birkhead wrote to Smith that Worthington had 'honored...[Blackwell] next unto me with a present of one of his bables [sic] in English', AAW A IX, no. 31 (pp. 77–8); see ARCR II, no. 171.

[207] The priests in the Clink prison who favoured the oath of allegiance.

[208] John Smyth had seceded from the Church of England and emigrated with his congregation to the Netherlands, R.J. Acheson, *Radical Puritans in England 1550–1660* (1990), 19–22. *Cf.* B. R. White, *The English Separatist Tradition* (Oxford, 1971), ch. 6; S. Brachlow, *The Communion of Saints* (Oxford, 1988), *passim*.

[209] Thomas Fitzherbert.

[210] Smith, *Prudentiall Ballance.*

desired.[212] some of yours are also scattered abroad in london by whome I know. Yf they could be sent in, m^r Buckl.[213] will make some sheift to utter them.[214] but there is vigilancie kept at the Custome house, that no such wares can escape. and so havinge no more at this tyme, and referringe the disposition of your returne to your selfe as I have written, albeit my frendes here will dislike it, for they I am sure will resist it, I leave yow to godes most holy protection. this 11 of April. 1610.
your lovinge frend
    Geo. Salvine.
(On p. 88)
    Addressed: To his verie good frend m^r Richard Baker geve these. att Rome.
Endorsed: (1) 11 Apr: 610 [sic]
        (2) Archpriest ii [= 11] Apr.

9 *George Salvin (Birkhead) to Richard Baker (Smith) (23 April 1610)   (AAW A IX, no. 35, pp. 91–4. Holograph)*

my Rev. good S^r your Last of the 6 of march both to my selfe and m^r west[215], whose presence yow now enioy of S Cuthbertes daie[216] againe to my selfe I have received, and together with them a duplicate from Card blanch.[217] of that which he had sent before unto me by m^r Swin.[218]

---

[211] Richard Smith, *Vita Illustrissimae, ac Püssimae Dominae Magdalenae Montis-acuti in Anglia Vicecomitissae* (Rome, 1609). It was dedicated to Cardinal Edward Farnese. On 7 December 1610 (NS) Smith reported to More that James I was greatly offended with this 'litle booke' which the Venetian ambassador was said to have presented to him, AAW A IX, no. 103 (p. 337).

[212] See **Letter 7**. In July 1610 William (Gabriel) Gifford OSB thanked Smith for 'the life and death of that woorthie ladie which trulie I red over verbatim not without teares', and said he had delivered a copy to Matthew Kellison, AAW A IX, no. 54 (p. 151).

[213] Ralph Buckland, secular priest. Buckland acted as a letter carrier. In October 1611 he lost 'a greate packett of letters' when he was robbed while going to the Continent, AAW A X, no. 135 (p. 387).

[214] John Redman had written to Smith on 24 November 1609 (NS) that he had tried to persuade William Cape to be a 'partenour' with the merchant John Fowler in an arrangement to sell Smith's books in England but 'we could not find out the price of eche copie for that he [Cape] knew not what monie m^r Bucland and m^r Archpriest had layed out so I requested him to enquire heerof at his arrival and then to thinke of my offre and requeste and to ioine with fouler in the hazard telling him to my iudgement that thei wil be no lousers', AAW A VIII, no. 183 (p. 693). For Cape, see A.F. Allison, 'Franciscan Books in English, 1559–1640', *Biographical Studies* 3 (1955), 16–65, at pp. 46–7; ARCR II, nos 117–20.

[215] Thomas More.

[216] 20 March.

[217] Cardinal Lawrence Bianchetti. See AAW A IX, no. 22; **Letter 8**.

[218] Thomas Fitzherbert.

and one from our protectour[219] to the Assistantes.[220] so that yo*w* may see how I have received all yo*u*rs, as I trust yo*w* have received myne. I have answered yo*u*r former letters two waies, one by paris, and have sent yo*w* ther inclosed a copie of my answere to blanc with another copie sent me out of wailes. the other by my old frend[221] for expeditions sake, both beinge dated the 11 of April[222] and in my old frendes a copie of blanch his letter to me, w*h*ich in this yo*u*r Last, yo*w* say was sealed before yo*w* could see it.[223] he exhorteth me as yo*w* may see to observe the breves of Clem and Paul[224] prout iacent in omnibus, and yet adviseth me to persuade yo*w* to accept againe of my old frend and Swin, and addeth D thornell w*h*ich how it will stand with the breves I cannot well conceive, as I have written in my other Letters unto yo*w*. now I send yo*w* this by the waie of bruxels by the meanes of yo*u*r frend m[r] heath.[225] As for yo*u*r staie there, I have told yo*w* my minde in my letter sent by the waie of my old frend. be yo*w* sure he getteth nothinge to pr*ei*udice our cause by me. yett I was content to do it now for more increase of frendeship, betwene yo*w* and him. w*h*ich I like verie well, and am glad yo*w* have alredie made it. and so much the more as his hol hath vouchsafed to crave it at yo*u*r handes. yo*w* know that I was alwaies redie to [five words deleted] submitt my selfe to his deter- mination, and I thanke yo*w* also for beinge so redie unto it as yo*w* are. I trust o*u*r brethren will concurre with us. write I praie yo*w* unto them to that purpose. I thinke verely Paul will like of us the better, when he seeth us so willingly yeeld unto him, in matters that do so much aggreve us. use yo*u*r owne discretion in com*m*inge or not com*m*inge awaie. yo*w* are sure to be welcome heare. m[r] west knoweth my minde, yf it so fall out. sith he is there, I shall like yt well enough that he remaine till I take other order, yf yow find he may do it with Conveniencie[.] he can mainteyne himselfe, he is trustie and faithfull, and as yet I know not whome els I could send thither. yf yo*w* iudge D thornell fitt to ioyne with him, I shall not mislike it. but yo*w* see what blanch. shooteth at. and verely I feare we shalbe crossed in everie thinge untill that be

---

[219] Cardinal Edward Farnese.

[220] On 9 June 1610 Birkhead's assistants William Bishop, John Colleton, John Mush, John Michell, Morgan Clennock and Edward Bennett wrote back to Farnese, assuring him that they had not caused division among the English clergy and attacking Bianchetti for inclining too much to SJ, AAW A IX, no. 41.

[221] Robert Persons SJ.

[222] AAW A IX, no. 32.

[223] See **Letter 8**.

[224] *i.e.* the breve of Clement VIII concerning the regulation of the English mission and Paul V's two breves denouncing the oath of allegiance of 1606.

[225] In 1611 Thomas Heath was posted to London (under the alias of Broome) to work as a conveyer of the secular clergy's letters. He also used the alias of John Baptist Fabian, AAW A X, no. 150.

performed but I know our brethren will be so hote against it, that I dare not yet so [p. 92] much condiscend. be not yett overhastie I praie yo*w* in departinge thence. I will not faile still to urge for you*r* manteinance what may be don. but I have no sure hold, but onely of our frend and m^r farington[226]. they are not come unto me as yett, but I looke daily for them. Seinge thinges go as they do, I wilbe quiet, and move nothinge any more unles they gett me all the handes of my brethren unto yt. the benedictins and we be verie good frendes. I take no disgust that we are barred from sendinge our letters by them. therfor the speeches given out to the Contrarie are false and mere Calumniations broched onely to sett us by the eares together. one in the north of that order called m^r Samuel[227] hath some quarrel against some of mine,[228] and myne against him. fath. Preston[229] and I have taken order to end the quarell. I trust it shalbe don. of late m^r Bruninges[230] preest m^r white[231] was taken by crosse and sett in the m*a*rshalsee but himselfe bound onely over to appeare when he was called. m^r Coll. and m^r fennell either by money or by potent frendes are released out of prison, to be confined the first in london, the other in the Countrie to houses where the owners be no recusantes.[232] they have both notwithstandinge stoutly denied the oath. m^r Ionson[233] a preest in prison at york by meanes of a scottsman hath offered an forme of an oath to the Kinge; who liketh it well. but I was not made privie unto it, nor have not as yett seen yt. I have ben admonished that no forme of oath should be offered up before the Inquisition had seen yt. this is don without my privitie, and so I praie yo*w* answere yf yo*w* heare any thinge thereof. I dare not deale with the Clinkers, I am told yf I do I shalbe in great daunger, and that yf any Censure shall

---

[226] Edward Bennett.

[227] Samuel (Bartholomew) Kennett OSB.

[228] *i.e.* against Cuthbert Trollop and William Ogle, two leading northern secular priests. See **Letter 15**.

[229] Roland (Thomas) Preston OSB, superior of the Cassinese Benedictines in England.

[230] Probably Richard Brenning of Denmead, Hampshire who married Eleanor, daughter of Anthony Uvedale of Hambledon, Hampshire, by Ursula daughter of John Norton. Richard Brenning appears in the first recusancy roll, CRS 18, 283, 291. He had, with the Uvedales, assisted the escape from Winchester gaol in late 1599 of the secular priest Edward Kenion, an intimate of the group around Viscount Montague. Kenion had shared a chamber in Winchester gaol with the imprisoned recusant Anthony Norton, brother of the priest Benjamin Norton, *CSPD 1598–1601*, 336–40; Anstr. I, 196–7.

[231] The secular priest Richard White, ordained in September 1587, Anstr. I, 378.

[232] Anthony Champney wrote to Smith on 6 July 1610 (NS) that Colleton 'may goe whither he will and abyd where he will the mayster of the howse where he lyethe goinge to churche', AAW A IX, no. 51 (p. 141).

[233] Cuthbert Johnson was regarded by the southern secular priests as one of their party. In 1624, however, he was nominated by SJ when Rome set about appointing a successor to the deceased bishop of Chalcedon, William Bishop, Allison, 'Richard Smith', 158.

come forth against them they will write and publishe books against it. they are but three or foure, and cannot do much harme but to them selves. I hope the Card will will [sic] hold me excused in these daungerous tymes; howbeit I meane to do what lieth in me, for the deutie I owe to the sea Apostoliqiue whereunto I hold my self bound alwaies to be an obedient child. and therfor do most willingly submitt my selfe to his hol decree, and will not move the matter of missions and doway till I see him Contented therewith. and I trust my brethren when they see yo*ur* letters, wilbe contented with this Course. I repose my selfe much [p. 93] upon yo*ur* discretion in the deliverie of all my letters sent unto yo*w* by m^r west. pe*r*haps Paules determination will prohibit yo*w* to do it. I am loth any thinge be don that may offend. Lett me know I praie yo*w* what is don in that point. what I wrote of m^r Rich[234] was written to me by one who is wholly for them.[235] <u>The bish. of</u> bath and wells[236] shewed of late a new booke to the kinge of D feildes.[237] the k bad him read it. and after he had hard him read a

---

[234] Probably Michael Walpole SJ (though Edward Walpole SJ also used this alias). In January 1610 Birkhead reported to Smith in Rome that Michael Walpole held an arguably lax opinion about the papal deposing power. Archbishop Bancroft had examined Walpole 'verie civilly', and 'asked him yf he wold take the oath [of allegiance], and he denyed yt. he questioned with him of everie branch of it, to wh*i*ch he replied in some. that not speaking particuiarly of our kinge, towards whome, in respect he was his subiect he owed all reverence, and deutie: but makinge the question generally of kinges, he saied, the best divins held opinion that for iust causes the pope might exco*mmun*icate, depose, and absolve subiectes from ther allegiance, that in some cases, [word deleted] subiectes might take armes against ther prince, in ther defence'. But 'the matter' was not 'defined to be of faith'. Walpole refused to identify himself as a Catholic cleric. Bancroft asked him again 'why he should refuse the oth, consideringe m^r Blackwell and m^r warmington had taken yt, and what he held of them. to wh*i*ch he answered that he held m^r Blackwell to be lerned, and that he once was earnest in the contrarie opinion, in regard of wh*i*ch, his act could not move others. then the b told him how well he had used m^r Blackwell in all frendly manner, to wh*i*ch m^r Rich answered, I dowbt not but your lordship hath plaied yo*ur* part well with him, I wish he had discharged his part as well. at the wh*i*ch the b laughed and dismissed him', AAW A IX, no. 2 (pp. 4–5). The Jesuits claimed that Walpole had replied to Bancroft's questions about the papal deposing power with 'firmness and prudence' whereas John Colleton had not, Foley VII, 1005. Smith wrote to More in September 1611 that one of his (Smith's) recent letters to More had evidently miscarried, in which 'I sent you a leefe or twoe of a booke set out by m walp wherin mariana [Juan de Mariana SJ] his opinion is defended flatly and they said to be enemies to Iesus who condemned his booke wh*i*ch the K. tooke very ill', AAW A X, no. 126 (p. 364). This is a reference to Walpole's *A Briefe Admonition to all English Catholikes, concerning a late Proclamation set forth against them* (St Omer, 1610), ch. 5. He had also written *A Treatise of the Subiection of Princes to God and the Church* (St Omer, 1608) which was probably never issued, ARCR II, no. 780. In June 1610 Birkhead reported that Walpole had been banished, AAW A IX, no. 43. By 1612 he had been appointed confessor at Douai and was the source of much conflict within the college.

[235] *i.e.* the Jesuits.

[236] James Montagu.

[237] Richard Field, *Of the Church. Five Bookes* (1606–10).

while, he interrupted him, and shewed great dislike of the manner of feild his writinge, saing it was bitter, nothinge but wordes etc*etera*, and asked yf he had no proofes. the b replied that the proofes followed. read them, said the kinge. and <u>after the b had read a</u> while the k staied him, and shewed great dislike and Contempt of the proofes: sainge they were but Cavills, sophismes etc*etera* and that he did not like that men should handle matter rather with Cunninge then good learninge, and after further readinge the k tooke the booke, and threw it on the ground in a great angre, and spake wordes w*h*ich were not to be disliked, as he hath don at other severall tymes. one D Butler[238] made a sermon before the k of Late against iustification by onely faith, and provinge workes of penance and namely satisfaction to god and the world. before he went up, the Arch. of Cant[239] said to one by him, that he should not find an heyrebreadth betwene the preacher and a papist. after the sermon ther was much speech therof, and in particular betwene the k and the L Souch.[240] the k defendinge what the doctor had said, and the L Souch speakinge against it, till they grew somewhat warme. thus much hath ben written to me by some of good intelligence. I will move my brethren when I see them to write a common letter to the Irish b[241] of thankesgevinge, and to others there besides where it may do good. by paris[242] also I have sent yo*w* a ['copie' deleted] letter to farnese.[243] I have written so much that I feare they will thinke me importune. but now I meane to cease, hopinge we shalbe frendes. God grant us all peace, in Christ our Lord. Com*m*end me to m[r] Geff.[244] and m[r] west. all yo*u*r frendes heare are in health and wish yo*w* all prosperouse successe and happie protection in the divine providence of Almightie God. this 23 of April 1610

yo*u*rs ever assured

   Geo. Salvine

(On p. 94)

Addressed: To his verie good frend m[r] Richard Baker give this. Ro.

Endorsed: (1) Apr: 23: 10:

       (2) Archpr*i*est 23 Apr.

       pr*i*est. Ionson by a Scots man presented to the K*ing* a new form of oath w*c*h He liked.

---

[238] Dr Richard Butler. For his last will and testament, see PRO, SP 14/70/66.

[239] Richard Bancroft.

[240] Edward Zouch, eleventh Baron Zouch.

[241] Peter Lombard, Archbishop of Armagh, who resided in Rome. See also Conway *AH* 23, 18–19.

[242] *i.e.* via Anthony Champney.

[243] AAW A IX, no. 21 (23 February 1610).

[244] Geoffrey Pole.

10 *George Salvin (Birkhead) to Richard Baker (Smith) (4 May 1610)*   *(AAW A IX, no. 39, pp. 105–8. Holograph)*

my Reverend Good S^r, since the receit of yo*u*r last, wherin yo*w* sent me the duplicate of bianchettes Letter,[245] I [word deleted] have written unto yo*w* thereof by yo*u*r meane att bruxels, w*hi*ch I trust will come to your handes. m^r farington[246] and the rest have ben with me of Late. I have shewed them all. they tell me yo*u*r wauntes shalbe better supplied, but will not have yo*w* returne in any case. I cannot yet gett them to take any thought for sendinge either money or Letters, but are content to Lett that burden still rest upon me. wherin surely I will do to my power, but I dare not give yo*w* my worde for an absolute performance thereof. yo*u*r six pound to m^r heath I have alredie paid by meanes of will[ia]m cape; and now father pr*e*ston and m^r vincent[247] beinge in prison,[248] I have sent them vi^li xiii^s iiii^d yf they will take it, for dischardge of our Letters sent by there helpe.[249] I told my brethren thereof, but they made me no answere how I should be repaied againe. the imprisonment of the two foresaid frendes wilbe a great hinderance. I dare not come at London, because the bishops send out there pursivantes in such nomber that no man can escape. the tyme was never so hard in that respect. but that the Lower house standeth so stifly upon it, it is thought the kinge wold have all the penal Lawes against us in his owne handes. yo*w* shall heare from our brethren as shortly as may be. yt greveth them that thinges go as they do. yo*w* shall know there mindes by there owne letters. sith ther is no remedie, I suppose they will like of the peace yo*w* have made, and I hope to gett them unto it heare, and to be content to rest from prosecuting the matter of the missions and the Colledge of dowaie. neverthelesse for bb they are exceedinge vehement, and most desirous now to prosecute that suit. Send me word I praie yo*w*, whether yo*w* think it convenient or no. me thinkes his hol hath no likinge unto it, or els he wold never have

---

[245] See **Letter 8**.

[246] Edward Bennett.

[247] Walter Robert (Vincent) Sadler OSB.

[248] They had been arrested by Anthony Rouse and sent to Newgate, AAW A IX, no. 43. Anthony Champney remarked on 6 July 1610 (NS) that Preston had expected that he would be released on the same easy conditions as John Colleton, but news of the assassination of Henri IV had prevented this, AAW A IX, no. 51. See also Foley VII, 1011.

[249] On 2 July 1610 Birkhead informed Smith that the superiors of the Cassinese congregation of OSB had again forbidden the English Cassinese Benedictines to carry the secular clergy's letters because of some 'preiudicial information…against us. but I meane never to trouble them any more', though he had recently sent Smith £65, by means of the Cassinese, to maintain him in Rome, AAW A IX, no. 49 (p. 132). See also **Letter 16**.

enioyned me to gett the consentes of all. w*h*ich in verie deed hath so many difficulties as I am not able to expresse them; a thinge no doubt forseen by them that have suggested that course to paul. howsoever I hope we shall resolve to be quiet w*i*th that w*h*ich he hath alredie graunted us, and for our partes will keepe peace with our opposites as well as we can. and so I desire yo*w* to do there with my old frend[250] and m^r Swynnerton.[251] but for feare of a worse event, I dare not follow the Counsel of blanchet,[252] that thinketh it the best for me to move yo*w* ['to' deleted] againe to Consult w*i*th the forenamed two frendes and to ioyne D Thornell unto them. the first I know well enough, but the doctor I never saw. wherfor what to say of him I know not. I referre it to yo*w*. for the other two the Counsell is flatt against the breve,[253] and the interp*r*etation thereof, or I am much deceived. our frendes [p. 106] heare also mislike the doctor. I perceive yo*u*r frend Beniamin[254] hath light upon my olde frendes Last Letter unto me,[255] and hath sent yo*w* the Copie. I praie yo*w* be warie in discoveringe it. such expostulations are onely betwene him and my selfe, and shall not impaire yo*u*r credit with me. I meane to answere it with silence because I wold Continue the peace yo*w* have begonne. it is straunge: both he and m^r Swyn. wrote verie kind Letters unto me of the 6 of march and now of the 20 he writeth as yo*w* see.[256] but pardon him; it is an answere to one, w*h*ich I writt to him, and sent yo*w* a copie therof, for as much as it Concerned yo*w*. As for supplie of money yo*u*r frendes have promised me not to faile, and as soone as it com*m*eth to my handes, I will use the best diligence I can to send it unto yo*w*. they are Loth yo*w* shold returne as yet, and I am as Loth yo*w* should be driven to that perplexitie w*h*ich yo*w* have suffered alredie. do as yo*w* shall see it convenient. yo*w* may be sure to be welcome to us so longe as we do stand. neither will it be ungratefull to us yf yow tarrie still as I have in other letters written unto yo*w*. Now the prisons are well filled againe w*i*th preistes. all god be thanked stoutly refuse the oath. m^r Coll. and

---

[250] Robert Persons SJ.

[251] Thomas Fitzherbert.

[252] Cardinal Lawrence Bianchetti. See **Letter 9**.

[253] *i.e.* Clement VIII's breve forbidding SJ interference in the secular clergy's affairs.

[254] Benjamin Norton.

[255] Robert Persons's letter to Birkhead written on Easter eve, 10 April 1610 (NS), Milton House MSS (transcript at ABSI), protesting that he departed 'out of this world with the same desire of love peace, and union betweene all you emongst your selfes and with all our fathers which alwayes I have had', and denying that SJ ever asserted superiority over the seculars in England. Champney wrote to Smith on 6 July 1610 (NS) that Christopher Bagshaw had told him 'that father persones before his deathe [on 15 April 1610 (NS)] had changed his opinion and designe', AAW A IX, no. 51 (p. 141).

[256] Persons's letters to Birkhead of 6 and 20 March 1610 (NS) are both in the Milton House MSS and are printed in part in TD V, pp. xcvii–c.

also m^r fennel two assistantes, have gotten there Libertie and are Confined upon 20 daies warninge. m^r Coll. is confirmed [word deleted] in his old opinion, that his Countrema$n$[257] is to stronge for yo$w$ and us, and therfor is Loth to strive against the streame. I told yo$w$ in another Letter[258] of an oath offered by m^r Iohnson at york. I am sorie he was so hastie, and have now since written my minde unto him, and do heare send yo$w$ inclosed the Copie of the said oath, w$h$ich I suppose will not be Liked there. yf yow can fitly shewe it to the inquisitors, I wold be glad to know there mindes. yt seamed not amisse to send it unto yo$w$, because I feare yo$w$ may heare of it els by some other waie. now also the talke goeth that the oath shalbe interpr$e$ted by the parlament that it must be taken in that sense as m^r black:[259] offered to take it at the first. namely accordinge to his maiesties intention, w$h$ich is onely to tie us to our temporall subiection. I write thus much of purpose that yo$w$ may enforme our superiours in matters of Conscience, and know there resolution, that I may the better be able to answere such as will repaire unto me in that respect. for by godes grace in these matters I meane to do nothinge but as I shalbe directed from thence. our brethren beinge with me of Late, wished me to signifie unto yo$w$, whome in my iudgment I thought fitt to be my successor, because albeit I have my helth indifferent well (I thanke god) yet they see me weake and [p. 107] feare that any little fitt of sicknes will putt me in daunger and to pr$e$vent the worst, are desirous I should nominate some. w$h$ich I was verie loth to do. but they urginge me therunto by some good reasons, I promised them to write unto yo$w$ to that effect, and they promised me to give there Consentes. wherfor yf it shall please god to call me out of this world, I nominate heare in secrett unto yo$w$, m^r D Bishope, m^r Colleton, and your selfe. that when yo$w$ heare such newes, yo$w$ may be redie to signifie to our Cheife pastor the desire of our brethren, and that he may make choice of some one of yo$w$ as he shall please. And this I do the more willingly, for that I hope therebie much discord and dissention may be pr$e$vented. for as my desyre is to be quiet my selfe in these my old daies, so is it also my desire to have all quietnes observed amongst yo$w$ after my decease. me thinkes it should be good for us now to make no more complaintes, but rather to stand upon our owne defence, yf any be made against us. and Let me once againe speake to yo$w$ of bb. a vaine thinge it is for any one to sue for a thinge w$h$ich he knoweth beforehand wilbe refused. wherfor once againe I praie yo$w$ Lett me know how yo$w$ find Paul[260] to be

[257] *i.e.* Persons. John Colleton was not yet aware of Persons's death.
[258] **Letter 9**.
[259] George Blackwell.
[260] Pope Paul V.

inclined therin. my Assistantes do still crave that they may proceede in the matter of suffrages. which I now am in doubt whether I may permitt or no, sith I am tied to observe the breves ad literam and also my faculties, which Conteine no such thinge. yf I be by this new determination, prohibited from makinge any petition for the helpe of our necessities, it will make us to muse. yet D wor.[261] offereth againe to Conferre with us in any thinge that may apperteine to the reformatiom of the Hierarchie of our Clergie. wherupon I see that they[262] will be consultors with us whether we will or no. I praie yow Let me have your opinion as soone as yow can. I wold be Loth to do any thinge which may either offend his hol or preiudice our Cause. before I do that I wold be glad to resigne my office, and yf either yow or my old frend could procure me leave to do it, I should hold my selfe much beholden to yow both. I wold adventure it of my selfe, but that I feare it wilbe ill taken. I have now Lately chosen m^r Cuthberte Trolope to be my Assist. in the north in m^r Parkers place.[263] his zeale, pietie, sinceritie, and discreet behaviour is such, that I could not have notice of any more fitt for that place then he. the k maiesties speach to the Lordes and commons at whitehall 21 of march. 1609 by our account is now come out in print.[264] of religion he saieth thus: As for religion, we have all great cause to take heed unto it: papistes are waxed as proud at this tyme as ever they were, which makes many to think they have some new plott in hand. & although the poorer sort of [p. 108] them be (god be thanked) much decreased, yet doth the greater sort daily increase, especially amonge the feminine Sex. nay they are waxed so proud that some say no man dare present them nor iudges medle with them, they are so backed & upholden by divers great Courtiers[.] it is a surer and better waie to remove the materials of fire, [word deleted] before they be kindled, then to quench the fire when once it is kindled. Nam levius laedit quicquid previdimus ante. it is to longe to write yow all in particular. he wisheth not stronger lawes then are alredie made, but those to be well executed. he misliketh the cowrse of blood notwithstandinge. he willeth yf there be any scruple touchinge the ministringe of the oath, that now they should cleare it. since I have (saieth he) with my penne brought the popes quarrel upon me, and

---

[261] Thomas Worthington.

[262] The Jesuits.

[263] Birkhead admitted to Smith that the former appellant Trollop was a controversial choice because he was 'guiltie of the Appele', AAW A IX, no. 58 (p. 164). According to Benjamin Norton, Trollop was a cousin of the priest Richard Broughton, AAW A XII, no. 204.

[264] James I, *The Kings Majesties Speach to the Lords and Commons, xxi. March 1609* (1609). See C.H. McIlwain, *The Political Works of James I* (New York, 1965), 306–25, at pp. 322–3.

proclaimed publique defiance to Babylon in mainteyninge it: should it now sleepe, and should I seame (as it were) to steale from it againe. As for recusantes Let them be all dewly presented. none ought to be spared from the danger of the Law, and then it is my part to use mercie as I thinke Conveniente. he maketh two ranckes of papistes, either old brought up in tymes of poperie, and such as in yonger yeares have never drunke in other milk. or such as become Apostates. the former he pittieth, and hateth not there persons yf they be quiet subiectes. but as for the Apostates he can never shew any favorable countenance towardes them, but will have the Law strike sureliest upon them. thus yow see in manner of an abridgment his whole speach in effect. God helpe us and give us stronge patience for upon his divine providence must we only relie. unto the which I shall ever commend yow. And so not forgettinge my commend. to m^r Geffrey^{265} and m^r more, I bid yow farewell the 4 of maie. 1610.

your lovinge frend

    G. S.

Addressed: To his loving frend m^r Richard Baker give this.

Endorsed: (1) Maii 4: 10.

        (2) Archpriest 4 may

11 *Richard Baker (Smith) to Thomas More (26 October 1610 (NS))*   *(AAW*
    A IX, no. 83, pp. 279–80. Holograph)

Deere Syr I wrote unto you from Florence^{266} and milan which letters I wold be glad were safely comen to your hands.^{267} As I tooke cooche at milan I saw F. Gerard^{268} passing by but spoke not to him, and touching my voiage hitherto I thank God and good praiers it hath bene very good and without any hurt or danger. For though ther be many thousands of soldiers in the state of milan and savoie^{269} and twoe

---

^{265} Geoffrey Pole.

^{266} Smith had written to More on 22 September 1610 (NS) from Florence where he was welcomed and entertained by the two younger Dormer brothers (Anthony and Robert), their tutor Francis Hore, and Edward Vaux, fourth Baron Vaux, AAW A IX, no. 75. The Dormers, Hore, Vaux and Thomas Sackville, with Sir Oliver Manners, were about to journey to Rome; *cf.* G. Anstruther, *Vaux of Harrowden* (Newport, 1953), 377–8.

^{267} Smith wrote to More from Milan on 30 September 1610 (NS) that he had travelled via Florence and Parma but could not afford to travel through Switzerland and so was compelled to continue through Savoy, AAW A IX, no. 77.

^{268} John Gerard SJ. In his letter to More from Milan on 30 September 1610 (NS) Smith reported that Gerard was there under the name of 'Francesco' with Thomas Owen SJ and one of More's Jesuit cousins, AAW A IX, no. 77.

^{269} See *Downshire MSS* II, 329, 362.

thousand French gathered about lions to pass into Piemont[270] yet we
saw none but in citties. In lions I found m^r woodward[271] sick of an ague
and his fellow maurice[272] had left him and taken his iorney towards
you. At first m^r wood wold not know me, after in talke he allowed the
moderation of missions and acknowledged the great necessities of
Priests[.] other talke litle we had except about the casting of my booke
into the Inquis:[273] It is thought that both he and maurice goe to informe
against there superiour[274] which in others wold be counted a serious
faction. D. worthington intendeth to mantaine some writers about him
as he hath hither written to m^r sacvil[275] wherof m^r woodward D
Singleton[276] m^r Ihonsen and one or twoe such others are to be the men.
But I find m^r sacvil the same man he was and rather better to us[277]

---

[270] Jean Beaulieu informed William Trumbull on 25 October 1610 (NS) that 'there is
now some new forces and levying to the number of 4,000 or 5,000 about Lyons' under
the Count de la Roche for action against the forces of Spain and Savoy, *Downshire MSS*
II, 382.

[271] Philip Woodward, secular priest. He had been banished in July 1610. He left Douai for
Rome on 13 September 1610 (NS) but died on the journey (at Lyons), Anstr. I, 386.
Champney enquired from More in a letter of 27 September 1611 (NS) whether he had left
any money, for James Morris [see next note] his travelling companion had said he left £100,
AAW A X, no. 127. Seven weeks later Champney wrote to More that the Jesuit rector at
Lyons had claimed 'that m^r woodwarde hadd not above 5^{li} sterling' but 'what his frends will
say thereunto I knowe not nor care not', AAW A X, no. 152 (p. 425).

[272] James Morris, secular priest, who was involved in the well-known Catholic disturbances in Herefordshire in 1605, Anstr. I, 237. Birkhead named Morris as one of the
priests, including John Muttlebury (professed OSB in 1610) and Paul Green, who were
opposed to the secular clergy's suit for the appointment of a bishop and 'who are used
as Instruments to carp at our Labours'. Morris, with others, had given their names to
John Bennett to subscribe to the suit for a bishop (AAW A IX, no. 23), but Morris
withdrew his support. Birkhead, though, had the papers with 'the handes of them that
gave ther Consentes', and thought such people could not 'goe back without blushinge',
AAW A X, no. 3 (p. 7). Champney wrote to More in September 1611 that Morris had
died at St Omer, AAW A X, no. 127.

[273] For the delation of Richard Smith's *An Answer to Thomas Bels late Challeng* (Douai,
1605) to the Inquisition (probably by Robert Persons SJ), see CRS 41, 122–3. In September
1609 Persons informed Birkhead that Smith 'hath been over liberal in talk here to divers,
especially about his opinion, that it is not *de fide quod papa ullam habeat authoritatem deponendi
principes*; and he hath defended the same before divers', TD V, p. lxxv.

[274] George Birkhead.

[275] Thomas Sackville, fourth son of Thomas Sackville, first Earl of Dorset. See A.J.
Loomie, *Toleration and Diplomacy* (Philadelphia, 1963), 12–13.

[276] William Singleton, secular priest, had been a zealous supporter of George Blackwell
against the appellants, CRS 41, 23–4 n. 6. In a letter to Thomas Fitzherbert of December
1607 he attacked the anti-Jesuit John (Augustine) Bradshaw OSB who was a friend to
the secular clergy. He also submitted reasons for rejecting any proposal to appoint a
bishop for England, ARSI, Anglia 31. I, fo. 314r–v, Anglia 36. II, fos 253r–64r. For the
hostility he aroused at Douai, Anstr. I, 318; TD V, p. lxxxi.

[277] Sackville also assisted SJ with money, Allison, 'Later Life', 88, 136. He became the
patron of SJ's scholasticate at Louvain after the move of the novitiate from Louvain to
Liège in 1614, McCoog, 78.

and willing to bestow his money in this place and upon more fit men.[278] The Earle of Anguish[279] I find here very kind but he hath bene sick thes 18 weeks and is feared that he wil not escape wherof I am ful sorie.[280] D. Boswil[281] is dep*a*rted hence for England and hither is comen m^r Constable.[282] The others are as before. In England ther is lately executed m^r Cadwalader[283] in Hereford <u>who was one of the Appellant priests so God</u> honoreth the*m* whome others wold make infamous, and in oxford m^r napper[284] a priest is condemned but reprived. F. Baldini[285]

---

[278] Smith refers to the project for founding a writers' college in Paris. On 9 November 1610 (NS) he wrote to More that Sackville's funding of the project 'perhaps wil bring him into as much troble or make him leese his lands w*h*ich as yet he hath not sould', AAW A IX, no. 87 (p. 291). On 20 July 1610 Birkhead had informed Smith that Sackville 'still holdeth his minde for the 500^{li}, but his meaninge is to employ it onely for the supplie of such bookes as he shall think necessarie for the writers', whereas, said Birkhead, £1,000 would be sufficient 'to place two or three to beginne a foundacion', AAW A IX, no. 53 (p. 147).

[279] William Douglas, tenth Earl of Angus, who died on 3 March 1611. He had been a leading member of the Catholic aristocratic party in Scotland which had caused King James so many difficulties in the 1590s. He had retired to the Continent in 1608, Cokayne I, 159. He was among the lay Catholic promoters of the Collège d'Arras, TD IV, 135. On 22 September 1609 (NS) Thomas More dined with him in Paris and found him 'importunate' for bishops. The earl, said More, had been told that Smith could, at his first presentation of the clergy's petitions in Rome, 'easelie have procured them'. Angus asked after Smith but 'tooke it somwhat il that he never receaved any letter from us'. More noted that the earl 'is by the king of England confined in France, and must not passe out of this realme otherwise he wold have seen Italie as having an especial devotion to Loretto, and Rome. He hath allowed him two parts of his lyving, and the third thereof is deputed for his sonns maintenance', AAW A VIII, no. 154 (p. 625). In June 1609 the earl had obtained for the nuncio Ubaldini a copy of James's apology for the oath of allegiance, Conway *AH* 23, 120.

[280] Champney reported on 1 March 1611 (NS) that Angus 'was buried yesterday at St Germans monasterie assisted w*i*th the most of bothe nationes and manie others' including the marquis of Hamilton, Lord Roos and Lord Clifford 'who were att the funerall oratione but not att mass', AAW A X, no. 22 (p. 53).

[281] John Bosvile, secular priest. He had been arrested in mid-1606 and, apparently, was banished since he arrived in Rome in November 1607, Anstr. I, 44–5. Subsequently he had been assisting Champney in Paris with the project for the writers' college, AAW A IX, no. 66.

[282] Henry Constable. Constable also assisted with the writers' college project, AAW A IX, no. 66.

[283] Roger Cadwallader, executed in August 1610. See **Letters 12, 12a, 15**.

[284] George Napper was executed on 9 November 1610. According to the Oxfordshire-based priest Anthony Tuchiner (formerly a servant of one of the branches of the Sussex family of Caryll, PRO, SP 12/160/25, fo. 57r) Napper had, after studying at Exeter College, Oxford, served as a gentleman to Anthony Browne, first Viscount Montague, AAW A X, no. 19. For Napper's relationship to other Oxfordshire Catholics, and his narrow failure to procure a pardon, see Davidson, 202–8, 444, 473. Joan Napper, George's sister, had married Thomas Greenwood, an Oxford lawyer, and their son Thomas married Grace More, the clergy agent Thomas More's sister, Davidson, 200.

[285] William Baldwin SJ. James I wanted him to be interrogated concerning his prior knowledge of the Gunpowder Plot, *CSPV 1610–13*, 14, 24.

is certainly in the Tower and one told me that the State sent hither to desire the*m* to send one to assist at his Examination for they dobted not but to find matter touching this K. his death so hard a conceit they seeme to have of that man. my l. wotton[286] hath here sworne a league defensive betwene France and England. It is reported that o*ur* K. is so earnest about the oathe as that he said he wold drive all Catholiks out of England that wold not take it or they shold drive him, and as the nuncio[287] told me new lawes are made for mens wives who also added that twoe priests were executed.[288] The banished priests[289] who were landed at Amsterdam affirme that there they found m[r] Alabaster[290] close prisoner but could not speake with him so far is [he] from pr*o*fessing him self a Protestant as some reported.[291] The Counte Palatin[292] who appr*e*hended F. Baldwin is dead and hath apointed a Calvinist tutore to his younge sonne, w*h*ich his uncle a lutheran[293] who

---

[286] Edward Wotton, first Baron Wotton. For his embassy, see *CSPV 1610–13*, 11–12, 18, 27, 31, 44, 51; *Downshire MSS* II, 354.

[287] Robert Ubaldini.

[288] For the 'Act to prevent the dangers that may grow from popish recusants', 7 & 8 Jac I, c. 6, allowing women to be tendered the oath of allegiance, and married women, convicted of recusancy, to be imprisoned without bail (though a husband could redeem his recusant wife from imprisonment for her recusancy at £10 per month or one-third of his estate), see M.B. Rowlands, 'Recusant Women 1560–1640', in M. Prior (ed.), *Women in English Society 1580–1800* (1985), 149–80, at pp. 155–6. Birkhead thought that this act would mean 'the oath will not be pr*e*ssed so much as it was', AAW A IX, no. 53 (p. 148).

[289] For these priests (including Cuthbert Johnson, Oswald Needham, and Gilbert Hunt), see CRS 10, 104–5; Challoner, *Memoirs*, 323.

[290] William Alabaster. He returned to England after quarrelling with Robert Persons in Rome, but maintained a vaguely Catholic stance for a time, AAW A X, *passim*; Questier, *Conversion, Politics and Religion*, 45, 55, 71, 95, 189, 190. Hicks speculates that the denunciation of Richard Smith's *Answer to Thomas Bels late Challeng* was a riposte for the use of Alabaster by Smith and More to lay charges against Persons before the Inquisition concerning Persons's supposed complicity in the Gunpowder Plot, and for their attack on Persons's *The Iudgment of a Catholicke English-Man* (St Omer, 1608), CRS 41, 123. In July 1608 Persons had sent to Paul V a letter of Alabaster to a Jesuit novice (Peter Worthington) which, said Persons, contained a com*p*lete account of Alabaster's heresies and his assertions that Christ appeared 'to him in visible form' and gave him 'commands as to this and that'. Persons also said that Alabaster had been teaching his doctrines to women religious in Flanders, Vatican Archives, Borghese MSS IV 86, fo. 30r (transcript and translation at ABSI).

[291] Sir Thomas Lake wrote to the earl of Salisbury on 2 September 1610 that King James thought Alabaster to be 'distracted'; he should continue to live at Amsterdam for the time being 'to see what will become of him', *Salisbury MSS* XXI, 237.

[292] For the arrest of William Baldwin at Heidelberg, and Frederick IV, Elector Palatine's delivery of him to James I, see *CSPV 1610–13*, 6, 13–14.

[293] Philip Ludwig, Duke of Neuburg. See *CSPV 1610–13*, 52, 56, 64. Neuburg's religious allegiances were perceived to be uncertain, *Downshire MSS* IV, 123. His son Wolfgang William defected from the German Protestant Princes' Union and declared himself a Catholic in 1614 after marrying a Bavarian princess, *ibid.*, *passim*; AAW A XIII, no. 108; R. Bonney, *The European Dynastic States 1494–1660* (Oxford, 1991), 185–6.

according to the order of Germanie shold have the care of the young
Prince taketh ill and therupon ther are like to grow warrs. The
Genevians fear that all this preparation between Spaine and Savoie is
for the*m* and have put out all such as could not buye corne for six
moneths befor hand.[294] This daie I have sent my man william[295] home
for to know and send me words how matters goe there. He desired to
be com*m*ended to you and D. Thornel. I have talked with BIPDYE[296]
but I find nothing to o*u*r purpose. I propose to staie here this fortnight
and then to goe to D. Kellison who at D. worth.[297] entreatie hath bene
lately at Dowaie for to settle some order, for it is thought they must
amend things but for their Credit sake must not doe it at our suite.[298]
But God be thanked for any amendment sive ex charitate sive ex
occasione. yo*u*r letters here I delivered to yo*u*r friends who were glad
to heare of your health and wish you all comfort and courage for
patience will overcome greater adv*e*rsaries than we have in so good a
cause. The nuntio told me there is [word omitted ? : 'scarce' ?] a Preist
in England of whome he hath not bene told some ill. Such ill occupations
some use and like scarabies are ever eating in dung. After I had written
thus far m[r] Sacvil came to tell me heavie news that my L. montacute
had dissolved his house and that the K. every daie spoke against him
for mantaining soe many Catholiks for sending to Rome about Bishops
and the like and that he was like to fall into troble and that him self
desireth to get leave to travel.[299]   God p*r*otect him and comfort him

---

[294] The Venetian ambassador in France was reporting in May 1611 that the duke of
Savoy planned to move against Geneva as soon as Huguenot disturbances in France
meant that Louis XIII could not intervene, *CSPV 1610–13*, 143. See also *Downshire MSS*
II, 247, *cf.* 329, III, 9, and *passim*. In March 1611 the Savoyard ambassador in England
had assured James (who had earlier promised assistance against an assault on Geneva,
Salisbury MSS XXI, 210) that the duke of Savoy would not attack the city, *Downshire MSS*
III, 47, yet in late August 1612 (and subsequently) William Trumbull was told that the
duke was still conspiring against Geneva and also against Berne, *ibid.*, 352, 355, IV,
passim.

[295] Identity uncertain.

[296] Not identified.

[297] Thomas Worthington.

[298] Smith wrote to More on 9 November 1610 (NS) that Kellison 'liked not the
conditions' at Douai, AAW A IX, no. 87 (p. 291), even though both Worthington and
John Knatchbull were offering him carte blanche to get him to remain there, AAW A
IX, no. 103.

[299] Though Hicks regards the report as alarmist, CRS 41, 6 n. 8, Richard Smith
confirmed on 9 November 1610 (NS) that 'the most heavie news wherof I wrote in my
last of my L. montacutes trobles and the dispersion of his house proveth too true'. Smith
said the cause was a well-known letter sent in 1605 by Viscount Montague to Paul V
petitioning for the appointment of a bishop over the English clergy and for the seminaries
to be reformed, AAW A IX, no. 87 (p. 291); CRS 41, 5–6 n. 8. On 22 November 1610

and his. I pray you do my humble dutie to my good L. Primat[300] and my hartie Commendations to m^r Pole m^r Fizherbert[301] F. Anselmo[302] m^r Isham[303] and all our freinds. And thus with my most hartiest to your self I leave you to the protection of our sweet Saviour. Paris 26 of 8^{ber} 1610

yours ever assured

  R. Bak

(On p. 280)

Addressed: Al Illustre Signor Nicolo Fierberto nel Ficho por il Signor
          moro   Roma

Endorsed: (1) of m^r Cadwallader martyr & Appellant
          (2) Dr Smith
          (3) Octob. 26: 1610:
          (4) Earle Anguish deadly sick

12 *Benjamin Norton to Geoffrey Pole (31 October 1610)*   (*AAW A IX, no.*
    94, p. 315. In hand of Thomas More)

Molto Ill^{re} signor. I have forgotten whither in my last letters I gave you warning or noe of a iourney which then I was to begin, and now I thanke god I have ended, by reason wherofe I have not satisfyed your expectation in writing unto you. I learn by a letter which some three daies since I receaved from m^r G. West[304] which was the first and last that ether I receaved from him or you, which was written the 21th of August last, that you are desirous to hear from me, which you shal by the grace of god, if god grant me libertie. In the iourney I spake of

Benjamin Norton reported a search at Montague House, **Letter 12a**. (Montague House, the Brownes' London residence, had been searched also at Easter 1610 by Humphrey Cross and twelve constables, and in September 1609, on the information of William Udall, and, before that, in April 1606, PRO, STAC 8/15/8; *CSPD 1603–10*, 310; Harris, 'Reports', 256–7.) Montague's real problems started as a result, it seems, of harbouring priests, rather than because of the famous letter sent to Rome, see **Letters 12a, 15**.

  [300] Cardinal Edward Farnese.

  [301] Nicholas Fitzherbert.

  [302] Robert (Anselm) Beech OSB.

  [303] Christopher Isham. Simon Willis, who was acquainted with him in Rome in 1609, described him as 'a poore syllie old man, whom in the absence of Mr. Nycholas Fytzherbert wee used to dyrect us in the streates', CRS 60, 197.

  [304] Thomas More.

before, I met with one Mr Smith,[305] which soone after was taken at or about Wallingford. who whiles the pursuivantes were searching in the house got out at a windoe, and had escaped, had not a simple clowne by chance espyed him who was cause of his apprehension. The first night in mine Inn I met with a gentleman who told me of Mr Kadwalladers death at Hereford for a priest, and refusing to take the new oath, and albeit he were apprehended long before the proclamation which set manie others at libertie[306] yet such was the malice of D. bennet[307] the usurper of that bishoprick that he was made away, who was often offered his life, if he wold have taken the oath. but it seemeth that they had some spleen against him for his burying of the dead in Wales at the first comming of the king, wherabouts ther was great adoe at that time.[308] Ther I understood likwise that one Hammon alias Henrie Pet,[309] presenting him self to the magistrat some two daies after the proclamation was expired was cast into a Dongeon in Gloster.[310] I pray god comfort him. Going forward in my way I understood that some few men, and woemen had taken the oath in the west, who I can assure you were by a letter from the Archp^r. forbidden to do it. but it seemeth that some other Divines which are not subiect to him may be the cause of it. For meeting with Mr Broughton he told me that one Lister a Iesuit (famous for a foolish booke which he wrote hertofore[311]) told him ([sic] as he will iustifie (as he saith) that men may take the oath having relation to certein words of the kings, in which it seemeth that he saith that he requireth onlie ther temporal alleadgiance[312] etcetera in which manner that whirligigde prefect of yours Mr Sheldon,[313] who was a broker for the Iesuites in getting monie for St O.[314] and rich

[305] Not identified.

[306] The proclamation of 2 June 1610, Larkin and Hughes, 245.

[307] Robert Bennett, Bishop of Hereford.

[308] The disturbances in Herefordshire in 1605 over the funeral of Alice Wellington, Anstr. I, 237.

[309] Henry Pett alias Hammond, secular priest and brother of the priest Robert Pett. He had recently been indicted and had taken the oath of allegiance with a qualifying protestation, and had then asked to be sent into exile, AAW A VIII, no. 25.

[310] He was still in Gloucester prison in April 1611, AAW A X, no. 36.

[311] Thomas Lister SJ wrote the manuscript tract 'Adversus Factiosos in Ecclesia' of 1598 (a polemic against the appellants, condemning their appeal against the archpriest, George Blackwell, as schismatical). The text of it survives only in Christopher Bagshaw, *Relatio Compendiosa Turbarum* (1601); Milward I, 117.

[312] In March 1611 Birkhead repeated to More that Lister was advising Catholics to take the oath, AAW A X, no. 24. *Cf.* CRS 51, 277, suggesting that in the 1590s Lister was regarded as politically unreliable by the Jesuits themselves, and that he had been approached for support by the opponents of Robert Persons.

[313] Richard Sheldon, secular priest.

[314] The SJ's college at St Omer.

Nunns for Bruxells, had taken it before. About that time it happned that diverse ministers were convented before the Bishop of Sarom[315] at a place called Shepinum [?][316], and al such as had two benefices were to pay as one told me v.[l] to buy the Prince bookes, but I rather think it was towards the building of a Colledg near unto London,[317] which is to be erected for learned Hereticks to write against Catholikes. About which time (and peradventure one of that convocation) a Minister being at Shepinum fel dronke in the Lord, and fearing least he might be fresh before he got home he carried a bottle of wine with him. It hapned soe by the way that he must needs untrusse, and in doing of his busine[s] he fel asleep. but mark I pray an extraordinarie kind of charitie, a stranger comming by drank up his wine, and pinned up his shirt to his sholder, and soe leaft him with his broad face bare. In my absence the pursuivantes keapt Rex in Hampshire, they sought manie places, and finding some churchstuff at M[rs] Udals[318] they got xx[li] of her. from thence they went to Georg Copes,[319] and came as they said to [word obliterated] him, and whiles they were busie within a searching a gentleman came in and passed by a cowntrifellow that was set to keap the dore. a child, or at the most a girle meeting with him in the hall asked him what he did ther the pursuivants being above a searching. he streight waies quietlie went out, and the fellow that sat at the dore said nothing unto him, and away he went as swift as an hinde. About that time in an In at Havant they tooke one M[r] white,[320] some say they saw him on his knees at his praiers, others say that they had taken him a little before, and got al the monie from him which he had or cold make but because he had not paid al that had bene promised they tooke him with them and carried him to Newgate wher he now lyeth. Since I came home I receaved a letter from m[r] G. West on St Simon, and Iudes eve,[321] & intending to answere him in the morning ther came an Allarum to get me gone, wheruppon I betook me to my heels, yet nothing was done that day, but indeed ther were six knaves which came to seaz upon mens goods, and purposed as al the neighbors said, who sent messages about it to enter into your coosen Rich.[322] howse, and to take away plate bedding, and houshold stuff, but he having warning to

---

[315] Henry Cotton, Bishop of Salisbury.
[316] Chippenham (?).
[317] Chelsea College.
[318] Possibly Ursula (Norton), wife of Anthony Uvedale of Hambledon. See Mott, fo. 449v.
[319] For the Cope family of Bedhampton, see Mott, fos 115r–18r.
[320] This may be the Richard White whose arrest was recorded by Birkhead in April 1610, see **Letter 9**. For the well-connected Catholic White family of Southwick and Havant, see Mott, fos 510r–14r.
[321] 27 October.
[322] Richard Lambe.

keep his doors shut did soe, and hath noe harme as yet. Those fellows got I know not what of Mrs Bruning,[323] and Roger woollescot[324] in Hampshire. They drave away Ihon Colpis his Cattel in the night, and kild him a mare, and got xxx^l from him.[325] They or the Shreefe had almost as much of poor Aling of Steedom.[326] They got fowrscore powndes of Ned wiburn,[327] and I know not what of others. They wold have had Ant. williamsons, and his mothers cattel,[328] but he sware by noe beggers that they shold pay dear for them, they drew ther woepons thrise one at the other, at the last one of the knaves diswaded his fellow from dealing with such a murtherous minded man, who as it is thought wold have dyed upon them, but he saved his Cattel and your Coosen Rich. saved his goods not soe much (as I thinke) by shutting up of doors, or drawing of swords as by reason ther commission was a little too stale, and was to be returned some day or two before, wherof I had intelligence before they came. your sisters are wel of whom I say nothing because I know that Mrs Marie[329] wil write. it were good you sent them a line or two somtimes. That modest child Mall woodward

[323] Eleanor Brenning, daughter of Anthony Uvedale.

[324] Roger Woollascott of Chidham in Sussex (apparently the husband of Eleanor Brenning's aunt Susan) was subjected to an exchequer commission at this time on account of his recusancy, PRO, E 368/539, mem. 147d, E 368/540 mem. 55a, and property belonging to him and Christiana Bruen was assessed. He managed, however, to get the commission's findings reversed by the exchequer court in London.

[325] John Colpis jnr of Stoughton. See PRO, C 142/223/69 (inquisition *post mortem* of John Colpis snr (1591)). On 12 November 1610 Colpis (described as of Watergate in the parish of Upmarden) conformed in front of Samuel Harsnett at Lambeth Palace, having already taken the oath of allegiance before Thomas Brigham, mayor of Chichester, and William Thorne, Dean of Chichester Cathedral, and certified his conformity to the exchequer barons, PRO, E 368/539, mem. 140a–b (where an assessment of Colpis's property made on 6 October 1610 is recorded). *Cf.* AAW A X, no. 29.

[326] John Ayling of the 'Shiphouse' in Stedham parish, who was subject to exchequer assessments for his recusancy in 1605, 1606 and 1607. He died on 1 March 1612, and his heir, William, was a conformist, PRO, E 368/521, mem. 280a, E 368/525, mem. 256a, E 368/528, mem. 231b, E 368/546, mem. 93a.

[327] Edward Wyborne, brother of the prominent East Sussex/West Kent recusant William Wyborne who died on 31 January 1612, PRO, C 142/140/183 (and, perhaps, Benjamin Norton's brother-in-law, see **Letter 1**). Edward, described as of Battle, was assessed, for his recusancy, on the same day as John Colpis, 6 October 1610, on personal property held at Battle as well as on estates at Tonbridge and Pembury in Kent, though some of his property was already held by Thomas Pope under a crown grant made in March 1610, PRO, E 368/543, mem. 109a.

[328] Anthony Williamson of Midhurst leased various estates in West Sussex from Anthony Browne, first Viscount Montague, BL, Additional MS 39415, fo. 26r. Elizabeth Williamson, Anthony's mother, was assessed for recusancy, like John Colpis and Edward Wyborne, on 6 October 1610, PRO, E368/539, mem. 147d.

[329] Mary Pole.

is latelie dead of the plague. Will. Lambe[330] _is returned_ from schoole with never a pennie in his purse, saving that he had xx[s] to bear his charges homward, nor anie learning at al. he brought with him a letter of commendation for his behavior, and that the fault was not in him who did his best etcetera. Trulie S[r] when I dealt with them about him, my bargain was that they shold trie him some months, and if they fownd him not fit, I wold pay them for the _time_ of his being ther, and have the remainder of the 40[l] which I gave with him again. they never complayned of his insufficiencie yea M[r] Vincent[331] being ther made enquirie after the boy, and they liked him wel, and now have they on a soden sent him back without anie pennie of his portion to doe him good herafter. whither I be wel dealt withal or noe, I report me to M[r] Anthonie Fletcher[332], and M[r] Philip woodward who were acquainted with al I did, and were present at the bargain making, and I pray you if you thinke that anie good may come [word deleted] therof, to acquaint ther general, or others of it which may tel it them in the best fashion. for my part if I have noe amends I wil lick [?] my self whole, ant [sic for 'and'] right my self some other way, and yet not omit as long as I have a tong in my head to tel the truth in this busines. your coosen Rich. wold gladlie hear some good news of Bucks[.][333] Our neighbors are wel, but I have not bene with them these x. weekes, nor intend I to be if I may chuse. I am not of ther cownsel. I am the quietter. we be great frendes and that is enough[.] I pray you commend me to M[r] W.[334] M[r] D. Ansel.[335] D. Thorne,[336] M[r] N. Fitzherb. and the rest and I pray you to acquaint M[r] W. ether with al or as much of the letter as may concern him. I shold take it for a favore to hear from you somtimes. sweet Iesus be with you and thus with al your good companies

[330] William Lambe, brother of Anthony, and son of Benjamin Norton's patrons Richard and Constance. In August 1609 Birkhead wrote to Smith in Rome that he was glad 'William applieth his singinge so well. his brother Iohn is now in flanders for the same end', AAW A VIII, no. 140 (p. 584); see CRS 54, 252. By November 1610 he was being presented as a recusant in Midhurst, WSRO, Ep. I/17/13, fo. 99v.

[331] Walter Robert (Vincent) Sadler OSB.

[332] Anthony Fletcher was a native of Westmorland but resided in Sussex where he served the Browne family at Cowdray. His son, Thomas Fletcher, was Birkhead's godson, Anstr. II, 114; AAW A XI, no. 62. Anthony entered the English College in Rome in 1609. Persons reported to Birkhead on 14 March 1609 (NS) that he had been welcomed at the college 'to show the desire we have to serve his Good Patron [Montague]', Milton House MSS (transcript at ABSI). He was ordained in December 1610 and was sent to England in September 1612, but was already being drawn into SJ, CRS 74, 171; see **Letter 35**.

[333] Not identified (though a 'Mr Buck' was assisting the seculars with their finances in 1609, AAW A VIII, no. 102).

[334] Thomas More.

[335] Robert (Anselm) Beech OSB.

[336] Edmund Thornell.

commendations under our roofe I leave you this last of October, 1610.

12a [On same sheet as **12**] *Benjamin Norton to Geoffrey Pole (22 November 1610)   (AAW A IX, no. 94, pp. 315–16. In hand of Thomas More)*

Molto Ill^{re} Signor. Since my last letters which were of the last of October or ther aboutes I have little to write of but that I purpose whiles I live and am at libertie (which can not be long) to write to you as oft as I can, I wold not have written yet this weeke at the least but soe it is good S^r that I may now wel fear that every letter wil be my last, and therfore take this one as my last unles things fal out better then I have reason to expect. About the time of my last letters your coosen S^r francis Hastings dyed,[337] and dyed a beggar too, and about that time your frend M^r [name obscured: possibly 'Hore']³³⁸ had a yong sonn Francis. The cowntesse of Kildare³³⁹ in Ireland dyed about that time; but al your poor frendes nere or about us live as yet dailie expecting such hazardes, and miseries as wold make a christians heart even bleed to thinke of them. In the beginning of this month the Catholiks of our parish were sommoned to appear at the Shirtowne,³⁴⁰ and for as much as they feared that the oath wold be tendred unto them they appeared not, and streight upon that contempt they were excommunicated in the church, and the names of above threescore in the parish wher I live³⁴¹ were set upon the Church doors amongst which your two sisters³⁴² with ther Coosins,³⁴³ and Companie were the first. The knaves that went then away out of the cowntrie have since that time renewed ther commission and are to come shortlie downe again. As yet ther have

---

³³⁷ Hastings was buried at North Cadbury on 22 September 1610, Hasler II, 272. A manuscript petition of 1606 addressed to Sir Francis Hastings, concerning toleration for recusants, was signed 'your well beloved countrymen, kinsmen, clients and friends the Catholic Recusants of this realm of England', *Downshire MSS* II, 444–6.

³³⁸ Francis Hore (?).

³³⁹ Gerald FitzGerald, eleventh Earl of Kildare, had in May 1554 married Mabel, the sister of Anthony Browne, first Viscount Montague. She died on 25 August 1610, Cokayne VII, 236–9. (Sir Anthony Browne, father of the first Viscount Montague, who helped restore the future eleventh earl to his estates after the death of Henry VIII, had taken as his second wife, Elizabeth FitzGerald, daughter of Gerald FitzGerald, ninth Earl of Kildare; *cf.* Foley VI, 712.) Francis Barnaby, one of the appellant priests, became Mabel Browne's chaplain and trusted confidant, C.W. Russell and J.P. Prendergast (eds), *Calendar of State Papers, relating to Ireland...1606–8* (1874), 393; Anstr. I, 23.

³⁴⁰ Chichester.

³⁴¹ Midhurst.

³⁴² Mary and Martha Pole, resident in Midhurst, were both excommunicated in November 1610 by the Chichester consistory court, WSRO, Ep. I/17/13, fos 103v, 106r, 106v.

³⁴³ The Lambe family.

none taken the oath in this cowntrie but Ihon Colpis and Ih. Loane.[344] In Hampshire they are warned to appear, and it is generallie thought that the oath shalbe generallie offered through al Ingland, and al that refuse it shalbe utterlie undone. In a letter which I receaved from M[r] More ther was a letter of your mans to his Father, which being saflie delivered to his hands he took it soe kindlie that he sent us the next day a fat goose for our dinner. yesterday Tom. Middlemore[345] came to my chamber, and with great ioy shewed me a primmer which you had sent him for a tooken, by which you may gather that the bearer therof is saflie returned, but soe are not his Master, and the other that wayted upon him. for I thinke they hear (or at least we hear say) that the ports are watched for them albeit the Nominalls[346] at S[t] O.[347] told this bearer of your token that the aforenamed which are not yet come might come when they wold being favored by the state, and cownsel which is a ranke lie, and coyned by them which dailie bacbite us at home, and abroad. M[r] Palmer[348] latlie told me that he differred the going to M[rs]

[344] In March 1611 Birkhead informed More that John Loane had had his 'ground driven by the officers and pursivantes, and 40 fatt oxen taken from him under pretense of some arrerages dew to the kinge' although he had already compounded for the same; the fact that he had taken the oath of allegiance was no benefit to him, AAW A X, no. 27 (p. 63); cf. **Letter 14**. Thomas Heath said Loane had lost property to the 'valew of 600[li]', AAW A X, no. 39 (p. 97). Richard Broughton noted in April 1611 that the commissioners' rapacity had led them since Easter to take from Loane at 'Battell in Sussex forty fyve Oxen worth eight pounds at the least a peace, & Henry Smith of Chinting [Chyngton] no Cath having thre & twentie bullockes neare to M[r] Loanes ground, are allso taken away from him by force', AAW A X, no. 36 (p. 91); see also **Letter 14**. In a letter to More of 3 March 1611, Norton said that Loane, who had just married a rich widow, 'was ever a fairespoken man yett I ever tooke him to bee more Iesuited than preestifyedd', implying that he had taken the oath under the influence of lax Jesuit casuistry, AAW A X, no. 19 (p. 45). There was a Kentish recusant family called Loane at Sevenoaks, but this man is probably to be identified with the wealthy East Sussex recusant called John Loane/Lone (written 'Love' in some records), whose immediate family came from Goudhurst in Kent. His wife had died very recently. His property was assessed by an exchequer commission in February 1611, PRO, E 368/541, mem. 114a, 124b. See also WSRO, Ep. II/9/12, fo. 8v.

[345] Thomas Middlemore, the youngest son of John Middlemore of Hawkesley, Worcestershire. Thomas now resided in Sussex, W.P.W. Phillimore, assisted by W.F. Carter, *Some Account of the Family of Middlemore of Warwickshire and Worcestershire* (1901), 238–40; BL, Additional MS 34765, fo. 43r. This individual may be identified with a servant of Jane Sackville, wife of Anthony Maria Browne, second viscount Montague, CRS 60, 145. 'Thomas Middlemore, gent' was one of the group of recusants at Battle (including Edward Wyborne, David Lomer, Edward Goldwyer, and Richard Vincent) who were indicted at the Sussex assizes in July 1605, Cockburn, *Calendar of Assize Records: Sussex Indictments: James I*, 18.

[346] *i.e.* Jesuits.

[347] St Omer.

[348] Identity uncertain. However, since in August 1611 Anthony Champney referred to William (Maurus) Taylor OSB by using the alias of Palmer, and Taylor was involved in the project for setting up a convent for English Benedictine nuns in Paris with which the

Catherine, and her Cowntes[349] because he had not yet receaved a relique which you promised to send etcetera. [p. 316]

The book which you sent was like to have bene taken on sonday last in a search at London wher ther were six preistes taken in secret places in one house which was somtimes called Montague house,[350] and for names [?] sake it is more then much feared that the Lord Montacute wil be called in question. for the last night newes came to that purpose. your coosin Richard[351] was taken at Mathew woodwards[352] that morning, & payed sweetlie for it. Mathew and his wife (although nothing was found in ther house) are committed to the Clink, and the prisons are ful, nether wil they be able to hold manie more unles some preists be executed, which is generallie expected. yet for al that I doubt not, but yt it is generallie said abroad that ther is scarse a priest but taketh or alloweth of the oath, wheras in my last letters I acquainted you of Mr Cadwalladors death for the refusal therof, and in these letters I acquaint you that Mr Georg Napper is latelie executed at Oxford for the same,[353] and because you shal give credit unto it I have sent you a little peece of a cloath which was dipped in his blood.[354] He dyed most resolutelie, and so I hope we al wil doe before we will take so abhominable an oth and I know none of ours (more then those three or four, which at the first interteined it that) [sic] doth or wil mantein it, but as I said in my last letters m^r Sheldon a forward fellow for the Nominalls took it, and m^r Lister alloweth (as Mr Broughton wil iustifie) the taking therof, and who knoweth not what Lister is, and what

seculars assisted, the reference here may be to him, AAW A X, no. 61; Lunn, 'English Cassinese', 63. But the secular priests John Bosvile and Richard Cooper also used the alias of Palmer.

[349] This may indicate Elizabeth Somerset, Countess of Worcester, a relation of Katherine Pole. (The countess was a daughter of Francis Hastings, second Earl of Huntingdon by Catherine, daughter of Henry Pole, first Baron Montague, first son of Margaret Pole, Countess of Salisbury.) See also **Letter 39**.

[350] Viscount Montague's London residence in Southwark, on land which formerly belonged to the priory of St Mary Overie.

[351] Richard Lambe.

[352] Birkhead told Smith in October 1609 to direct his letters 'to Mathew Woodw. at S marie overies', AAW A VIII, no. 161 (p. 643). Elizabeth, the wife of Matthew Woodward of Lodsworth parish in West Sussex, near to Midhurst, was denounced excommunicate in January 1601, CRS 60, 117, and was a convicted recusant, J. Cockburn (ed.), *Calendar of Assize Records: Sussex Indictments: Elizabeth I* (1975), 334.

[353] For the most comprehensive account of the arrest and execution of Napper, see Davidson, 463–77.

[354] At the beginning of January 1611 Birkhead sent More 'for [Cardinal] Farnese a peec of mr Nappers shert dipped in his blood, and a straw moistened with the blood of those two last [martyrs] m^r [John] Roberts and m^r [Thomas] Sommers', AAW A X, no. 2 (p. 3), the retrieval of whose remains by London Catholics is well documented, Challoner, *Memoirs*, 321; *Downshire MSS* II, 407.

Sheldon may be wel thought to be[.] of those that were taken at London three are said to be Monks, and Gregorio [or 'Gregorie'],[355] and Robertes[356] are said to be two of them. M[r] Vincent[357], and an other Whitfellow[358] scaped but hardlie. when the tearm is ended we expect al those Raskehells in the cowntrie. I pray you to tel M[r] west[359] that I have receaved a great, and little from him since my comming home, and I pray you to acquaint him with such newes as I doe or shal send ['you' deleted] unto you to whom I wold write but for trobling of my frends, and how things goe I know not until I see the Doctor, but shewerlie I fear that ther is somthing amisse some wher or other because I cold never receave anie one letter from you albeit I have sent diverse unto you, nether cold I ever understand that you had receaved anie from me had not M[r] west in his letter given me some comfort therin. Trulie S[r] it were good (albeit I wil not assume so much to my self as to be worthie of a letter) that you writ somtimes to your sisters, for they live by hearing from you. your coosin Constance[360] desireth that her sonn Anthonie may rather goe to Rome then Spain, and desireth me to write unto you that you wil procure that he may be sent for to Rome when he is readie, which she thinketh wil be the next mission, but I doubt it[361] but because such a message is sent to her, I pray you to doe what you may before the time to get him to be sent according as she desireth. I have not bene at my great Neighbors these three monethes but I hear from them, and I fear me that Bianchetto wil breake our backs if your Cardinal[362] help us not. Adieu good S[r] and I pray you to remember me in your best devotions, & to commend me to m[r] West, m[r] Beach and the rest of my frends, not forgetting me to m[r] Fitzherb.[363] which waited somtime on Cardinal Allen and to Doct Thornel. this 22th of November 1610.

yours ass BN.

Addressed: All Illustrissimo Signor il Signor Ganfre Polo.

---

[355] Robert (Gregory) Hungate entered OSB in 1610; William Estmond, whose name in religion was also Gregory, had left the English College in Rome in 1606 for Venice to enter OSB. But neither was in England at this date. The correct identification may be Thomas Law jnr, a son of the bursar at Douai, and brother of William Law, Lunn, 'English Cassinese', 65; *cf.* **Letter 6**.

[356] John Roberts OSB.

[357] Walter Robert (Vincent) Sadler OSB; *cf.* **Letter 10**.

[358] Not identified.

[359] Thomas More.

[360] Constance Lambe.

[361] Anthony Lambe entered the English College in Rome on 7 October 1612 (NS), Anstr. II, 181.

[362] Cardinal Edward Farnese.

[363] Nicholas Fitzherbert.

Endorsed: (1) Octob. 31. et Novemb*er*. 22. 1610.
(2) of mr Cadwalladors death. Constauncy about refusing the
oath.
my Cosen B. Norton to my cosen Poole.

13 *George Salvin (Birkhead) to Thomas More (3 March 1611)*   *(AAW A X,*
no. 18, pp. 41–4. Holograph)

my verie Good S[r], I have of Late receyved two large and lovinge
Letters from yo*w*. one of the 1 and [word deleted] the other of the 15
of Ianuarie. yo*w* still seame to compleyne of want of intelligence and I
am overwearied with writing for I keepe the same course with yo*w* that
I did with m[r] Baker.[364] yf my Letters miscarie, what remedie? yet I find
the [word deleted] way of bruxels verie sure though slow. yt is not to
be told how often I have written, as I hope yo*w* see by this. our frendes
must be content that we do as we may. these tymes grow so perillous
that we cannot putt anythinge in execution. and therfor I am of opinion
that it is better for us to proceede Lente as we doe then then to propose
or demande any thinge. for both the tyme is not for it, and I see [word
deleted] wee shalbe crossed propose what we will. what yo*w* write of
m[r] Ratcliffe[365] I feare is overtrue in some respect. for he hath given his
Censure that the oath may be taken, when the taker meaneth no more
but temporal allegiance to the kinge. and in this reservation he referreth
himselfe to the definition of his hol.[366] in my other Letters I have sent
yo*w* in particular what he hath don[.] how it wilbe taken I wold be
gladd to know. for heare by diverse it is condemned, and my selfe did
never like of such haltinge, as he knoweth well enough.[367] I pray yo*w*
Lett me know what Censure is given therof. yf he be guiltie therin,
others of all sortes will hardly scape free. how to behave my selfe in
this and such like eventes I know not. miserie maketh many to com*m*itt
a nomber of absurdities. m[r] Abbotes of London is now (as I am told)
mad b of Canterburie.[368] he is the sorest enemie that ever we had. I
sent in my former Letters much relation about the death of 4 of our
brethren one onely (namely m[r] Rob) beinge a benedictine:[369] and I

[364] Richard Smith.
[365] John Mush.
[366] For Mush's views on the oath of allegiance, see **Letter 18**.
[367] Birkhead was agitated because some of the priests imprisoned in the Clink were claiming Mush as 'of the same opinion with them', AAW A X, no. 24 (p. 57). In April 1611 Birkhead noted that Mush was doing more harm in this respect than the more extreme and less reputable Richard Sheldon and Edward Collier, AAW A X, no. 37.
[368] Abbot was officially nominated to Canterbury on 4 March 1611.
[369] John Roberts OSB was executed on 10 December 1610 with Thomas Somers. Their execution had followed their attempt at escape from Newgate prison, *Downshire MSS* II, 407. The other two martyrs referred to are Roger Cadwallader and George Napper.

thinke I shall send yow word shortly of moe. for it is said that Abbotes will have more bloud, and one david Ringsteed by his means they say is like to be executed for harboringe preistes.[370] a quarter of m^r Napper was sett upon an old arch in oxford besides Christ Church, and his hand hanginge perpendicularit*er* downe to the ground. under the same did arise a springe of most excellent faire water, where never any was before. one of the most impiouse fellowes in all the towne had great helpe to his eyes by means therof [in margin, in different hand: 'a miracle of mr Napper']. but m^r D King vicechancelour and deane of Christes Church com*m*inge home from london hath stopped upp the springe, and removed his quarter to another place.[371] In Newgate are at this pr*e*sent 11 pr*e*stes and in the Clinck v or six besides m^r blackwell and his Companie who are little respected by reason of there opinions. both prisoners, and Lay catholiqus are in extreme want. for my owne part Little com*m*eth to me for ther releife. and yet for all that they live. I cannot send such p*ar*ticular discorses as yow wold have. trust me there is no stirringe abroad; but with extreme daunger. all the old pursivantes are changed into new, and one Hierom[372] D Worthingtons man is one of the Cheifest. Alabaster (as I think I have written in other

---

[370] This may be the Hampshire recusant and former under-keeper of Winchester gaol David Ringsteed (or possibly his son) who in the early 1580s was living in the same parish in Winchester as the future priest Benjamin Norton, PRO, SP 12/160/26, fo. 56r. The under-keeper had been imprisoned in 1586, and was still in the Clink prison in the early 1590s, Mott, fo. 333r. A Hampshire Catholic, and presumably relation, Edward Ringsteed, went surety for a priest arrested by the pursuivant John Wragge at Easter 1610, PRO, STAC 8/15/8, mem. 2a. A man named Ringsteed was the keeper of Montague House when it was searched in April 1606, PRO, SP 14/20/20.

[371] Benjamin Norton recounted that a monk had confirmed the story of 'Nappers Well', in which 'many washt theire eyes & drunke of the water & gott good therebye' till John King 'caused [it] to bee rammed upp, and flunge the quarter of that saincte into the Theames', AAW A X, no. 29 (p. 67). Within a month a new version of the facts was reported by Richard Broughton: 'about the time one of his quarters was hanged on an old wall by Christchurch ther brook forth many litle springes under a wall hardby & one even under th*e* hand wher it did hange, wherof th*e* children made a litle well, but after th*e* quarter was taken away by Cath. th*at* spring did dry up', AAW A X, no. 36 (p. 92). The day before his execution Napper had sent Birkhead his voice for bishops and his nomination of those he thought fit for such a dignity, AAW A IX, no. 88.

[372] Jerome Prestman. The high commission pursuivant Lewis Owen had arrested him in early 1610 for importing Catholic books. Prestman was imprisoned in Newgate but was swiftly released, PRO, STAC 8/15/8, mem. 2a. Birkhead noted on 17 March 1611 that Archbishop George Abbot had charged the secular priest George Fisher on Prestman's evidence that he 'made an oration at doway' in praise of Hugh O'Neill, third Earl of Tyrone, AAW A X, no. 24 (p. 57). Subsequently Prestman deserted Abbot's service, was reconciled to the Roman Church and travelled to Rome to join as a 'lay brother ... some howse reformed', AAW A XII, no. 101 (p. 224). Abbot was furious at Prestman's defection and the priests who had been 'tampering with him'. In May 1613 Abbot ordered William Trumbull to ruin Prestman's credit by spreading rumours that he was still spying for the regime, *Downshire MSS* IV, 114.

Letters) yet keepeth his faith, but is much dowbted of many. this day m^r [p. 42] higgons is said to preach at poules Crosse.[373] the b of Ely,[374] d overall[375] deane of poules and one Casebon[376] a french huguenote conferr about reforminge france to the discipline of England. the Earle of dunbar[377] and Lord of kenlos[378] m^r of the Rolls are dead. we look for nothinge but extremitie, and yet by godes helpe, we live as yo*w* left us. I marvell our protector[379] is so hard to be wonne. I hope tyme will give him occation to understand us better. yf yo*w* meane bianchetto (as I thinke yo*w* do) I beleive yo*w* easily. for he is induced to credit others more then us. in some of my Letters yo*w* shall receive a longe Letter[380] to him from me for an appologie against the Compleintes of fa: p.[381] and m^r Tho fitz.[382] yf yo*w* have received yt and delivered yt

---

[373] Theophilus Higgons's sermon (published as *A Sermon preached at Pauls Crosse* (1611)) lasted '4 hours long at the least', *Downshire MSS* III, 31–2. On 9 April 1611 (NS) Francis Hore wrote from Venice to More in Rome, that 'Mr Higgins (our Oxford minister) you may please to tell m^r [Humphrey] leech is fallen back againe' and 'become an arrant relaps', AAW A X, no. 32 (p. 78). Edward Bennett wrote to More on 26 October 1611 that Sir Edward Hoby had engineered Higgons's recantation of Catholicism through the bribe of a 'fatt benefice' and that on 'the same day that' Higgons 'made his sermon' Hoby 'made also a great feast 'at the enstallm[ent]' of the 'Bushop of Canterbury' [George Abbot] and 'there lik another Baltassar bibens vinu*m*...comending his own religion, crieing owt against catholickes, & exclaiminge that the lawes weer not w*ith* mor diligence putt in execution against them, especiall[y] abowt the oath, at last as it showld seem half drunck (an humor wherewith he is often trubled) he began to brag of his own forwardnes in setting fowrth the gospell, & saied that the same day he had two sonnes born, on to the spirite & the other to the fleshe, ['for that' deleted] he meant Higgins w*hich* that morninge had made his recanting sermon, & a sonne of his own wherof that morninge alsoe his lady was delivered...for before he had never had any' [he had, in fact, fathered an illegitimate son, Peregrine, by Katherine Pinckney]; yet 'behowld the iudgmentes of god, as he was thus railinge & bragginge at the Archbushop tabl ther cometh on of hi[s m]en in great hast sweating & towld hym his sonne was dead', AAW A X, no. 139 (p. 396). *Cf.* T. Birch, *The Court and Times of James the First* (2 vols, 1849), I, 110–11; McClure, 306. For Hoby's assisting Higgons to his benefice, AAW A X, no. 26 (reputedly worth £126 a year) and procuring of his pardon for going abroad, see PRO, SO 3/5 July 1611. Richard Broughton said Higgons, in his sermon, held 'some Catholique pointes', AAW A X, no. 36 (p. 91), while John Sanford said that he 'gave ample satisfaction to all that were well affected' with 'abundance of tears in his contrition'. Catholics planned to distribute his Catholic published works near Paul's Cross, but Abbot prevented this, Birch, *Court and Times of James I*, I, 108.

[374] Lancelot Andrewes.

[375] John Overall.

[376] Isaac Casaubon. *Cf.* A. Milton, *Catholic and Reformed* (Cambridge, 1995), 265.

[377] George Home, first Earl of Dunbar, who died on 20 January 1611.

[378] Edward Bruce, first Baron Kinloss, who died on 14 January 1611.

[379] Cardinal Edward Farnese.

[380] AAW A IX, no. 98 (copy of Birkhead's letter of 6 December 1610 to Bianchetti). For Bianchetti's answer, see AAW A IX, no. 99.

[381] Robert Persons SJ.

[382] Thomas Fitzherbert.

unto him, I wold be glad to know how he taketh it. I ment nothinge but moderation therin, yf he take it not so, I shalbe sorie. my desyre is to be frendes with all, so farre as our owne cause may be free from preiudice. I am told that the two gentlemen[383] to whom yow Lent your stock have now supplie sent unto them. yow must lerne herafter to take heed, and to keepe your owne in your purse. they will have meanes when yow can have none. I perceive that yf your pension were increased, it might be, yow may happely be exalted. I dare give yow no assurance, but I verely think that 45 poundes more wilbe made amongst us more then your ordinarie pension. and I know some who are redie to give there worde for so much. me thinkes that yf yow could obteyne the pension for me that m^r blackwell hath had heretofore, yt wold serve the turne verie well. I marvell for two causes, first that it lieth in the deck. and no memorie is had therof. I beleve some have yt all this while that are Loth to part from yt. Labour for it, and see now againe what yow can do. yt wold serve your turne verie well. secondly I marvell, how they can thinke one able to supplie my place in these tymes without any helpe, either for sending Letters, or for usinge the assistance of such as will look for rewarde at my hand. I have now ben three yeares in this place come the 13 of this moneth, and as yett never had pennie of the Common for any helpe therin. & how shall I finde any one to serve me, when I can make them no recompence. No man but my selfe taketh paines in this kinde. some tymes some do write, but I can do nothinge els but write, and yett yow compleine. I have couradge neverthelesse to hold out as longe as I may. Commend me I pray yow to m^r Geoffrey.[384] I see he is our frend. yow and he shall alwaies have me redie to do yow any office of Courtesie that lieth in me. And so commendinge me and my companie to your praiers I leave

---

[383] Anthony and Robert Dormer. See **Letter 17**. They were conducted on the grand tour in 1610–11 by Francis Hore, a fellow of Exeter College, who had met Smith in Oxford when Smith journeyed there to visit Elizabeth Dacres, AAW A IX, no. 26. Hore was closely acquainted with several of the correspondents whose letters are in AAW A, notably Smith, Thomas More, John Bosvile and Anthony Champney. The Dormers were financially assisted by More, and also Sir Edmund Lenthall, an Oxfordshire connection (cf. CRS 60, 210), because their parents kept them very short of cash, AAW A IX, no. 26, X, no. 6 and passim. They returned in March-April 1611 from Rome via Florence, Venice (where Hore was assisted by Sir Dudley Carleton's secretary, and was courteously treated by Carleton himself on the grounds that they were both Oxford men), Milan and then through France, AAW A X, nos 32, 38. Hore told Carleton that he and the Dormers had visited Cardinal Bellarmine, J. Stoye, *English Travellers Abroad 1604–1667* (1989), 80–1. They were with Champney at Paris in mid-May 1611, AAW A X, no. 47. In March 1615 Edward Bennett noted that Hore had made hostile remarks about him and 'fawneth upon the padri [Jesuits], when he is with them', AAW A XIV, no. 46 (p. 133), something which in a letter to More of January 1615 Hore seems to confess to have been true (in the past), AAW A XIV, no. 10.

[384] Geoffrey Pole.

yo*w* to the providence of our saviour. this 3 of march 1611.
yo*u*r lovinge frend
    Geo. Salvin
[p. 43]
m^r baker[385] is not yett returned but tarrieth at paris upon occasion as
yo*w* know. I hope to good purpose. they will make no great shew, and
therfor I trust no great matter wilbe made of ther doinges in pollicie.
yet am I of yo*u*r opinion, and cold say more then I can write. one
impediment unto that new erection [word deleted] I feare may arise
of some of our Countrewomen addicted to S^t bennettes order. who
meane to take an house there as yo*w* are like to heare shortly.[386] the
prior of doway[387] hath ben with me. he offereth me all service. he
seameth a reall and plaine man in his wordes. the Congregation Italian
and they are not yett wholly united so farre as I can perceive.[388]
(On p. 44)
Addressed: To his verie good frend m^r Thomas Moore give these at
            Rome.
Endorsed: March: 3: 1611. G. Sal:

14 *Benjamin Norton to Thomas More (12 April 1611)   (AAW A X, no. 33,*
     pp. 81–4. Holograph. The middle section of this letter is badly damaged in
     places)

My good frende, if heeretofore for wa*n*te of meanes of sendinge
imediatelye to yo*u*r selfe I have ben thought remisse nowe I hope I
paye yo*w* whome & I wright the moore bicause I have promised o*u*r
Archp^r. that if I have libertye I will not faile to wright unto yo*w* for a
quarter of a yeare but afterwards I bidd him & his Rabbies [?] doe
what theye will them selves & expecte noe moore at my handes. nowe
therefore to beegin my le*tt*res I tell yo*w* that yo*u*rs of the 26th of Febru:
came safe to my handes the 7 of Aprill & revived my feeble spirits for
I had travailed the too dayes beefore very harde on foote & comm*inge*
to my dames[389] thinkinge to have reste newes came the nexte morninge
that the knaves weare in the towne w*hic*h made me flee to the place

   [385] Richard Smith.
   [386] See **Letter 23**.
   [387] John (Augustine) Bradshaw OSB. In August 1607 he had thrown his weight behind
the anti-Jesuits in the selection procedure for a new archpriest to replace Blackwell,
Lunn, *EB*, 75–6.
   [388] For the efforts to unify the English Benedictines of the Spanish and Cassinese
congregations, see Lunn, *EB*, ch. 4.
   [389] Constance Lambe.

wheare I laste lefte yo*w*[390] *&* so spende 4 dayes with my frende Leptye[391] Tipt[392] etc*etera*[.] my Cosin Thomas[393] pr*e*sentlye offered to sende my *lett*res if I woulde wright. & iudge y*o*w when I have donne whether I accepted off his offer or noe[.] In my beeinge abroad I understoode of the takinge of a cople of pp. the one was Mr Henrye Mayhewe[394] at widdowe Cables[395] in Wilteshire. the other one Mr Frauncis & as I suspecte it is Mr Kennion[396] at Mr Edwarde Keynes[397] his howse in summersetshire. the first was taken on Easter daye the 2de the frydaye after. soe that y*o*w maye see that in the cheefeste feastes & solemnityes bee ower greatest daingers soe all thinges goe the co*n*trarie waie in o*u*r miserable cunntrye. I wonder at my selfe how I escape[.] I thinke god hathe a finger & a thumbe to in thease businesses otherwise I hadd beene longe eare this [word illegible] a silogisme to Bocardo.[398] well godes will bee done[.] I owe a deathe & once I muste die but whiles I live I intende to make some sporte amongst the*m* & when I shall chaunce to die (if I maye be soe happye as to die at the gallhowse for either beeinge a preeste or refusinge the othe w*h*ich godwillinge I nev*er* intende to take) I hope I sha[ll] take moore co*m*forte therin then if his H*olin*es woulde beestowe a red capp uppo*n* me. Yt is no smaule co*m*forte unto me that y*o*w have had a sight of my *lett*res of Oct*o*ber & November for I muche feared that they had miskarried. I take it kindelye at m^r Ieffreyes[399] handes th*a*t hee woulde showe them unto y*o*w. I have noe good newes at all to wright of late [save?] that o*u*r Archpr*i*est.[400] is well in helthe & all my neigbo*u*rs live. I hearde latelye of the takinge of a p: m^r sliffeelde[401] I knowe not whoe hee was nor wheare it was. abought the hollye weeke Mr Thulis[402] was taken in Essex. The knaves havinge

---

[390] Presumably this refers to Cowdray, Viscount Montague's Sussex residence.

[391] AAW A X no. 29 (Benjamin Norton to Thomas More, 26 March 1611) identifies 'Leptye' as Richard Smith, who had temporarily returned to England from Paris, see **Letter 17**.

[392] Not identified.

[393] Thomas Heath.

[394] Henry Mayhew, secular priest. See Anstr. I, 223; TD IV, p. clxx. Mayhew was from Dinton in Wiltshire.

[395] Presumably this is Joan Cable of Whiteparish in Wiltshire, CRS 60, 125.

[396] Edward Kenion, secular priest. See **Letter 16**.

[397] Edward Keynes, recusant, of Compton Pauncefoot in Somerset, CRS 61, 211–12; CRS 54, 193.

[398] Bocardo: both the name for the prison in Oxford's city walls and a mnemonic word in logic (OED), a conclusion which is inescapable (hence the use of the word as a name for the prison).

[399] Geoffrey Pole.

[400] George Birkhead.

[401] Not identified. William Newman, an anti-Jesuit secular priest, used the alias of Slyfield, but he was permanently based at Lisbon at this time, Anstr. II, 230–1.

[402] Christopher Thules, secular priest.

latelye beene in the easte of sussex have driven awaye 45 fatt oxen of m^r
Loanes^{403} woorth 16 poundes a yoke. xxx fatt sheepe & 23 bullocks off
Harrye smithes of chintinge[.]^{404} the oxen bee solde gett the moneye
of them whoe can. & although I heare that H. smithe have arested
them that drove awaie his cattell, yett can I not learne although hee
bee a protestaunt that hee hathe gotten them againe but theye will
beare him in hande that the cattell are Mr Loanes which I assure my
selfe hee will sweare by by [sic] Golde & by golde againe to bee
untrue, & if swearinge will recover them I thinke hee will not spare for
that. [p. 82] they gott abought Battell some 8^l of Ned Goldew: for a
horse & mare which they founde of his.^{405} [word illegible] off Dick
Vinc^{406} I knowe not for whatt. theye learned [?] owte wheare I. Kape^{407}
[?] as wise as hee is had fower keyne & theye gott moneye for them.
they have undone Davie L:^{408} in Regarde his livinge is cheefelye gotten
in keepinge Cattle abought him which hee can not nowe doe. theese
men beeinge knowen to your selfe maye make yow to Commiserate
them. the olde man [word illegible] waye (as northeren men saye) is
lame still. & m^r Formalityes^{409} I thinke muste beetake him againe to
the northe theare to learne how to deale with scots. for none can
matche them any whitt but northeren men. & I thinke it was a Northeren
man that cosenedd [?] a scott in this manner. One there was that came
to a scotte opened his boosome & shewedd him thatt he had some 8^l
in his boosome sayinge that he woulde (as I take it) make it upp an C
if the scott woulde procure him to bee made Knight[.] the hungrye
scott was for him, & wente abought to effecte it verrye eagerlye. badd
him withall to come to the Courte & awaite in suche a place untill the
kinge might bee mooved thearewith & hee doubted not but it shoulde
bee effected within halfe an hower. s.^{r} quothe the Northeren man to
the scotte I can not beeinge here provide my selfe on suche a suddayne

^{403} See **Letter 12a**.
^{404} See **Letter 12a**. Henry Smith is recorded as bailiff of Seaford in 1608, ESRO,
SEA 104 (for which reference I am grateful to Christopher Whittick).
^{405} Edward Goldwyer. An exchequer commission in October 1610 had already seques-
trated property worth 5 marks belonging to him at Battle, PRO, E 368/539, mem. 147d.
In February 1611 another commission, led by Sir Barnard Whetstones and John
Langworth, seized moveables of his valued at £4 including a horse 'with a partie white
face & two white feete', PRO, E 368/541, mem. 124a. Richard Broughton reported this
sequestration in April 1611, AAW A X, no. 36.
^{406} Richard Vincent of Catsfield. He held property by lease from Anthony Browne,
second Viscount Montague, PRO, E 368/541, mem. 124a–b.
^{407} The exchequer commission sitting at Lewes on 6 October 1610 found that John
Cape had goods at Battle worth eight pounds, thirteen shillings and four pence, PRO,
E 368/539, mem. 147d.
^{408} David Lomer. He held property at Battle worth five marks (according to the
exchequer commission's inquisition at Lewes on 6 October 1610 [see previous note]).
^{409} See **Letter 30**.

[?] provyde [sic] my selfe of apparrell sutable to my caulinge. yett coulde yow procure mee a Velvett cloake heere in Coorte to hide my other apparrell that maye sarve for this [word illegible]. the scott made haste & gott him a verrye faier velvett cloacke & goinge in to learne howe longe it woulde bee eare the Kinge woulde bee reddye to dubbe this craftye countryman of yours your good countryman showed him a tricke of that cuntrye & wente away with the scotts velvett cloke & soe too knaves partedd [?], yet bicause yow shall not thinke I speake of anye spleene againste your countrye & countriman I thinke in my Conscience your countriman was the honester man. <u>Wee looke for a Commission to come downe in to the countrye to have the othe tendered to all</u>. which my Dame[410] not longe since understandinge of she played in my absence this prancke thatt foloweth. she wente to consulte with my neighbour whether ['shee' deleted] it were good shee did that which afterward in deade shee did. my frende diswaded her from it. well that satisfied her noe whitt, butt she woulde needes goe to a chappell of S^t. Frauncis not many miles from her house & praye to that s^t. to directe her. shee did soe. & when she was at her prayers in came the patrone of the chappell & asked her what shee made there. shee tolde him whatt she was abought & howe shee prayed to bee directed by that s^t. butt seeinge hee was come she mente by the s.^{ts} leave to aske his counsell. hee answered thatt he sawe noe greate harme if shee followed that course that my fre[n]de hadd diswaded her from. Whereuppon shee tooke harte at grasse, came home gott her horses & men and wente to a Iustice of peace his howse which neither knewe her nor shee him [p. 83] & thus she beegan. S^r quoth shee I am suche an one (beutifull yow knowe & faier as any breste of backon[411]) a strainger unto yow. & hearinge that a Comission was to come downe to yow to offer the othe to all Recusants, I hasted my comminge to give yow to understande that if hee ['yow' inserted] shoulde then sende for her ['mee' [?] inserted] shee ['I' inserted] intended not to come unto him, not owte of contempte, but for Conscience sake for that she never intended to take that othe. whye quoth the Iustice yow maye take the othe. it is nothing to doe[.] yes quoth shee it is moore then I minde to doe. whereuppon hee fetcht the statute booke & readinge the othe with her shee as hee redd it unto her, misliked this, & thatt, and delivered her opinion plainlye concerninge the Authoritye of the pope over princes etcetera. pease quothe the Iustice for yow maye runn into the premunirie.

---

[410] Constance Lambe.

[411] Norton frequently stressed that Constance Lambe was not physically attractive, AAW A X, no. 29 (p. 70) (relaying her request to More that her son Anthony Lambe should be educated at Rome, 'who is likelye to prove a hansommer man' than 'ever shee was woman'), XI, no. 170 (p. 499) (that Anthony Lambe 'is sayed to have robd his mother of a greate deale of her bewtye (for shurelye shee hathe scarse any lefte)').

Runn whither I will quoth shee I will ne*ver* take it & although I bee
threatned by the refusall heereof to loose all [word deleted] the landes &
goods I have, w*hi*ch truly are butt smaule for my husbande[412] is butt
poore & hadd but 15ˡ in Marriage w*i*th mee yett lett that goe in godds
name. yea theare is a greater matter w*hi*ch might moove mee, thatt is my
children. yett rather the*n* I woulde take this othe I woulde rather see them
all kilde beefore my face. well q*uo*th the Iustice there is noe dealinge w*i*th
yow the*n*. noe q*uo*th shee for I verelye thinke if I tooke the othe I shoulde
soe looke noe waie butt I shoulde see the divell readye to catche mee
awaye. Well the iustice understandinge whoe shee was & how well des-
cended made her good [?] there & tolde her hee woulde doe her any good
hee coulde & whome shee came. & trulye y*o*w [will ?] not beeleeve howe
I laughed att her but w*i*thall I ioyed ex[t]raordinarilye at her Resolutio*n* &
I [word deleted] make mutche of her & shee of [word obscured: mee
[?]] & I thought good to tell y*o*w this storye hopinge that y*o*w will co*n*ceale
her name & [word illegible] laudare homine*m* in vita but weare shee well
gone to heave*n* the*n* weare it fitt that the Resolutio*n* of suche wome*n*
shoulde bee knowen. Will [y*o*w] knowe [?] any more good qualities of
hers? the*n* whe*n* y*o*w returne enquire after her & yt may bee shee will have
some by thatt tyme for as she groweth younge soe she amendeth &
groweth good butt as she groeth olde soe shee groweth wrinkoled &c. I
had once writtne to y*o*w to acquainte mʳ poole w*i*th some newes. butt
nowe I intende to wright to him my selfe. forgett not to sende mee the
copye of my Notarishipp[413] & bee able [?] in y*o*ur lett*e*rs to answere my
directio*n* that y*o*w oute of the sharpenes of y*o*ur witt maye pr*o*pose soe that
when y*o*w have pr*o*posed & answeredd al doubts I maye knowe what to
doe. ytt woulde have stoode some of my frendes in some stead a whiles
since if I hadd knowen howe farr the authoritie thereof extended & what
it was to bee a Iudge. &c[.] playe y*o*ur p*ar*te well as y*o*w will deserve [p.
84] well at my handes. I will bee loathe to tell y*o*w the cause of all the
adoe untill I receive the copye of that authorytye w*hi*ch is ['sub sig' deleted]
graunted sub sigillo Collegii Archivii but when I shall receive the copye
in a legible hande of the former copye the*n* will I tell y*o*w howe my mark
sarved mee & showe y*o*w a prettye prancke that the Nominalls[414] played
me or at the leaste a follower of theires. y*o*w muste bee sile*n*te untill I have
it agane in a plainer hande for this is not to bee understoode. Adieue my
good frende & Comende mee not to any but my frendes for of my frendes
I reckon for my foes I care not[.] I will [two words deleted] wright my
minde to M.ʳ poole in a lett*r*e w*hi*ch shall bee se*n*te by y*o*ur meanes bicause

[412] Richard Lambe.
[413] Norton wrote to More in June 1611 to say that the pope could assure himself that
unless 'hee have true newes of...matters fro*m* Notaryes or men of creditt', he would be
'to muche abused', AAW A X, no. 61 (p. 167).
[414] Jesuits.

I will give roome to his sisters to wright by the other waye. Commende mee to M.ʳ D Ansel:[415] Doctouʳ Thornell M.ʳ Nicholas fitzherbert & my countryman (yf not kinsman) Father Owen.[416] for his Father marryed my Awnte to whome I doe not wright bicause I knowe not howe it will bee taken but if at any tyme yow thinke it good that I wright unto him tell me what yow woulde wishe mee to right of & I will doe accordinglye. if hee liste to deale with mee as a true hampeshire man or kinsman Relligiouslye & reallye I will give him correspondence. but I will not deale with one that hath duplicitatem personii though hee have withall duplicem spectum Eli[ ] [word partly obliterated]. Adieue good s.ʳ 12ᵗʰ of Aprill. 1611.
yours B N.
Addressed: To his muche Respected [f]rende Mʳ Thomas Moore
Endorsed: April: 12. 1611. Ben.

15 *George Salvin (Birkhead) to Thomas More (25 June 1611)*   *(AAW A X, no. 76, pp. 201–2. Holograph)*

My Rev Sʳ I have received your two last of the xi of may and all the rest that came before. I wrote as much in comm. of mʳ pett[417] as I could. I thought in · that letter or rather petition there neded no Complementes. not three daies before I had sent one sufficiently furnished with them. I thanke yow for laboring that those odiouse thinges be not sent to me. for it wold overthrow me quite. in my opinion there need no ordinarie processe in that matter, which is so evident and notorious. mʳ black. bookes[418] are sufficient testimonies of his error. and now your frend mʳ Sheldon hath published a worse, and one mʳ Roger widderington a laick, one more perillous then them both.[419] do yow not therfor think it tyme for S Peter to draw his sword by any means of iustice he can? the quarrell in the north is almost appeased, but such relations as yow speake of will sturre up the coales againe. mʳ Troll[420] and all his fellowes at the first did but onely relate unto mʳ Sam[421] superior what offence was given in the countrie. and

[415] Robert (Anselm) Beech OSB.
[416] Thomas Owen SJ.
[417] Birkhead's commendation of Robert Pett was contained in his letter to Cardinal Edward Farnese of 14 June 1611, AAW A X, no. 72.
[418] See **Letter 2**.
[419] Richard Sheldon, *Certaine General Reasons, proving the Lawfulnesse of the Oath of Allegiance* (1611); Roland (Thomas) Preston OSB, *Apologia Cardinalis Bellarmini pro Iure Principum* (1611). For Preston's use of the name of the Northumberland gentleman Roger Widdrington (to whom he was related by marriage) as a pseudonym, see A.M.C. Forster, 'The Real Roger Widdrington', *RH* 11 (1971–2), 196–205; Lunn, *EB*, 41.
[420] Cuthbert Trollop.
[421] Samuel (Bartholomew) Kennett OSB.

since Contrarie to ther intention the matter hath ben exaggerated by
m^r Sam so much that it is come to a monstrous Contention. but as I
sayd now almost appeased.[422] and if fa preston will ioyne with me to
put them both to silence, I hope it will be quickly ended. but I feare
he will stand so stiffly for m^r Sam creditt and there disgrace for
slanderinge him which they do mordicus denie, that I feare the worst.
some notes I send yo*w* herinclosed onely to give yo*w* a tast ['and to
lett' deleted] of what is written to me. I could send yo*w* many such
thinges, but that it maketh my packetes to thick, and then our frendes[423]
do grumble. I hope yo*w* have received the notes I have sent yo*w*
concerninge m^r Cadwallader, and yo*w* shall have moe as opportunitie
serveth. I have sent the Italian copie of fa Iones to our brethren there,
who dowbtlesse wilbe sturred up by that, to send a better information.[424]

[422] Cuthbert Trollop took a firm line against the oath of allegiance. He attacked the
lax John Clinch, the chaplain of Roger Widdrington, see **Letter 33**, and also John
Mush, who had been appointed by Birkhead to resolve the quarrel over the oath between
OSB and the secular priests in the North, see AAW A XI, no. 139; **Letter 18**. Trollop
and other seculars said that Kennett's penitents, including Sir John Claxton, took the
oath 'soome privatlye before the Bishop, soome publiqlye'; and so did John (Thomas)
Hutton OSB's penitents. (Hutton belonged to the Spanish congregation of OSB.) One
of Hutton's penitents told Trollop that it was wrong to condemn those who took the
oath as guilty of mortal sin, AAW A X, no. 130. The secular priest Cuthbert Crayford
was equally vehement against the oath and Benedictine laxity therein, AAW A XI, no.
3. On 14 October 1611 Birkhead again told More that 'I have in some sort staied my
brethren of the north in ther quarrel against m^r Samuel the bened. and m^r Mush M^r
Trollope and m^r [William] Ogle the especial agentes therin, rest well contented therewith'.
But Crayford was not satisfied and wanted to carry his grievance to Rome. Crayford
accused Birkhead of being affected to OSB while Birkhead retorted that SJ had a hold
over Crayford, AAW A X, no. 133 (p. 383). Richard Smith later said he heard Crayford
'wholy depended on m^r [Richard] Holtby [SJ]', and promised More to do his best to
thwart his purpose if he showed his face in Paris, AAW A XI, no. 20 (p. 51). Crayford
had been named in the appellant controversy polemic as a supporter of George Blackwell,
Persons, *Briefe Apologie*, fo. 106v; J.C.H. Aveling, *Northern Catholics* (1966), 168. He was
referred to in the North, by Protestants, in the late 1590s as the 'Busshopp' of Grosmont
Abbey, the house belonging to the Cholmley family which was used by the northern
priests in the mission largely organised by Holtby, PRO, SP 12/170/120, fo. 201r.
[423] *i.e.* OSB, on whom the seculars still relied for carriage of their letters.
[424] Robert Jones SJ wrote an account of Cadwallader's martyrdom (AAW A IX, no.
74). In it Cadwallader is tacitly enlisted as a favourer of SJ because he had been visited
in prison by a Jesuit before his death and because he had come to some arrangement
with SJ concerning the disposal of his books. Birkhead said that, on the contrary,
Cadwallader had been visited by one Vaughan alias Grisold, AAW A X no. 3, either
George or Roger Grisold (Warwickshire secular priests) or, more probably, Lewis
Vaughan. See **Letter 16** (Edward Bennett's version of the story). John Jackson also
narrated these events, AAW A IX, no. 125. John Gennings OFM, who worked in both
Sussex and Wales, said that Cadwallader had often complained to him of SJ's 'unkyndnes'.
As for his books, Cadwallader had sold them for £10 when he was arrested, on condition
they should be returned if he were released, AAW A IX, no. 84 (p. 281); Allison,

our frend[425] lieth fast in the fleet,[426] but everie day in hope to be delivered for his money, as I have written unto yow alredie.[427] the b of Canturb[428] hath commission to search in any mans house of what degre so ever. so that we shall still be exercised. the oath is like to be generally bought out for money. yf our great frendes abroad wold presse hard in our behalfe with there intreaties, it is thought that some tolleration in deed might be obteyned. the La Arbella is in the tower, m[r] Semer hir husband is gon.[429] Charles of Sweden hath given the k of denmark a

'Franciscan Books', 16. William Bishop said Cadwallader had given them to someone who was not a Jesuit, AAW A X, no. 45. In early 1612 Thomas More was still collecting affidavits to show that Cadwallader had not been abandoned by his brethren. Cadwallader's last letters were being collated as conclusive proof of this, AAW A XI, nos 22, 23.

[425] Anthony Maria Browne, second Viscount Montague.

[426] Richard Broughton had written in mid-April 1611 that the king had recently spoken sharply to bishops and the privy council against noblemen and noblewomen harbouring priests who were a threat to his life, AAW A X, no. 36. William Bishop noted on 29 May 1611 that a high commission pursuivant had been to Cowdray to arrest a specific priest, though 'having a nescio hominem, [he] departed with a fly in his eare', AAW A X, no. 48 (p. 119). The next day Birkhead wrote that, through Archbishop Abbot's malice, Viscount Montague had been commanded to appear before the privy council but he fell into a 'tertian fever, which shreudly handled him for eyght or nyne fittes as they say', and so he could not travel. Friends tried to secure a deal by which he would not be confronted with the oath, AAW A X, no. 51 (p. 125); cf. CSPD 1611–18, 32.

[427] On 14 June 1611 Birkhead had written to More that Montague had been interrogated by the privy council 'and at the first protested his fidelitie to his Maiestie in most effectuall wordes and manner, but desyred to be excused touchinge the oath quia multa continet contra fidem'. Henry Howard, Earl of Northampton (who, a Jesuit newsletter writer noted, intervened on behalf of Thomas Strange SJ when he was questioned about the deposing power, Foley VII, 1025) then spoke on Montague's 'behalfe how loial he had shewed himself, adding that perhaps in tyme more might be obteined of him'; but Montague said 'that by godes grace he wold ever be the same man that now he is, and requested them to have no other conceit of him. And when my Lord Zouch asked whether he had refused the oath, my lord with a loude voice said yes my lord I do refuse it', AAW A X, no. 73 (p. 193). After refusing the oath, Montague was sent first to Dorset House and then to the Fleet prison, AAW A X, no. 87. A composition of £6,000 was levied on him in place of the full penalty for praemunire; it was promised that he would not be offered the oath again, CSPD 1611–18, 51; PRO, SO 3/5 June 1611. (For the arrangements which Montague made to pay the £6,000, see A.A. Dibben, The Cowdray Archives (2 vols, Chichester, 1960), I, p. xi n. 1.)

[428] George Abbot.

[429] For the escape of Arabella Stuart and William Seymour, grandson of Edward Seymour, second Earl of Hertford, see Larkin and Hughes, 266 n. 2. Robert Pett reported that Seymour left the Tower using 'a false haire and beard in a docter of physikes habit', AAW A X, no. 77 (p. 203). Seymour converted to Catholicism when he got abroad, as William Trumbull feared that he might. He was reconciled to the Church of Rome by Anthony Hoskins SJ. The conversion, however, was delayed and kept secret so as to avoid scandal, Downshire MSS III, 90–1; B. Fitzgibbon, 'The Conversion of William Seymour, Duke of Somerset (1588–1660)', Biographical Studies 1 (1951–2), 117–19; Belvederi, 231.

great overthrow of 8000 men.[430] I longe to heare of the receit of those
Letters which I have alredie sent to vives[431] and the primate.[432] yow
have a good zeale, but as our case standeth now, yow could do no
service in London.[433] yow shold not escape 4 daies. yow do well where
yow are. yf I knew his hol wold heare of such a matter, I could send
him a great number ['of voices' deleted] of our owne voices for bb. I
have written so much in other letters, that I have no more to say, and
so commendinge me to your praiers I bid yow farewell. this 25 of Iune
1611
your loving frend
    Geo. Sal
(On p. 202)
Addressed: To his verie good frend m[r] Thomas moore give this Rome.
Endorsed: Iune. 25: 1611.
        G. Sal

16 *Edward Farington (Bennett) to George West (Thomas More) (26 June
    1611)   (AAW A X, no. 78, pp. 205–6. Holograph)*

Good Syr: my last to you was of the first of Iune,[434] as I take it, at least
no longer agoe. wherin I did acquainte you with such occurrentes as
then did happen amongst us. yester night I receaved two from you,
thon of the 9 of Aprill, thother meant for m[r] Lea,[435] but directed to me
of the 16 of the same: I see by boath how much we are behouldinge
unto you, boath for your payns in our affayres, as alsoe for the good
advise you give how heere we should follow our busines. for my own
parte, I doe what I can, & will not cease hereafter to sett forward the
cause all that lieth in me: although we be reasonable well combyned,
yeat fewe we have that will take payns, which it may be is the occasion

---

[430] In May the Danes had declared war against Charles IX of Sweden, alleging
breaches of the Treaty of Stettin. Birkhead here, it seems, refers to the siege of Kalmar,
CSPV 1610–13, 155, 168–9, 175.

[431] John Baptist Vives. Thomas More resided with him in Rome at Vives's house in
the 'rue de popolo'. For a possible identification of Vives, see L.F. von Pastor, *The History
of the Popes from the Close of the Middle Ages* (40 vols, 1891–1953), XXV, 369–70, XXVI, 84–
5.

[432] Birkhead had written to Cardinal Edward Farnese (from whom he had recently
received two letters, AAW A X, no. 64) on 14 June 1611 (AAW A X, no. 72, enclosed
with his letter to More of the same date, AAW A X, no. 73) *inter alia* narrating Viscount
Montague's troubles.

[433] More had presumably suggested that he should return to assist with the bishops'
suit.

[434] AAW A X, no. 58.

[435] George Birkhead.

that yo*u* receave so few relations as yo*u* doe: in my last I towld yo*u* how d Bushop was taken;[436] and in this yo*u* shall receave a part of his letter to me by w*h*ich yo*u* may p*a*rtly understand how it fareth w*i*th hyme.[437] heer hath been latly taken 3 or 4 preestes[438] wholy by it, on of them is a frier,[439] a Ieswett[440] alsoe was mett w*i*th but was lett goe by the knaves as some think for 40 or 50[li]: they are so well stord that they can easlier redeem them selfes then other poor prestes can. yo*u* seme to say we ar heer to remedy matters, & not f[or] to seek from

[436] On the day before he was due to leave England for France, William Bishop had been arrested by the renegade secular priest Anthony Rouse. He was sent to Newgate prison. On 30 May 1611 Birkhead believed that £100 would have secured his release but it could not be raised, AAW A X, no. 5. Richard Smith said that Bishop had nobly refused to secure his release by offering a bribe, AAW A X, no. 52. Birkhead noted that though Bishop had written against George Abbot's brother Robert, and now refused George Abbot's demand that he should take the oath of allegiance 'geving many sufficieant reasons why it ought not to be taken', George Abbot had actually said Bishop's reasons were 'the best he had heard for the denial therof'. Bishop had offered to 'sweare to his m*aies*tie all the temporall allegiance that can be exacted of any Christian subiect'; James approved of his answer, AAW A X, no. 51 (pp. 125–6). Smith repeated the point about Abbot's approval but said that 'ytt is so calumniated as though he had said that he thought the oathe lauful w*h*ich is very false', AAW A X, no. 52 (p. 129). Birkhead said Bishop 'found no other favour but to be sent free prisoner to the gathouse, where he remaineth with much credit amongst Catholiques for his absolute answer against the oath. yet not without hope of being shortly banished', AAW A X, no. 51 (p. 126). Bishop's examination in the State Papers records that he refused to take the oath. His main reason was that he did not want to damage the credit of the secular clergy at Rome in their battle with SJ, PRO, SP 14/63/74. Bishop later claimed that he was delivered 'out of prison against Cantreburyes will...who is well knowen to beare mee...deadly hatred...because I writing aga[in]st his brother [Robert Abbot] touched their beggarly descent', AAW A XII, no. 138 (p. 309). See Milward II, 139–42.
[437] This letter has not survived.
[438] Henry Mayhew, Edward Kenion, John Thules and John Gennings OFM. See **Letter 14**. Kenion was released into exile in February 1612, though he appears to have returned to England by September 1615, **Letter 22**; TD V, p. ccii. (Matthew Kellison attempted in 1614 to use Kenion and Joseph Haynes as replacements for Edward Weston and William Singleton at Douai, Allison, 'Later Life', 115–16.) Like Richard Smith, Kenion enjoyed the patronage of Armand-Jean du Plessis, Bishop of Luçon, the future Cardinal-Duc de Richelieu. (Anthony Champney had been offered this place in the bishop's retinue before Kenion, but the other members of the Paris writers' college would not allow him to take it up, AAW A XI, no. 113; **Letter 32**.) Birkhead recounted that Henry Mayhew 'denied the oath directly, and for sayinge it was absurd and that no christian could take yt, the b [George Abbot] told him he deserved to be hanged'. Mayhew was imprisoned in Newgate. But 'm[r] kenyon answeringe in the b Conceit more moderately was sent to the Clinck' (*i.e.* where the principal Catholic clerical favourers of the oath were incarcerated), AAW A X, no. 51 (p. 125).
[439] John Gennings OFM. He refused the oath and was sent to Newgate, TD IV, p. clxx.
[440] Not identified. On 1 June 1611 Benjamin Norton listed various priests who had recently been arrested and released for cash payments, including his 'neighbo*u*r M.[r] Michael' for £40. John Floyd SJ and John Falconer SJ had paid larger sums to remain at liberty, AAW A X, nos 52, 61 (p. 165).

you that thinges showld be sett in order: alas we have gatherd voices, we have brought our brethern, the gretest part, to an union, we be ioyned with our superior, we have & doe propose our necessiti[es] to the sea Apostolick, & this is all the remedy we can give to matters, if thence you doe not sett some order amongest us, then must all perishe, & be owt of all order. you need not fear the ioyninge of fitzherbert[441] with you to handle our comon affayers, for our superior nor our selfes will ever agree unto it, have we labored so much to remove hym, & can you imagyn we will admitt hym agayn? no no: we would leave all first [?] then suffer either hym to have any doing in our cause or his patrons the Iesswetes either: for seing we have shaken of ther yoke we will keepe our selfes free if we can. mr whit[442] hath written to mr Lea latly & offereth us all curtesy, he saeth he hath written to ther ['protect' deleted] proctor general with you to be your frend, & saeth further that if the Italian monckes[443] tak against us he will not be good frendes with them. soe that I think you shall have frendship from hyme. mr morgan[444] never writt nor spok to me abowt the comon cause. ther hath been much a doe to gett mr Cadwalladers head who most constantly died only because he refused the oath[.] I would paul[445] had it in his hand:[446] ['the' deleted] on mr muskett[447] on of our brethern looketh this sessions to be called to his triall: if it be soe I pray god give hym constancye. is it not straing that we showld send an agent to paul, spend so much money, make soe many supplications & he retorn withowt on thinge grauntd? that must be urged. I have written another letter to Card farnes[.][448] I think mr Lea will send it with this. he writes unto me that myn to paul[449] cometh towardes you: I suppose it cometh open into

[441] Thomas Fitzherbert.

[442] John (Augustine) Bradshaw OSB.

[443] The Cassinese congregation of OSB.

[444] Possibly a reference to Morgan Clennock, who had become an assistant to George Blackwell in 1600.

[445] Pope Paul V.

[446] Birkhead wrote to More on 6 October 1611 that Robert (Anselm) Beech OSB had shown 'a peece' of the recently martyred John Roberts OSB to Paul V; 'I could shew him the whole heades both of Mr Cadwallader and Mr Napper, yf tyme & place wold permitt me which though they be not in my handes, yet can I make good means to fynde them out', AAW A IX, no. 81 (p. 273). On 20 May 1612 Birkhead reported that Lewis Vaughan, who was about to set out for Rome (see **Letter 56**), was the man that 'got the Iewell of mr Cadwall. and perhaps...both it, and mr nappers may follow him in winter next'. Birkhead thought More and Vaughan should present them 'to the highest', because Vaughan 'ventured his life three tyme for one of them. yett his desyre will be to bringe' Cadwallader's head 'back, because the Countrie will take it in evill part to be deprived wholly therof', AAW A XI, no. 83 (p. 237).

[447] George Fisher.

[448] No copy of this letter survives in AAW.

[449] Edward Bennett wrote to Paul V on 13 June 1611, TD V, pp. cxlvii–l.

your handes & soe I need not tell you the contentes. it is straing to me to heer that don Ans[450] is soe much our back frend,[451] I have been his Frend, & showed hym kyndnes litl thinking he would prove as he doth. I see all these religious are of on humor & sett all against the clergy, only m^r whit showeth hym self lovinge. I would desyer you to urg this point to paul that we ar much trubled that d smith showld return from his feet & bring us not on benediction: I urg for ordinary iurisd[i]con which granted all will follow: doe not think that the president of doway[452] will ever ioyne further with us then the Iesswetes will give hym leave: he is altogether for them & his goverment must goe on as they direct.[453] I marvaile you did expect any good from hym: within thes 6 week[es] he expelled 3 preestes & sent them away withowt ther faculties.[454] I would paul did well understand the estat of that colledg. but if we had bush[o]ps all would easily be amended. the lady Arbella is taken agayn, m^r Seamer her husband escaped: the lady of Shroosbery comitted to the bushop of Canterbury,[455] now ther is no talk but of that matter. ther is a proclamation that the oath must be offered to every body: the litl lord[456] hath refused it[.] he payeth 6000^{li}:[457] I thinck hereafter there is no dainger of taking the oath with interpretation, for they will have it taken secundum litteram: money they would have, therfor supposing it will not be taken as it lieth, they will put every man to it. & they

[450] Robert (Anselm) Beech OSB.
[451] In May 1611 Birkhead was furious with 'the Italian benedictins for denyinge to send our Letters, and much more at m^r beach for yeeldinge to the humor of others against our proceedings, haveinge receyved so much kyndnes of me', AAW A X, no. 51 (p. 125).
[452] Thomas Worthington.
[453] The seculars' perceptions of Worthington varied quite a lot. According to Birkhead in November 1610 Worthington had conceded that Douai College ought to be reformed, though his plan for priests to live in community there was unsuitable, AAW A IX, no. 86; cf. Belvederi, 224. Robert Pett in June 1611 was impressed with Worthington's concession that there should be a visitation made of the college, AAW A X, no. 77. Champney thought Worthington was infinitely preferable to other pro-Jesuit seculars such as John Knatchbull (whom it was rumoured would be made president in Worthington's place), AAW A X, no. 109. And in September 1611 Smith thought Worthington reasonably cooperative, AAW A X, no. 117. At the end of February 1612 Champney noted that Worthington had preached 'upon St Thomas his day lamentinge muche the want of Bishopes in our countrie...which ys an argument that he ys of another opinione then heretofore', AAW A XI, no. 29 (p. 76). In March 1612 Edward Kenion expressed the view that Worthington was now free of Jesuit influence, **Letter 22**.
[454] They were John Warham, Lewis Williams and Francis Greaves, CRS 10, 110. Bennett believed that they were dismissed because they had, with seventeen others, supported a scholar whom Worthington had expelled, AAW A X, no. 58 (p. 159). Worthington claimed he had sent them away only temporarily, AAW A X, no. 79. Birkhead thought Warham was of 'good understandinge', AAW A X, no. 97 (p. 274). The three students wrote to More on 4 May 1611 (NS), AAW A X, no. 42.
[455] Mary Talbot, Countess of Shrewsbury, was sent to the Tower, CSPD 1611–18, 48.
[456] Anthony Maria Browne, second Viscount Montague.
[457] See **Letter 15**.

that deny it fall into the premuniry & soe must either lose all or mak a hard composition as the litle lord did: he lieth for the present in the fleete [p. 206] but we hope upon this agreement of 6000^li he shall out. it wer [?] well [?] paul knew of it. my best Frend^458 houldeth her self wonderfully bownd unto you for your kyndnes to her litle ones, a great while a goe ther is order taken that they discharge all places where they ar bownd. I hope they have satisfied your self amonge the first: I will do any thing I can for [word obliterated] them. ther goeth a speech of a proclamation ['for the' deleted] that is to come fowrth for the banishing of all these preestes in prison. soe m^r [name illegible]. I heer m^r Iohns^459 hath written much of the charity of a brother of his to m^r Cadwallader the martyr & that non of us would come at hym, withall that he submitted hym self to the Iesswetes: this last is most false, only he wished all thinges to be forgotten, & that we should all agree & goe on lik brethern in the harvest. for the second in the very assises week two or thre of our brethern attended abowt the prison to have come to hym but could not. & this Ieswet cominge [?] by chance gott in, & soe hard his confessions & se how they bragge: I see a letter of his ['m.^r Cadwallader' written above] written to on of our brethern viceassistant^460 in those partes, & it was written in the assises week, wherin he giveth most [word illegible] thankes to the kynd vice assistant^461 for his charity, & that for some fyve weekes or there about beinge sent hym he wished hee should otherwayes dispose of it for they [sic for 'that' ?] he soe suppli[e]d his wantes that ther was no such need. withall he took gratefully ther desyre to come to hym, but seinge it could not be, he sayed he thancked our lord, ther was no such need, & that they should truble them selfes no further: letters of [word illegible] receaved within thes 10 dayes. soe that I marvail at m^r Iohns if it be true he hath charged us with carlessnes to help the holy martyr: And soe withall good wishes 26 Iune 1611.

yours ever

Ed Farington

Addressed: to the worshipfull my espetiall Frend m^r west thes
Endorsed: Iune 26. 1611 Ed. far

---

^458 Lady Elizabeth Dormer.

^459 Robert Jones SJ. See **Letter 15**.

^460 John Bennett.

^461 Birkhead had written to More in January 1611 that Cadwallader 'remained the same man at his death as he was before, as may appeare by a Letter which he wrote to m^r Iohn bennett after he was in prison', a letter which Birkhead had sent to the priest John Jackson and which he expected Jackson would pass on, AAW A X, no. 3 (p. 7). Jackson had translated this letter into Latin 'out of the copie which he [Cadwallader] wrate with his owne hand. and which our Superiour hath in his keeping', AAW A IX, no. 125 (p. 396).

17 *Richard Orontes (Smith) to Thomas More (7 July 1611)   (AAW A X, no. 86, pp. 237–8. Holograph)*

My good Syr. Since my returne[462] I have sent divers letters[463] unto you and receaved also some from you but none in answer to mine doe come[.] Now I am shortly to go over[464] having left things as I hope in good forwardnes. you shal ether with this or soone after with the first securitie receive the <u>voices of 112 for Bish.</u>[465] you I know will expect more and surely more might have bene gotten if <u>some were more diligent</u> or the Pursivants did not so range [?] about as they do daily that nether london nor the countrie can afford any safetie or possibilitie to meet[.] yet this is certain that the nu<u>m</u>ber of pr. is nothing so great as was imagined and that it hath very smally increased <u>since</u> the span. sem:[466] began. yett this number wil shew that it is not ambition w*h*ich maketh so ge*n*eral a desire. I hear <u>of scarce six</u> that deny to have the*m*[467] and two for fear of offending withold their hands yet give their consents. I have also left my man Thomas[468] behind who shalbe mantained in lond to hold correspondence with you w*h*ich is the greatest matter that

---

[462] *i.e.* to England.

[463] AAW A X, nos 12, 17, 23, 52, 66, 67.

[464] According to Birkhead, Smith left for France by 3 August 1611 (though Thomas Heath said it was on 6 August, AAW A X, no. 150). He should have left on 3 July, but he delayed in order to be present at the christening of Viscount Montague's daughter, AAW A X, nos 97, 99, 103; *cf.* AAW A X, no. 71.

[465] In his next letter to More, Smith said that there were 115 signatures to the petition for a bishop, but there were many others which had not been obtained, AAW A X, no. 92. AAW A XI, no. 253, provisionally assigned, however, by A.F. Allison to 1612, contains 115 names of secular priests, each signifying his preference for choice of bishop, but lists twenty-four others who would indicate privately their nomination. On 30 May 1611 Birkhead was still hesitating to send the collected signatures, AAW A X, no. 50. On 6 July 1611 he told More he would be sending the names shortly, AAW A X, no. 84. On 17 July Birkhead wrote that he and Smith had finally sent the petition with the appended names, AAW A X, no. 93, though subsequent letters are somewhat ambiguous about whether they have been despatched or not, and in mid-November 1611 Birkhead was expecting his 'great packets' to have gone only as far as Paris, AAW A X, no. 146 (p. 411). Only by January 1612 did Birkhead expect the 'great packetts' to have arrived in Rome, AAW A XI, no. 10 (p. 23); More acknowledged their receipt in a letter to Birkhead of 21 January 1612 (NS), AAW A XI, no. 26. More confirmed in a letter of 29 February 1612 (NS) that the petition material had now all arrived safely, AAW A XI, no. 67.

[466] St Alban's College, Valladolid.

[467] See **Letter 7**. John Bavant, however, in his letter to Robert Persons SJ of 28 March 1610 claimed that underhand means were used to extract consent from the secular priests when Thomas More went canvassing in late 1609, CRS 41, 99. In July/August 1610 a Jesuit newsletter said that subscription was forced out of all who did not positively object, and that an indifferent survey would show that 'the half of them would deny having had any such a thought', Foley VII, 1018.

[468] Thomas Heath.

hitherto hath wanted[.]⁴⁶⁹ And I hope for other matters you shal find more diligence in divers namely in mʳ Nels:⁴⁷⁰ and mullin.⁴⁷¹ To whom I wold have you to write. I have write to Signor vives, and others have promised me to do the same for to encourage him, but I doubt that none wil goe from hence to accept his allowance. Ben:⁴⁷² goeth now over with mʳ Poles sisters⁴⁷³ and whither he wil goe further or no I can not tell. lately I sent you the proclamation to put all to the othe and now the Iustices are verye busie about it[.] mʳ Bruning and his sonne⁴⁷⁴ and mʳ Ih: Cotton⁴⁷⁵ are cited to appear and others otherwher. The L. montacute is now lett out of the fleet and partlye hath paid partely must paie within this twelv moneths six thousand pounds for denial of the oathe which he denied at the Co[un]cel table very constantly in so much as when one of them having not wel heard him asked whither he hath refused it or no he speakinge aloud said yes my L: I have refused it, and others saying that in time they hoped he wold be otherwise mynded he fell on his knees to desire them ['to' deleted] not to be so conceited of him but that he trusted in God to continew in

⁴⁶⁹ Heath's first extant letter was sent to More on 25 April 1611, AAW A X, no. 39. In late 1612 Birkhead wrote they were no longer able to maintain Heath in London, and Birkhead was at his 'wittes end how to receyve or send' letters, AAW A XI, no. 228 (p. 657). Heath, however, had still not left London by the beginning of September 1613, and he was arrested in October 1613 carrying letters for Benjamin Norton, AAW A XII, no. 160; **Letter 46**.

⁴⁷⁰ John Jackson.

⁴⁷¹ John Almond alias Molinax, secular priest.

⁴⁷² Benjamin Norton.

⁴⁷³ Katherine and Mary Pole, Geoffrey Pole's two youngest sisters, *Downshire MSS* III, 124, and perhaps also at this time Constance, who was noted in 1613 by William Rayner and Anthony Champney as being in Paris, AAW A XII, nos 90, 103. Norton notified More on 24 June 1611 that he proposed to 'accompany the gentlewomen to ther brother', AAW A X, no. 74 (p. 195). Geoffrey Pole had gone to Caen in early June 1611 to see to their coming over, AAW A X, no. 63. With others (including Anne Bluet and Elizabeth Dacres) Pole's sisters were intending to enter OSB, AAW A X, no. 62. See **Letter 23**; Lunn, 'English Cassinese', 64. The negotiations for the (soon defeated) union between the OSB congregations included a project for 'the erectinge of a monasterye of Women which shoulde bee of the Englishe congregation', AAW A X, no. 74 (p. 195); Lunn, 'English Cassinese', 63–4; Lunn, *EB*, 97. Pole travelled to Paris with them in mid-August. After the project's failure, Mary Pole lived with Geoffrey Pole at Paris for seven years, returned to England and then went, with Mary Lambe, her cousin, to the Augustinian house in Louvain. She was professed in 1622, A. Hamilton (ed.), *The Chronicle of the English Augustinian Canonesses Regular of the Lateran, at St. Monica's in Louvain 1548–1623* (1904), 243–4. Katherine Pole returned to England in 1613, **Letter 39**.

⁴⁷⁴ Presumably Richard Brenning, husband of Eleanor (Uvedale), and his son Anthony, Mott, fo. 62v. In late 1612 Anthony Brenning appeared before the exchequer court as the son and heir of Richard Brenning (of Hambledon), and, by virtue of the 1604 recusancy statute's provision for conforming heirs, claimed discharge of recusancy forfeitures levied on his deceased father's property, PRO, E 368/547, mem. 162a.

⁴⁷⁵ John Cotton, the second son of the recusant George Cotton of Warblington, Hampshire.

the same opinion.[476] Some few daies after, <u>my L. william[477] tooke the oathe saying</u> that no considerat man wold refuse it.[478] m[r] widdringt. booke[479] doth much harme and if no greater auth*ori*ty be sett here more such bookes [wil]l come forthe and now m[r] widerington[480] is said to have put m[r] olivars[481] notes together and to have given the*m* to my L. of Canturb[.][482] He hath gott libertie and licence to abide at a house wher the husband is no recusant. w*h*ich libertie also m[r] Sheldon and m[r] Collier[483] do expect. The Sco[c]h Capucin[484] out of the tower[485] and Frier Graie[486] are sent over by order of my L. Treasurer[487] as is saide beesid w*h*ich ther are almost thirtie more in prison in london. The <u>Iesuits</u> escape for they fine wel when they are taken.[488] I pray you demand the letter of mar mercant[489] and the other papers of F. Anselmo[490] and keep the*m* yo*u*r selfe and when you hear I am at Paris

---

[476] See **Letter 15**.

[477] Lord William Howard of Naworth.

[478] Birkhead wrote to More on 3 August 1611 that 'those of greater worth, being winked at by some, can finde distinctions to take it by way of modification. yea some of them stick not to say, that no man of Consideration will refuse in that sence', AAW A X, no. 97 (p. 273).

[479] Preston, *Apologia Cardinalis Bellarmini*.

[480] Roger Widdrington.

[481] Oliver Almond, secular priest. Birkhead made him his assistant in Staffordshire in September 1612 in place of Ralph Stamford, though by June 1613 Birkhead had replaced him with Roger Suffield because Almond had been arrested and imprisoned, AAW A XI, no. 171, XII, no. 111. In late July 1613 William Bishop believed Almond's release could be purchased for a small sum of money, AAW A XII, no. 138. Anthony Champney notified More in November 1613 that Almond, Bishop and other secular priests were suspected of agreeing with Preston's opinions, AAW A XII, no. 205. (In June 1591 the priest John Cecil had informed Sir Robert Cecil that Almond was a loyalist, *CSPD 1591–4*, 53.)

[482] George Abbot.

[483] Edward Collier, secular priest. Birkhead reported on 3 August 1611 that Collier had published a book in defence of the oath, AAW A X, no. 97. If so, it has not survived.

[484] John Chrysostom Campbell.

[485] Campbell was delivered through the agency of Louis Gallacio de l'Hospital, Marquis de Vitry, recently in England on diplomatic business, AAW A X, no. 98. In August 1611 Campbell went with Thomas Sackville to Douai to ensure that Thomas Worthington was not replaced as president of Douai College with the hated John Knatchbull alias Norton, a future Jesuit; thence Campbell went to Rome, AAW A X, no. 109. The seculars wanted Campbell to help persuade the Cassinese Benedictines, principally Robert (Anselm) Beech, that the appointment of a bishop in England would not be prejudicial to OSB's interests, AAW A X, no. 183.

[486] Robert Gray OFM. See **Letter 35**.

[487] Robert Cecil, first Earl of Salisbury.

[488] See **Letter 16**.

[489] Robert Persons SJ. On 28 August 1812 (NS) Smith wrote to More thanking him for the letter in question, AAW A XI, no. 140. According to Christopher Greene SJ Thomas Owen SJ also used the alias 'Mercante', ARSI, Anglia 37, fo. 314v.

[490] Robert (Anselm) Beech OSB.

send them to me, but not otherwaies then secretly, for they impart much. Here ['our' [?] inserted] the back freinds tell the <u>pore pr: that their superiors</u> and others might <u>provide for them if they wold but being wel them selves care</u> not for others, ther <u>they say none want and here they teech them</u> to murmure. And one comen from Bav[491] <u>writeth to me that</u> one of that howse cursethe and b[l]ameth [?] me for that which I goe about to do at Paris[492] by which you may see their charity and the importance of the worke. F. Bauldin[493] in Tower but no wordes of him. Ther is also ladye Arbella and with more libertie than at first, and my La: Shrewsberie who was ther for her sake now sent to the Fleet. Here is the Lansgraves sonne[494] pretending as is said a mariage with our Princesse, for whom also the Prince of Savoie maketh suite and as it is said is to come hither for that purpose. my Goddaughter[495] is this daie gone for her abode upon fear that my L. of Cant. who is now of the Co[un]cell wold send for her having gotten notice of her determined iorney which she with four others was to undertake for Paris within this moneth.[496] God speed them wel in the worke in which I fear they will find more difficulties than yet they imagin. m[r] Faringt[497] hath written to me that he will send me 40[l] in leiu of that which you lent to his freinds[498] which he saith was 120 Cr. but you write of 130. And I hope it shalbe sent for you to Florence with far lesse <u>losse</u> than otherwaies. And I doubt not but every day we shal plaine waies hitherto so full of difficulties, and that you shall have better intelligence of our affaires. Be you as [you] have bene hitherto of good couriage and you shall see things wil amend. A secret talke here is of one comen from Paul that hath much talke with his maiestie but this is rather thought a surmise and that he cometh for Savoye. Tomorow the B: of Chichester[499] cometh to midhurst to urge the oathe.[500] m.[r] wib[501] hath bene very sick[.] m[rs] Gage is not yet married. This letter is to signor vives[.] read and seal it[.] do my humble

[491] John Bavant.

[492] The foundation of the writers' college.

[493] William Baldwin SJ.

[494] Otto, son of Maurice, Landgrave of Hesse-Cassel. See *CSPV 1610–13*, 175.

[495] Elizabeth Dacres.

[496] Smith reported on 17 July 1611 that Elizabeth Dacres had got a licence 'to goe over', AAW A X, no. 92 (p. 261).

[497] Edward Bennett.

[498] Francis Hore and Anthony and Robert Dormer.

[499] Samuel Harsnett.

[500] Newsletters written in July and August informed More that sixty Catholics in Midhurst had been summoned to take the oath, thirty in Easebourne, and all the Catholics in Battle, AAW A X, no. 110. According to Birkhead, in October a certificate of ninety refusers of the oath at Midhurst had been 'given to his maiestie', though they were all of the 'poorer sort', AAW A X, no. 136 (p. 390).

[501] William Wyborne, who died on 31 January 1612, PRO, E 368/545, mem. 122c.

duty to my l. Prim.[502] to whome I write long since. and my commendations to m^r Nicol[503] F. Ansel m^r Isham.[504] stay D. Thornels coming hither for it will prove pleasing nether to him self nor to others. Thus with my hartiest to your self I bid you adeiu 7 of Iuly. yours ever

R. oronte

(On p. 238)

Addressed: Al Illustre Signor. Signor mio observandissimo Tomaso Moro *Endorsed*: Iuly. 7. 1611. Oron

18 *John Ratcliffe (Mush) to Thomas More (19 August 1611. The date is taken from the endorsement)   (AAW A X, no. 105, pp. 307–8. Holograph. Printed nearly entire in TD IV, pp. clxxvi–xxxi)*

R^d S.^{r}

And my muche respected frend. I received yours written Anno d: 1611 [altered from '1610'] feb. the Kal of Iuly. 1610 [sic for '1611']. since which I received none from you to my selfe. yett have I seene some of yours to other our frends. we suffer greate difficultie in sending to you & receiving from you. And verie often our watchefull frends intercept bothe yours and ours for they ar more vigilant in this evil office than the heretiks. they have their hierlings for this purpose in france, flanders Italy & Rome. I wrote to you about Michelmas 1610 touching what I had conselled in the oathe[505] but I knowe not whether our frends sent it, or not, or whether you received it or no. my desire was to certifie you of the whole matter that you might knowe how to answere for me against the calumniations of our adversaries, which I doubted not would be most diligent to slander & calumniate me, wher they had farr worse

---

[502] Cardinal Edward Farnese.

[503] Nicholas Fitzherbert.

[504] Christopher Isham.

[505] For John Mush's explanation of his views about whether a Catholic might take the oath of allegiance, see AAW A IX, no. 71 (18 September 1610), a letter to Paul V enclosing a formula which he says is approved by many Jesuits and Benedictines. John Jackson said that Mush had written to him that 'diverse gentlemen proposed unto him a maner of swearing and asked his advise thearin which he delivered to some of them verbatim' but Richard Holtby SJ and others, to stir up trouble, have censured him 'after their old fashion' and 'm^r Holtby hath written 10 reasons against it', AAW A IX, no. 125 (p. 395); AAW A X, no. 16. On 30 May 1611 Birkhead wrote to More that although Cardinal Pompeo Arrigoni, 'the secretarie as yow terme him of the holy office', had instructed that all English Catholics must absolutely reject the oath of allegiance, Birkhead had sent More 'of late by the way of Bruxels a longe Letter [AAW A X, no. 56] from m^r Mush' to Arrigoni to be delivered at More's discretion, AAW A X, no. 51 (p. 125). (Arrigoni had been a friend to the appellants in Rome in 1602, AAW A VIII, no. 88; Law II, 10. In 1612 he favoured the appointment of bishops for England, Conway *AH* 23, 41.)

deserved them selves. for their cheefest meane to hinder our good desires & petitions, is by defayming us here but principally wher you ar. In that business I neither knowe nor heare as yett but that I did which may easely be iustified which was this, for perhaps you received not my formar. Aboute Michaelmass 1610 ther was terrible a doe about the oath every wher, but this persecution (as it ever haith bene) was more hote in yorkeshire & the northe, than elswhere[.] And even so it is at this present by reason of a new proclamation to tender the oath most diligently[506] to all catho: without exception or delay. In truth catho: were never in like terrour & frights as then, & are now. neither man nor woman knowing which way to turne them, or how to avoide utter ruine of them selves & posteritie. In this wofull confusion & desperation, divers of the best catho: in yorkshire desirous by any lawful meanes to save them selves bothe from temporall subversion, & spiritual damage of soule devised waies how they might both satisfie the king in taking an oath of temporall allegeance, & not offend God by any unlawful oathe. which they thought might be done, if first before they tooke the kings oath, they made this protestation. I will take this oath so farfurth onely as it concerneth my temporall dutie or obedience to the king. after which they thought they might kneele downe & take the oath verbatim. In this matter they asked fa: Tho. Steavensons[507] an old Iesuite sent lately from Rome his opinion whether they might in conscience take the oath thus or no: He (as they say) an old vertuous & learned Iesuit (for I knowe hime not) answered they might sweare thus without sinne. Thus upon his resolution they stood prepared to sweare when the magistrate called. But before they were cited to appeare, it fortuned that I was sent by m^r Archpriest[508] into the northe to compound certaine scandalous contentions which m^r samuel[509] a Benedic: of the Italian congregation (which we find more troublesome than the spanishe.) had rased against some of our most vertuous bretheren m^r Ogle & m^r Trolop.[510] passing by

---

[506] Larkin and Hughes, no. 118 (proclamation of 31 May 1611).

[507] See Anstr. I, 335; Foley I, 471–5. Stevenson had expressed extreme views (written in a manuscript tract for Robert Catesby) on the allowability of the deposition of monarchs, J.P. Sommerville, *Politics and Ideology in England, 1603–1640* (1986), 71.

[508] George Birkhead.

[509] Samuel (Bartholomew) Kennett OSB.

[510] See **Letter 15**. By 20 August 1612, when Mush penned an impassioned letter to Birkhead defending himself, Trollop had attacked Mush for being of the same mind concerning the oath as George Blackwell (though Mush claimed that he had never expressly declared his opinion in the matter) and for lenity towards his penitents who were not prepared to affirm Rome's line on the oath. Mush admitted he knew them 'resolved to yeld the state satisfaction of theire alleadgeance to his Maiestie even in the question of deposition, which the[y] held but an opinion, & yet undecyded by tha Church'; nevertheless he felt able to give them the sacraments 'upon theire extrinsicall principels, albeit theire opinion weare repugnant to the intrinsicall whereon I might settle

thes gentilmens houses, they propounded the question to me also: my answere was, that, I thought they could not lawfully sweare with that-protestation, & that I thought the Iesuit was deceived in his opinion, bycause the act of swearing to the whole oathe verbatim after that protestation, did contradict & reverse what they had before protested in words. & so their protestation was in vaine, for that after it they tooke the whole oath.

what remedy then said they. God knoweth quoth I. Then they propounded an other invention. What <u>if, when the magistrate dothe tender us the oath</u>, we pray him that we may heare it readd or that we may privately read it our selves. without making any signe or shewe of swearing or reverence at all. And after we have hard it readd say. <u>This oath contayneth</u> many difficult points which we do not understand (as in truth ther be as many divers expositions of every parte therof, as ther be heades emong us) but to so muche of it onely as doth truly concerne our temporall alleageance to the King we will & do sweare sincerely & willingly. & without more a doe kneele downe & lay their hand upon the booke. To this my answere was (salvo SS^{mi} D. N. iudicio) that I thought it might be lawfully done. bycause in this manner they tooke not the oath verbatim. nor no more therof, but so muche onely in generall tearmes, as concerned meere temporal alleageance. And if the magistrate would yett descend to particulars & aske what the points were which they meant of, Then I tould them that they should specifie That they acknowledged him to be their lawful king. 2. That they would kepe faith & tru allegeance to him, 3. That they would defend him against all his Enimies, 4. that they would discover all treasons &c. my reason for approving this manner was, bycause by thes generall tearmes they sweare onely temporal allegeance, & by the same excludid all other matters conteyned in the oath.[511] And I tould them that surely the magistrate would say that swearing onely thus, they excludid all poynts in the oath which concerned the popes authoritie, & would never admitt them thus to sweare[.] And so it proved in deed. for they would admitt no mans oath in this manner so that no harme is come of my advise, suppose it had bene unlawful. Yett not standing upon my owne iudgement herein, I propoundid the case to manye of the secular & religious, & the most of them were of my opinion. I ever condemned the whole oath, & have opposed as muche against it, & the approvers of it, as any in England. And my

my selfe'. In any case, he knew that, if he rejected them, they would simply find another priest, AAW A XI, no. 139 (p. 385).

[511] In October 1611 Champney told More that Mush recommended people not to 'take the oathe proposed but only by occasione of the oathe offered to sweare a temporall and civil obedience to our kinge as dothe evidently appeare by the thinge yt self', AAW A X, no. 132 (p. 379).

owne onely brother & sister aged folks almost 70. ar condemned to perpetual prison, & have suffered utter shipwracke of lands & goods, for refusing this oath. which irreparable damage peculiar onely to them emong all catho: of England [p. 308] (for none have suffered losse of all but onely they) I could have averted easely with one word to them, if I had houlden (as the Iesuits slander me) the oath to be lawful. I perceive by m^r Nelson,[512] that you have had long that which I sent under my hand in this matter (which I purposely did to prevent all mistaking & calumniating that I had done worse then I did) [word deleted] & that you feared I knowe not what how it would be taken & censured. but of the event I heare nothing at all. This I assure you, here is greate division & varietie of opinions aboute this oathe & sore pressing all to take it. those flie that can escape, & appeare not but this muche exasperateth the king. & some sharp course is expected to bring all to the stand. you ar happie you see not thes calamities. paule quite undooeth this poore churche, by depriving it of ordinarie pastors, by which our saviour appoynted all particular churches to be governed. verely here is nothing but most lamentable confusion debats & factions emong bothe clergy & people[.] And every day much worse then other, whiles everie one is left to them selves, & none to governe or to have care of the whole. we ar all immediately under paule. He is farr absent, can he then with saifetie of his owne sowle keepe this charge without sending & appointing some other bisshops in his place to minister necessaries unto so greate a people. if he can do this, then surely may he in like manner be sole bisshope him selfe over all Europe & deprive all nations of their ordinarie pastors. if I were with you, thus muche surely would I tell him. Our miseries ar greater by his denying us necessaries, & reformation of our colleges, than by the persecutions of he[re]tiks. At Doway they expell our most towardly young priests 3 at a clapp,[513] & this without crime. Singleton & Snatchepole[514] in their furie will have it so. Here was by the Iesuits & Benedic: exceding Ioie & insultation at the emptie returne of D.S.[515] He haith therby discomforted all his bretheren, & muche discontented them. You send us no word how D. Bissh. letters & myne were accepted by his Ho:[516] & the protectours[517] & Card. Arigone.[518] will they

---

[512] John Jackson.
[513] See **Letter 16**.
[514] John Knatchbull.
[515] Richard Smith.
[516] See AAW A IX, no. 71 (Mush's letter of 18 September 1610 to Paul V).
[517] Cardinals Farnese and Bianchetti. AAW A X, no. 106 (endorsed 'Redditae Novemb. 1611') is Mush's letter of 26 August concerning the oath directed to the vice-protector Bianchetti. On 26 February 1612 Birkhead wrote to More that 'm^r mush hath don verie well', *i.e.* in opposing the oath, 'ever since m^r farinton [Edward Bennett] and I gott him to write that Letter' to Bianchetti, AAW A XI, no. 25 (p. 64).
[518] AAW A X, no. 56 is Mush's letter to Cardinal Arrigoni of 30 May 1611.

have no pittie on us? you still harpp of uniting & combinyng. we were so, as you may see by the voices. but what avaleth this? Surdis canimus. what can be done against the clinkars before their reasons be hard & confuted. If Barcley & widdrington be not soundly confuted ther books will do muche harme in that point. The Iesuits reporte that paule haith prohibited all here to give the Kinge any oathe of temporall allegeance unless it be first approvid at Rome. This <u>scandalizeth all sortes of Catho: excedingly</u> <u>that he</u> should so litle regard our afflictions. for they looked rather his Ho: should have sent them a lawful oath of alleagence which every one might have had in readiness at all assaies & wherby ther might have bene conformitie emong us: than to forbid a lawful thing we being in so greate extremities, & our meanes of sending to Rome so litle & so difficult or rather impossible till all be undone. The axe is over our heades, to fall if we refuse, & we must send to Rome. o how great care whether we perishe or be saife. But I & other can not beleeve his Ho: commanding us to obey him as our king will forbid to give him an oath of temporal allegeance. sure it is some fiction of the religious to dishonor his Ho: & trouble our staite. for it is not likely he would forbid a thing wherin few or none ['will' deleted] thinke them selves bound to obey him. & thus we ar enforced to defend his Ho: honor in this pointe. Here be no newes but a contynewall increase of persecution, & an hourely expectation of greater miseries abowt this infortunate oathe. for the tyme appointed is now at hand. the catchepoles increase their numbers. the prisons at london ar ful of priests. Great almesses ar given, but they vanishe owt of the Archpriest secular priests & prisoners sight, none of us can tell what becometh of them. some great summes ar now & then intercepted as they passe over, & then the religious will not acknowledg them to be sent by them. though we all thinke the contrarie. God forgive them that will send monye out of this poore realme[.] I wishe my selfe manye tymes with you that wee might have an absolute answere whether paule will do us any good or no. remember mee to mr Nic: fitz. & most kindly to your selfe I have me recommended & rest ever your most assured Rat. 19 Aug. 1611.

At the same tyme <u>fa: Nicol Smith</u>[519] <u>Iesuit held that the whole oath</u> might be taken <u>with</u> equivocation, bycause he thought no parte <u>of it was</u> against faith. [one line deleted.] for the clinkars. it is an odious matter for mr Archp. to deale in. it will scandalize muche & breed greater trouble & Schisme, if they be any way punished before their actions be convinced to be evill their reasons hard & confuted, & they found obstinate & incorrigible. the Iesuits may best steale [?] & be doers in this odious matter as they have bene & are in all other. a dio.[520]

---

[519] Nicholas Smith SJ.
[520] This paragraph was presumably intended as an addition to the preceding text, perhaps within the passage on Thomas Stevenson SJ, but no precise indication is given.

when I had written thus farr, I was called for to meete our R. Superior[521] ther with him & other Assistants to consult about proceding with the clinkars according to his Ho: mandatum. which business we have done as you shall heare. then & never before truly I saw certane lettres of yours touching the calumnie rased against me in Rome of defending or approving the k. oath. by your writing I perceive muche adoe is made of it. which I marvell at considering in expresse words I condemned in that note & ever, the taking of the whole oath. And then in that necessitie gave onely my opinion for taking some lawful pointes in it. till suche tyme as his Ho: might be asked his iudgement therin & expressely saing that if he should not like it both I would & all ought to conforme our iudgements to his. my opinion was never put in practize, nor ever will. besids I never hard of it since, nor any matter was made here about it. but onely by the Iesuits who doing worse them selves yett laboure all they can to defame us here & more with you. I never defendid it but was & still am most desirous to knowe what his Ho: iudgeth of it. his iudgement god willing shall ever be myne in this & all other. And therfore you need not doubt of temeritie in me or any the least swarving from the sea Apostolike. yett cannot I stay the malice of calumniating tounges. Truly I muche commend your most diligent & painful labours in our affaires. would to God D. S.[522] had done soe. It comforteth us that you have hope of some good. I have smale yett more than I had this morning, upon reading many of your letters. I would I were with you a while. I write often out of the north but whether they here send them or not I can not learne, it seemeth you receive none of myne. for I write verbatim to you all I did or said of the oath in winter last. a dio. saving any quarrel, that you forbeare to write & admonishe me your old frend, bycause you are Iunior.[523] non sta bene tra noi

No address

Endorsed: (1) (in margin of p. 307) Ratclif alias Mushe
(On p. 308)
        (2) Recea. Oct. 28: frid
            Answea: Oct: 30. sond
        (3) Aug. 19. 1611. Ratcl. (in different hand) alias Mushe.

---

[521] George Birkhead.
[522] Richard Smith (?).
[523] By May 1612 Mush was instructing More 'to lett that busines of my opinion touching the oath...die rather then further to stirr in it', AAW A XI, no. 71 (p. 207).

19 *John Jackson to [Thomas More] (No date (8 November in text)*
   [1611])   (AAW A X, no. 177, pp. 485–6. Holograph)

my very Reverend and worthely beloved S^r

   I am ashamed th*a*t we hold noe better correspondence w*i*th yo*w*
then wee doe, but yow know the difficulties we travayle in, and I am
much afrayed wee shall have a sharp winter wh*i*ch is already begun
w*i*th some stormes. m^r [sic] vaux her howse surpriz'd, her alter taken
and 2. Iesuites m^r Io. percy & one m^r Hart.⁵²⁴ D. Bish. is in th*e*
Gatehowse, m^r Martin⁵²⁵ & other 13 preists in Newgate, many in th*e*
Clink th*a*t are noe Iurors as m^r Coll. m^r Leak,⁵²⁶ m^r Kenian, m^r
Haynes⁵²⁷ ['all' deleted] m^r stamford⁵²⁸ as I take it an Assistant. much
mischeef by pursuivants, in th*e* citie and country. we greiv and groan
to think th*a*t his hol. shewes soe litle co*m*passion of ow*r* afflictions as
not to co*m*forth us w*i*th th*e* graunt of any one petition thowgh never
soe iust. but if we wear united wee shold have any thing. first it is a
slaunder if any give owt th*a*t wee are at variance. 2^{ly} wee have made
some iust suites wh*i*ch require neyther consent nor knowledge of any
other bodie, as the repealing of th*a*t Breif against th*e* proceeding of
doctours, though they have the voyces of the unive*r*sities whearin they
have studied and done their acts.⁵²⁹ what a disgrace is this not only to
us but to any unive*r*sitie in christendome th*a*t if an Inglish preist banish'd
his country or wearied by long persecution & willing to retyre himselfe
awhile, or otherwise drawen to goe to some unive*r*sitye & thear live
orderly & studiously, doe all his acts w*i*th applause and be thowght

---

⁵²⁴ See **Letter 20**.

⁵²⁵ Thomas Martin, secular priest. He had in June 1611 composed a memorial on the
need to reform the secular clergy's low educational standards, AAW A X, nos 68, 69.
Cuthbert Trollop alleged, without supporting evidence, that Martin was a 'partaker' of
John Clinch's lax opinions (about the oath of allegiance and about occasional conformity),
AAW A X, no. 130 (p. 376).

⁵²⁶ Thomas Leek had been arrested in Gray's Inn 'by the benchers' on 27 March 1611.
He was taken to confer with Richard Sheldon in the Clink prison in the hope that
Sheldon would persuade him to take the oath of allegiance, AAW A X, no. 31 (p. 73).
His stance on the oath was doubtful. See **Letter 4**.

⁵²⁷ Joseph Haynes, secular priest, a close relative, possibly nephew, of John Bennett,
Anstr. II, 153; AAW A XVI, no. 162.

⁵²⁸ Ralph Stamford was arrested in early October 1611, TD IV, p. clxxxiii. (Curiously,
in June 1607, Stamford had been accused by Richard Blount SJ of allowing Catholics to
take the oath of allegiance and to attend Protestant churches, ARSI, Anglia 37, fo. 102v;
Foley VII, 1003.)

⁵²⁹ For the breve of Clement VIII of 19 September 1597 (NS) regulating whether and
how the English missionary clergy should proceed to the degree of doctor in continental
universities, see TD III, pp. cii–iv; CRS 51, 301–2; CRS 41, 53, 120–1. The degree of
doctor could not be conferred without a licence from the cardinal protector and the
approbation of the superior of the seminary. The removal of this restriction was one of
the seculars' principal aims.

worthy by the whole universitye to proceed, yet must this man stay, expect, make freinds, and sute to R. before he can have leave to proceed. wyll succeeding ages ever beleiv that such a breif shold be graunted owt by one of <u>an other bodie</u> his intercession, against the cleargy. and that his hol. wyll not see it recalld after soe many petitions, being made to know how uniust it is. <u>But his hol. did graunt that</u> it shold be repealed![530] <u>why is it not then? under officers can not be wrought. why shold not his hol.</u> be told soe much? yow know wee have many difficulties and enough to doe in studying cases, controversies scriptures etcetera to enable us to encounter with our adversaries who grow dayly more strong & able, having all meanes and encouragements, & also to confirme such as are owrs, Notwithstanding thease & many other buisinesses & difficulties yet must we spend tyme, and imploy all owr meanes in writing & suing to his holines, & after this obtayne nothing. surely if his hol. did truly understand & compassionate owr state wee thinke he shold rather at the first least notice of the iustnes of owr requests graunt them then eyther suffer us to imploy owr tyme & other ['men' deleted] abilities in renuing the same suites, or leave us without comforth in the middest of soe many discomforths. If owr requests did concerne them of an other bodie, or if they wear for any mans private interest then their might be reason to linger. but being meerly for the advancement of owr cleargy & consequently of Gods church, we can not but think it strange. Owr k. being a temporall prince useth all meanes to promote his cleargy and their cause. and it is much to see how his examples doe encourage them and advance learning. wee have many discouragements but noe encouragements but God himselfe. what I speake of this [sic] matters of Doctours is also understood of owr other requests of the colleges, <u>of sending insufficient men</u> to the great disgrace of our cleargy and scandall, besides the weakning of owr cause, of Bishops etcetera. If God had not rays'd yow & bestowed on yow an extraordinarie spirit, in what case had wee been ere this? Thear is a rumor that owr viceprotectour[531] wyll doe what he can to hinder the howse at parise. verely if I <u>wear thear I think I shold tell him, & his hol. also, that</u> noe <u>better service cold be done at this tyme for the hereticks, they wold</u> be thankfull to him for it, I warrant yow. Thear is some hoope of <u>m^r Alabaster yet, if</u> any place wear provided beyond seas in tuto loco, whear he shold not be sent for, and competent maintenance. he is much greived at his hol. for censuring

[530] Presumably Jackson refers to the modification of the breve, made as a result of Richard Smith's petition, concerning the attestation to be granted by the superior of the seminary, CRS 41, 53 n. 5, 120 nn. 15–18. Anthony Champney, about to proceed doctor at the Sorbonne, gained a licence from the cardinal protector through Geoffrey Pole's and Robert Ubaldini's good offices, AAW A XI, nos 64, 65; Conway *AH* 23, 97.

[531] Cardinal Lawrence Bianchetti.

his booke,[532] and tells strange storyes of the Ies. surely it is pittie that wee have noe more care of keeping such men. [p. 486] we see what means our adversaries make to get them from us and thearby much disadvantage owr cause. O how Heresie insults upon such an occasion. at the report of a Higgens or an Alabasters coming back litle think they at Rome how much owr poore church is scoffed at, and weak ones scandaliz'd. I imagine if this wear told them, we shold have exhortations & good lessons of patience etcetera. but in the mean tyme religion goes to decay and unles his hol. take some more regard, that remnant of cath: which are in owr country will grow to a small numbre, & remedies wyll be thowght upon perhaps when the disease is desperate. Doe but consider how few sonnes pay the statute whose fathers did, how few keep preists whose parents did and yow shall find that prests (such as they are increase) and Cath. decrease. they are soe conceyted that at Rome on the one side and among the Ies. on the other, the greatest respect is had to matters of pollicie as they begin to turne polliticks with the rest. they call to mynd that when the Appeall was followed unles they had been cowntenanced with the k. of France they had done litle good thowgh their cause was most iust. and diverse such instances of the proceeding against D. Bish. & M^r charn: and the like do work noe good effects in our country. when I think seriously of thease things my hart akes to think what our country wyll come unto with [sic for 'without'] Gods speciall providence. Good S^r labour to enforme his hol. & to move him to loke this way with compassionable eye. The savoy Imbassadour[533] went to the Court this day which is the 8^ve of all saints[534] but because thear is a report of a cross match concluded between france & spayne it is thowght he shall not speed, some think if our prince might have had a daughter of spayne, this wold have gone forward, but I can write nothing certayne, thear is a report that they look to match the La: Eliz: her grace with the now king of spayne.[535] Thear hath been hear one Caussabon a Humanist & linguist invited owt of France by our k. and well enterteynd[536] who hath published a booke Against the Apollogie for the Iesuites written in French, it is by

---

[532] William Alabaster, *Apparatus in Revelationem Iesu Christi* (Antwerp, 1607). This book was declared heretical by the Roman Inquisition in January 1610, ARCR I, no. 5.

[533] Claudio di Ruffia, Count of Cartignana.

[534] McClure, 313; *CSPV 1610–13*, 241.

[535] *CSPV 1610–13*, pp. xiii, 254.

[536] John Jackson had previously noted Isaac Casaubon's receipt of a Canterbury prebend at James's direction worth £100 annually. Also, Sir Henry Savile 'who is setting forth S. Chrisost. in Greek sent his coach severall tymes for him (as I was told) to goe to windsour whear the bookes are in printing and whear D. [Andrew] Downes & the best grecians are togither', AAW A IX, no. 125 (p. 395); *cf.* Milton, *Catholic and Reformed*, 354 n. 121.

way of an Epistle to Fa. Fronto Duceus a Iesuite of name in paris.[537] whear he is very sharp against diverse of their writers about the doctrine of deposition & the powder plott, but most of all he seemes to inveigh against Andreas Eudemo Ioannes.[538] thowgh Bellar:[539] and others have their shares al[so]. it stands them upon to reply. if I thowght it wear opereprecium I wold relate the cheif particulers, but I think it wear fit that yow shold have such bookes sent to note owt such things as they observe in owr writers which breed the most scandall & that they might be avoyded as much as may be. satis, saith he in the last leaf, ah plus satis studio partium utrinque hactenus est datum.[540] wtherin I fear me he saith too true, fear me? nay I see it, & sorrow it. Assure Bellar. that an answer is expected both to the first booke of the Bish: of Ely[541] (for as for the second[542] I can say litle) and also to mr withringtons[543] or els it wyll much redound to their discredit & leave diverse staggering at the least. the Bish. goeth branch after branch to shew how the oath may be taken in a sence allowed by Cath. & though thear be in his booke both impious impertinent and idle stuff, yet thear be many things which some doe stand upon. It is an idle conceipt to think that mr withr: booke was done by mr Blackwell. Noe. Noe. it hath an other maner of proceeding.

No address

Endorsed: (at top of p. 485) 'shewing cleargies most uniust oppression'.

20 *George Salvin (Birkhead) to Thomas More (18 November 1611)*   *(AAW*
    A X, no. 147, pp. 413–16. Holograph)

my verie good Sr, I have alredie written unto yow, how one told me upon your puttinge fa persons wordes to be Censured, that all the laitie

---

[537] Casaubon replied to [Pierre Coton] *Response Apologetique a l'Anticoton* (Paris, 1610) with his *Isaaci Casauboni ad Frontonem Ducaeum S.J. Theologum Epistola* (1611). See Milward II, 119–28. Enclosed with this letter of Jackson to More was AAW A X, no. 178 (observations on the controversy between Casaubon and Fronton du Duc SJ).

[538] Andreas Eudaemon Joannes SJ, who had defended Henry Garnet in *R.P. Andreae Eudaemon-Ioannis.. Apologia pro R.P. Henrico Garneto Anglo* (Cologne, 1610), replied to Casaubon with *R.P. Andreae Eudaemon-Ioannis, Cydonii e Societate Iesu Responsio ad Epistolam Isaaci Casauboni* (Cologne, 1613).

[539] Cardinal Robert Bellarmine SJ.

[540] Casaubon, *Isaaci Casauboni ad Frontonem Ducaeum*, 171.

[541] Andrewes, *Tortura Torti.*

[542] Andrewes, *Responsio.*

[543] Preston, *Apologia Cardinalis Bellarmini.*

wold forsake us, and leave us destitute of all helpe.[544] this was not of himselfe, but he had it from beyonde the seas. for my part I shall relie upon godes providence, and wishe that everie man may be respected accordinge to his desertes. but no man I thinke can iustly blame yo*w* for that, so many heare groundinge upon those wordes, the lawfullnes of the oath. but his frendes are angry supposinge it com*m*eth of splenne, in w*h*ich sense I cannot beleve yo*w* wold do it. they may see as much don to m*r* Mush, and yet they will not say we do it of malice to him. his hol saieth in plaine terms the oath may not be taken with any restriction: the foresaid father seameth to averre the Contrarie, whose credit yo*w* know is greater in this Land then the credit of xx such as yo*w* and I. who can then blame either of us for craving direction in that matter.

yt seameth they are moved, and feare that some advantadge may be taken against them. a yeare since one wrote to me that m*r* broughton should say that m*r* Lister was of opinion that the oath might be taken accordinge to the Limitation set downe by his m*a*ies*t*ie in his book: but I above a yeare agoe intreated D bavan to lerne the truth of that matt*er*, m*r* broughton now com*m*eth after all this tyme, and writeth unto me that he never said so: ['whether' deleted] wheras in verie deed he uttered as much to m*r* beniamin,[545] as I thinke he hath alredie written unto yo*w*. but it is best for us to Lett them alone, for otherwise we shalbe accounted factious and busie. yet in a thinge so apparantly true, me thinks I am loath to yeeld. aske Counsell of our frendes, what

---

[544] More had recently written to Birkhead that he 'had given fa persons his wordes about the oath to be censured' by the Inquisition, which caused Birkhead some anxiety, AAW A X, no. 146 (p. 411), though Edward Bennett and Robert Pett were delighted, AAW A X, no. 148, XI, no. 5. The book censured was Persons's *Iudgment of a Catholicke English-Man*, CRS 41, 122–3. In January 1610 Birkhead had got Geoffrey Pole (returning to Rome with More) to take one of Persons's books, presumably the *Iudgment*, to give to Smith, and informed Smith that an offensive passage in it, which More had previously copied out for Smith's use, was being cited by the priests in the Clink to justify their own position in favour of the oath, AAW A IX, nos 1, 7. (AAW A VIII, no. 205 is a memorandum concerning priests who had justified their taking of the oath of allegiance by citing Persons's *Iudgment*.) However there is also in AAW A X a memorandum (AAW A X, no. 165) received by More on 22 December 1611 (NS) entitled 'Doctrina P*a*tris Personii Iesuitae in libro excuso in lingua vulgari Anglicana, cui Tit*u*lus est Tractatus ad mitigandum', *i.e.* Persons's *Treatise tending to Mitigation* (St Omer, 1607) which More may have used subsequently to bolster his case. It listed and quoted certain passages that could be taken to allow the oath of allegiance. Since there is in AAW a submission from Richard Smith dated 20 December 1611 (NS) in defence of his book against Thomas Bell (*An Answer to Thomas Bels late Challeng*), AAW A X, no. 164, More was probably presenting the case against Persons in context of a justification of Smith; see **Letter 11**. In May 1612 Birkhead said he had heard a rumour that Smith's book was 'putt againe into the inquisition, in revenge of that w*h*ich was don to fa persons', AAW A XI, no. 82 (pp. 233–4).

[545] Benjamin Norton.

is our best to do in such cases. fa whyte[546] [word deleted] gott the
victorie of his adversaries with patience, and so must we do, Lett them
say what they will. yf yo*w* saw what iuggling ther hath ben about this
oth [?], yo*w* wold say ['I' deleted] we have had good cause to demande
direction.

me thinkes I forsee that we shall have great Contradiction in our
suit for bb. the religiouse cannot abide it, for that they feare to have
some matters ripped up w*hi*ch they have no list to heare of. Some are
discontented partly being addicted to them, and partly emulous of
those w*hi*ch are no*mi*nated by us because them selves are Left owt.
these especially are those beyond the sea. but who hindreth them to
put up a petition, or to no*mi*nate such as they like. yf yo*w* knew how
some w*hi*ch hold the oth to be lawfull, little care for any thinge that I
can do, yo*w* might easily persuade our Superiors to herken to that suit.
I send yo*w* ['hereinclosed' deleted] by m^r bakers[547] means a letter[548]
sent me out of the north. [p. 414] by yt yo*w* shall perceyve both how
difficult a charge is imposed upon me and also how necessarie it is for
this poore church, to have some greater autoritie amongst us. yt is no
matter yf yo*w* shew it to the viceprotector,[549] he may see therbie how
confidently [word deleted] we deale within, that neither spare one or
other for the zeale we have to the Sea Apostolique. but I leave it to
you*r* owne better consideration. I told yo*w* in my other Letters that
m^res vaux[550] her house was searched by order from the Counsell,[551] and
that two Iesuites m^r fisher[552] and m^r hart[553] were found there. now I am
to tell yo*w* that she [is] com*mi*tted to the fleete,[554] and they close
prisonners to the gatehouse and many do think that the one of them
shall be executed before c*hris*tenmasse. m^res vaux is a most constant

[546] John (Augustine) Bradshaw OSB.
[547] Richard Smith.
[548] Presumably Birkhead means the letter of Cuthbert Trollop to Birkhead, dated 10 October 1611, concerning the laxity of the Cassinese Benedictines in the northern counties, AAW A X, no. 130.
[549] Cardinal Lawrence Bianchetti.
[550] Elizabeth, widow of George Vaux. She was resident at Harrowden Hall, Northamptonshire.
[551] The search was, apparently, for John Gerard SJ, who was rumoured to have returned to England. *Cf.* **Letter 26**.
[552] John Percy SJ.
[553] Nicholas Hart SJ. For Hart's association with the gunpowder plotters, see M. Hodgetts, 'Shropshire Priests in 1605', *Worcestershire Recusant* 47 (1986), 24–36, at p. 29. According to Henry More SJ, the regime had no intention of prosecuting Hart and Percy for treason, Foley I, 171.
[554] Edward Bennett wrote to More on 26 December 1611 that Elizabeth Vaux had been freed because she had been 'begged' by Philip Herbert, first Earl of Montgomery, with whom she had evidently compounded for her offence, AAW A X, no. 166 (p. 458); McClure, 313; *Downshire MSS* III, 180–1.

gentlewoman and both zealous and wise and will I dowbt not deserve much honor both before god and man. in which course the L montague hath troden the path before her, albeit I perceyve by your Letters that some hath performed no charitable offices in denigratinge and diminishinge the honor dew unto him for so noble a confession. One S[r] steven Proctor of yorkshire condemned the last yere by parlament to the towre and Losse of his eares[555] (as it is said) havinge gotten his release by frendes, hath this terme accused certen yorkshire knightes to be guiltie of the powder treason as S[r] william inglebie, S[r] Iohn yorke, S[r] Iohn mallorie, and S[r] francis Trapps, who with there wives and servantes are all imprisoned some in one place and some in another.[556] they be all fearefull men and wise and therfor it is supposed that Little wilbe proved against them. it is also said that the iustice[557] and his sonne for there service in apprehendinge m[res] Vaux and those Iesuites shalbe knighted.[558] yow may gesse by all these circumstances in what miserie we are. the Iesuites are not so bold about the oth as some of myne, and the benedictins of the Italian Cong. for what soever they have don in secret, I cannot perceive that they do openly avouch yt. it much vexeth them that yow have delt so with fa pers. but albeit to my remembrance I did not provoke yow unto it, yet sith many grounded there opinion upon his wordes, I see not why either yow or I should be blamed. fa preston dealeth verie strangly about m[r] Samuel.[559] he beleveth all he saieth, and so do I of myne and therfor we shall never end the matter.[560] howbeit myne are resolved to be quiet and to trowble them selves no more: and yett he provoketh them much by contestinge against them still. I perceive some probabilities that the Iesuites would

[555] See E.R. Foster, *Proceedings in Parliament 1610* (2 vols, 1966), I, *passim*.

[556] Thomas Heath reported that these men were 'accused by s[r] Stephan Procter for receaving' John Gerard SJ 'after proclamation', AAW A X, no. 150 (p. 421). In April 1612 Richard Smith remarked that Heath had further informed him that three of Sir John Yorke's servants were imprisoned in the Tower and racked concerning the Gunpowder Plot and the harbouring of Gerard, though some people thought it was all on account of Yorke's words spoken against Scotsmen, AAW A XI, no. 66. (In February 1614 Procter was called in question over his accusations that Henry Howard, Earl of Northampton was not free of blame concerning the Gunpowder Plot, *Downshire MSS*, 351, allegations which were first made in 1612, *CSPD 1611–18*, 147; McClure, 508–9; C. Howard, *Sir John Yorke of Nidderdale* (1939), *passim*.)

[557] Gilbert Pickering of Titchmarsh.

[558] John Chamberlain, who reported that John Pickering was 'dangerously hurt' during the search, said the honour was bestowed on 10 November 1611, McClure, 313. *Cf. Downshire MSS* III, 180 (John Thorys's report to William Trumbull of 13 November 1611 that Pickering jnr was 'not dead nor the father knighted but brought into the Council, who thought it fit he should have some grace showed him to weigh down the disgrace that is wont to accompany this kind of service'). For Pickering snr's triumphant account of his 'servyce' and his knighthood, see BL, Additional MS 15625, fo. 3r.

[559] Samuel (Bartholomew) Kennett OSB.

[560] For Preston's defence of Kennett, see TD V, p. clxxiv.

faine be frendes, but are Loth to beginne. and for my part yf they wold keepe them selves with there owne bandes, I should not mislike it. because I see verie well, that we shall never have any thinge graunted, untill some such Course be taken. yow wrote unto me in one of your Last, that I should write unto his hol. and some one or two of the Card. as for his hol, I hope yow shall find two in my great packetes that will serve the turne, after my plaine fashion. as for the Card, I meane to write as soone as I shall fynd it requisite. Card. bellarmins book against berclaie[561] giveth us great satisfaction, and yf his grace wold please [p. 415] to do the like against witherington, it might worke exceedinge much good to the satisfaction of many. witherington of him selfe is knowen to be unable to write so lernedly, and to colour in such fit termes so bad a cause. but who it is that hath don it, as yet we cannot lerne. when I know it, yf he were my owne brother, I wold not forbeare to detect him. for in my poore opinion, his presumptuous spirit deserveth much correction. thus yow see I cannot but write unto yow for your better information, which yow may use discreetly to the helpe of our Cause. yet wold I have yow to do thinges in moderation, for otherwise as I have allredie signified, we may happe to loose many frendes of the better sort, which yow may easily conceive by the foresaid threatninge before mentioned. And so commendinge my selfe to your best devotions, and not forgettinge my dew rememberance of all service to your monsignor,[562] whome one of thes daies I meane to salute with a poore Letter, I leave yow to godes holy protection. this 18 of novemb. 1611.

your lovinge frend
  Geo Salvine
the Letter out of the north I have desyred m[r] baker to convey unto yow, for feare of makinge my packet to great. therfor yow shall expecte from him, in Companie this as I hope
(On p. 416)
Addressed: To his verie good frend m[r] Thomas moore give this. Rome.
Endorsed: (1) Rec. mond. febr. 13.⎤
                 Answ. wedn. febr. 15. ⎦ 1612
           (2) Novemb. 18. 1611. Sal.
           (3) Contentes A lay man threatning M[r] Archp[r] to forsake us moved from some on this side the seas because of the putting up of a book into the inquisition[.] my excuse. of m[r] Lister. contradiction in our suit for bb. the letter out of the north wishing if I thinke good to

---

[561] Cardinal Robert Bellarmine SJ, *Tractatus de Potestate Summi Pontificis in Rebus Temporalibus. Adversus Gulielmum Barclaium* (Rome, 1610), answering Barclay, *De Potestate Papae*. Birkhead informed More in early 1612 that Bellarmine's book had helped to persuade John Mush to oppose the oath of allegiance more vigorously, AAW A XI, no. 25.

[562] John Baptist Vives.

shew it to the viceprot. of M^rs vaulx and the Ies taken in her house. of my Lo. noble confession[.] the foure knightes accused by s^r stephen Proctor. the Ies not soe bold about the oath. ther il taking of the book prefering to the Inquisition. of m^r Br. dealing in m^r Sam. case. of the Ies. desire to be frendes. of his writing to his ho. and some one or two of the Card. Card Bell. book against Berclay liked and wished an answer against withrington. promise to write to our Monsignor.

21 *George Lea (Birkhead) to Thomas More (15 December 1611)*   *(AAW A X, no. 160, pp. 441–2. Holograph)*

my verie Rev good S^r, it is now so longe since I hard from yow, and I have written so often, that I beleve I am now even with yow in your nomber of Letters, yf mine be safely come unto yow. I have had such checkes of late concerninge your puttinge fa pers. wordes to be censured,[563] that I feare some false measure. yett yf yow communicated the matter first to our vicepr.[564] as it seameth yow did, it will helpe the matter well. I could wish yow to take heede how farre yow deale with vives. the vicep. meant somethinge when he advised yow to the contrarie, a yonge Carmelite called m^r dowghtie[565] here in London sendeth me word that your monsignour[566] is wholly crossed in his designes, and therfor I feare yow cannot gett any great favour in dealinge with him though yow fynd some perticular releife. yet this forenamed Carmelite assureth me that his superiors favour your monsignour much, and he offereth me to write unto them in our behalfe, for that vives is now altogether bent (as he saieth) to convert his charitie to the furtherance of our countrie. which Courtesie I could verie well ['like' deleted] like of, but that I feare the issue therof.

   It is not amisse yf yow move his hol in my name to give me as ample faculties as the religiouse have viz that I may give to some of myne facultie to give a plenarie unto them when they heare firste confession: item the same to them whome they heare in there death bed. because these prerogatives draw away our ghostly children; and the last cause is the disposition of some pious worke to fall into there handes. I know not whether I have these faculties or no. I have all that m^r blackwell had. but [word deleted] I am not sure whether he had these or no.

---

[563] See **Letter 20**.
[564] Cardinal Lawrence Bianchetti.
[565] Thomas Doughty alias or *vere* Dawson, whose name in religion was Simon Stock, Anstr. II, 83.
[566] John Baptist Vives.

In declaring this matter[567] to m^r blac: and the rest of the clink I have don what I can, and more then I need, upon so slender a commission. so it is accounted. I have written to my Assistantes of it, that they may admonish all both clerkes and laickes in there circuites. yow have the copie I hope by this.[568] my selfe hathe told diverse of all sortes of it. and finally I have in particular written to m^r blackwell as a frend in private therof. which he hath taken verie unkyndly at my handes, sainge that but for that letter he neded not to have taken any notice of yt. but he careth little, and as I am told, runneth on his course as he did. yet yow see I have don with my great daunger what lay in me. I heare not as yet of any exception, which the magistrate taketh against me. I am told that m^r <u>Sheldon and Colier are gon to church</u>. master warmington is confined to his brothers in dorsetshyre, and there I warrant yow for all this declaration, will practise his faculties. yet it hath don much good. for both m^r Charnock and others doe stagger, and they say, are redie to relent. for my part I shalbe ever redie to shew my self obedient to the sea Apostolique. m^r blackwell thinketh yow his great frend, and pretendeth to have other intelligence from yow, but I beleve nether him, nor those that tell me so.

The matter in the north betwene my fellowes and the benedictines goeth not so well as I could wish. yet have I don what lieth in me to appeese them. m^r Preston and I were to be arbitratours in the matter. we made choyce I of m^r mush[569] and he of don Augustino alias Smith[570] to heare the matter and we charged them to do no more but to take in writinge what they said [p. 442] and without further interrogatories to send it to us. when they mett, Don Augustino beinge somewhat of an hote spirit wold not heare them but upon there othes, which formall course for my part I did not intende. my frendes were unwillinge, but at the last m^r mush perswaded them unto it. herupon they sett downe there informations upon there oathes; which maketh them on both sides to stand so stifly to there assertions, that I see no end. whereupon I beinge greeved at that kynd of proceedinge, wrote to fa preston, that the best way to <u>end the matter</u> were to enioyne them, he m^r Samuel[571] and I those which are <u>subiect to</u> me, to silence and to burie the matter, and ech one to looke to his owne vocation without any further exceptions of one against another. which in myne opinion is the onely way for peace. which course yf it be not observed I have told m^r preston that I will deale no more therin. Now commeth m^r Samuell againe with a replie to m^r Trollops and m^r Ogles last replie. m^r Preston wold have

---

[567] *i.e.* that oath-favouring priests were deprived of their missionary faculties.

[568] See AAW A X, no. 101.

[569] See **Letter 18**.

[570] Edmund (Augustine) Smith OSB.

[571] Samuel (Bartholomew) Kennett OSB.

me to read it, which I denye, because this way of writinge will discover
all in the end to the enemie, and prove scandalous and preiudicial to
the whole contrie. he taketh this verie evil at my handes (as I am told)
and giveth out great wordes[.] what he will do I know not, but this
discourse I make to yow, that yf he make any compleint there, yow
may be able to certefie our protector of my doinges, which I still take
to be the best course for peace. and hereunto I have wonne both m^r
mush and m^r Troll. and m^r Ogle. onely m^r Crawforth[572] will needes
prosecute the action against Samuel. and therfore of Late hath moved
me to ioyne with the padri[573] in that respect, or els to give him licence
to use what means he can there with our superiors. the first I like not.
the latter way I have graunted him. because he appelinge to our
superiors, I dare not resist him. yf yow heare of any such suit, yow
neede not take notice thereof, unlesse his frendes and sollicitors impart
it unto yow, and then yow may deale accordingly as yow shall fynde it
most convenient for our cause.

the b of Canturb[574] hath gotten a copie of the precept[575] yow sent me
about those of the Clink, they say he had it from paris. but I hope they
will make no great matter of it, because it is so slenderly autorised. one
day I meane to send yow a copie of my letter to m^r blackwell[576] who
still holdeth that the pope is not well informed. the pursivantes are
intollerably busie. no catholique can passe in the street this Last terme,
but they will force him to ransome himselfe, or els carrie him to a
magistrate to have the oath offered unto him.[577] no more, but desyringe
yow to commend us in your praiers, I leave yow to god this 15 of
decemb 1611.

your assured frend
    Geo. Lea.

m^r blackwell asked him which caried my letter unto him, for writinges
and seales, and said my commission had not therfor sufficient autoritie.
howsoever, he saieth, they may here the confessions of them which
have but venial sinns, and that he will do. yt semeth by him that yow
have written somewhat in there favour. for they will hardly beleve that

---

[572] Cuthbert Crayford. See **Letter 15**; AAW A XI, no. 82; **Letter 27**.
[573] The Jesuits.
[574] George Abbot.
[575] AAW A X, no. 189.
[576] No copy of this letter exists in AAW.
[577] Edward Bennett wrote on 26 December 1611 that the high commission pursuivants
now had more extensive powers than before (though cf. **Letter 1**). He said John Greaves
SJ had recently been arrested and had bought his freedom for £20, 'being taken for a
layman', AAW A X, no. 166 (p. 457).

yo*w* have written this to me. yo*w* were best to write unto them againe,
and tell them what daunger they are in.   m^r [sic]
No address
Endorsed: (on p. 441 in left hand margin at end) 'm^r moore'.

22 *Edward Kenion to [Thomas More] (2 March 1612 (NS))*   *(AAW A XI,*
no. 31, pp. 79–80. Holograph)

Rnd S.^{r} having heertofor beinge prisoner pr*e*sumed uppon no acquaintance to deliver you my pouer opinion concerning our English affaires
in an imperfecte letter,^{578} which I the*n* desired to conclude with some
more leasurable oportunitie I make my selfe the more bould at this
pr*e*sent allthough with the neglecte of that discurse to troble you with
matter more imp*e*rtinente. for my self [?] I latelie arrived at Paris where
I intende godwillinge to make my abode[.] wee were ['six' deleted] 6
in nu*m*ber banished vz my self out of the Clinke. & out of Newgate M^r
francis foster Mr Thomas wood.^{579} Mr Craford^{580} a moncke. Mr Green
alias forscu.^{581} Mr Whright^{582} who in his passage from St Sebastians
(where hee lived) in to flanders by misfortune was caste in at Portsmouth.
the means of our banishmente was by the duke of Savois Embassadoure,^{583} but the Archbush changed tow of those whom he begged[.]
Mr Blacwell died before my departure[.]^{584} he celebrated the same
morninge,^{585} and the afternoone passinge over the courte to M^r
heborne^{586} to be co*n*fessed tooke coulde com*m*inge to his chamber fell
in to a sounde, and within the space of tow howrs died. being demanded
by M^r warmingto*n* his iudgmente of the oath he answered that if he
hadd donne amisse hee cried god mercie but hee did (as he affirmed)
accordinge to his conscience. hee departed before hee hadd extreme-

^{578} This letter has not survived.
^{579} Not identified.
^{580} William (Maurus) Scott OSB. See Lunn, *EB*, 63.
^{581} Presumably Thomas Green OSB.
^{582} Richard Wright alias William Yarwell, secular priest, generally known as William
Wright.
^{583} Claudio di Ruffia. See *CSPD 1611–18*, 112. On 3 February 1612 Birkhead had
reported that the ambassador secured the release of 'm^r blunt, m^r Craford a benedictine
[William (Maurus) Scott OSB], m^r Foster, m^r warren, m^r Wright, and out of the Clinck
m^r kenion', AAW A XI, no. 13 (p. 35).
^{584} Blackwell died on 25 January 1612, AAW A XI, no. 7.
^{585} Birkhead had told More in August 1611 that Blackwell had no penitents, and 'saieth
masse, but never any with him save the partie that helpeth him. w*i*th secrecie he
observeth for feare of Canturburie [George Abbot]', AAW A X, no. 97 (p. 273).
^{586} Anthony Hebburn, secular priest.

unctione.[587] M[r] Sheldon is becom*m*e a most rep*ro*bate Apostata. hee hath painted his splinative spirite in a booke of his motives which hee intitleth the novell and hereticall rule of the Romaine faith.[588] feare. wante. Rancore and an overfloinge pride have brought him in to these desperate tearmes. M[r] Collier is in like man*n*er fallne and goeth to Church. M[r] Iohn Cople[589] to the greate grefe of his freindes increaseth the nu*m*ber of these forlorne me*n*: M[rs] moune with whome hee liveth hath beene the means of his overthrowe[.][590] finallie a waye is made and manie me*n* have loste shame[.] I feare we shall not easelie stope the gappe. M[r] warmington hath write*n* a booke in defence of the oath.[591] it is by som*m*e me*n* reasonablie liked. hee had a learned

---

[587] Birkhead told More at the beginning of February that 'it is thought by some that m[r] blac. called m[r] hebburne, and by others that he called for m[r] Colleton to be with him at his death', AAW A XI, no. 13 (p. 38). Birkhead thought, however, that it was Hebburn he called for 'in articulo mortis', 'whome he knew to have lost his faculties, havinge m[r] Colleton and others in that prison untowched in that kynd', AAW A XI, no. 25 (p. 65). So he showed no real remorse. He was 'conditionally penitent' only for his defence of the oath, AAW A XI, no. 26 (p. 68). Edward Bennett on 11 February 1612 sent More a narrative rather different in tone: Blackwell 'fell sick on the sodayn, m[r] collington [Colleton] & others beinge w*i*th hyme havinge newly been at confession w*i*th m[r] Hebbwrn: he desired m[r] Collington to forgive hym, and all the world besides he had offended. further he added for the book I have written I sayd nothing but what in my conscience I thought true: yeat if [I] have offended I am sorry for it, & desire to dye a child of the catholick church: w*i*thall [he] desired extreme unction. they went p*re*sently to supp*er* who were w*i*th hym, but before they came up agayn he was dead. he could never abyd Sheldon w*i*th the reste to come to his chamber, byddinge them avoid, ever calling of them columnas declinantes', AAW A XI, no. 17 (p. 45). In Paris, Anthony Champney also avoided harshness in narrating his death. Relying on Kenion and Francis Foster (a bitter opponent of SJ), he wrote that Blackwell died 'upon the co*n*versione of S[t] paul' and 'asked m[r] Colleton pardon for those thinges wh*i*ch hadd passed betwixt them about and since the appell and beinge asked of his proceedinges in the matter of the oathe sayd that he had donn nothinge agaynst his co*n*science, wherein notw*i*thstanding yf he had erred he desired pardon of god'. While Birkhead noted the providential suddenness of his death, Champney mentioned merely that 'he died without anie great sickness', AAW A XI, no. 29 (p. 75). For Roland (Thomas) Preston OSB's account of his death, see Preston, *A Theologicall Disputation concerning the Oath of Allegiance* (1613), 252–3. George Abbot reluctantly allowed Blackwell to be buried in a London churchyard, because he had been a 'frend to the state', AAW A XI, no. 13 (p. 38).

[588] Richard Sheldon, *The Motives of Richard Sheldon Pr.* (1612). He subsequently preached, on 29 March 1612, a Paul's Cross recantation sermon, published as *The First Sermon of R. Sheldon Priest, after his Conversion from the Romish Church* (1612).

[589] John Copley, secular priest.

[590] John Chamberlain had written on 29 January 1612 that Copley, a domestic chaplain to the second Viscount Montague, 'falling in love with an auncient Catholike maide...that attended the children, they have both left theyre profession and fallen to mariage', McClure, 331. According to Birkhead, 'the woman that seduced m[r] Copley was comended' by one 'm[r] byrd to the place where she was to be interteyned, and by the Jesuit wh*i*ch reconciled her to m[r] Copley him selfe, who by her allurementes is become an heretique', AAW A XI, no. 1 (p. 3).

[591] William Warmington, *A Moderate Defence of the Oath of Allegiance* (1612).

phisitions papers[592] and and [sic] all the helpe Mr Blacwell could yeld him. The heigh commission is strenthned with more ample aucthoritie. The pursivants appeale Catholickes of beste sorte in the streets to appeare before the bushops who minister them the oath[.] the[y] were never more busie. My Lorde Strange[593] immediatlie uppon his returne was called to appeare before the councell. the[y] tendred him the oath[.] hee required respecte[.] the[y] granted him time, and offered him Mr Blacwell to conferre with all, or if it pleased him to accept Canterburie or London.[594] The Bushoppe of Canter moved the kinge for the triall of Mrs Vaus and the tow Iesuits which were taken in herr howse but the kinge replied that hee hadd allreadie beene to forward to take bloode and woulde noe more: The Bushoppe allsoe was againste oure banishemente but the Treasurer overswaied him: he bendeth allsoe his whole strench againste doctor Bushoppe to keepe him in prison.[595] uppon my arrivall in france I tooke my yornaye towards dowaye by order from Mr Sack[596] doctor Bush. Mr Colling.[597] and Mr Nelson[598] to signifie unto him[599] their generall desire of the cleargie to intertaine his love. I found him beyonde my expectation readie to yoine with us, hee desired nothinge more then a generall meetinge wherein wee mighte consult of the affaires of the cleargie. hee esteemeth it trecherie to deliver the colledge in to the Iesuits hands. hee is readie to take a vicepresidente at oure appointmente and readers allsoe when so ever it pleaseth us to sende them. he feareth nothinge more then oure delaies. doctor Norton[600] is takinge his yornaye as it is reported towarde Spaine god grante hee maye intertaine him self there. there is nothinge more of which I canne give you informatione. wherefore with my kindeste commendations to youre self, not forgettinge to remember in my prayers youre worthie desertes, which daylie bindeth us more unto you I leave you saluted desieringe you to give mee notice of what passeth concerninge widdringtons booke[.][601] Martii. ii.

---

[592] This may be a reference to the poet and doctor of medicine Thomas Lodge, who took the oath of allegiance on 1 January 1612, T.H.B.M. Harmsen, *John Gee's Foot out of the Snare (1624)* (Nijmegen, 1992), 295.

[593] Evidently a reference to Edward Vaux, fourth Baron Vaux, who had returned from abroad after he received news of the search of Harrowden Hall, Anstruther, *Vaux of Harrowden*, 394–5; **Letter 20**.

[594] *i.e.* with either George Abbot or John King.

[595] As early as May 1611 Abbot had blocked an initiative to release William Bishop, AAW A X, no. 48. Bishop had been negotiating to be allowed to cross to France, AAW A X, no. 97.

[596] Thomas Sackville.

[597] John Colleton.

[598] John Jackson.

[599] Thomas Worthington.

[600] John Knatchbull.

[601] Preston, *Apologia Cardinalis Bellarmini*.

youre assured freinde
    Edwarde Kennion
I thinke my laste letter bare the name [of] francis Smith
No address
(On p. 80)
Endorsed: (1) Martii. ii. 1612. Ed. Ken.
            Recea. frid. April. 6 ⎱
            Answ. twesd. April. 10⎰ 1612

23 *Richard Orontes (Smith) to Thomas More (13 March 1612 (NS))*   *(AAW*
       A XI, no. 39, pp. 103–4. Holograph)

my deerest Syr I have yours of the 15 of ['Ian:' deleted] Febr: And am
very sorie of that ill happe of our Protector, and shal for my owne parte
be glad to see m^r Chamberl[602] albeit some that have hertofore knowne
him well be but hardly conceited of him and I pray God he rather
deceave their expectation than yours.[603] I shold have bene glad to have
had some of the Copies of my good la. life[604] but I wold not have you
seeme troblesome or importune to any for them. Here you shall receive
Mr Kenion his letter[605] who relateth I hope the affaires of England. He
I hope will prove a fitt subiect for our purpose. since his coming over
m^r warmington his booke for the oathe[606] and m^r Sheldon his booke

---

[602] John Varder alias Robert Chamberlain and Jones, secular priest.

[603] Varder, who had acted in a secretarial capacity for Birkhead, had been arrested by
the renegade priest William Atkinson in May 1609 in Smithfield, Anstr. II, 326. Sent into
exile, he came to Rome to assist the secular clergy's petitioning programme, AAW A X,
no. 96. He was viewed with suspicion by Edward Bennett who warned More against
him in December 1611, AAW A X, no. 166, as, earlier, had Anthony Champney, AAW
A X, no. 98, and also Richard Smith who thought Varder had been a spy for Robert
Persons, AAW A X, no. 162. Birkhead's recommendation, however, was enough to ensure
that More accommodated him at Rome, though even Birkhead thought that More
should use 'his helpe in such thinges as cannot much harme us', AAW A X, no. 99.
Shortly after, in September 1611, Birkhead had to inform More that 'a Iesuite hath told
me of a ringe which he [Varder] tooke from a gentlewoman. she is like to incurre her
husbandes displeasure for it', and he must give satisfaction or risk scandal, AAW A X,
no. 128 (p. 367). Even in February 1612 Birkhead had extracted only a provisional apology
(and the ring was returned only in 1613), AAW A XI, no. 13, XII, no. 45. Smith informed
More that Varder 'is thought to be unsure to you and now laboreth for a pension for to
settle him self' in Rome, AAW A XI, no. 14 (p.39). By the end of February 1612 he was
making his return to England via France, AAW A XI, no. 29, and he arrived in May.
See also **Letter 31**. Birkhead regarded him as a liability, in fact, for his furious antipathy
to SJ, AAW A XI, no. 83. (This, however, may account for Edward Bennett's more
positive view of him by May 1612, AAW A XI, no. 69.)

[604] Smith, *Vita Illustrissimae, ac Piissimae Dominae Magdalenae Montis-acuti.*

[605] **Letter 22**.

[606] Warmington, *Moderate Defence.*

for his Apostasie[607] is published[.] This last I have seene but not read, they say it is most spiteful and that he is an other Bel.[608] He insin[u]ateth that Rouse Atkinson and such like do against their conscience but he from his hart detesteth our religion and had thes 16 years suggestions against the masse, m[r] Copley and Collier accompany him in his revolt. Thes are the fruits of our Anarchia. And as the K said in the Conference at Hampton Court no Bishops no King so I fear his Hol. wil find in tyme that no Bishops no Pope. For as the K thoughe present could not bridle his ministers without Bish. so nether wil the Pope keep in order so many Humors without some authority present. And it is a slender reason which m[r] Preston useth that the P in policie wil give us no Bish because he may immediatly by him self command us the better.[609] For if he had good Bish to his likinge (as he may if he please) he shold then have twoe strings to his bow, his owne authority absent and an other present which by reason of the presence wold perhaps swaie more than his absent. And m[r] Ken: addeth that he knoweth divers to incline to liberty which maketh me the more desirous you shold commence the suite[610] [word omitted ?: lest ?] it be granted too late. And as for the Conference with m[r] Presid.[611] nether is it to be so shortly nether doth he shew any desire to concur for Bish. as he uttered in his speech with m[r] Ken:[612] and in his letters to England in which he requested that the consent of the laitie shold be demanded which is the shift of thos that would not have it take effect.[613] And howsoever you begin it now, I suppose the suite wil not be answered before the Conference be ended, at what time if we shold agree upon that as I ['hope not' deleted] have no hope (For m[r] Preston sheweth plainly an aversion and averteth others) we might then renew the suite agayne. you there best see what you have to doe, but my desire is that you set upon the matter and God dispose it as he pleaseth. Here it is reported that our Engl. Embas. in Spayne[614] hath killed a spanyard in the field in defence of the K. of

---

[607] Sheldon, *Motives*.

[608] *i.e.* the secular priest Thomas Bell, who renounced Catholicism in late 1592, Anstr. I, 29–30.

[609] Paradoxically Preston (an exponent of quasi-gallican ideas about limiting the papal deposing power) is here credited with a papalist argument concerning the extent of the pope's ecclesiastical authority. See Allison, 'Richard Smith', 149–50.

[610] *i.e.* the suit for ordinary jurisdiction.

[611] Thomas Worthington.

[612] See **Letter 22**.

[613] For the conference held at Douai in 1612 in order to establish some degree of consensus among the clergy about a papal grant of ordinary jurisdiction to a secular priest, see TD V, 30–2.

[614] Sir John Digby. Samuel Calvert wrote from London on 26 February 1612 to William Trumbull for news 'of a bruit of some discontentment or disaster happened to Digby in Spain', *Downshire MSS* III, 249.

Engl. and is therfor in ward, and that the Spanish E[m]bas. in England is therfor handled in like sorte.[615] Here is in towne a Copie of the Proclamation which our K hath made touching the Hollanders that if they will not banish one Vorstius who a[t] [?] leiden teacheth Arianisme and hath sent one of his scholers into England that he will call away his Embas. and osum erit de omnino.[616] It is also said by persons of intelligence that the French Embas.[617] in England hath written to the Q: to call him home because he can do her no service ther and that his abode ther is with her honor.[618] Dr Bish also writeth that in london they speak of a breach with Spaine for ilusage of the merchants.[619] Here shalbe great triumphe on the Anuntiation day for the declaration of the Crosse mariage with Spayne. God speed it well. Card. Peron hath now published his epistle to Causibon touching our K: disavowing thos Copies which befor had bene printed.[620] I did your Commendations to m^r Pole who returneth them very kindly. m^rs Dacres and her company are yet at Rhemes and their busines no more forward than five moneths agoe.[621] Thomas[622] writeth to me that ther is great pressing of the oathe

---

[615] On 1 March 1612 (NS) Antonio Foscarini, the Venetian ambassador, reported that a false rumour had been circulating that Alonso de Velasco, the Spanish ambassador, had been imprisoned in the Tower, *CSPV 1610–13*, 299.

[616] James I, *His Maiesties Declaration concerning His Proceedings with the States Generall of the United Provinces of the Low Countreys, in the Cause of D. Conradus Vorstius* (1612). It was published in French and Latin as well as English.

[617] Samuel Spifame, Seigneur des Bisseaux.

[618] Cf. *CSPV 1610–13*, 335 (Antonio Foscarini's report in April 1612 that Spifame was in 'very slight favour' at Court).

[619] See *CSPV 1610–13*, 287, 324.

[620] Cardinal Jacques Davy Du Perron, *Lettre de Monseigneur le Cardinal du Perron, Envoyée au Sieur Casaubon en Angleterre* (Paris, 1612). This edition superseded two earlier editions which had been published without the approval of the author, ARCR I, nos 1521–4. The secular clergy in Paris regarded Du Perron as a patron, AAW A XII, no. 39. It was said that Casaubon in Paris had alleged that Du Perron had expressed approval of James's polemical defence of the oath of allegiance with the exception of his 'digression...touching Antichrist', *Salisbury MSS* XXI, 288; cf. Patterson, *King James VI and I*, 99. John Jackson had claimed, in a letter to More of 8 June 1611, that 'the ambassador of Venice [Antonio Foscarini], who came lately from France, told Mr. Preston that divers cardinals, amongst others Monsieur Peron, and Monsieur Joyeux [Cardinal François de Joyeuse], and the pope's nuncio at Paris [Robert Ubaldini], said to him that the point of deposition was a thing indifferent, and that either opinion might be holden', TD IV, pp. clxxiii–iv.

[621] For the obstruction of the proposed English convent at Paris, see Lunn, 'English Cassinese', 63–4. By mid-1612 the project was failing for want of finance, AAW A XI, no. 94. Also, Antoinette d'Orléans-Longueville, the sister of Catherine Gonzaga, the Duchess of Longueville, 'under whose protectione they thought to live saythe that shee cannot help them unless they will be content to admit as manie frenche as Inglishe that yt may not be sayd to be an house' for the English alone, which Marie de Médicis 'will not permitt', though Champney said 'some do think ther ys some other reason' (in other words Jesuit interference). He noted that Edmund (Augustine) Smith OSB was in Paris trying to rescue the venture, AAW A XI, no. 216 (p. 617). On 19 October 1612 (NS) Thomas Floyd notified William Trumbull from Paris that Geoffrey Pole had departed

and that some negotiat composition about penal statuts but see so intricate difficulties and most dispaire of good successe.[623] my l: Treasurer[624] hath bene lately sick as is said of a dead paulsey but now recovered.[625] my brethren will needs have me one of the Conferencers which to tell you is quite against my mynd. Sic notus ulisses [?]. D. Norton[626] is expected here shortly to goe to Spayne, but wherfor I know not. If that were true that his Hol. wold have the Archpr.[627] to entermedle in Doway perhaps it was the Cause [?] that moved the Rector to carrie the scholers to him, or els to demand some such thing as D. Norton may be thought to negotiat in Spayne. wil Gale[628] is dead

for Rome 'leaving his sisters in great assurance, as he thought, to be nuns; but I think they will find a rub they were not aware of', *Downshire MSS* III, 379. In December 1612 Beaulieu told Trumbull that Sir Thomas Edmondes in Paris had lobbied effectively to stifle the project, *Downshire MSS* III, 440. Robert Pett reported on 5 January 1613 (NS) that Champney had informed him that 'our English gentilwomen are returned agayne to Rhemes' because Edmondes had 'prevayled with Vilroy [Nicolas de Neufville, Seigneur de Villeroi]' to 'procurer ther remove from Paris unles they would have remayned with such conditions as they could not except of', AAW A XII, no. 2 (p. 4). Anthony Champney said on 12 February 1613 (NS) that Elizabeth Dacres was considering returning to England, AAW A XII, no. 34, but she entered a Benedictine house at Douai in March 1613, and was clothed in April, **Letter 42**.

[622] Thomas Heath.

[623] Edward Bennett had written to More on 26 December 1611 that 'heer is some speech of a composition' to be offered by lay Catholics to the crown to be free of all penal statutes. The sum of £20,000 was being mentioned. Bennett, however, had told William Bishop that such a scheme was worthless unless liberty of conscience was granted as well and the priests were comprehended in it, AAW A X, no. 166 (p. 458). Birkhead made the same point in January 1612, AAW A XI, no. 1. Champney and Smith were talking about such a scheme in February 1612, AAW A XI, nos 19, 20 (Smith's mention that Thomas Heath had written 'of some composition with Cath: for 30 or 40 thousand poundes yearly for remission of al penal statuts which inflict not death and that some principal persons labor in that matter with hope to effect it wherby they may live at more quiet and the Kinges rents so much increased'). On 29 February 1612 (NS) Champney reported to More that 'for the compositione in poenall statutes whereof I writt in my other these two are of divers opiniones mr [Edward] Kenione beinge towld by one who ys nere the lord of northampton that there would be nothinge donn therein' but Francis Foster had said that 'Sr Hughe Biston [Beeston] speakinge to the l Treasurer [Robert Cecil] for on mr Geneson [William Jenison] who ys condemned in premunirie for the oathe entreatinge that he might compownde was willed to expect till the matter was heard or concluded for all which shortly would be some speeche of marienge our ladie Elizabethe to the kinge of Spayne', AAW A XI, no. 29 (p. 75).

[624] Robert Cecil, first Earl of Salisbury. On 20 February 1612, Benjamin Norton was expecting William Herbert, Earl of Pembroke to succeed Salisbury as treasurer and Sir Henry Neville to become principal secretary, AAW A XI, no. 24. By 9 April Norton thought the new treasurer would be either Archbishop Abbot or Edward Somerset, Earl of Worcester, AAW A XI, no. 54.

[625] See McClure, 338.

[626] John Knatchbull.

[627] George Birkhead.

[628] Not identified.

at home and m^rs Coppinger.[629] Thomas wold gladly be here with me, and my maister[630] wold gladly have me from heare[.] Thomas saith he hath delt with your brother[631] about the money you me[n]tion and daily expecteth rec[ev]ando [?], but I have sent the alteration of your mynd touching the manner of the sending it to you. A while since the oathe was tendred to my L. vaux who required respit til lent which he hardly obtained and now what he wil answer I can not tell but his answer wil revelare ex multis cordibus cogitationes[.][632] Hitherto none of worth have refused the oathe but thos who were the priests[633] Ghostlye chidren. There is one Scotish Capucin comen into England. Alabaster is said to be turned to naught. Commend me I pray you to m^r Nicolas[634] and thus with my kindest to your self adeiu 13 of march.

Yours assured

   R. orontes.

(In margin) If there were 300 Ies. without a superior and all order as there are Prests in Engl perhaps as many scandals wold they shew.

(On p. 104)

Addressed: Illustre e reverendo Tomaso Moro

Endorsed: (1) Martii. 13. 1612. Oront.

      (2) Recea. frid. April. 6.⎤
                  ⎬ 1612
        Answ. wed. April. 11⎦

      one only to his and Ant. Ch.

24 *John Nelson [Jackson] to Thomas More (20 March 1612)*   *(AAW A*
    XI, no. 45, pp. 121–2. Holograph)

v. r. and beloved S^r.

   I went of purpose in feb: last to see old m^r Dolman[635] whose

---

[629] Not identified.

[630] Anthony Maria Browne, second Viscount Montague.

[631] Christopher Cresacre More.

[632] Edward Vaux, fourth Baron Vaux, was imprisoned in the Fleet for this refusal, McClure, 339. On 21 March 1612 Birkhead told More that Elizabeth Vaux was 'condemned in the premunire, and yet she answered that she wold sweare her allegiance, albeit the kinge were excommunicated. my L Vaux answered that he wold take the oath, according to the kinges interpretation, and yet nether of these modifications wold be accepted', AAW A XI, no. 46 (p. 123). Edward Bennett on 11 April 1612 said that the earl of Montgomery had petitioned to be allowed to compound with Vaux (as he had with Vaux's mother), AAW A XI, no. 57. For Vaux's opposition to the oath, strengthened by the advice of Edward Weston, see Allison, 'Later Life', 112–13.

[633] *i.e.* the secular clergy.

[634] Nicholas Fitzherbert.

[635] Alban Dolman, the Marian priest who had acted in May 1595 as one of the arbitrators during the 'Wisbech stirs', CRS 51, *passim*. In 1593 Robert Gray confessed to the authorities that Dolman had visited Cowdray in 1589 or 1590 and was known to Anthony Browne, first viscount Montague, PRO, SP 12/245/138.

auncientnes yow may coniec[ture] by th*a*t he was preist at Rome when
D. Sanders[636] was made preist and assisted him as his father when he
said his first mass. I conferred w*i*th him about th*e* point of Bishops and
he told me th*a*t at th*a*t tyme pius 4th as I take it or 5th and as farr as
he remembres the whole College of Cardinalls did hold it requisite th*a*t
some Inglish Bishops shold be made to continew th*e* succesion,[637] and
th*a*t some I know not who besides th*e* L. Mountague[638] who was then
thear or had been thear thowght it fit to be stayed tyll they had th*e*
opinions of the confessours th*a*t at th*a*t tyme wear in prison hear, of
who*m* some wear Bishops. and also because they wold not in those
dowbtfull tymes (hooping [word deleted] and dayly expecting a change)
exasperate the state against those they had in prison. what thear answer
was from hense he knowes not, but it is probable th*a*t the opportunitie
being lett slipp those th*a*t followed did not urge the busines. post est
occasio calva. but howsoever th*e* pope himselfe did then intend it, as
he[639] very seriously & religiously told me & willed me to signifie soe
much unto yow & and gave me liberty to write a l*ett*re in his name to
his hol. and th*a*t he wold avow it. div*er*se other informations I had from
him w*hi*ch I doe not now well reme*m*bre. Yet I reme*m*bre th*a*t he told
me th*a*t going to church had been declared by publick decree unlawfull
had not th*e* said Lord Montague hindred it, for exasperating the state
(forsoth)[.][640] He told me of a gentlema*n* who had appointed & promised
to give eyther 200 or 300[li] (I have forgot whether) to th*e* prisonners at
wisbich & th*a*t fa Gerard growing (after him) acquainted w*i*th the p*ar*ty
gott it all to him selfe or his societye. & another who m[r] Dol. reconciled
bequeathed (as I take it by way of satisfaction) <u>200[li] to the same</u> prison &
father Gerard growing acquainted w*i*th th*e* heyr or executor after the
said gentlemans death gott th*a*t also into his owne hands for himselfe
or society. <u>other such knowne relations</u> he hath <u>of him w*hi*ch</u> <u>wold</u>
<u>discredit others if they had th*e*</u> like against them. I have <u>written what</u>

---

[636] Nicholas Sander, Catholic polemicist.

[637] A draft paper, now in the Vatican archives, which relied on information supplied
by Nicholas Sander to Cardinal Giovanni Morone in summer 1561 (or was perhaps even
drawn up by Sander), contains proposals for the appointment of imprisoned Catholic
clerics as bishops in England, C.G. Bayne, *Anglo-Roman Relations 1558–1565* (Oxford, 1913),
127, 282–5; T.M. McCoog, *Monumenta Anglia* (forthcoming), appendix III.

[638] Anthony Browne, first Viscount Montague, who had been an ambassador at Rome
in Mary Tudor's reign, Cokayne IX, 98.

[639] *i.e.* Dolman.

[640] For the petition (concerning attendance at Protestant service) to Rome in 1562 by
English Catholics, see A. Walsham, *Church Papists* (1993), 22; Bayne, *Anglo-Roman Relations*,
163–81; McCoog, *Monumenta Anglia*, appendix III.

is hear reported of m^r Th. Fitz. to m^r champ.[641] who I hoope hath signified th*e* summe thearof unto yo*w*. D. Bish. hath his warrant for banishme*n*t procured by the sorbons means.[642] m^r wilford (who was wholly Iesuited) hath taken the oth & defends it, iudge the*n* whether th*e* sec: pr. or others doe more approve it.[643] I praye send me some word of one Raphe Green[644] in th*a*t colledge of whom I wold be glad to hear. thear was burn'd in smithfeild 3. dayes since one legate An Arrian a rude, prowd obstinate fellow.[645] yow have hard I suppose of the kings booke agaynst conrad*us* vorstius the Hereticall reader at Leiden in th*e* lowcountries, set forth both in Inglish & french.[646] thear are many things in th*e* booke worth the noting & such as if other kings wold doe the like wee shold be at greater quiet. pag. 5. he saith thus. & que nous nous sentons obligez en honneur & conscience de tascher d'obvier à un si gran mal autant que nous pouvons, (comme celluy qui est prince chrestien, & qui à presté aux dits Sieurs Estats en toutes leurs occasions, toute faveur et assistance Reale,[647] à cause de leur Religion). doe other princes the like to us? pag. 30 Car sa Maiestè [sic] estant par la grace de deiu[648] protectrice de la Religion (thease be the Imbassadours words) du quel tiltre elle se vant[649] plus, que non pas du tiltre du Roy de la grand' Brettaigne) [sic] se tient oblige de proteger touts ceux, qui quand & luy font profession de la mesme religion.) pag. 35. L'alliance entre sa Maieste et voz provinces, [';laquelle'[650]] estant fondeé [sic] sur la co*n*servation, et manutention de la Religion reformée etc. pag. 40.

---

[641] The rumour was the one spread by Roland (Thomas) Preston OSB that Thomas Fitzherbert 'is Card. or at least bb w*i*th autority over o*u*r cause as Card Allen had', AAW A XI, no. 30 (p. 78). On 5 May 1612 (NS) Anthony Champney passed on John Jackson's report that Fitzherbert may have been made cardinal 'and that some Iesuite showld say thereuppon lett them nowe gett Bb. & spare not for he shalbe sup*e*rintendant over Ingland and dispose of all'. This was highly distasteful, said Champney, considering that Fitzherbert 'hathe so disorderly a sonne [Edward] as he ys reported to be and no cath(olike) as ys sayd', AAW A XI, no. 73 (p. 211). Edward Bennett remarked that Edward Fitzherbert was 'owt of gods church' and unlikely to return, though, in August 1613, Bennett attended his death and reported that he 'died very well, and repentant althoughe his lief had been most scandalous', AAW A X, no. 148 (p. 417), XII, no. 154 (p. 345).

[642] See **Letter 25**.

[643] Possibly the recusant James Wilford of Lenham, Kent. The Wilfords were not part of the secular clergy's network of patrons.

[644] Ralph Green had entered the English College in Rome in October 1607, having been reconciled to the Church of Rome by John Jackson, CRS 54, 186–7; CRS 37, 148–9. In November 1610 he had left the college in order to enter SJ, CRS 75, 196.

[645] Bartholomew Legate. See McClure, 337; **Letter 26**.

[646] See **Letter 23**.

[647] 'Royale' in printed version (James I, *Declaration du Roy, touchant le faict de C. Vorstius* (1612)).

[648] 'Dieu' in printed version.

[649] 'vante' in printed version.

[650] in printed version.

le principall lien de nostre coniunction[651] estant nostre uniformité en la vraye Religion. pag. 49. Et nous esperons en la misericorde de Deiu[652] que nul chrestien (ie parle en cecy tant pour les papists que pour nous) n'errera en aucuns de ce[653] grands points. [p. 122] pag. 53. he saith that in the parts of Hungarie & Boheme, vivent un[654] infinité de sectes, (s'accordants seulement en leur union contre le pape)[.] in other places he presseth much the authoritie of the church and the auncient Doctors. I cold wish yow had the booke thear, thowgh I [word deleted] doubt not but that diverse thear have it. m^r Sheldon was brought by the Bish. of Bath[655] to kiss the kings hand 5 dayes since & the k. talked with him a long tyme & had done longer if one had not brought him a lettre in a napkin upon the receip whearof he withdrew himselfe. If these that come to us from them had the like or halfe the like countenance & favour shewed them that owrs which fall have at their hands, Higgens had never return'd to scandalize religion as he did. & though men shold not respect it yet it wear fit to give it. & we cannot looke to have them saincts at the first. I praye remembre me kindly to my frends thear & to m^r Ra:[656] by name if he be return'd from Naples. pray him not to measure my love by lettres[.] I have noething to write but complement which I know he regards not. tell him the couple at whose marriage he was have a daughter between them to begin the world with. I suppose yow hear of the Bish. & preist that wear executed at Divelin in Ireland.[657] & of the miracles that wear wrowght at the same tyme.[658] they urge the oath

---

[651] 'conjonction' in printed version.

[652] 'Dieu' in printed version.

[653] 'ces' in printed version.

[654] 'une' in printed version.

[655] James Montague.

[656] Thomas Rant, Oratorian priest. Rant wrote to More on 20 November 1612 (NS), AAW A XI, no. 209.

[657] Cornelius O'Devany, Bishop of Down and Connor, and Patrick O'Lochran, executed on 1 February 1612. Both were Franciscans. The reason for O'Devany's condemnation was, according to John Finet, that 'he was titular bishop of Downe during Tyrone's rebellion, guilty of his treasons, and received a conditional pardon that he should take the Oath of Allegiance', which he had subsequently refused, and was 'found otherwise machinating', *Downshire MSS* III, 285; cf. D. Murphy (ed.), *Our Martyrs* (Dublin, 1896), 238–56. Benjamin Norton thought the cause was 'suspicion of powder treason', AAW A XI, no. 24 (p. 60).

[658] On 26 February 1612 Benjamin Norton wrote to More that O'Devany had shown exemplary courage. He refused a reprieve which was offered to him on condition that he conformed, and he stiffened the resolve of O'Lochran. 'A creeple was cured beeinge at his deathe' and 'the people toke awaye his quarters', and the 'probabilities of truth', wrote Norton, 'are for that one tolde me this from my Brother Neddes [see **Letter 1**] mouthe, whoe had it of his sister whoe as I have writne in my laste lettres is a widdowe & shee had it from a Irishe lordes mouthe & as I thinke hee was the Lorde Melvyn [Richard Nugent, fourth Baron Delvin, great-nephew of Anthony Browne, first Viscount Montague]

in th*a*t country also,[659] & hear it is much press'd. some take it, & a few
refuse it. Thus w*i*th my best remembrances & th*e* like wishes praying yo*w*
hartely to be recom*m*ended at those holy places I rest 20 martii 1612
yo*u*rs faithfully
N.

Addressed: To the right worship*full* my assured good freind m^r Thomas
         Moore give thease.
Endorsed: (1) Mart. 20°. 1612. N.
         (2) Rec. sond. Iuly. 1° ⎫
              Answ. wed. Iuly. 4°. ⎬ 1612
                                      ⎭
         (3) herwith a note of two names for b*i*sho*p*s.

25 *George Salvin (Birkhead) to [Thomas More] (31 March 1612)*   (*AAW A*
       XI, no. 50, pp. 131–2. Holograph)

Rev. S.^r in my last, w*hi*ch I think was of the 22 of march or therabout
I told yo*w* of a bruite raised against m^r pr*e*ston for beinge the maker of
widderintons booke, w*hi*ch holdeth still, but himselfe denieth it.[660] and

whoe was at the execution', AAW A XI, no. 24 (p. 60); *cf*. Murphy, *Our Martyrs*, 255–6.
Edward Bennett wrote to More on 1 March 1612 that at the execution, which took place
after sunset, a Protestant clergyman 'who accompanied them to the place of execution
w*i*th intent to have p*er*verted them was him self soddenly stroken dead as he fixed his
eies upon them when they were hanging. after ther death alsoe a straing miraculous
accident fell owt, to [w]it, that on whose arme was lame going owt w*i*th others to cutt
of some part of them for devotion: returned back with his arme whoale', AAW A XI,
no. 30 (p. 77).
    [659] *Cf*. C.W. Russell and J.P. Prendergast (eds), *Calendar of State Papers, relating to
Ireland...1611–14* (1877), 192.
    [660] On 21 March 1612 Birkhead had narrated to More that Edward Vaux, fourth Baron
Vaux, had been ordered to discuss the oath of allegiance with Roland (Thomas) Preston
OSB, and Preston 'wold neither persuade nor disswade him, but rather wished him not
to take it. at his returne to the b [George Abbot] he asked whether he wold take it or
no. he denied it. the b demanded what m^r pr*e*ston said unto him, he told him as before.
then the b raged and was much offended against him, & said in the hearinge of the said
lord vaux and of a great nomber of people that preston was a traytor both to the kinge,
and the pope, because he made the booke [*Apologia Cardinalis Bellarmini*] w*hi*ch he fathered
upon widderington', AAW A XI, no. 46 (p. 123) (cited by Lunn, *EB*, 42). Later, according
to Anthony Champney in August 1612, Preston gave out a rumour that William Bishop
'had approved his book [perhaps referring to Preston's new book, *Rogeri Widdringtoni
Catholici Angli Responsio Apologetica*, which had appeared by July 1612] before yt was printed'.
This was, apparently, Preston's revenge for Bishop's presumed part in spreading George
Abbot's 'carelesse' outburst that Preston wrote under Widdrington's name. Bishop had,
according to the Jesuits, been trying to create a rift between Preston and the other Cassinese
Benedictines, particularly Robert (Anselm) Beech. In reply Bishop wrote 'true it is that I did
speake of such a matter, but was far to short of being the...divulger of it', because it was
already common knowledge in London; in fact, Bishop claimed, he had done as much to
hinder the rumour as to spread it, AAW A XI, nos 141 (p. 391), 149 (p. 409).

some are redie to beleve him.[661] whether the Archp[662] hath any autoritie to looke in to such defectes amongst the religiouse or no yet the wordes of his commission are ut admoneret omnes et singulos sacerdotes Anglos etc. now whether religiouse prestes be comprehended as well as the secular, it is to me uncerten. at the least it were necessarie that some should have an eye therunto, when as there verie superiors are deamed so much to halt in that respect.

one legate An Arrian[663] and infected with many other heresies besides was burned of late in Smithfeild. the Lawes against that iustice were repealed in the quenes daies, and therfor he pleaded they could not burne him. but it is said he was onely condemned for withstandinge the Councel of Nice, which with the three other of Const. Ephesus and Calcedon are allowed by the parlament.[664]

the Chaplains to the Embassadours especially from spaine and the low countries come sometyme hither with out faculties to heare confessions of there countrimen, and they make recourse to the Archp to have them of him. but he havinge no iurisdiction over outlandish preistes, is forced to denie them that courtesie. which perhaps they take more greevously then they seame. wherefor in my opinion it were not amisse yf yow could procure him some speciall licence for that end.[665]

I have given yow to understand in my former Letters, of diverse written by the Archp to all those great men whome yow named,[666] and I hope they are almost with yow by this: now I heare that one of our brethren hath written a latine letter, which the Archp hath willed to be sent to yow, and that yow should conveigh it to Card Arrigona whome [he] had Left out himselfe, whome m^r mush thinketh an especiall frend of ours.[667]

upon the 22 of march m^r mullinex,[668] his man Roger thersbie, and m^r hart[669] m^r henley,[670] and m^r Cooke,[671] were all apprehended by

---

[661] On 20 April 1612 Birkhead was still saying that Preston's authorship was denied, and that Blackwell was believed by some to be the author, AAW A XI, no. 62.

[662] i.e. Birkhead.

[663] See **Letter 24**.

[664] Chamberlain noted that 'some lawiers are of opinion that we have no law to execute heretikes, and that whatsoever was don in that kinde in Queen Elizabeths time was don de facto and not de jure, yet the King sayes yf he be so desperate to denie Christ to be God he will adventure to burne him with a good conscience', McClure, 337.

[665] Birkhead repeated this request to More on 23 April 1612, AAW A XI, no. 63. See also **Letter 37**.

[666] See AAW A XI, no. 12, for Birkhead's letters to Cardinals Sfondrata, Bellarmine and Aldobrandini, to Don Francisco de Castro, the Spanish ambassador in Rome, and to John Baptist Vives. For this attempt to raise support in Rome, see TD V, 53–4.

[667] See **Letter 18**.

[668] John Almond.

[669] Not identified.

[670] Not identified.

[671] Identity uncertain. In December 1610 one William Cook of St Andrew's parish in Holborn was indicted for recusancy, CRS 34, 54.

Tarbox the pursivant;[672] so as m^r Cookes house in Southamptons house is now quite spoiled. m^r mullinex and thersbie were committed to newgate, the rest it is thought were bailed.

doctor bishope was bannished upon the 23 of march.[673] he is now therfor gon. god speed him well. I trust his presence will do much good both for the settinge up of the house at paris, and also for the Conference with m^r president.[674] yow know how zealous our superiors there, are for the maintenance of the dignitie of the sea Apostolique, and how ill it wilbe taken at the handes of these that (thowgh they be in the fornace of persecution) are fownd to be cold in the defence therof. wherfor me thinkes yow should do well to give that new companie at paris some Caveat about that matter. for yf we be founde deficiente in that respect, all our Labours will come to nothinge. many both of the secular and religiouse preists are to backward in condemninge the bookes of berclay and widderinton, which maketh such a stoppe in the zeal of the laickes, that verie few do stand against the oath. and now yow shall see that how manifestly soever it appeareth, that m^r prestons case wilbe huddled by his frendes.

D bishope immediately before he went awaie, wrote this unto me. I have god be [p. 132] thanked, great hope of my speedie deliveraunce. for the L of Canturb[675] called me before him yesterday, and told publiquely that the K maiestie had graunted my enlargment unto the french Embassadour at the instance of the Sorbon doctors, which he wold not (as he said) in any case contradict, but wold he tell me that I was most unworthie of it. first because I threatned his maiestie with open warre yf wee might not have our wills. 2. for refusinge the oath twise. 3. for writinge to the popes hol, and therin callinge the oath iuramentum dicam, an potius iuramentum infidelitatis. (this Letter was by him intercepted). Lastly for my disloiall hand to the state, and my manifold seducinge of the kinges subiectes by wordes, <u>writinges, and deades. and all for severall</u> endes which I had proposed to my selfe. these pointes and some others he thundered out against me in a longe speech. when he had spoken him selfe almost out of breath, then I demanded him yf it were his pleasure to heare my answere. he bad me speeke. I first shewed that I was much beholden to his maiestie for my enlargment, consideringe how he might be informed against me. and that I as [sic for 'as I'] had in former tymes shewed my dewtifull affection towardes him, so I wold do hearafter in prayinge for him and his and in all other good offices. then I began to answere the pointes,

[672] See CRS 53, 174.
[673] See **Letter 24**.
[674] Thomas Worthington.
[675] George Abbot.

but that he was not willinge to heare. so I passed most of them over to that point wherin <u>he said that for our owne particular endes we wold continew</u> our seducinge of the people. to w*h*ich I answered, that it was clere to all indifferent weighers of that matter, that we disabled our selves by our function of all preferment in our Countrie, where we might have lived well enough, yf we wold have followed the tyme. and I thought that [there] were few, but wold quickly understand, that yf wee wold forgoe our religion and imbrace thers, we might be able to live well enough. finally my request to his hol of bishops trowbled him much. I told him that we did not desyre bb that should disquiet there estate any more then pr*e*stes. for they wold not not [sic] come to demande bishoprickes here nor to meddle w*i*th there matters, but onely to see good order kept amongst catholiques. this is in effect that w*h*ich passed. I had almost forgotten to tell yo*w* that said L had to shew me a particuler of all them that had given voices to be bishops. m^r Copley belike was privie to that matter.[676] thus farre he. w*h*ich was true indeed for he was trusted to range them in order. I send yo*w* herinclosed part of a latine letter written to some great personage, by m^r washington,[677] as it hath ben told me. yo*w* may peruse the reasons for yo*ur* better information. the L vaux and his mother are still in newgate. some saie they have absolutely denied the oath, w*h*ich is most like, because of there endurance. yf yo*w* be mindefull to speake for the forsaid speciall facultie, that the Archp may grant it to the almoners of the Embassadours, it wold helpe our cause in diverse respectes. he[re] cometh Don petro de Cunega[678] out of spaine, the duke of bullion[679] out of fraunce and divers others,[680] what to do god knoweth. And so with my

---

[676] Birkhead had already reported to More on 21 March 1612 that John Copley had 'bewrayed what he knew to the Lord of Canturb who obiected to d bish that he knew how many voices, everie man had', AAW A XI, no. 46 (p. 123).

[677] Paul Green.

[678] Don Pedro de Zúñiga Palomeque y Cabeza de Vaca, created Marquis of Floresdavila in April 1612; see CRS 64, 48. Zúñiga's embassy was to announce the conclusion of the Franco-Spanish matches and to patch up Anglo-Spanish diplomatic relations, and also to offer a match between Henry, Prince of Wales and Maria, the second infanta of Spain, *CSPV 1610–13*, 324, 342, 413; CRS 64, 199; *cf. Downshire MSS* III, 263, 265.

[679] Henri de la Tour, Duke of Bouillon. At the beginning of March 1612, Bouillon was despatched to assure James that the double dynastic match between France and Spain would not 'disturb...friendly relations' with the English Crown, and also to offer a marriage between Princess Christine and Prince Henry, *CSPV 1610–13*, 299, 302, a marriage originally projected in August/September 1611, *Downshire MSS* III, 133. Antonio Foscarini thought that Bouillon would also negotiate for the Elector Palatine to marry Princess Elizabeth, *CSPV 1610–13*, 318, a project in which he had been involved in 1611, *Downshire MSS* III, 151, *cf.* 249. After considerable delay, he arrived in London on 6 May 1612 (NS), going 'to the cowrte with 100 coches', *CSPV 1610–13*, 348; AAW A XI, no. 69 (p. 203); *cf. Downshire MSS* III, 286. For Bouillon's career, see Adams, *passim.*

[680] *CSPV 1610–13*, 332, 342, 350.

lovinge Commendacions to your selfe, m^r D perse,[681] m^r beech, m^r
fitzherb.[682] and all other good frendes, I beseech god ever to preserve
yow to the good of our poore afflict Church. tell the gentleman I have
don his commendacions upon the token of a fish dinner at stains. this
31 of march 1612.
your lovinge frend
  G. Sal.
No address
Endorsed: (1) Mart. 31. 1612. Salv.
          (2) Rec. th. Iune 28. ⎤
          (3) Answ. sat. Iune. 30. ⎦ 1612

26 *Richard Sara (Edward Bennett) to Thomas West (More) (11 April
    1612)   (AAW A XI, no. 57, pp. 169–72. Holograph)*

very deere Syr. I have yours of the 14 of Ianuary havinge some 3
weekes a gon acknowledged & awnswerd yours of the 20th of the same.
I thanck the gentleman that lay with us of chrismas was twelvemonenth
for his kynd comendations, what curtesye was showed hime, (howsoever
his affection were other wayes bestowed) was playn & sincere. some 4
monethes a gon I have been towld that he was departe[d] this life,
wherupon I sayd a masse of requiem for his soule. but now I am very
glad to understand of his good healthe wher with f. Griffyn[683] had some
senight a goe acquainted me who is saffly arived in these partes. I was
on of the first that he came to: he is not dissmissd but with leave ['is
come' deleted] (against the likinge of some) arived. he is a good
religiouse, playn, & sincere honest man: if his brethern were of his
dictamen in the managinge of Englishe affayers we should soone have
peace with them. I heere nothinge of the dimission of those 6 you
mention in your last. I marvaile you say nothing of 4 or 5 letters I sent
you synce the begininge of winter.[684] but I suppose it fareth with me,
as it doth with your self. for I had yours of the 20 of Ianuary some 3
weekes or a moneth before the 14 of the same monenth came to my
handes. I cowld wish m^r Ratcliff[685] with you, but our wantes be soe
great for money that I fear me we shall not send hime. in my last I

---

[681] William Percy.
[682] Nicholas Fitzherbert.
[683] Griffin Floyd. Floyd had been dismissed from SJ in February 1612, CRS 74, 172, 184.
[684] The four surviving letters from Edward Bennett to More since the beginning of November 1611 are AAW A X, nos 148, 166, XI, nos 17, 30.
[685] John Mush.

towld you howe that Canterbury[686] towld openly the body of the
cownsell befor my L vaux that m[r] preston is the autor of wideringtons
booke,[687] wherof I suppose his holl is informed by the Iesswettes: I
would gladly understand what is conceaved of it in those partes: I fear
me the Italian monckes will fare the worse for it. I heer nothing of any
awnswer of Ely to Capella.[688] m[r] denton[689] is gon with comission to
meet d worthing[.] our lord send them good lwck. m[r] mwllenex[690] is
taken who hath refused the oath most constantly. m[r] Batty[691] alsoe is
taken they be boath in newgate. heer is lessius[692] come over, & on that
hath redd hime sendeth me word that he howldeth fide catholica
tenendum that the pop hath autority to depose princes. but that he
doth not prove it. even now a gentlman towld me that in oxfordshyre
the Iudges gave a most terribl[e] charge not only abowt the oath, but
alsoe abowt ['taking' deleted] receavinge the comunion, soe that ther
be warrantes gon from the Iustices to all c[o]nstables & parish ministers
comandinge them to give notice of all that doe not comunicate this
Easter or removed against the tyme. soe that our persecution in all
kynd doth still increase withowt hope of any temporall consolation: god
of his goodnes give us patience. My best frend[693] with the younge
gentlemen[694] most kyndly remember you. it is feared m[r] Gerard is come
into England, if it doe prove soe, this searchinge for hime wilbe an

[686] George Abbot.

[687] See **Letter 25**.

[688] Mark Anthony Capello, who had published *F.M. Antonii Capelli...Adversus praetensum
ecclesiasticum Regis Angliae liber in quo Iacobi Regis & eius Eleemosynarii [Lancelot Andrewes]
confutantur scripta* (Bonn, 1610).

[689] William Bishop.

[690] John Almond.

[691] Reginald Bates.

[692] This must refer to Leonardus Lessius, *Defensio Potestatis Summi Pontificis, adversus Librum
Regis Magnae Britanniae, Gulielmi Barclaii Scoti, & M. Georgii Blacuelli* (St Omer, 1611), though
Rome had suppressed the book and it was not generally distributed. Anthony Hoskins
SJ wrote *A Briefe and Cleare Declaration* (St Omer, 1611), which is an abstract of Lessius's
book, ARCR I, nos 1505, 1534, but this had been sent to England as soon as it was
published, A.F. Allison, 'Leonardus Lessius of Louvain and his English translator', in S.
Roach (ed.), *Across the Narrow Seas* (1991), 89–98, at p. 96. Anthony Champney noted in
July 1612 that Preston's new book, *Rogeri Widdringtoni Catholici Angli Responsio Apologetica ad
Libellum cuiusdam Doctoris Theologi, qui eius pro iure Principum Apologiam tanquam fidei Catholicae
aperte repugnantem...criminatur* (1612), not only refuted Edward Weston's views on the oath
of allegiance (see **Letter 32**) but 'shakethe up also an Inglishe treatise which mentionethe
a larger discourse writen of the same subject by Lessius which discours as he [Preston]
saythe ys delivered from hand to hand to frends only and not permitted to be seene by
day light', AAW A XI, no. 121 (p. 329). On 4 August 1612 (NS) Robert Pett also remarked
that Lessius's own book had arrived in England, Allison, 'Leonardus Lessius', 96 (citing
AAW A XI, no. 132).

[693] Lady Elizabeth Dormer.

[694] Anthony and Robert Dormer.

occasion to overthrowe many. he hath him self sued much with his
superiors that he might come[.] if they have yeelded to hys request they
have litle feeling of the pressures we suffer because of ther pollicy &
practise. heer hath been an Arrian[695] bwrned at Smithfeeld & another[696]
showld have been bwrnt at Coventry, but when the fier came neer
hyme he cried owt & recanted, & soe was saved: but yeat it is thought
he is litle amended.[697] if I can meete with the articles they were
condemned for I will send you them. my l of mongymry hath begged
the L vaux, what the composition wilbe, that as yeat is not knowen.
surly many wilbe overthrowen both spiritually & temporally abowt this
oathe. temporally in refusing it, spiritually if they tak it. it is the opinion
of most that if f parsons had not procured the first breve, ther had been
no speech of it. our lord keepe you Easter eve being the 11 Aprill:
yours ['faringt' deleted] Sara

(On p. 170)
Heresies mantayned by Edward wrightman of coventry dioces where
being condemned & fire sett to hyme: after he had been well scorched
he cried owt that he would recant: wherupon they had much a doe to
save hyme.

1. That ther is not the trinity of persons in the father the sonne &
   holy gost.
2. That Iesus christ is not the true naturall sonne of god, perfect
   god & of the sam substance & maiesty with the father in respect of
   his godhead.
3. That Iesus christ is only man & a meere creature, & not god &
   man in one person.
4. That christ took not flesh of the substaunce of the virgyn mary: &
   that, that promise, the heel of the woman, shall break the serpentes
   head, was not fulfilled in christ.
5. That the person of the holly gost is not god coequall, coeternall, &
   coessentiall with the father & the sonne.
6. That the 3 creeds vz. the Apostles, the Nicen & Athanasius are the
   heresies of the Nicholaites.[698]
7. That the said Edward wrightman is the prophet spoken of Deu

---

[695] Bartholomew Legate.

[696] Edward Wightman.

[697] On 13 May 1612 Bennett notified More that Wightman had relapsed and 'was
caried agayne to the stake where feeling the heat of the fier again would have recanted,
but for all his crieinge the sheriff tould hyme he showld cosen him no more & comanded
faggottes to be sett to him whear roringe he was burned to ashes, whose dome alsoe I
wish all heretickes that will never repent', AAW A XI, no. 76 (p. 218).

[698] Presumably Wightman is referring to the sectaries mentioned in *Revelation* 2: 6, F.L.
Cross (ed.), *The Oxford Dictionary of the Christian Church* (1958), 958.

18[699] I will raise them up a pro[p]het e[t]c. & that that place of Isay I alone have troden the wyne presse & that, that place. whose fann is in his hand are proper and personall to hime the sayed wrightman, & that he is that person of the holy gost spoke of in the scriptures & the comforter spoken of Io 16.[700]

8. That these wordes the wordes of christ of the sinne of blasphemy against the holly gost are meant of his person.

9. That the soule doth sleepe in the sleep of the first death: as the body doth. & that the soule of christ did sleepe in that sleepe of death as well as the bodye.

10. That the sowles of the elect saintes departed are not members possessed of the triumphant church in heaven.

11. That the baptisme of Infantes is an abhominable custome.

12. That there ought not to be in the church the use of the lordes supper, to be cellebrated in the elementes of bread & wyne. & the use of baptime to be celebrated in the ['use' deleted] element of of [sic] water as they now use in the church of England: but the use of Baptisme is to be administred in water, only to convertes of sufficiente aige & understandinge converted from infidelity to the faith.

13. That god hath ordayned & sent him vz wrightman, to perform his part in the work of salvation in the world, to deliver it by his teachinge, & admonition from the heresies of the Nicholaites: as christ was ordayned & sent to save the world: & by his death to deliver it from sinne & to reconcile it to god.

14. That christianity is not wholly professed in the church of England but in part. & this much of this fellows wickednes.

The heresies of Bartholomew Legate (bwrnt at London) certified into the Chauncery by the Bushop of London 3 Martii 1611

1. The Creedes to [w]it Nicen & Athanasius contayn not a profession of the tru christian faith therfor will not professe his faith according to the same creedes.

2. That Christ is not god of god: begotten: not made: but begotten & made.

3. That ther are no persons in the godhead.

4. That Christ was not god from everlasting, but began to be god when he took flesh of the virgin mary.

5. That the world was not mad by christ.

6. That the Apostles teach crist to be man onlye.

7. That ther is no generat[ion ?] in god. but of creatures.

[699] Deuteronomy 18: 18.
[700] John 16: 7.

8. That this assertion / god to be made man / is contrary to the rule of faith & a monstrous blasphemye.
9. That Christ was not before the fullnes of tyme except by promise.
10. hat Christ was not god, otherwise then annointed god.
11. That Christ was not in the forme of god equall with god, that is in substance of god, but in righteousnes & givinge of salvation.
12. That Christ by his godhead wrought no miracles.
13. That Christ is not to be prayed unto.

These notes I thought good to send you, it may be such novelties when they see them will give our Frendes with you occasion to pitty us who live amongest these combustious spirittes.[701]
(On p. 172)
Addressed: To the worshipfull my worthye Frend m^r Thomas Weste these
Endorsed: (1) Apr. ii. [= 11] 1612. Sara.
　　　(2) Rec. Sat. Iulii. 7° ⎫ 1612
　　　　　Answ. wed Iuly. 18°.⎭
　　　(3) Letters written in the yeare 1612 To Mr Thomas More concerning the oath of alleageance

27 *George Salvin (Birkhead) to Thomas More (20 May 1612)*　　*(AAW A XI, no. 84, pp. 239–42. Holograph)*

my verie good S^r, after my longe desyer to heare from you I have now receyved two of yours (not missinge those you have sent before), the one of the 16 of march, the other of the 28. so that I make account to have receyved all which you have sent. as for answere to the first, be you sure that albeit I begynne to grow dymme, yet when iust occasion forceth me, I will not omitt to visit you with my letters, beinge not ignorant of the consolation that such correspondence bringeth with it. for the sturre about the booke you presented[702] take you no great thought, it can do you no harme, neither need you to prosecute that matter for your credit, for I do not conceyve you have lost it by that means. the sturre about that point is not so great heare as I perceyve you imagin, albeit one of Late of no small reputation hath once againe obiected the same unto me. but I am not moved ther with, but Lett

---

[701] For another copy of the articles laid against Wightman, Bodleian Library, Oxford, Ashmolean MS 1521 (B), item 7, pp. 5–9. Bennett misses out one article: 'That the place the fourth of Malachy, of Elias to come, is likewise meant of his person', and combines two others. For copies of the articles against Legate, almost identical to Bennett's list, see BL, Lansdowne MS 255, fos 442r–3r; G. Roberts (ed.), *Diary of Walter Yonge* (Camden Society, Old Series 41, 1848), 25. I am very grateful to David Como for this information.
[702] See **Letter 20**.

such speeches passe, wherin I fynd much good, and therfor could wish yow wold also deale no more therwith. for I am told yt will but breed amongst us increase of combustions. your zeale against the oath giveth me great edification, and causeth me iustly to see what the generall opinion is in that place [word deleted], which by the grace of god I meane to hold so longe as I live. In that sense yow say yow are a frend to those of the Clinke, I am also a frend, and I thinke I have shewed the same in as good termes as any other of my brethren hath done. but I see yow imagin the Contrarie by the tenor of my letter to our viceprotector,[703] which in verie deed was all true, but yett made not such a strepitus as yow conceyve, neither hath as yett putt me to any great hazard: yf I fall in the handes of the persecutors, and then they obiect the same unto me, I hope by the grace of our lord Iesus to qualifie there heate with some reasonable answere or other. that which I wrote of your geving them notice of matters, was but mr blackwels bragge, and for any thinge I know it hath not prevailed to your hurt.[704] beleve me I consider well enough who they be that say divide et impera: I will have an eye unto them I warrant yow, and yet make no disturbance of our peace so farre as lieth in me. yow need not molest your selfe in that kynd any more, what I wrote was onely for a caveat to your selfe. I am glad your monsignor[705] continueth so well for us, remember me unto him in the best manner, and tell him that albeit I write not unto him, because of molestinge him in his greater affaires, yett both my selfe and all belonginge unto me shalbe ever redie to acknowledge his charitie and to be alwaies gratefull for his singular benevolence towardes us. The Carmelite[706] I never saw as yett, but I understand he speaketh kyndly of me, and sent me the booke of Teresia for a token.[707] he behaveth hinselfe well, and as a religious person of that order. and perhaps I shall gett him to write a word or two to his generall in our behalfe. I like well of your advertisment concerning the

[703] Birkhead wrote to More on 9 January 1612 enclosing a letter to the viceprotector Bianchetti certifying what he had done about Blackwell, AAW A XI, no. 3.

[704] See **Letter 21**. In early January 1612 Birkhead had warned that More should 'take heed what yow write to mr blackwell. he giveth out ill speeches, as though yow were wholly for them', AAW A XI, no. 1 (p. 1); and that Blackwell 'told a frend of the Iesuites...the intelligence yow send to me, is nothinge in respect of that which yow give to them', AAW A XI, no. 2 (p. 5). In February 1612 Richard Smith also warned More that the oath-favouring priests in the Clink prison regarded More as a friend, AAW A XI, no. 20.

[705] John Baptist Vives.

[706] Thomas Doughty alias or vere Dawson.

[707] Probably [Michael Walpole ?, trans.], *The Lyf of the Mother Teresa of Iesus* (Antwerp, 1611), ARCR II, no. 783.

choice of a viceprotector.[708] but I dowbt not but that for your part, yow have don by this your endevour for our good, alwaies remittinge your selfe to his hol pleasure. As towchinge m[r] Crawforth[709] yow still write as yf yow were molested with feare of his comminge thither. but I have satisfied yow in diverse Letters, and now I breifely tell yow againe, that the good old man hath don, and meaneth no such longe iorney, and I think also wilbe quiet, albeit he still taketh him selfe to be wronged by m[r] Samuell.[710] Commend me to don Anselmo[711] and thank him for his to me, and tell him that fa preston and I have resolved to agree in the generall, though we differ in some particulars. m[r] Sam still urgeth against my brethren, but I have willed them to be quiett, and so I trust they will remaine. m[r] Copley is desperate in his Apostasie, but I am enformed he will do no harme against us, though the pursivantes much urge him therunto.[712] Surely I perceyve that these [p. 240] benedictins of spaine are our great frendes, both by that which yow write of ther procurator, and also by many courtesies from fa white.[713] we must shew our selves gratefull as well as we can. for any thinge I know, the matter is quyte dashed as towchinge our frend at Brucxels, and so it is good it shold rest. your monsignors and Card Arragons letters never came to me; and yett I have caused the partie to be demanded, that shewed me once a letter to himselfe from the said Card. yow say well concerninge our frendshippe with the padri.[714] what soever I write I meane no other thinge. And therfor I can not but give my old frend m[r] d perse[715] many lovinge thankes for his good advise and so I praie yow tell him from me. I am gladd yow conferre in our matters with him, for I am assured of his love to me, and I am perswaded that we may reape much good by his iudgment and experience. I will do what lieth in me to satisfie the gentleman named m[r] Thomas Rant, but yt cannott be speedily don because my intelligence from those partes is little and seldome.

    now a word or two to your other letter of the 28 of march. I rest much contented in that yow tell me of the receit of myne of 23 of Ianuarie,[716] but I marvell yow make but mention of five in a coople.

---

[708] Cardinal Lawrence Bianchetti had just died. He was buried in the Church of the Gesù in Rome next to Ignatius of Loyola. I am grateful to Thomas McCoog for this information.

[709] Cuthbert Crayford.

[710] Samuel (Bartholomew) Kennett OSB.

[711] Robert (Anselm) Beech OSB.

[712] Copley made a point of his determined neutrality in this respect, John Copley, *Doctrinall and Morall Observations* (1612), sig. ¶4r–v.

[713] John (Augustine) Bradshaw OSB.

[714] Jesuits.

[715] William Percy.

[716] AAW A XI, no. 6.

for as I remember ther were above 7 or 8 in them both.[717] I wrot to the holy office, to Card. Bellar. and to your monsignor of which because yow make no mention, I suppose that second packet was not come when yow wrote this Letter. [In margin: now I reme[m]ber it was by the way of Brux I wrote these last.] yf they be miscaried I can be but sorie. I hope they were all to verie good purpose. and that which yow iudge was defective in my letter to the Spanish Emb,[718] I hope I have in some sort supplied in that Letter to your monsignor. I leave all thinges to the wisdome of your frendes and your selfe, and therfor in that yow delivered my letter to Conti[719] which was for Sfondrata,[720] I cannot but imagin yow had good reason to do it. yow stand upon our direction from hence, but it will come alwaies to late, and therfor we must relie upon the confidence we have in your sinceritie. macte igitur animo and do your best in our principall suit,[721] and I trust god will blesse yow with good successe. Card. melino (as I take it) is he that a few yeares since was employed in Austria. I hope his experience he had in that countrie of the heretiques will make him to have the more compassion of us.[722] I could wish the Cappucine had respected our necessitie in his sermon for the residence of BB. perhaps it might have don us much good. what he should be (whose Letter so well penned m[r] Geffrey[723] sent unto yow) I cannot imagin. I wold he had discoursed of other countries, where he should have had much more matter then either of dorsett or Sommersett.[724] it is not unlike (as I have signified in some of my other Letters) that yow shall have a gentleman there [word deleted] shortly who seameth both able and well prepared to enforme of our present calamities.[725] yow wold have us to sett downe

[717] See AAW A XI, nos 6, 12.

[718] Don Francisco de Castro. See **Letter 25**.

[719] Cardinal Charles Conti.

[720] Cardinal Paul Emile Sfondrata, nephew of Pope Gregory XIV.

[721] For the appointment of a bishop.

[722] Giovanni Garzia Millini had been created cardinal in 1606 by Paul V. An influential figure in the curia, he was, however, as secretary of the Inquisition, a leading opponent of the project for appointing a bishop for England and, in 1623, when Gregory XV reversed the policy of Paul V in this respect, he still opposed any such episcopal appointment, Allison, 'Richard Smith', 159–60.

[723] Geoffrey Pole.

[724] Perhaps Birkhead is referring to the (now badly damaged) letter to More of March 1612 (AAW A XI, no. 52) in the first part of which the writer deals extensively with the condition of the Catholic gentry in Dorset and Somerset and the shortage of residences for priests. T.F. Knox identified the writer as Edward Kenion.

[725] Birkhead wrote to More on 20 April 1612 that a Catholic 'gentleman' who had written to Cardinal Bellarmine was intending to visit Rome; More should assist him since 'his zeale is extraordinarie, and therfor I beleve, yf he may be hard, he will roundly describe the manner of our persecution (yf it may be) to paule himselfe', AAW A XI, no. 62 (p. 182).

what course ['wold' deleted] were best to be taken for the satisfaction of all in our disputes, which wilbe hard for us to do, ubi tot sunt sententiae quot sunt homines. the safest waie for us in matters of doctrine, or of fact, concerninge doctrine, wilbe still to relie upon the Censure of that holy sea. but our disputes are not so manifest, and I have good hope to suppresse them, especially amongst them that belonge to me. but will yow know what we do? for certen, the greatest and best part of mine adheare to the breves. but most gentlemen and such as have any thinge to loose do make a nomber of sheiftes to take the oath. the sheift which is now most common and carieth most men awaie, is to fynd out some Iustices there frendes, before whome [p. 241] they sweare onely there temporal alledgiance, excepting that in the oath which concerneth the popes autoritie, and the iustices admitt this manner of swearinge underhand, but yett openly make a certificate to the Superior magistrate that such parties have taken the oath of alledgiance, meaninge this parlament oath. this forme [word deleted] is currant with the laitie, and is thought by them to be Lawfull. yf this course wold serve, I know no other that will satisfie there humors. but to this we may not give our consentes it beinge both against his hol breves, and also that order which yow sent last to me about declaringe those of the Clinck to have lost ther faculties. for it seameth to insinuate that the said oath ['or modification' deleted] is not to be taken in any sense, or with any modification. this is all which I can say of this matter, if his hol. will beare with this, or give us leave to winck theratt, there wold not be any such shrinkinge as there is. I assure yow men are so bent upon this sheift, that those which resist it, are most like to be deprived of there interteynment, for my owne part I utterly mislike it. for it is nothinge in verie *deed but* plaine dissimulation, which I think will not be iudged by the highest to stand with the service and pleasure of god, unto whome neverthelesse I submit my selfe in all thinges. [In margin: 'both religiouse and Clergie men hold that this oth is not the parlament oath, and so not against the breve'.] some have gotten licence from thence (as it is said) to suffer a minister to preach in there howses, and so avoid the oath. yf the highest do accept of this, there wilbe nombers redie to embrace it.[726] but then (o Lord) how will the enemies of the Catholique religion bragg and insult against us for not havinge zeale and Couradge to professe our faith accordinge to the veritie of the gospell?

yow do well to say, that yow hope yow may say God have mercie on m^r black.[727] soul. many heare do dowbt whether they may say so or

[726] *Cf.* A.J. Loomie, 'A Jacobean Crypto-Catholic: Lord Wotton', *Catholic Historical Review* 53 (1967), 328–45, at pp. 333–6.
[727] George Blackwell. See **Letter 22**.

no. he is dead in deed long since, but <u>unpenitent</u> and havinge no remorce for the Combustion he had made amongst us. still he thought his opinion good, and the last confession he made was to m^r hebburne, whome he knew to have Lost his faculties. what God may do in extraordinarie power and accordinge to his manifold mercies we do leave to his divine wisdome, but m^r bl dyinge in the sight of others (as many do hold) in contempt and disobedience of the sea Apostolique, yt maketh some scrupulous persons to leave his estate and condition onely to god.

as I remember in my last to yo*u*r monsig*n*or (if it be come) I have taken notice of the miscariadge of his and the Car. Arr. to me. m^r Baldwin lieth still in the tower, and no speech what shall become of him. m^r Alabaster holdeth catholique still in shew, albeit he converseth altogether with men of the Contrarie opinion. m^r pr*e*sident^{728} giveth good wordes and hath told d bish he is contented to conferre,^{729} without a mandat*um* from thence. what wilbe the end god knoweth; in divers to me he hath much stood upon, nihil innovandu*m*,^{730} but by a generall consent of all sortes. now we shall see at this Conference, what his meaning is[.] I am glad of that w*h*ich yo*w* write of don mauro.^{731} thus yo*w* see I have in some sort answered both yo*u*r longe letters, now onely and lastly I tell yo*w* that we are still perplexed in our distresses everie day increasinge. com*m*end us therfor I desyer yo*w* in those holy places, that we may persever to the end. And so I leave yo*w* to god this 20 of may 1612.

yo*u*r assured frend

Geo. Salv.

(On a separate slip marked p. 241*)

what I have written in this letter concerninge the secret licence to heare a sermon in that sort, I desier yo*w* to keepe it to yo*u*r selfe. for it is not manifest, but onely muttered and whispered from one to another, but doth exceeding much harme. I cannot beleve that any such licence is graunted.

yo*w* do well to take no notice of the Iarrs betwene the benedictins, neither do I also. those that belonge to me are so constant against the oath, that the laie catholiques eschew there advise, and make ther recourse to others of the same order that be well lerned, and are by such lerned laickes resolved to take the oath in that forme w*h*ich I have

---

^{728} Thomas Worthington.

^{729} Birkhead refers to the forthcoming conference at Douai.

^{730} A reference to the initial ruling communicated (24 September 1610 (NS)) by Cardinal Lawrence Bianchetti to Birkhead in reply to the two petitions for reform of Douai and the sending of priests to England, AAW A IX, no. 76.

^{731} William (Maurus) Taylor OSB. See Lunn, 'English Cassinese', 63–4.

sett downe in my letter. which pleaseth me nothinge at all, but yett havinge no good meanes to helpe, I take no great exceptions at there doinges, save onely that I tell them, I dare not approve them.
(On p. 242)
Addressed: To his verie good frend m^r Thomas Moore give this. Rome
Endorsed: (1) May. 20. 1612. G. Sal.
      (2) Recea. thr. Sept. 6. }
          Answ. thr. Sept. 13. } 1612
      (3) Of m^r Blackwells death

28 *Robert Clerk (Pett) to Thomas More (9 June 1612 (NS))*   *(AAW A XI,*
no. 96, pp. 273–4. Holograph)

Very Reverend and beloved Sir. yours of the 19th of may beinge salfly arived unto my handes I would not omitt according to my accoustomed manner to geve yow notice therof, as alsoe to geve yow to understande that the inclosed with yt to Sir w:^m Roper,[732] f: Augustine,[733] m:^r Rant and m^r Ishams sonne[734] are all sent already accordinge as they weare addressed. and now in requitall of your packet I send yow an other as well fraughted yet with the greater part for your self which may make me presume that they shalbe the better welcome; yow shall therfore

---

[732] Sir William Roper of Eltham, a grandson of Anthony Browne, first Viscount Montague and a great-grandson of Sir Thomas More, had started paying recusancy fines in November 1600, CRS 57, p. lxxxiv. After another recusancy conviction in February 1605, PRO, E 368/555, mem. 253a, and resulting assessments of his property, he conformed in front of Archbishop Richard Bancroft at Lambeth on 17 November 1606, PRO, E 368/525, mm. 241a–3a. He presented his conformity certificate to the exchequer in 1607, and then again in November 1611. It is not clear when Sir William and Lady Roper first travelled to the Continent, but in July 1611 they went to Spa. Lady Roper returned briefly to England in October 1611 while Sir William was at Cambrai, AAW A X, nos 95, 140, 149. The Ropers were friendly with the English Benedictines of the Spanish congregation and John (Augustine) Bradshaw OSB sometimes carried letters for them, AAW A XI, nos 5, 16, 21. Sir William with his wife came back to England in June 1613, but returned almost immediately to the Continent and by October 1613 was in Cambrai again. However he must have returned to England again because he presented his 1606 conformity certificate to the exchequer once more in 1614. On the basis of his original conviction for recusancy he had been, on 24 September 1614, assessed on his landed estate, PRO E 368/555, mem. 253a; *cf.* J.J. La Rocca, 'James I and his Catholic Subjects, 1606–1612: Some Financial Implications', *RH* 18 (1987), 251–62, at p. 257. See also CRS 68, 89–90 (a Spanish account of Sir William Roper conforming in July 1617 to avoid a grant of his property, on account of his recusancy, to Sir John Ramsay, first Viscount Haddington). From the constant correspondence between Sir William and his son Thomas, who resided with More in Rome, it seems the Ropers were heavily involved in promoting the secular clergy's causes.
[733] John (Augustine) Bradshaw OSB.
[734] Either William or Francis Isham.

understand that some few dayes past I receaved from m:ʳ william Howard[735] a Letter dated from doway certefiyinge me of his acquaintance with yow at Rome[736] and Late departure from thence cravinge withall my help for the directinge of a little packet from him unto yow which now with the rest I here send yow together[737] with one from m:ʳ Mayney[738] to m:ʳ Roper.[739] then further I have receaved this week two Letters together in one packet from our R: Archpriest of two general dates the one of the 16ᵗʰ of March the other of the 22ᵗʰ of Aprill ether of them especially concerninge the matter of the meetinge at doway[740] and noe newes mentioned in them but souch as Longe since I have written unto yow; with thes Letters I receaved alsoe two for your self from him which heare alsoe I sende yow. then further ther is one little Letter addressed unto yow by the name of west which came as I take yt with the same packet from Tho: Heth together with a little note written to his brother[741] which likewise I have sent yow that therby yow may sea what he writeth as concerninge your mony matters, And now from our frendes at doway I received this weeke newes asconcerninge ther affayers ther, and with ther letters one directed to your self from M:ʳ Champney[742] and an other from F: white[743] which likewise with this packett I send yow accompanied with the copies of two petitiones[744] to

---

[735] Fifth son of Lord William Howard of Naworth. See R.E. Grun, 'A Note on William Howard, Author of a Patterne of Christian Loyaltie', *Catholic Historical Review* 42 (1956–7), 330–40. On 21 July 1612 (NS) Robert Pett wrote to More that William Howard had 'bene sent for expresly from my Lord his father'. Roger Widdrington was the messenger sent for him. (Widdrington was a friend of Lord William Howard, and Howard's library may have supplied Roland (Thomas) Preston OSB, who used Widdrington's name as a pseudonym, with the books he needed for his tracts on the oath of allegiance, Lunn, *EB*, 41–2; *CSPD 1611–18*, 347.) Pett said that 'this hastie sendinge for him did proceade from a letter which I convaied for him into England' which had signalled his intention of entering OSB. John (Augustine) Bradshaw had notified Pett of Howard's 'forwardnes. . .to have bene a monke and with what expedition his father hath labored to prevent yt', AAW A XI, no. 124 (p. 337). See also **Letter 32**.

[736] On 14 September 1611 (NS) Champney had informed More that, on that day, there 'parted from hence [Paris] 4 or 5 yonge gentlemen towardes Italy[.] they will not come so farr as you as yett but purpose to stay in Sienna one of theme ys my lord wiliame his sonn' (by whom Champney sent More 'one of mʳ witheringtonn his bookes'), AAW A X, no. 118 (p. 341).

[737] William Howard had written to More on 26 May 1612 (NS), AAW A XI, no. 87.

[738] John Mayney.

[739] Thomas Roper, son of Sir William.

[740] The conference at Douai which met in May 1612.

[741] Jerome Heath.

[742] AAW A XI, no. 81, written from Douai on 17 May 1612 (NS), printed in TD V, pp. cxii–xiii.

[743] This is apparently John (Augustine) Bradshaw OSB's letter of 21 May 1612 (NS), AAW A XI, no. 85, narrating the proceedings of the conference held at Douai in this month.

[744] The petitions are written out in AAW A XI, no. 78, printed in TD V, pp. cxiii–xiv.

be exhibited to his holynes; and Lastly I send yo*w* heare w*i*th the rest a Letter directed to a franciscan frier one F: w:ᵐ Thomson a scottishman[.]⁷⁴⁵ yt is from one of the same order and natione heare [in margin: 'called f: Iohn Ogleby'⁷⁴⁶] who is my goostly fatther and very good freand and therfore I ame bould to recommend this Letter unto your care as alsoe his busines yf in any thing yo*w* may further yt w*hi*ch is in procueringe him and an other of his bretheren permission and facultyes for ther country as he to whome this letter is addressed will I thinke imparte unto yo*w*[.] otherwise I doe not request yo*w* to troble yo*ur* self therin but only to procuer us an aunswer of the letter and to let him understand yo*ur* willingnes to asiste him from whome the letter commeth in what yo*w* may. for truly I have byn much beholdinge to him for his Love and kindnes since my comminge hether and he is a very good religious man and of good esteme in his order. I have written to our freandes at Paris of the Late arivall of ther Letters from doway hether[.] that of M:ʳ Champneys to my self was of the 17ᵗʰ of may and that from f: white to my self wherin they were inclosed did beare date of the 28ᵗʰ of the same moneth w*hi*ch doth argue him to have reteyned the Letters more then ten dayes in his handes and unto myself they arived not untill the second of this moneth in the eveninge beinge saterday and becaus they came the same day after the post was [word deleted] departed towardes yo*w* I was constreyned to kepe them till this next Saterday followinge and soe by fault of delay at doway they have had at the Leste three weekes hinderance all w*hi*ch I have written and signified unto them.

for m:ʳ Ishams daughter I intend not to troble my self any further, M:ʳ Minors hath of Late written unto me that he and his brother in Law are now very good freandes⁷⁴⁷ and that he hath written to his

Champney's letter of 17 May 1612 (NS), AAW A XI, no. 81, enclosed copies (AAW A XI, nos 79 and 80) of them.

⁷⁴⁵ See W.J. Anderson, 'William Thomson of Dundee, Friar Minor Conventual', *Innes Review* 18 (1967), 99–111. When Thomson returned to Scotland from Rome in 1613 Thomas More prepared a commendatory letter for him, dated 19 April 1613 (NS), addressed to Birkhead. Thomson proposed to travel through England. More thought that, since Thomson was experienced in Roman politics, he might be of use to Birkhead, AAW A XII, no. 77.

⁷⁴⁶ See W.E. Browne, *John Ogilvie* (1925), 268, 270.

⁷⁴⁷ In March 1611 it was proposed that Christopher Isham's daughter should attend upon the wife of a new ambassador who was about to be appointed to go to England from the archduke Albert in Flanders, AAW A X, no. 20. She discharged herself from service in July 1611 (AAW A X, no. 87) and married, in early 1612, one Walter Minors of the 'Inglish Companye' at Rheinberg (North Rhine, Germany). This was a marriage which was against her father's wishes since he had intended that she should enter religion, AAW A XI, nos 5 (p. 13), 43, 59. She replied, through Robert Pett, in March 1612, that, sorry as she was to have offended, she could not 'repent' her choice because she had matched with 'one whome she loveth' and that his birth and good qualities made him

father in ther behalfes but for my part I have not receaved any letter from him: M:ʳ minors hath a brother[748] of Late come over gone to the spaw to make preparation for the Countes of worcester[749] whom he serveth[.][750] he is a proper gentilman and seameth to be in good credite with the Countes. Sir Charles Sommerset and m:ʳ Arundel passed this way lately towardes England.[751] and Lately also ther hath ben with me one m:ʳ Bradbery[752] newly come from your partes and goeinge towards England. I have retorned answer to m:ʳ William Howard of his and presented him withall my ready and willinge service. The proces here of d: Norton[753] agaynst the president[754] was for an abuse offered him (as he sayed) by an old servant of the hous called Lewis becaus he could not by the presidents meanes get dew satisfaction to be made

suitable, AAW A XI, no. 33 (p. 83). She left for Rheinberg where her brother William (ordained in September 1602 at Valladolid) was also resident. On 18 March 1612 (NS) Pett wrote to More that he had assisted Walter Minors in clearing his name of rumours grounded 'only upone the dislike which m:ʳ wm Isham toke of the mach betweene m:ʳ Minors and his sister'. Minors claimed to have paid her debts and 'he is contented that' any marriage portion 'be soe imployed and disposed of as that he never have use…of any one peny therof', AAW A XI, no. 43 (p. 111). By March 1613 Isham snr's daughter had given birth to a son, something which still did not placate her father, AAW A XII, no. 50.

[748] Ralph Minors.

[749] Elizabeth, wife of Edward Somerset, fourth earl of Worcester, and daughter of Francis Hastings, second Earl of Huntingdon. John Chamberlain noted on 23 July 1612 that the countess had gone to Spa, McClure, 372.

[750] See M.G. Brennan, *The Travel Diary (1611–1612) of an English Catholic Sir Charles Somerset* (The Leeds Philosophical and Literary Society, Literary and Historical Section, Leeds, 1993), 7. Ralph Minors appears to be the steward mentioned by William Jones to William Trumbull in November 1612, *Downshire MSS* III, 415. Walter Minors wrote to Trumbull from Rheinberg on 2 December 1612 (NS) asking whether his brother Ralph had left a sum of money with Trumbull, *Downshire MSS* III, 425. See also *ibid.*, 445; **Letter 6**.

[751] Brennan, *Travel Diary*, 13–15, pointing out that the identity of Sir Charles Somerset's travelling companion is problematic. He notes that Sir Dudley Carleton informed Chamberlain from Venice on 3 April 1612 that Somerset and 'my Lord Arundel's son' had left for England; *cf.* M. Lee, *Dudley Carleton to John Chamberlain 1603–1624* (New Brunswick, NJ, 1972), 127. Brennan speculates that the reference is to a son of Thomas Howard, first Earl of Suffolk, possibly his third son, Henry, who had been accompanying Somerset's eldest brother, Sir Thomas, at Paris in September 1610, and then travelled with his brother-in-law Lord Cranborne to Italy, and could have joined up with Sir Charles on a return journey. Yet Henry Howard had arrived back in London in February, McClure, 337. Edward Chaney suggests that 'm:ʳ Arundel' is Thomas Arundell, future second Baron Arundell of Wardour. In 1607 he had married Blanche, daughter of Edward Somerset, fourth earl of Worcester. (I am very grateful to Edward Chaney for this information.) See also **Letter 53**.

[752] Not identified.

[753] John Knatchbull.

[754] Thomas Worthington.

unto him and therfore came hether to complayne to the Nuncio[755] unto which complaynt when the president had replied the proces was ended and the doctor glad to retorne as wise as he came.[756] the Marques Spinola[757] and Count of Bucquoy[758] are sayed to be now arived to Mariemont[759] wher the Archduke this summertyme remayneth.[760] and this week passed this way from out of England the Ambassador of Mantua.[761] F: white certifieth me that he heareth of the apprehendinge of three of his bretheren[762] in ther entry into England, as alsoe of Mr Iames fitzeIames[763] with others at ther comming out at Dover. [p. 274] And now in requital of your scottish miracles yow shall receave from me some scottish newes which is that of Late yt hath ben rumored here that the Lord Haddington[764] which ['was' deleted] is maried to the Erle of sussex his daughter[765] had most cruelly murthered his wife: & that therupon all the portes were shut up for his apprehendinge but the truth of this matter is sayed to be that the Lord sancher[766] who some yeares past had receaved a publike disgrace by one Turner a fenser in a publike prise before the kinge to the Losinge of one of his eyes to revenge him self of this dishonor then receaved, did by a trayne get this Turner into a Taverne wher after he had bene a little made mery one prepared for the purpose shot the sayed Turner with a pistol in at the back in souch sort that he fell presently dead without speakinge any one word; the manner of this murther beinge presently related to the kinge his maiesty commanded presently the portes to [b]e [word

[755] Guido Bentivoglio.

[756] John (Augustine) Bradshaw OSB reported on 21 May 1612 (NS) that the Jesuits, as also Knatchbull and Singleton, were furious at Worthington 'because he goeth not those wayes which they would have him. he desireth exeedinglie to ridd them out of the College', AAW A XI, no. 85 (p. 243).

[757] Ambrose Spinola, Marquis of Benaffro, Duke of Santa Severino.

[758] Charles Bonaventure de Longueval, Count of Bucquoi. See *Downshire MSS* III, 303, and *passim*.

[759] In Hainaut, Belgium.

[760] *Downshire MSS* III, 303.

[761] Carlo di Rossi, Mantuan ambassador to England, *CSPV 1610–13*, 342, 359.

[762] On 21 May 1612 (NS), Bradshaw noted the arrest of the three Benedictines, 'fr maurus de la Sagun [William (Maurus) Scott]. fr Edwardo de Obarenes [Edward Ashe]. and fr Iuan de S millan Hijo [John Harper]', AAW A XI, no. 85 (p. 243).

[763] Perhaps a relation (one of the brothers?) of Nicholas FitzJames OSB, Davidson, 657. In mid-January 1612 Pett had written to More that James FitzJames was with him in Brussels pursuing some private suit or matter of his own, though it was likely to be hindered by King Philip III, AAW A XI, no. 5.

[764] Sir John Ramsay, first Viscount Haddington.

[765] Elizabeth Radcliffe.

[766] Robert Creighton, eighth Baron Sanquhair. In 1608, Sanquhair had married Mary, the daughter of Sir George Fermor of Easton Neston, Northamptonshire, a Catholic family which, through Sir Francis Lacon of Kinlet, had a connection with the Brownes of Cowdray, Davidson, 595.

obscured: 'barred' ?] and proclamation to be made that whosoever could take or cause to be apprehended alive the Lord sancher should have five hundred poundes for his reward; or yf in resistinge he toke him dead he should have 250^li. likewise whosoever should take him alive which shot the pistol should have 100^li. yf dead, 50^li.[767] now becaus at this tyme the L: Haddington was retiered some 30 miles from London with his wife[768] and some circumstances with all occurringe which might geve occation to suspect that he had done yt upon dislike or discontentment with her gave likewise occatione that this rumor was raised of him; the Lord sancher as is sayed hath yealded himselfe to the Bishop of Canterbury and is committed and haveinge confessed the facte yt is likewise reported that he shall undouptedly be executed; yet some say that he standeth upon his purgation as not haveinge byn accessarie therunto but that beinge a catholike this is framed agaynste him[.] I shall hereafter informe yow further hereof as I come to learne more certaine truth of the matter. since that tyme happened an other accident which is that at a banquett at the french Embassadors an English gentilman[769] chansed to Let fall somethinge upon a scotish gentilman[770] his silke stockinge which he takinge in yll part upon multipliyinge of wordes tooke the English gentilman by the eare and pynched him soe sore and with souch violence that he drew his head almost unto the grond and tore the skyn in souch sorte that much blod Issued forth, this likewise is sayed to be brought before the kinge who hath willed the gentilman to come before him and that he will sea him to have all honorable satisfaction made him;[771] The Lord Vaux is condemned in a primunire and removed to the Kinges Beanch. divers others are committed as Sir Hen: Iames[772] of whome yow write, M^r

---

[767] For Chamberlain's accounts of the murder and the trial, McClure, 348–9, 362, 364. This murder is the subject of a forthcoming article by Michael Bowman, 'The Murder of John Turner'. See also **Letters 28, 30**.

[768] It had been reported in May 1612 that Viscount Haddington had (inexplicably) taken his wife from London to Farnham Castle and had not returned, *Downshire MSS* III, 290.

[769] James Hawley.

[770] James Maxwell.

[771] McClure, 348: James Maxwell, 'a sewer or gentleman usher upon very small occasion pluckt or pincht one Hawly a gentleman of the Temple by the eare at the feasting of the Duke of Bouillon' and 'the bloud followed freshly'; *Downshire MSS* III, 297, 306, 341. See **Letter 29**.

[772] For Sir Henry James's refusal to take the oath of allegiance, see H. Bowler, 'Sir Henry James of Smarden, Kent, and Clerkenwell, Recusant (*c.* 1559–1625)', in A.E.J. Hollaender and W. Kellaway (eds), *Studies in London History* (1969), 289–313, at pp. 307–8.

Berry M:ʳ Chester,⁷⁷³ M:ʳ Vaviser⁷⁷⁴ with others⁷⁷⁵ god Comforte and help them all. the Duck of Bouillion ['his' deleted] is departed from England[.]⁷⁷⁶ the gyftes which the kinge bestowed one him self and his trayne are sayed to amount to thirty thousand crounes. The Count of Henault⁷⁷⁷ Embassador from the Palatin⁷⁷⁸ is alsoe retorned and as is sayed for a further commission for makinge the full conclution of the mach betwene the Palatine and the Lady Elizabeth⁷⁷⁹ which as yt is thought will undouptedly take effecte unles the spanishe Embassadors⁷⁸⁰ arivall doe hinder and breake yt, god dispose all to the best unto whos holy protection I doe recommend yow and soe take my leave restinge ever

yours most assueredly
    Rob: Clerc
Bruxells this 9ᵗʰ of Iune 1612
[In margin] yf that spanish epistle written to father generall beare not to great a bulke I pray send me one of them or yf hereafter any thinge of the Like arive with yow.
No address
Endorsed: (1) Iune. 9. 1612. R.P.
        (2) Rece. thurs. June 28.⎱ 1612
            Answ. sat. Iune. 30. ⎰
            herwith one to mʳ Wil. Thomps. dilvr. Iu. 29. and a letter
            to my coosen Th.⁷⁸¹ from Mʳ Mayney dd. Iune 28.

---

⁷⁷³ *i.e.* one of the Chichester family of Arlington in Devonshire. On 15 May 1612 Edward Bennett wrote to More that, in this drive to enforce the oath, 'mʳ Bery & mʳ Chichester gentlmen of the west [are] boath in prison', AAW A XI, no. 76 (p. 217); *cf. Downshire MSS* III, 298.

⁷⁷⁴ William Vavasour of Hazlewood, Yorkshire offered a composition to the crown of £700 for his refusal to take the oath, BL, Lansdowne MS 153, fo. 87r; Foley IV, 689–90.

⁷⁷⁵ Richard Broughton wrote to More on 5 May 1612 that many gentry were through favour being allowed to compound for refusal 'as fower out of yorkeshire, Mʳ Sayre [John Sayer of Worsall]; Mʳ Vavicer, Mʳ Gascoyne, the fowrth name I have not hard [in fact, William Middleton of Stockeld, BL, Lansdowne 153, fo. 80r]', AAW A XI, no. 72 (p. 209). For Middleton's pardon for refusal to take the oath, see PRO, SO 3/5 (26 November 1612). See PRO, SP 14/70/9 (a list dated 18 July 1612 of those who were to be offered the oath).

⁷⁷⁶ See **Letter 25**.

⁷⁷⁷ Philip Lewis, Count of Hanau, brother-in-law of the Duke of Bouillon.

⁷⁷⁸ Frederick V, Elector Palatine.

⁷⁷⁹ Princess Elizabeth.

⁷⁸⁰ Don Pedro de Zúñiga.

⁷⁸¹ Thomas Roper.

29 *Benjamin Norton to George West (Thomas More) (6 & 10 June 1612)   (AAW A XI, no. 95, pp. 271–2. Holograph)*

My good frende: thease seven weekes I have beene far awaye from my good neighbours & a meere strainger to my man & dame.[782] from whome I have receaved noe lettre in all this tyme by reason whereof I can saye nothinge of any thinge in those partes neither of any other matters but of suche as I have by the relation of an olde acquaintance of yours one I: Younge[783] to whome I give greate creditt. whoe tellethe mee firste that he hathe rec. xxˢ in silver from the Clarke for yow. I saye in silver bicause had it beene in golde ytt had beene worthe 22ˢ, which moneye I have & desire to knowe whatt I shoulde doe with it. secondlye hee tellethe mee that a little before & after Ester that theare was muche a doe in the easte of sussex vz breakinge uppe of howses at midnight by the Counstables at Mʳˢ Brookes of Asson[784], and some of her sonnes at Berricke farme[785] to fe[t]che [?] her & them to take the othe. some fledd, some weare taken, and some tooke, & some refused to take the othe. aboughte that tyme thear was searche at Bentlye[786] by a pursephant and ii Iustices of peace for seminary pp. for informations or lettres of information from beyonde the seas, & for libellous bookes, but theare was noe harme donne there and the poore scott dyed some weeke beefore. over all the Cuntrye theare was sittinge of Iustices & caulinge all kinde of howseholders beefore them to take the othe as well at other places as at Battell where amongste diverse protestants some of susewell[787] weare brought but none of the towne meddled with all, beefore the sittinges off which Iustices theare was watche & warde to staye all roges & wanderinge persons but for all that none weare stayed but Catholiques & some people weare not far from Robertsbridge brought thither (whome I muste not name) whoe I thinke [word deleted] made butt bad shifte & in some sence tooke the othe. The thursdaye beefore the Assention the Lorde Vaux was con-demned in a premunire for refusinge the othe[788] albeeit some saye (howe trulye I knowe not) that hee offered after a sorte to take it. that very Daye Nedd Goldwire loste his coppy holde at Selscome[789] beeinge overthrowen by lawe, soe that hee muste sticke to his wifes portion &

---

[782] Richard and Constance Lambe.
[783] Possibly John Young, recusant, of West Firle.
[784] Probably the widow of Robert Brooke of Frog Firle in Alfriston, who died in 1610.
[785] Berwick is a parish north of Alfriston.
[786] Bentley in Framfield, Sussex, the property of Edward Gage. See **Letter 30**.
[787] Shoyswell hundred (in Hastings Rape in East Sussex), virtually coterminous with the parish of Ticehurst.
[788] See **Letter 23**.
[789] Sedlescombe.

welthe, whoe was a widdowe some tymes the wife of one Mr Dounte[790] or suche a name, whoe dwelte I thinke in that parishe. Yow have hearde I doubte not that there is one saukell or saukewell[791] a Iesuit whoe hathe offered him selfe to the Bisshop of London[792] & remaynethe with him.[793] of whome (leeste the reporte of his doinges might discreditt his brethren) yow muste speake nor thinke noe yll, untill the discreditt (if any bee) bee by tyme worne owte. From London yow maye heere howe a scott[794] at a horserace strooke the Earle of Mountgummerye[795] over the face with a ridinge wan[d] & howe the sage wise erle putt upp the disgrace.[796] howe likewise a scottishe Lorde[797] caused a Fenser[798] to bee murdered for an olde grudge,[799] & lastelye howe an other scott did moste groselye abuse a gentleman of the Indes of the Coorte by bytinge his eare[800] all which is talked of & not well digested by the Englishe, but howe shall theye amende them selves? The right honorable Lorde

[790] Probably John Downton of Sedlescombe, steward of the Battle estate. His will was proved on 11 January 1611, ESRO, Lewes Archdeaconry Wills, A 13, fos 99r–100r; Henry E. Huntington Library, Los Angeles, BA 56/1623 (for which reference I am grateful to Christopher Whittick). His wife's name was Mary.

[791] John Salkeld, formerly a Jesuit, who had now abandoned Roman Catholicism. See CRS 75, 287, 349. For Salkeld's arrest, see *Downshire MSS* III, 331; *CSPD 1611–18*, 124. On 20 May 1612 Birkhead was still not sure whether Salkeld was in fact leading a Jesuit mission. He had no faculty or permission from his superiors, 'yett he saieth that he doth nothinge, but which the best lerned in Spaine did approve, before his departure thence', AAW A XI, no. 83 (p. 237).

[792] John King.

[793] John (Augustine) Bradshaw OSB told More in July 1612 that Salkeld was with Archbishop Abbot and was writing against the Jesuit Francisco Suarez. Salkeld was said 'to have asked leave of his Generall to be a Carthusian and coming to Maclin with ill wether was carried into England so that you see he is no Iesuit', AAW A XI, no. 110 (p. 303). Salkeld had a brother, Henry, whom Anthony Champney and Christopher Bagshaw used in September 1613 to take correspondence to More in Rome, and who later renounced his Catholic priesthood in order to join the Church of England, AAW A XII, nos 166, 168; Anstr. II, 276.

[794] William Ramsay.

[795] Philip Herbert, Earl of Montgomery.

[796] The earl of Montgomery had quarrelled with Ramsay at a horse race in Croydon, *Downshire MSS*, III, 269. Robert Pett noted that there 'were more then a hundred swordes drawen', and that 'undouptedly yf one stroke had ben given ther had much harme ensued therof for that one in the Company cried out downe with the scot' but Charles Howard, first Earl of Nottingham had imposed order, AAW A XI, no. 59 (p. 176).

[797] Robert Creighton, eighth Baron Sanquhair.

[798] John Turner.

[799] Of the original quarrel, years before, which led Sanquhair to harbour thoughts of revenge, Richard Broughton noted that when Sanquhair was 'exercisinge weapons with a fencer in a prise, the fencer confessed he could not hurt him but in the face'. Sanquhair 'gave him leave not to spare any part of him, so they continuinge to play, the fencer put out one of his eyes', AAW A XI, no. 103 (p. 289). See also Benjamin Norton's account, **Letter 30**.

[800] See **Letter 28**.

Treasurer[801] is nowe righter then ever hee was as beeinge stretched to rights beeinge dedd, whoe was ever a crooked Apostle whiles hee lived. hee dyed (noe doubte) in the lorde, & stuncke soe muche on the earthe that hee was fayne to bee interred at Marrleborrowe in Wilkeshire as hee was comminge from the Bathe.[802] A parlamente shall bee in November nexte or els my brother brazen face[803] lyethe whoe tellethe mee that hee hearde soe muche at London. Condemne mee not for my not comminge unto yow untill yow knowe moore, what ever the gentleman which givethe the 3 Currs Currente shal wrighte against mee of whome I have deserved better measure then I finde as yett. Nowe good s[r] for wante of paper I muste make and [sic] ende[.] Wherefore I desire yow to remember mee to all my frendes & especiallye to that good zealous & learned Doctor m[r] doctor Thornell[804] of whose wisedome & sinceritye I heere soe muche that I am halfe prowde that sometymes I was acquainted with him. & I woulde hee knewe in howe kinde a manner I take the salutations which in yours [sic] lettres of the 7 of Aprill (which are the onleye one since Ianuary: which I received) hee sente unto mee vale 6 Inii 1612

BN.

(On p. 272)

I have had an other pull of sicknes which hathe brought mee lowe. I am to remayne untill I bee older by a monethe & stronger by an ownce with my sybella[805] whome some of the kinde of the three currs current have soe snarled att that I feare mee theye will never doe her good answerable to the harme which by them & theire meanes shee hathe receaved. Yff ever I returne to my olde neighbours I make accoumpte to finde newe kinde of deelinges for I have an inkelinge that all is not well beetwixte them and mee butt whatt the matter is I knowe not & knowinge my one innocencye I will care lesse then they Imagine howe ever thinges fall owte. I speake it to yow as to my true & sincere frende oro in utraque fortuna fidelis. Olde Roelande[806] & my bretheren are scarce cater Cosins.[807] the cause I dreeme to bee the Northeren quarrells maynetayned or not sufficientlye appeased by the

---

[801] Robert Cecil, first Earl of Salisbury.

[802] See McClure, 351. On Salisbury's departure for Bath, Edward Bennett noted that James was as close to his lord treasurer as ever, AAW A XI, no. 69.

[803] Norton's brother-in-law. See **Letter 1**. Norton refers to him also as 'Ned Godface', AAW A X, no. 29.

[804] In February 1612 Birkhead had informed More that Thornell was trying to organise financial assistance for the secular clergy, AAW A XI, no. 25.

[805] Sybil, Norton's sister. See **Letter 1**.

[806] Roland (Thomas) Preston OSB.

[807] i.e. good friends (OED).

Wizardes in the southe.[808] howe matters nowe goe beetwixte them I knowe not, for I have not had a lettre from m.[r] Rola[n]de thease 12 monethes. Theare was a speeche beefore Whitsontyde that one m[r] Craforde[809] & some other pp shoulde bee arrayned, but whatt is done I doe not knowe livinge wheare I doe & hearinge nothinge from thence or any other place & as I can not heere from them soe doe I not knowe howe to sende unto them, and whatt shifte I shall make to have this lettre conveyed unto yow I knowe not, for any tyme this moneth I have studyed howe to sende unto yow & yett coulde not compasse howe to doe it, wherefor good s.[r] have mee excused if yow heere from mee but seeldome al[t]howgh I desire as muche to give yow correspondence as any here whosoever. Commende mee in this side [?] to D Ansel:[810] of whome & from whome I can heere nothinge. vale 10 Inii 1612.

Addressed: To his approoved good frende M[r] George Weste
Endorsed: (1) Iunii. 6. et 10. 1612. BN.

(2) Recea. thr. Sept. 6. ⎱
    Answ. thr. Sept. 13. ⎰ 1612

30 *[Benjamin Norton] to George West (Thomas More) (9 July 1612*   (AAW
   A XI, no. 118, pp. 321–4. Holograph)

My deare s.[r] I am butt yesterdaye come home from my s.[r] sib:[811] to my dames[812] wheare I founde to lettres of yours sente thither for mee vz one of the 23 of May the other of the 6 of Iune. & at my sisters I receaved to others from yow one of the 7 of Aprill which came unto mee very speedilye & for in Iune I received an other of the 28 of februarye for all which lettres I thanke yow. & I assure yow that I have writtne unto yow everye monethe this newe yeare Maye excepted & that I omitted bicause at the place where I then laye theare had beene watche & warde to staye recusantes & I durste not ve[n]ture to sende by any of them that weare knowen to bee suche. In thease of yours I understood that myne have not come to your handes which makethe mee to sende yow woorde againe & againe that I have receaved xx[s] in silver for your Ringe & woulde faine knowe what I shoulde doe with it. yow guesse right of matters for in deede I have omitted to wright of newes which Londoners might wright of bicause I thinke that they knowe the newes better then my selfe and that it would bee stale newes eare it came

---

[808] See **Letters 15, 20, 21, 27**.
[809] William (Maurus) Scott OSB. See **Letters 30, 31**.
[810] Robert (Anselm) Beech OSB.
[811] Sybil, Norton's sister. See **Letter 1**.
[812] Constance Lambe.

unto yow. wherefore I sayed nothinge of the martirdomes of m.^r
Crayforde alias scot[813] a benedictine monke & m.^r Nuporte[814] whoe had
some tymes lived where m^r Formallyes[815] lived since whose deathes this
is a certane newes & admirable too, that there is in the westerne seas
a streame of bludd which many have seene & dipte theire handes in
it & this newes I speake of [word obscured: 'it' (?)] bicause a lorde of
the Counsale & a knight of my Acquaintance saye it is moste certane.[816]
I could sende yow many Epitaphes writtne uppon the ded Treasurer
but theye are sluttishe ones[817] & if heereafter yow doe wright for them
yow maye have them. Theare hathe beene searchinge againe & againe
at Bentlye[818] & lastelye one taken but not m.^r Warde[819] but a Browner
man.[820] theye had warninge and forwarninge of it butt theye wente to
shutt the stable dore when the steede was stolen. The scottishe Lorde[821]
is hanged[822] beefore the coorte gates for the murtheringe of Turner the
fenser whoe made a good ende & I will bee bolde to tell yow what I
heare of this matter. some 6 yeares since this Lorde (sankey I thinke
theye caule him) came to Turners scoole of fense to playe with him &
after theye had played some tyme the Lorde perceaved that the fenser
seemed to favor him. Whereuppon the Lorde used these wordes unto

[813] William (Maurus) Scott OSB.

[814] Richard Newport. Viscount Montague and Thomas Howard, Earl of Arundel
attended the execution (30 May), McClure, 355.

[815] Unidentified. In September 1612 Norton wrote to More that the priest Thomas
Manger's host had mistaken the approaching 'm^r Formality' for the pursuivant Anthony
Rouse, and forced Manger to depart in haste, AAW A XI, no. 170 (p. 500).

[816] See **Letters 31, 34**. Although the secular priests looked enthusiastically on Scott's
martyrdom, he had been on good terms with SJ, and, shortly before his execution, he
affirmed his goodwill towards the Society, Stonyhurst MSS, Collectanea N II, no. 14.

[817] See **Letter 34**.

[818] Edward Gage of Bentley in Framfield was one of six Sussex recusants who were to
be required at this time to take the oath of allegiance, PRO, SP 14/70/9, fo. 25v. In
August 1606 he had been granted a licence to go abroad with his family, *CSPD Addenda
1580–1625*, 486, and was at Liège in June 1612 from where he wrote to the exchequer
official Henry Spiller concerning the oath of allegiance, BL, Lansdowne MS 153, fos 81r,
83r.

[819] This may be William Webster alias Ward, secular priest, who was banished in
August 1613 and travelled to Rome in September 1614, Anstr. II, 344; AAW A XIII, no.
210.

[820] Edward Bennett reported that, during this search, George Tias was arrested and
Edward Weston only just escaped, **Letter 31**. The Tiases were closely attached to the
Mores of Barnburgh, Thomas More's family, and had followed them from Barnburgh to
Low Leyton in Essex in the early 1580s, D. Shanahan, 'The Family of St. Thomas More
in Essex 1581–1640', *Essex Recusant* 3 (1961), 71–80, at p. 74. (In April 1614 Tias's mother
was resident at Michelgrove in Sussex with Sir John Shelley, AAW A XIII, no. 72.) In
October 1613, according to Birkhead, Tias, imprisoned in the Clink, was opposing the
priests there who favoured the oath of allegiance, AAW A XII, no. 187.

[821] Robert Creighton, eighth Baron Sanquhair.

[822] See **Letters 28, 29**.

him Thowe seemeste to favor mee in thy playe but doe thy beste or
woorste & hitt mee if thowe canste. I can hitt your Lp. quoth the fenser
if I liste, where quoth the Lorde, marrye [p. 322] quoth the fenser in
your eye. doe then quoth the Lorde. the fenser forthwith made noe
more a doe butt thrust owte his eye. the lorde wente awaye & seemed
nothinge discontented or at leaste not malliciouslye bent against the
fenser. Not longe after the lorde beinge in Fraunce with the Frenche
Kinge (for it is sayed that hee had a pension of him) my Lorde quoth
the Kinge howe have yow loste your eye? marrye quothe hee at Foyles
in a fensers skoole. what my lorde quothe hee & dothe the man live
yet that did it? the Lorde sayed nothinge but it sturred coles in him.
afterwar[d] the lorde comminge to London hearde one saye theare
goes Turners one eyde Lorde. & an other tyme this lorde beeinge to
take water and certaine watermen expectinge his cominge longer [than]
they woulde one of the watermen sayd it ['is' deleted] weare noe matter
if Turner had putt owte bothe his eyes seeinge hee colde not with his
one eye see to come. Thease thinges [word obscured: 'netled' ?] the
Lorde when hee hearde of it by his man. whereuppon hee offerde 40[l]
to a follower of his to murder the fenser which the fellowe did not doe
in five yeares nether was hee urged any more to doe it[.] in the meane
tyme the lordes mallice [?] was allayed & nowe at the laste when hee
thought nothinge the hyred fellow murdered the fenser for which facte
bothe hee & that Lorde that sett him a woorke loste their lives but at
diverse tymes & differentlye. for the Lorde did dye singular well as
beeinge reconciled by the pp in the gatehowse[823] where hee was prisoner.
whereuppon when hee made profession of his faithe & desired domesticos
fidei to praye for him some sayed [two words illegible: 'see here' ?] the
fruites of his Relligion. noe quothe the lorde theese are the fruites of
the Relligion which I followed theese nyne yeares of yours. for in deede
in former tymes I was a Catholique & some nine yeare since [?] I
followed the tyme & foorsooke the Catholique Relligion. in all which
tyme theare was scarse any sin soe greate or badd butt hee had had
some snatche of it & spente all thatt tyme most sinfullye by reason
whereof & for wante of grace hee comitted this foule facte & came to
this shamefull ende. but god bee thanked that hee had meanes to enter
into the right awaye againe. which he intended though hee weare to
live never to forsake againe & beeinge sorrye for the facte hee gave a
C[l] to the fensers wife to make her some amendes & soe he dyed not
beeinge suffered to praye as hee was goinge to deathe in a Catholique
booke which was given him in prison which the shreefe tooke from him.

---

[823] See **Letter 37** for John Jackson's information that John Colleton (not a prisoner in
the Gatehouse) was Sanquhair's 'cheif & I may say soole helper', *i.e.* principally responsible
for Sanquhair's reconciliation to the Church of Rome.

whereat some man of note took exceptiones & sayed that it was a
strainge coorse that a man goinge to dye coulde not bee sufferede to
commende him selfe to god in his kinde but all was to noe purpose for
the shreeve kepte the booke still & some saye beadis [?] too, & the
poore penite*n*te p*er*adve*n*ture fared the woorse [p. 323] amongst them
for beeinge a catholique & to putt him to the moore paine I am tolde
that theye hanged him w*i*th a greater rope the*n* ordinarye & woulde
not suffer the executioner to dispatche him speedilye[.] Requiescat in
pace. Ame*n*. I am furthermoore tolde by my Nedd[824] at his beeinge in
London that the pp[tes]. in Iustice haule[825] beeinge many in a smaule
roome did make a petition to the b of Canterburye whose answere was
that theye shoulde lye one uppo*n* an other & that hee that was
undermost when hee was wearye might lye at the topp et*cetera*[.][826]
furthermore it is sayed (I hope th*e* Londoners will give y*o*w p*er*fecter
informations) that the prisoners of Newgate wear like to bee starved. a
newe keeper putt o*ver* them & newe graite[s] made beefore the entrye
unto them and a porter sett their that none colde see them et*cetera* &
that one tyme theye had some brothe se*n*te th*e*m of the w*hich* soe many
as tasted felte the smarte & weare like to bee poysoned, loste theire
heear, & suche matters.[827] this muche of recente matters[.] nowe [?] to
tell y*o*w what hapned at the place where I lived theese xii weekes a litle
beefore I came thither[.] this it was. theare was a poore woman cauled
goodwife <u>Cornes</u> dawghter of olde m[trs] <u>Tywrye</u>[.][828] this woma*n* lyinge
in was sente for to take the othe beefore the Iustices, shee makinge a
iuste answeare that shee was not in case to come, the Iustices came to
her whereof the poore woma*n* havinge some little warninge we*n*te oute
of her bedd & tooke her childe w*i*th her & hid her selfe under a tubb
or kiver or some souche thinge & what w*i*th cold & feare & I knowe
not whatt els shee gott that that coste her her life. Theare was in
hampeshire breakinge open of a howse in Winchester w*hich* is cauled
m.[r] Warnefords house[829] for M[trs] Cheyneye[830] to have her to sweare
butt shee beeinge the*n* warned to come beefore the officers did not goe
for all thatt knowinge right well that if shee we*n*te shee shoulde bee

---

[824] See **Letter 1**.

[825] In Newgate prison.

[826] See also Foley VII, 1065.

[827] *Cf*. **Letter 35**.

[828] Alice Cornes and Henry, her husband, and one Mercie [or Mary] Terrie, a widow,
all of Battle, were presented for recusancy in July 1605, Cockburn, *Calendar of Assize
Records: Sussex Indictments: James I*, 18, 19. The Battle parish register records the burial on
15 November 1611 of Margaret, daughter of one Mrs Cornes, ESRO, PAR 236 1/1/1
(for which reference I am grateful to Christopher Whittick).

[829] For the Warnford family of Portsmouth, Warblington and Southwick, Hampshire,
see Mott, fos 465r–8r.

[830] Not identified.

committed as one Chidden the father to dicke ussher[831] & to poore
maydes with others are wheare theye fare full harde for owght that I
knowe neither is one Catholique able to helpe an other[.] My paper is
spente & I have noe [word obscured: 'Roome' ?] to wright any thinge
of my neigbours whoe ar well for owgst [sic for 'ought'] I knowe
wherefore desiringe yow to Remember to M^r D Thornell I commit yow
to god 9 of Iulye 1612
(On p. 324)

Addressed: T[o] his approved good frende m^r George Weste.
Endorsed: (1) Iuly. 9. 1.1612. BN
(2) Rece. Sat. Sept. 22.°⎫
     Answ. wed. Sept. 26. ⎬ 1612
                           ⎭

31 *Richard Sara (Edward Bennett) to Thomas West (More) (17 July*
1612)   (AAW A XI, no. 122, pp. 331–4. Holograph)

very Rd Syr. my last[832] was owt of Sussex wherin I informed you of
such occurrentes as then hapned in these partes, but especially of the
recovery of m^r lea[833] who had been most daingerously sick of a hott
fever which had lik to have taken hime away from us. now I have
receaved a coople from you together, thon of the 10 of Aprill, thother
of the 6 of Iune. I see still how laborious you are in our affayers & soe
doe we all, which maketh us perpetually bownd unto you, & how soever
our sutes doe consort & fall owt, yeat for my own parte can not I see
but that you tak all the means that may be to doe us good, which if
they doe not tak place as you desyre we doe altogether impute it to the
litle care is had by the highest of our pressures, & soe most goe on with
contentd patience till it shall please our sweete lord to mak better
provision for us. you cowld say no more too paul[834] then you did, &
although you cowld not hinder, but that he would give us a vice
protector, yeat I doe not dowbt but your speches hath moved hime soe
much that he hath taken order with melino,[835] that he will prove farr
more indifferent to our cause, then ever we found Bianchetto. therfor
in any ['cause' deleted] case seeme to be confident with hime: & it

---

[831] Benjamin Norton reported to More in August 1612 that, at the summer assizes at
Winchester, 'three were condemned in a premunire for refusinge the othe' including 'one
of your acquaintaunce Dr. Ushers father', AAW A XI, no. 133 (p. 358).
[832] Bennett's previous extant letter to More is AAW A XI, no. 105, dated 20 June 1612.
[833] George Birkhead.
[834] Pope Paul V.
[835] Cardinal Giovanni Garzia Millini.

may be our great sute[836] beinge the first matter that he hath to deale
for us, he wilbe the more forward to helpe us to bringe it to passe, that
therby he may wynne us hearafter to have the mor liking unto hime.
assure your self at the first he wilbe loath to give you the least disgwst
in any sute you have: ther for in the name of god propose your great
sute, for I hope ere this you have doct worthingtons allowaunce, which
I suppose wilbe to good purpose. I pray god the monckes prove sure
to our cause. I lik exceeding well your awnswer to paul of our resollutions
to submitt all thinges to his ordinaunce, yeat for myn own part am I
nothing dawnted nor will not be, howsoever our busines fall owt;
howbeit if thinges be not granted unto our cause which we have neede
of, they most be content, that the blame of the inconveniences that are
like daily to fall owt amongest us, be laid altogether upon them selfes,
who, by reason of ther place, ought & should, (beinge informd as they
have been) have taken other order then as yeat they have.

we are all much bownd to that good prelate your monsig,[837] our sweet
lord the rewarder of all good deedes, reward hime for the payns & travaile
he taketh in our behalfes. I think that m[r] president[838] is altogether for us, &
that he liketh nether Sing[e]lton, nor yeat Norton.[839] I cowld have wished
m[r] d kell had accepted of his profer. you have sayed very well if they graunt
us not our requestes, we will <u>never leave movinge. no</u> more we will if my
advise be followed, they most be importuned, ells nothinge wilbe don. I
hope in tyme matters wilbe brought to that passe, that non shalbe welcome
into these partes without your comendations, & for those 4 that came
away in that manner, if you find the protector[840] kynd it were not amisse
you glaunced a litle at them, tellinge him that the Arch[841] expected to
heere from your self of the particular condition of every man that came
hether to live under his charge. abowt the discowrse you speak of, for the
equity of our demandes, to be made by some of us, I will deale with m[r]
lea abowt it. I tak the padri[842] to be the men that soe dislik of Card perons
cowrse in dealinge with Cassabon.[843] nothinge pleasethe them but what
is don by them selfes.

you doe well to keepe a kind of ordinary correspondence with d
Thorn, but for any thinge that he goeth abowt, heer is but litle regard
had. in m[r] dentons[844] [in margin: 'D. Bishop'] place d Boswell[845] is

[836] i.e. for the appointment of a bishop.
[837] John Baptist Vives.
[838] Thomas Worthington.
[839] John Knatchbull.
[840] Cardinal Edward Farnese.
[841] George Birkhead.
[842] Jesuits.
[843] Du Perron, *Lettre de Monseigneur le Cardinal du Perron.*
[844] William Bishop.
[845] John Bosvile.

made assistante, but in d smith place non: save only m[r] Norton[846] goeth
up & down that circuit but not with the autority of an assistant: as for
that matter of m[r] widdringtons gostly father,[847] I can give you no
accownt of it, but I doe suppose his facul[t]ies be not taken away, nor
can I thinck m[r] lea would proceed soe rigurusly withowt iust cause.[848]
for my self I am nothing acquainted with his proceeding in that matter.
even now as [p. 332] I receaved yours on of our gravest brethren at
newgate have [sic] written unto me to the same purpose you did, telling
me withall that widdrington had been with hime to complaine of m[r]
lea his hard dealinge: but shortly I will informe my self better & deal
with our superior to that purpose you mention. thus much in awnswer
to boath your letters.

At Bentley within this fortnight on m[r] Tias was taken,[849] & d weston[850]
escaped very hardly. m[r] Chamberlayne[851] is taken latly [five words
partially deleted: 'at on m[r] [ ] ho'] in London but realesed, we heer
litle of hime. d weston had written a litle pamphlet against widdrington,
but as I heere widdrington hath replied upon hime very bitterly in
print, as I take it, for I have not seene the booke.[852] at m[res] vaux wher
she lieth prisoner[853] the 29 of Iune was taken on m[r] Cornford[854] a
Ieswett who is comitted to newgate. the very day that m[r] Newport, &
m[r] Scott were executed, which was upon whitson eve, in the west part
abowt plimowth for 3 miles the sea appeared as red as blood, wherat
the people wondringe they took of the water in twbs, wherin standinge
but a whil it congeald lik putrified blood w[hich] did cast such a stenche
that no man cowld abyde the smell & sent. it maketh many to wonder, &
feare alsoe that it is a signe of some hevy plague to fall upon us.[855]
although all this yeer they have beene busy abowt the oath: yeat at the
last assise with us which hath been very latly ther was but litle sayed
against recusantes, whether it will prove to a calme we cannot imagyne:
talke ther is, upon the arivall of the Spanishe embassadour,[856] that there
is speech of maraidge between the lady Elizabeth & the kinge of Spayne

---

[846] Benjamin Norton.
[847] John Clinch, chaplain to Roger Widdrington.
[848] For the case of John Clinch, see **Letter 33**.
[849] See **Letter 30**.
[850] Edward Weston. Benjamin Norton informed More on 5 August 1612 that Weston
was 'pluckt oute of a hole by the legg yett for a greate somme of moneye lett goe. . .bycause
they knewe him not to bee the man which then & nowe still they looke for, but they
tooke awaye one Mr Browne or Tyas', AAW A XI, no. 133 (p. 358).
[851] John Varder.
[852] See **Letter 32**.
[853] *i.e.* at 'her lodginge or prison near Newgate', AAW A XI, no. 133 (p. 358).
[854] Thomas Cornforth SJ.
[855] See **Letters 30, 34**.
[856] Pedro de Zúñiga.

how true god knoweth. they say further that this Spanish Embassadour cometh to expostulate abowt our sendinge to virginia, as alsoe to redeeme those towns of the lowe cuntres which be in the kinges handes.[857] A Scottish lord called Sancher was in the end of this last terme hangd at westmi[n]ster,[858] he had caused on twrner a fenser to be murthered. he died exceding penitent, & in the presence of all the people which wer innumerable of all sortes, he confessed he had ever been a catholick, but this nyne yeers had had no use of his religion, & therfor not lived as his religion taught him. he desired ['all' deleted] publickly as he stoode upon the cart all roman catholick to pray for hime, he gave great almes, & died soe penitent that the very protestantes did much bewaile hime. y[es]terday we heer that at oxford a scott killed the Erle of essex base sonne being newly arived from beyond the seas.[859] The pursephantes rune soe up & down that ther is noe security for them.

I understand that there is some litle unkyndnes between m[r] Baker[860] & m[r] denton[861] abowt ['abowt' deleted] a kinsman of m[r] Bakers on m[r] Raynare[862] as I tak it. I pray writ to m[r] Baker, that you have hard of some such matter, & exhort hime & them peacbly to take up all matters amongest them selfes. what scandall would it be if they should fall but to the least disagreement amongest them selfes. I have in deed beene written unto abowt it, & that I showld write unto them, to cary matters lovingly on with another. alas syr they be farr my awncientes, & therfor am loth to tak notice of it, yeat I will writ to m[r] lea, who may in a general maner exhort them to a pecbl unitye, & when any difficulty falleth owt gravely & piously amongest them selfes mak an end of it.

they say m[r] Copley beginneth to play his parte, he hath written a book[863] which as yeat I have not seen, & thretneth the Arch.[864]

in lanchashyr at a gentlewomans howse wher a preest resided, the gentlman having a doughter, & she being alone on day sowing in a parlur, ther were three knockes given hard by her: she frighted with the noise [in margin: 'M[ris]. Piget[865] – now Religious'] [p. 333] rann up

[857] See CSPV 1610–13, 402, 408, 427–8, 435.
[858] See **Letters 28, 29**.
[859] Edward Bruce, second Baron Kinloss, was said to have stabbed 'Mr Devorax', apparently over 'words' about the recently executed Baron Sanquhair, Downshire MSS III, 332.
[860] Richard Smith.
[861] William Bishop.
[862] William Rayner, secular priest. See **Letter 32**.
[863] Copley, Doctrinall and Morall Observations.
[864] George Birkhead.
[865] Not identified.

to the chamber where the preest & her father were, she towld them what hapned. & they not belevinge her, the 3 knockes were there hard agayne. whosoever was in the gentlwomans company, & h[e] upon her report would not beleeve her, presently the three knockes wer hard: soe that there were non in the howse who took not notice of it. The gentlewoman being often trubled with this noise demanded of her gostly father what she should doe, for she feared some thinges would appear unto her, her gostly father exhorted her to speak to it, if it did appear unto her, wherupon she being fearefull desired of god all mighty that if any thinge appeared that it might appear in the liknes of a child, soe very shortly she hearing of masse, it appeared in the liknes of a very affable child, but yeat she was soe freightd, that it dwrst not demand what it would have. after she towld the preest what she had seen, who exhorted her agayn bowldly to speak to it, which she did upon the second apparation which was something more grimme then before, when blessing her self, she sayd in the name of god: what art thow: wherunto he awnswered he was a preest, & in his lif tyme he receaved money for saing masse, but not performed it, & that he had long appeard to an owld man at Rome, ['but' deleted] who would never speak unto hime: wherfor he was forced to sollicite her to have a masse sayd in satisfaction of his neglect, & the better to satisfy her that it was no illusion, he putt her in mynd, how that she was wont to deeme preestes happy, as having power to absolve them selfes, which you may perceave now said he is not true. hearupon repayring to her gostly father she acquainted hime with what hapned, who the next morning saieing masse for hyme, she being present ['after' deleted] at consummation of the holy sacrifice the vision appeared unto her in the same form of a child, who went to the alter, thence ascending into the challice, mownted up to heaven, & after was never seene. this straing discowrse a vertuous preest sent unto me afferminge it to be most true & latly hapned. thus I truble you with my news which If I had not thought would be gratfull unto you, I had not been soe forward: And soe thanckinge you for the payns you tak to releeve our afflictions with hartiest comendations from all frendes I comend you to our lordes protection this 17 of Iuly
your true frend
    Rich Sara
(On p. 334)
Addressed: To the worshipfull my assured Frend m^r Thomas Weste
        Esquier these
Endorsed: (1) Iuly 17. 1612. R Sar.
        (2) Rec. thr. Oct. 25 ⎱ 1612
            Answ. sat. Oct. 27. ⎰
        (3) The relation of an apparition

32 *Richard Orontes (Smith) to Thomas More (31 July 1612 (NS))*   *(AAW*
    A XI, no. 127, pp. 343–4. Holograph)

My deere Syr. I hope you wi[l] have me excused that I have not my
self written to you this long time for knowing that D. Champney and
others have acquainted you with all things that were done at Doway
or were otherwise knowne [?] [.]⁸⁶⁶ I perswade my self that you wold
and will account a letter from ether of us as come from us both as we
do your letter unto us. wherfor omitting all other complements. God
be thanked we have obtained for our company four hundred crownes
yearly of the Clergie of France.⁸⁶⁷ our good brethren opp here opposed
against us what they could but especially D. Roger whome we leest
doubted of and whome we most kindly used ever more.⁸⁶⁸ It was told
the Bishops that we were Iesu[i]tted men and I in particuler a powder
traiter which last sensles and unchristian calumnie is thought to have
comen from D. Roger who openly professed that he would ioyne with
Ies: against us and he truly ioyned with some of them in calumnies.
what this calumnie may hurte me in England I knowe not but here it
hath done no harme but to the Author. I was warned of him by letters
from Flanders to beware of his malice, but I suspected no such thing
in him by reason of his good speeches and frequent visits which now I
perceave were a welsh trick. God forgive him. Here is another scruple
amongst us[.] For D Bish. wold not have my Coosin Fen⁸⁶⁹ of our
company albeit he heere [?] comen out of Engl for that purpose and
hath bene admitted by our founder⁸⁷⁰ and hath endured a hard years
entertain[m]ent with me, And so hath left out his name in the Request
to the Clergie and given it unknowne to me. me thinks this is more
than needs and I having spent my money time and paines in this
matter do look to be acquainted with the affaires therof and not to be
wronged ether in my self or my kinsmen. long it were to discourse of
all this matter and to shew what exceptions firs[t] for learning then for
headines shold be taken against my Coosin.⁸⁷¹ But we refer all to mʳ

---

⁸⁶⁶ Anthony Champney's account of the conference at Douai in May 1612 is contained
in AAW A XI, no. 81 (17 May 1612 (NS)) printed with some omissions in TD V, p. cxii,
and AAW A XI, no. 94.

⁸⁶⁷ See Allison, 'Origins', 12.

⁸⁶⁸ In September 1612 John Jackson, at Brussels, wrote to More that among the various
difficulties the Paris writers' college faced was opposition from people such as Roger
Smith (also John Cecil and Christopher Bagshaw) who were excluded from it, AAW A
XI, no. 147. William Bishop told More in July 1613 that 'mʳ d. Roger Smith' lives 'in
this towne like a diogenes, scarse in good tearmes with any man of us', AAW A XII, no.
227 (p. 508).

⁸⁶⁹ William Rayner.

⁸⁷⁰ Thomas Sackville.

⁸⁷¹ Rayner had returned to the Continent from England and arrived in Paris on 2

Tho:[872] his coming whome we looke for shortly and hope that by him no wrong shalbe done. we presently [?] expect the allowance from our Protector[873] of D: Kellisons going to Doway. The Pres.[874] is said to stand constant and some dozen Engl: Gentlemen that live in the towne purposely to hear their devinity in the Engl. Colledg. m[r] Archpr[875] hath bene of late very sick but now God be thanked wel recovered. He writeth to me that some letters are sent for to recall me home but yet I have not seene them, And if I can I will differ my returne some what longer till this worke be better setled. our nunnes here are now in good hope to settle for La: longavil[876] giveth eleven hundred pounds to buye their house and procureth licence for their abode. marie Franks[877] returneth home, and one other is coming over to them. some disgust ther is betwixt m[r] Pole and D mauro.[878] m[r] withrinton came lately over to Doway to fech home m[r] Howard[879] and thence sent hither to D. Bush[880] and m[r] Constab two new bookes of his in answer to a litle treatise made ag[a]i[n]st his former booke by D. weston as is thought,[881]

October 1611 (NS), AAW A X, no. 131. Thanks to Thomas Sackville, rooms were prepared in the writers' college for both Smith and Rayner, AAW A X, no. 137. In May 1612 Rayner told More that Geoffrey Pole, Rayner's close friend, had solicited for him 'to bee the queen margarets [Marguerite de Valois, first wife of Henri IV] chaplein', AAW A XI, no. 75 (p. 215). But on 11 September 1612 (NS), John Jackson recounted that 'm[r] Reyner stoode for a place [in the college] & m[r] doc. Smith stoode for him' whereas Birkhead '& some assistants (who wear pleasd also to take me to the consultation) had named others'. A compromise was patched up to allow Rayner 'to live with them (not as one of them)', AAW A XI, no. 147 (p. 403). Rayner hated William Bishop, and implied in a letter to More in September 1612 that Smith hated Bishop as well, and would prefer to return to Cowdray than live in community with Bishop in the college, AAW A XI, no. 173. Bishop's objection to Rayner was not only that his 'learning & conversation' were insufficient, and he 'had not either by writing or any other publick triall in England recomended himself to the good opinions of others', but also that he favoured SJ 'over much', i.e. he would be a spy for SJ in the college. Rayner sympathised with Worthington and thought well of Thomas Fitzherbert who finally joined SJ in 1613. Bishop claimed that even Birkhead conceded Rayner's failings, though Birkhead was responsible for sending him over to Paris, AAW A XII, no. 8 (p. 19). Bishop eventually bowed, after the rules of the college were suitably amended, to pressure from Smith and persuasions from Champney and agreed to admit Rayner, AAW A XII, nos 106, 140, 156.

[872] Thomas Sackville. According to Bishop in January 1613, it had been bruited, initially, that Thomas Sackville had recommended Rayner for the college but now Sackville denied any such thing, AAW A XII, no. 8.

[873] Cardinal Edward Farnese.

[874] Thomas Worthington.

[875] George Birkhead.

[876] Antoinette d'Orléans-Longueville, sister of Catherine Gonzaga, Duchess of Longueville, Lunn, 'English Cassinese', 63–4.

[877] Identity uncertain.

[878] William (Maurus) Taylor OSB.

[879] See **Letter 28**.

[880] William Bishop.

[881] Champney wrote to More on 17 July 1612 (NS) that Roger Widdrington, while at

in which booke he is far more eager than in his former and as is thought changeth the question which now he maketh to be onely whither it be herresis temeritas error aut pec*catum* mortale to deny the P. power to depose, in which he defendeth the negative; and not about the absolute p*roposition*. In this booke he hath put the names of the 13 preists who subscribed to a forme of oathe in Q. Elizab. time[882] and nameth D. Bush: and D. Champ: which wil do nether them nor us any good, and withall wrongly wresteth their falt to defend his design.[883] But of this one of them will write more. m^r Kenion is gone a moneth agoe with the Bishop of luzon[884] who is a very go[o]d prelate and giveth him very good allowance. what the spanish Embass.[885] doth in England we heare not. Thither is gone also Counte maurice.[886] Mr Faringt[887]

Douai to collect William Howard, brought a copy of Roland (Thomas) Preston's *Rogeri Widdringtoni Catholici Angli Responsio Apologetica*. See ARCR I, no. 926.3. Champney remarks that 'yt ys an answer to a certayn letter writen as some say by Doct [Edward] weston agaynst his booke whom m^r widerington handlethe rowndly and roughly yf not rudely', AAW A XI, no. 121 (p. 329); Allison, 'Later Life', 112. See **Letters 26, 35**. For Weston's anti-gallican inclinations, see Allison, 'Richard Smith's Gallican Backers', part I, 353‑4. Robert Fisher had claimed in 1598, however, that Weston had been favourable towards his dealings on behalf of the appellants, CRS 51, 249, 260; and in 1610 Weston petitioned the cardinals of the Inquisition (though half-heartedly) in defence of Richard Smith's book against Thomas Bell which had been denounced at Rome, AAW A IX, no. 13; Allison, 'Later Life', 111‑12. Weston left the country soon after his near arrest at Bentley, see **Letters 30, 31**; for Weston's own account, see Weston, *Iuris Pontificii Sanctuarium* (np, 1613), preface (cited in Allison, 'Later Life', 112‑13). Champney reported to More that Weston was 'driven out by widerington his last booke which was agaynst him verie bitter and truly made yt not safe for him to stay', AAW A XI, no. 180 (p. 525). Allison suggests that Weston's manuscript opinion on the oath was written for Lord Vaux, and that this explains why Preston had to reply to it, *i.e.* to satisfy Archbishop Abbot after he (Preston) had not persuaded Vaux to take the oath, Allison, 'Later Life', 113.

[882] The Protestation of Allegiance of January 1603. See Bossy, *English Catholic Community*, 39‑41.

[883] Preston, *Rogeri Widdringtoni Catholici Angli Responsio Apologetica*, in section entitled 'Praefatio ad Lectorem', sig. b7r. Preston again named the priests who made the Protestation of Allegiance of 1603 in his *Disputatio Theologica* of 1613 (in a separate part entitled 'Rogeri Widdringtoni Catholici Angli Apologeticae Responsionis...', sig. Br‑v), which was originally intended for inclusion in the *Responsio Apologetica*, ARCR I, nos 925.6, 926.3. In mid-1613, just as the members of the Paris writers' college were about to move into the Collège d'Arras, given them by the Benedictine abbey of St Vaast at Arras, Philippe de Caverel, the abbot of St Vaast, was informed that the priests were out of favour with the Holy See. Preston's citation of the names of Champney and William Bishop 'in the margent' of his *Responsio Apologetica* [*i.e.* in the section naming the priests who had signed the Protestation of Allegiance] had been shown to him 'by some of our good frendes', said Champney sarcastically, AAW A XII, no. 139 (p. 311). The seculars petitioned Cardinal Borghese to write to the abbot in their favour, AAW A X, no. 169.

[884] Armand-Jean du Plessis, Bishop of Luçon, future Cardinal-Duc de Richelieu.

[885] Pedro de Zúñiga.

[886] Maurice, Prince of Nassau.

[887] Edward Bennett.

writeth to me to call upon you for commencing your great suite,[888] but now perhaps in this vacation it were noe fitt time. But al to your discretion. The scholers wherof the scot talked died in Dow. of the scurvey which one brought from Engl. and infested twoe or thre. my L. Sanker a scot was hanged at westminster for killing an English man. he died Catholik and very repentant.[889] my L. montgomeries hart served him to see him hanged though not to draw his sword against ane other of his co[n]trie.[890] I pray you commend me to m^r Nicolas[891] m^r white[892] m^r Robert[893] and al acquaintaunce[.] And thus with my hartiest to your self I end 31 of Iuly

yours truly

   R. orontes

(On p. 344)

Addressed: Al Illustre e molto Reverendo Signore Tomaso Moro Sacer-
      dote Ingles   Roma

Endorsed: (1) Iuly. 31. 1612. Oront.
      (2) Recea. thr. Aug. 23°⎫
                         ⎬ 1612
         Answ wed. Aug. 29°⎭
      (3) herwith one to my L. Primate

33 *George Salvin (Birkhead) to Thomas More (3 August 1612)*   *(AAW A XI, no. 131, pp. 351–4. Holograph)*

Rev. S.^r

I hope by this tyme yow have receyved an answere from me of all your Letters, now I am to advertise yow, oportere te caute ambulare, and not to offer any dowbt in this matter of the oath to be Censured, but in such termes (yf it be in my name) as I shall deliver yt unto yow.

---

[888] For appointment of a bishop.

[889] See **Letters 28, 29**.

[890] See **Letter 29**.

[891] Nicholas Fitzherbert. In November 1612 Fitzherbert was accidentally drowned near Florence. A violent quarrel began in Rome over his will, made three years before, in which he left everything, to the value of about £100, to the English Benedictines, though Richard Smith was convinced that Fitzherbert must have left him a legacy, AAW A XII, no. 30 (p. 69); Foley II, 230. A quarrel erupted also over his papers, which Thomas Fitzherbert, Thomas Owen SJ and Roger Baynes conspired to obtain, but were opposed by Nicholas Fitzherbert's friends, including Robert (Anselm) Beech OSB, AAW A XII, no. 28 (p. 65). In 1625 Thomas Rant warned Thomas White (who was about to become the secular clergy's agent in Rome) 'have alwayes your will & testament by yow. and name in yt, that thes writings [*i.e.* the agency's papers] are, as indeed they are your Clergyes, for, in any wise, theis must be left in such hands, as they may never come into the Iesuitts hands', AAW A XIX, no. 83 (p. 252).

[892] John (Augustine) Bradshaw OSB.

[893] Robert (Anselm) Beech OSB.

m^r widderington[894] hath ben beyond the Sea of Late, and since his comminge home hath to a frend at neugate charged me with an absurd Censure, as yf I should have Censured m^r Clinche for holdinge the lawfullnes of the oath in his mynd secretly. and saied yf I wold not recall it, there wold be thinges sett forth in print or writinge to my disgrace. but I have don nothinge but iustice and accordinge to the tenor of my commission sent by your selfe by order from his hol. namely to declare not onely m^r blackwell and those of the clink, but also all others of there opinion to have Lost ther faculties. now cometh out the said m^r Clinch with great contempt of my assistant m^r Trollope, for admonishinge him twice or thrice, and to the scandall of the Countrie, ['and' deleted] mainteyneth that notwithstandinge he will nether teach nor defend the oath, yet in his understandinge he ioyneth in opinion with m^r blackwell and the rest, and having expressed thus much in plaine wordes outwardly persisteth in this error verie obstinately. hereupon after much a doe I caused m^r Trollope to declare m^r Clinch to have Lost his faculties. wherin I thinke I did him no iniustice, nor Censured him [word deleted] for his inward thoughtes as m^r widderington meaneth to putt in his bookes. his secret he might have kepte to himselfe. therefor iudge yow whether I have not don accordinge to the Last mandatum yow sent me. this I write because both in your Letter to me, and in that to m^r Bennet[895] yow speake verie timide, as though I had committed some great error in the execution of my office. marck I praie yow the case, and how I sett it downe, and then propose it to our Superiors. for otherwise yow may cause them to repute me verie simple. I am ielaouse that m^r widderington or others by his incitement hath given yow some bad information. but yf yow credit him more then me yow do me great wronge. O miserie of miseries. this writing of bookes by him and others, ariseth of prowd disobedience to the sea Apostolique, and is the greatest plague that ever befell us. Salceld the Apostata Iesuit is now writinge for the lawfulnes of goinge to church, and takinge the oath. the enemie hath sett [word deleted] us one against another, and laugheth us to scorne, and crieth out in pulpites and everie where against our waunt of charitie: yf I be not backed by yow and my brethren heare, I may as well sit still and do nothinge. what comfort can I take when some followe widderington, some underhand wink at the oath, and thinke me over precise in

[894] Roger Widdrington.

[895] Edward Bennett wrote to More on 6 January 1613 to excuse himself 'abowt that sharp letter', presumably this one, which 'you mention to have receaved' from Birkhead about Clinch, 'wherof you say I was cause'. Bennett admitted he had informed Birkhead 'what your opinion was of the cowrses he showld take for the keepinge of our company together', in other words More's view that Birkhead should not proceed harshly against Clinch, AAW A XII, no. 3 (p. 5).

observinge my commission. I am not yett well recovered of a daungerous
sicknes, and forced for weaknes to keepe in, and hence forth not Like
to be an able man. I wold to god my unfittnes for this office, were well
considered, and that it wold please his hol now to take some other
order. thinges are so confused and perturbed that I feare that bb will
be as much contemned as my selfe. yf we had had them longe since,
this great disorder might have ben easily prevented. which now will not
be compassed but with abundance of martirs bloode. I make this
discourse [one and a half lines deleted] onely to give yow some taist of
the dispaire, which oppresseth me with greife. yet do I put [word
deleted] my trust in god, and by his helpe will hold on my course as
well as I can, and yf I were a stronge man, I wold make a iorney my
selfe, [p. 352] to utter my greife to paul.[896] two disgustes increaseth my
greife verie much: one that it hath ben told me to my face, by a frend
to our opposites, that I have not a preist that so precisely adhereth to
the breves as I do: and therfor wisely resembled me to Lucifer
Calaritanus.[897] the second, that by the same partie the religiouse are
reputed to be as backward as myne, but yett can conceale it better.
some of them heretofore most earnest against the oath, are now
exceedinge cold. this maketh me feare that they have some secret
direction from thence to beare with mens frailties for saving of there
goodes. yf this sheift had ben used in the primitive church, never had
there ben so many martirs. it seameth they of ould were fooles, and
we onely wise. yett god be thanked we have heare a great number of
such fooles, in all sortes, who most couradgeously abide the afflictions
which are laid upon them. good S[r], be of good couradge, beleve not
the reportes which yow heare of me, I wilbe as carefull as I canne to
observe my commission aright, and so I beseech yow enforme our
Superiours, yf any such Calumnie as this of widderingtons be brought
against me. yf I might speake with yow, I could tell yow that which
yow cannot apprehend. malice against some of my zealous brethren is
the cause of m[r] widderingtons onset upon me. I meddle not with him,
I marvell he is so busie in my affaires. o+ [a mark in the text referring
to the postscript]

some chardge hath ben given by the iudges against us at the sessions:
they say that all papistes are gladd my L treasorer[898] is dead, and hope
for a tolleration, and therfor must be well Looked unto. now after the
sises the pursivantes swarme in everie countrie. God send yow good

---

[896] Pope Paul V.
[897] Lucifer of Cagliari who died in 370 or 371. He was an anti-Arian bishop whose
violent opposition against the Arians (even repentant ones) led him eventually to withdraw
to Sardinia and, it seems, form a schismatic sect called (by St Jerome) Luciferians.
[898] Robert Cecil, first Earl of Salisbury.

speed with your suit: yow have had the helpes that we can afford yow. yf nothinge be obteyned, godes holy will be don who knoweth what is best and most convenient for us. the Colledge at doway and the new house at paris are like to stand in good termes. I presume yow are enformed by our frendes from thence how all thinges goe. Commend me to m^r D perse[899] and all my other good frendes. and so desyring to be partaker of your praiers, I leave yow to the tuicion of our blessed Saviour. this 3 of Aug 1612

your assured frend

   Geo. Salv

o+ but Lett me yett declare unto yow more at large our doinges with m^r Clinch. I assure yow, that m^r Trollope and the rest of the preistes in that Countrie have often told me of his bad dealinge in many thinges: but I still gave no eare unto them till they wrote unto me of much hurt by his opinions both about goinge to church and this of the oath. in so much as I wrote to my assistant m^r Trollope that yf he wold not desist, that he shold tell him, he shold be deprived ['otherwise' deleted] of his faculties. whereupon he seamed to yeld a little, and said he wold nether defend nor teach the oath, but yett in his understanding was of opinion with m^r blackwell and the rest. and published and expressed outwardly this his inward minde which he might have kept to himselfe, and not ben liable to the censure of the church upon which discoverie of his opinion, and obstinately persistinge in yt to the weakninge of many of his people, beinge at the last enformed therof by m^r Trollope, I wrote backe that yf he did not nor wold not recall that opinion as towchinge the lawfulnes of the oath and uttered in so manifest wordes in the presence of sundrie persons, he shold by vertue [p. 353] of the Last mandatum sent from his hol by our viceprotector[900] and your self, declare him to have Lost his faculties. for by it am I commanded to declare not onely m^r blackwell and those of the clink, but all other also of there opinion to be deprived etc. now yf m^r Clinch can purge himselfe and prove he spake no such wordes, then is the Censure void and to no effect, and so I have written unto him. for the order which I gave to m^r trolloppe was but conditionall.

   m^r widderington proposeth the case to better purpose then yow have proposed it but yet falsly and iniuriously: for he said to a frend in newgate, that I had either given or approved a censure in them that gave yt wrongfully [word deleted] against one holdinge in his understandinge the Lawfulnes of the oath, though he no way expressed yt outwardly: plainly insinuatinge therbie, that yf it be any way expressed outwardly, then may it be subiect to censure, which I take to be true.

---

[899] William Percy.
[900] Cardinal Lawrence Bianchetti.

but yo*w* seame to be of another minde: for yo*w* say that in this case it seameth to yo*w* that the delinquent must be proved to have taken the oath, or to have persuaded others unto it, (whereof also ther is no smal pr*e*sumptions) and yo*w* further add, that yo*w* never knew our Superiours autoritie extended so farre as to inflict such a punishement, onlesse faultes were more scandalous and notorious. for the scandall of his doinges, it is to longe to shew the particulars: for the notoriousnes of them, his open confession of his inward minde is sufficient according (as one may collect) to the doctrine of Tolledo [in margin: Lib 1 de instruct. sac. cap. 15. 2 parte decr. causa ['2' deleted ?] q 1 c. 15. 16. et 17. gloss.].[901] howbeit yf yo*w* give me sufficient testimonie that our Superiours iudge the case to be as yo*w* say, then shall the Censure be recalled with speed. but to tell yo*w* the truth, I have good cardes to shew from our Superiors to the contrarie, unlesse they recall the instructions they have given me, w*hi*ch I think they will not. to what purpose I praie yo*w* serveth the autoritie his hol hath imparted unto me, yf I may not execute the same upon iust occasion? yo*w* were ever remisse in havinge any thinge don against m*r* blackwell and the rest, and yet it seameth yo*w* are still in that vaine to those w*hi*ch follow his footestepps; a thing that maketh me at my wittes end: yo*w* com*m*end me for my dealinge in our principall suit, and tell me that yo*w* can require no more at my handes, but in these cases yo*w* give me much disgust. verily strange to my understandinge it is, that one may outwardly confesse to hold an error or haeresie in his minde, and yet not be subiect to Censure? it is a thinge well knowen, that a secret haeretique, yf he but utter his haeresie to himselfe, is excom*mun*icated ipso iure, and shall one protest his heresie or error in manifest termes to the great offence of many and not be subiect to the Censure of his Superiour? when a man is forced to abiure heresie, will the iudge permitt him to affirme that he retayneth it in his mynd? o but he saieth he will neither teach nor defend it: and I say (my Reverend S*r*) that herin Lieth his equivocation: for in verie deed he dothe absolutely both teach and defend the oath, by outwardly confessinge the Lawfulnes of the oath in his owne opinion, and so all that heare him appr*e*hend of his wordes, as his neighbours by experience can witnesse. to be short, I am wearie with writinge, onely this I must tell yo*w*, that albeit I have putt great confidence in yo*w*, yet yf yo*w* proceed thus in distrust of my executinge the office wherwith I am chardged, I shalbe compelled to use some other means to enforme his hol in these kyndes of actions. yf

---

[901] Cardinal Francis Toledo SJ, *Franciscus Toleti S.R.E. Cardinalis Summae de Instruct. Sacerdotum libri vii* (Milan, 1599), bk. 1, ch. 15, 'Quibus casibus incurratur suspensio'. Ch. 16 is entitled 'De eo qui potest absolvere à suspensione', and ch. 17 is entitled 'De degradatione & depositione'.

his holines mislike the order he hath given me, as soone as he shall please to alter it, I am redie to obey. otherwise by godes grace, I meane not to infringe his directions, for any mans pleasure; this coldnesse, and wilie sheiftes about the oath, are the bane of our cause. m^r Clinch wrote to my selfe, that his penitentes makinge no scruple [p. 354] to take the oath, he Left them to there owne dictamen. iudge yo*w* whether such a pastor is fitt to have faculties or no! yf I should tell yo*w* of his dissimulations, of his coldnesse about goinge to church, of his enstranginge himselfe from his brethren, of his froward, perverse and contemptuous dealinge towardes my Assistant,[902] and the rest of my brethren in that Countrie, I shold never make an end. I deale not with the Laitie, I marvell how it com*m*eth to passe, that wheras they ought to ayd me in manteyninge the autoritie of S^t peters chaire w*i*thout pr*ei*udice to his m*ai*es*t*ie, they leave me to my selfe without any comfort at all. why should m^r Clinch repine, beinge so often in most gentle manner admonished to desist, before the punishment was inflicted upon him? m^r warmington blameth his hol and me for that he was not told of his fault, and because I did not prosecute my admonition to all preistes, against them att the first. yo*w* seame to be affeard for me, but yo*w* neede not. I was provoked by divers of good Counsell, before I did it.

Addressed: To his verie good frend m^r Thomas moore give this
    Rome
Endorsed: (1) Aug. 3. 1612. Sal.
       (2) Recea. thr. Oct. 25. ⎫
          Answ. frid. Oct. 26. ⎭ 1612

34 *[Benjamin Norton] to George West (Thomas More) (16 August*
   1612)   (AAW A XI, no. 136, pp. 369–72. Holograph)

My deare s.^{r} yt is not longe since I sente yo*w* a le*tt*re[903] of many matters the confirmatio*n* whereof I daylye expecte[904] or if yo*w* have none

---

[902] Cuthbert Trollop.
[903] AAW A XI, no. 133.
[904] Norton had reported to More on 5 August 1612 that he had already delayed writing for a week hoping to ascertain the truth of several providential portents during the year.

heereafter the*n* I praye y*o*w not to reckon of that that hathe beene writtne. Nowe I hasten theese *lettr*es bicause I heere that if I can dispatche this *lettr*e in any tyme I maye chance to have him se*n*te & if I omitt this tyme I knowe not howe or when to sende p*ar*telye by reason of the difficulties theese tymes afforde but cheefelye bicause I was but yesterdaye in as weeke a case as almoste ev*er* I was by reason of an ague w*hi*ch hangethe uppo*n* mee & hathe brought mee lowe & drivethe mee daylye into many lothesome colde swetts & what will beecom of it & of mee by reason of it I knowe not but hopinge thatt y*o*w will reme*m*ber mee when I am dedd I intende to keepe tuche w*i*th y*o*w whiles I live. & I assure y*o*w that I have not fayled to wright to y*o*w everye monthe this yere (Maye excepted) w*hi*ch I repeete in div*er*se *lettr*es bicause I feare my *lettr*es miskarry⁹⁰⁵ & I woulde fayne by one meanes or other y*o*w shoulde knowe the care I have to satisfye y*o*w in this kinde. I likewise have writtne div*er*se tymes unto y*o*w to tell y*o*w that I have receaved xxˢ in silver fro*m* the clarke for y*o*w & I fayne wold knowe howe yo*w* woulde have it disposed of. mʳ sc.⁹⁰⁶ was w*i*thin a flight shott of mee yett came not unto mee but se*n*te mee a *lettr*e w*hi*ch y*o*w wrought unto him to reade & woulde have mee to tell y*o*w that yf heereafter y*o*w woulde wright unto him y*o*w shoulde inclose his *lettr*e in some *lettr*e to mee. the meaninge of thease matters I knowe not. Theare was abought the 7 or 8ᵗʰ of this moneth greate adoe in Oxforde shire some thinke by reason of some complainte that the Puritane Iustices have made to the Archepuritane (and yet a busshopp) the lorde of Lambithe⁹⁰⁷ wheruppo*n* some three Iustices of the peace

---

At Chilgrove near Midhurst some harvesters saw a red cross in the moon. At Kingsland in Middlesex someone found an abandoned child who (before dying) prophesied approaching environmental disasters, which Norton found credible in the light of the present summer drought which was destroying the harvest and making pasture and water scarce. On 26 February at Chichester 'there was an Eagle seene in the ayer & then a Lion was seene to encounter w*i*th him and goe awaye againe, & afterwarde come againe & goe againe & the Eagle keepe her place still'. He repeated that at Penzance, on the day that William (Maurus) Scott OSB and Richard Newport were executed, a 'bluddye streame' appeared in the sea, three miles in length and many miles long (a story which Norton had first narrated on 9 July 1612, **Letter 30**; see also **Letter 31** (Edward Bennett's account)). On these stories Norton commented 'in the necke of this there is greate expectation of warrs & commandemente is given for musteringe of souldiers & w*i*thall there is a rumor abroade (w*hi*ch I take to bee false) that there is some doinges in Irelande'. Norton expected that the visit of the Spanish ambassador Zúñiga (who had his first audience with the king on 5 July 1612, McClure, 366) would 'leave wares beehinde him', AAW A XI, no. 133 (p. 357).

⁹⁰⁵ Between 25 March and 16 August 1612 there are four extant letters in AAW A from Norton to More: 9 April (AAW A XI, no. 54), 6 June (AAW A XI, no. 95 [**Letter 29**]), 9 July (AAW A XI, no. 118 [**Letter 30**]), and 5 August (AAW A XI, no. 133).

⁹⁰⁶ Identity uncertain.

⁹⁰⁷ George Abbot.

came to s.ʳ Frauncis Stonars[908] over night & lodged there & seemed to
make the cause of there comminge to bee to see whither theye might
doe any good (or rather bad) with the Ladye.[909] butt in the morninge
six other Iustices comminge thither theye beesett the howse and searched
extreemelye for preestes & as some saye a chambermayde that had
latelye dwelte theare had revealed whatt shee knewe but as god woulde
there was nether preeste nor churchestuffe in the howse butt the searche
beeinge ended theye woulde have Sʳ Frauncis to come in bande to
bringe his Ladye & others of that sexx foorthecomminge some fortenight
after & theye weare to caule a sessions of purpose for them. I thought
therefore thatt the Ladies shold have kepte theere owne houses untill
then but I heare since that they have committed to the prison the
forsayed Ladye Stoner, & her daughter the Ladye Lentell (or suche a
name)[910] & other gentlewomen theye founde theare. I heere alsoe thatt
they have committed the Ladye Blunte[911] and one Mʳˢ Poore & her
daughter.[912] From thence they wente to sʳ Harrye Stoners[913] to have
mett with his ladye[914] but shee fledd havinge notice thereof as alsoe
others did in the night tyme into other shires. Ytt is thought that theye
ayme at this marke vz by vertue of the laste statute to make gentlemen
schymatikes [sic] to paye xˡ a monethe for theire wives or els to committ
them to prison & to make theire husbandes to redeeme theire vexations
with moneye or els to leave the companye of theire wives.[915] tyme will
discover all shortelye. [p. 370] Ytt is moneye which theye principallye
woulde have for hee which shoulde bee Richest is an extreame beggar &

[908] Sir Francis Stonor was generally a conformist but was indicted for recusancy as a
result of this search, CRS 60, 210.
[909] Martha (Southcote), Sir Francis Stonor's wife, CRS 60, 209–10. On 17 August 1612
Henry Howard, Earl of Northampton, commented to Robert Ker, Viscount Rochester,
on the 'sharpe course of procedinge' in Oxfordshire which had induced many to conform,
and in particular that Lady Martha Stonor had taken the oath of allegiance, Davidson,
106–7.
[910] Elizabeth (Stonor), the wife of Sir Edward Lenthall of Pyrton. Sir Edward was
noncommmunicant in 1612. Alan Davidson speculates that he might have provided a
London house for John Gerard SJ in 1599, Davidson, 140, 396.
[911] Cecily, the wife of Sir Richard Blount, and daughter of Sir Richard Baker of
Sissinghurst. On 26 February 1613 (NS) Champney sent More 'a breef narratione of the
ladie Blunt her troble for her conscience', and noted that she was William (Gabriel)
Gifford OSB's niece, AAW A XII, nos 42 (p. 89), 65. For the complexity of the religious
opinions of the Blounts of Mapledurham, see Davidson, 80–90.
[912] 'Mrs Poore' may be Prudence the wife of Francis Poure, though there were several
recusant members of this Oxfordshire family in this period, Davidson, 149; CRS 60, 230.
Francis's son, Richard, was required to take the oath of allegiance in July 1612, Davidson,
149.
[913] Sir Henry Stonor of Blount's Court, Sir Francis Stonor's heir.
[914] Elizabeth Wodehouse of Waxham, Norfolk, a convicted recusant.
[915] See **Letter 11**.

by hooke or crooke moneye muste bee hadd as some good gen[t]lemen feele to theire costes amongste [w]home a kinseman of myne Mr Francis Beningfeelde[916] payed 5C^l bicause theye founde one m^r Everarde[917] in his howse; & an other vz. m.^r Morgan of Lanternam[918] whoe married one of the Earle of Worcester his daughters[919] payed a thousande pounde not to bee trubled aboughte the othe[920] & when his frendes weare uppon the pointe of Compoundinge with the kinge theare was an horrible honeste man which spoke to the kinges face or soe that the kinge hearde of it againste these compositions. butt the kinge As hee is wise answered that hee woulde have the moneye & it shoulde bee payed him in golde too. for quoth hee the man will take the othe if hee weare muche urged. still theire is a speeche of a Parlamente & questionles it is principallye to gett moneye either by subsedies or by redeeminge the wardeshipps for the which some saye theire is demanded 5 hundred thousande pounde presentlye & to C thousande poundes by the yeare. the Puritanes make whatt meanes theye can to gett Burgesshipps & questionlesse Puritanisme will putt harde for it butt theye will have some ierke at the Protestantes & all thinke that when Recusantes bee thoroughlye ransacte then theye will have a flinge at the Bisshops & Englishe Clergye. yow maye guesse whereat theye ayme by thatt followethe. one Doctor Howsne[921] or suche a name tooke occasion in a sermon at Oxforde to showe that in the Annotations uppon the translated bible of Geneva hee coulde finde 32 places tendinge to Arianisme. Doctor Abbotts[922] & Doctor Ayery[923] sente for him & tolde him thatt hee might doe well to qualifye his late sermon with an other and that hee did yll to give the adversarye thatt advantage for whatt will men thinke butt thatt there weare division in theire Churche where in truthe (if yow will beeleeve them) theare was none. Doctor Howson answered that whatt hee had preached hee woulde

---

[916] Francis Bedingfield of Redlingfield. He had married Katherine, daughter of John Fortescue (nephew of the former chancellor of the exchequer, Sir John Fortescue) whose mother was Katherine Pole, daughter of Sir Geoffrey Pole of Lordington. Subsequently, Francis's son John would marry Susanna, a daughter of the Kentish recusant Edward Wyborne, CRS 7, 433; PRO, C 142/776/89.

[917] This may be the Suffolk Jesuit Thomas Everard who left England in either 1611 or 1612, CRS 74, 163.

[918] William Morgan.

[919] Frances, daughter of Edward Somerset, fourth Earl of Worcester. She was converted to Catholicism by Robert Jones SJ, Foley V, 905.

[920] Edward Morgan, William's father, offered his composition of £1,000 on 15 June 1612, BL, Lansdowne MS 153, fo. 85r. Possibly Norton is confusing the two.

[921] John Howson, a canon of Christ Church, Oxford.

[922] Robert Abbot, Master of Balliol College, Oxford, and brother of Archbishop George Abbot.

[923] Henry Airay, fellow of Queen's College, Oxford.

maintayne & putt in printe & desired thatt he might speake in thatt
matter beefore the Kinge him selfe.[924] theye answered that hee shoulde
not printe it for the Reason beefore mentioned. & shortelye after one
Doctor Goodwin[925] firste & Doctor Abbottes afterwarde spake in theire
sermons as muche as theye thought fitt againste Doctor Houson & soe
the matter hangethe yett & soe it will hange if Puritanes bee not hanged
or burned for theire inducinge firste to Arianisme & afterwarde to
Turcisme. butt theye havinge the Cheefe Prelate in theire side dare
doe any thinge butt good [p. 371] and that I assure my selfe theye will
never doe. I coulde if I liste tell yow as merrye a tale in an other kinde
of a [blank in MS] that beeinge in a forreste a huntinge & havinge
taken upp his stanninge to shoute when the deare shoulde bee browght
unto him, it happned that a Londiner knowinge nothinge ride a longe
throughe the forreste & marde theire spoorte. wheruppon one sayed
the Divl, the Divil, the Divill fetche mee heether that Divel & I will
take him by the nose as Dunston did the Divill wheruppon horsemen
pursued the Traveler & brought him beefore this newe Dunston. whoe
tooke him by the nose with his handes & beate him pittifullye in the
face. was not this manlye donn? but enoughe & to muche of this. ytt
was thought S.ʳ Thomas Lake shoulde have beene cheefe Secretarye[926]
butt nowe it is sayed that Vicownte Rochester[927] a scott shall bee the
cheefe & that S.ʳ Harry Nevill a greate Puritane shall execute the
office.[928] of the laste lorde Treasurer & secretarye theire is a booke
writtne in his prayse[929] & there bee a multitude of Epitaphes scarce
turninge to his praise.[930] the shortest is. Thatt to crookebackt RR in
sittinge at the helme the one overthrewe the nobles & the other the
Realme.[931] And an other (yea & one of the cleaneste) is.

---

[924] For this controversy and the subsequent disputation between John Howson and
George Abbot in front of James I in June 1615, see N. Cranfield and K. Fincham (eds),
'John Howson's answers to Archbishop Abbot's accusations at his "trial" before James I
at Greenwich, 10 June 1615', *Camden Miscellany* XXIX (Camden Society, 4th series, 1987),
320–41, at pp. 321–31.

[925] William Goodwin, Dean of Christ Church, Oxford.

[926] John Chamberlain believed on 9 July 1612 that Sir Henry Wotton and Sir Thomas
Lake would be appointed secretaries, but by 15 July Chamberlain was saying that Lake
had 'left of the canvasse', McClure, 367, 369. Wotton's candidacy was ended by the
failure of the proposed Savoyard dynastic marriage alliance which he was promoting,
Adams, 234.

[927] Robert Ker, Viscount Rochester, created Earl of Somerset in November 1613.

[928] For Sir Henry Neville's candidacy for the secretaryship, see Adams, 232–3.

[929] Sir Walter Cope wrote 'An Apology for the late Lord Treasurer Sir Robert Cecil,
Earl of Salisbury', printed in J. Gutch (ed.), *Collectanea Curiosa* (2 vols, Oxford, 1781), I,
119–33; *CSPD 1611–18*, 138.

[930] See P. Croft, 'Libels, Popular Literacy and Public Opinion in Early Modern
England', *Historical Research* 68 (1995), 266–85, at pp. 275–6.

[931] For John Chamberlain's version of this libel, see McClure, 356.

Heere sleepes in the Lorde beepepperde with pox
a Ciciliane monster beegott of a fox
some caulde him crookebacke & some litle Robbin
hee bore on his backe a packe like ower Dobbin
yett none coulde rule him, ride, or beestride him
butt he beestrid many or els they beelyde him
by crafte hee gott creditt, & honor by moneye
& much hee delighted in huntinge the Cunniye
but Rotten with ruttinge like sores in september
hee died as hee lived with a faulte in one member.

yow shall have noe more of thease unlesse yow sende for them. I will
make an ende not forgettinge to tell yow thatt latelye in the yle of
Weight the cheefe towne there was a fyer & threescore howses burnt.[932]
Forgett me not to my Dearest D. Thor: farewell
    16 of August. 1612
(On p. 372)
Addressed: To his approoved good frende m[r] George Weste.
ndorsed: (1) Aug. 16. BN.
        (2) Recea. thr. Oct. 25.⎱
            Answ. sat. Nov. 3. ⎰ 1612

35 *Robert Pett to Thomas More (30 September 1612 (NS))*   (*AAW A XI,*
    no. 174, pp. 511–12. Holograph)

Very Reverend and beloved si:[r] I have two of yours of which I ame at
this present to retorne yow answer, the former of the 25th of August the
later of the 8th of September[.] the reason why accordinge to my
wonted coustome I fayled to advertise yow of the receipt of the former
I hope yow have understood by one from m.[r] Nelson[933] and the week
followinge at our retorne[934] I was soe full of busines by reason of his
departure towardes England and of m[r] Colfords towardes Spayne[935]
that possibly I could not have commoditye to write; M:[r] Colford is
gone with my permission but not without geveinge me souch caution
as that his absence can [two words obscured] be preiudicial unto my
busines but as I hope beneficial[.] he pretendeth to [two words obscured]

[932] Not listed in E.L. Jones, S. Porter and M. Turner (eds), *A Gazetteer of English Urban
Fire Disasters, 1500–1900* (Historical Geography Research Series no. 13, August 1984).
[933] John Jackson. His letter to More of 11 September 1612 (NS ?) (AAW A XI, no. 147)
described his arrival in Brussels.
[934] Jackson had accompanied Pett to Zichem, a shrine near Louvain, AAW A XI, no.
147.
[935] See *Downshire MSS* III, 354.

spayne within fower monethes and is in hope at his retorne to geve us all satisfaction he haveinge obtayned a decree for the payment of his dept upon three next folowinge Indian fleetes[936] and therfore doth hope to receave the third part upon the fleet which is now expected in the moneth of October next and of the other two parts to make sale unto the marchants of Genua who are accoustomed to deale in souch bargaines and thus much astouchinge my apologie and this busines and now to the particulers of your letters; of M:[r] flecher[937] I heare nothinge as yet; the Prince Peretti[938] is sayed to be retorned from England to Paris but not to have seane or saluted our kinge by reason he was in progres and himselfe remayned in England very private acquaintinge him selfe only or in especial with the spanishe Embas-

[936] In June 1610 Birkhead recounted to More the cause of the dispute between Pett and Colford: Anthony Fletcher [see next note] had delivered the sum of £2,000 to Colford with, according to Colford, 'condition of hazard to employ it in trafique for cloth to the kinges [Philip III's] use, and out of the profit therof to pay' back both the capital and interest. Colford was evidently responsible to Pett for this money. But 'now the kinge not painge him neither principall nor rent, he likewise is destitute of means to paie either, and neither can nor will', AAW A IX, no. 43 (p. 117). Colford had apparently borrowed this money in order to supply clothing for Spanish troops in Flanders, and had not been paid for supplying it, *Downshire MSS* II, 57, 464. For the financial difficulties of Philip III's regime which led to Colford's problem, see R.A. Stradling, *Europe and the Decline of Spain* (1981), 33–42, esp. pp. 39–41 (for which reference I am very grateful to Albert Loomie). For Colford's attempt to secure payment by going to Spain, see *Downshire MSS*, III, 185–6, 261, 301, 313, 366, and *passim*, IV, *passim*; AAW A X, no. 161. Colford arrived in Paris on 15 September 1612 (NS) where Edmondes 'made him very welcome in return for his courtesy at Brussels, and gave him a letter of recommendation to Sir J. Digby', *Downshire MSS* III, 373. Pett noted in December 1612 that 'm[r] Colford brake his righte arme in his Iournay to spayne but is now agayne well recovered and in good hope of well effectinge his busines', AAW A XI, no. 234 (p. 675). By July 1613 Champney could tell More that Colford 'shale have his money in the space of one yeare so that he wilbe att libertie then att least to doe us service in some other place thoughe for this present he dothe well there where he ys', AAW A XII, no. 139 (p. 312), though 'certayne newes' that Colford had been paid in Spain reached Pett only in April 1616, AAW A XV, no. 61 (p. 161).

[937] After his ordination in December 1610, Anthony Fletcher's inclination towards SJ (which he entered in late 1612/early 1613, CRS 74, 171) did nothing for his credit at Cowdray where he had formerly served the Browne family. Birkhead told More in November 1612 'I am sorie m[r] fletcher is in his way home: he will fynd great difficultie heare of a place. I could wishe he provided himselfe in the Low Countrie for a tyme', AAW A XI, no. 201 (p. 577). Fletcher carried with him a demand direct from Pope Paul V that the seculars must settle their quarrels with the religious, AAW A XII, no. 68. This was not well taken. Champney reported to More that on Fletcher's arrival back in England he 'presented to his owld lord [Anthony Maria Browne, second Viscount Montague] a crucifix from his Ho and would gladly have hadd entrance and enter-taynement but was refused', AAW A XII, no. 72 (p. 154).

[938] Brother of Andrea Peretti, Cardinal Montalto, McClure, 378; AAW A XI, no. 138. In August 1609 Champney had suggested to Smith that Montalto should be petitioned for financial assistance for the proposed writers' college in Paris, AAW A VIII, no. 142.

sadors.[939] m:[r] sacfi[940] hath ben here as I suppose m:[r] Nelson hath written unto yo*w*[.] we had some conference together and I hope we shall have further at his retorne hether w*hi*ch he promised should be towardes the latter endinge of the moneth of October. yo*w* harp often upon one stringe asconcerninge the president[941] w*hi*ch I ame afrayed yo*w* will never bringe to any [word illegible] musicke yet I have always ben of yo*ur* opinion that yt is most necessarie and will urge yt unto m:[r] sac: at his comminge. f: white[942] hath ben in Britanie and by a letter w*hi*ch yesterday I receaved I understand he is now in Lorayne,[943] m[r] Oglebies[944] newes astouchinge the poysoninge of our priests in newgate w*i*th a salade[945] is held douptfull althought [sic] certayne yt is that many of them surfeted therof w*hi*ch many impute rather to some herb that was in yt then otherwise and m:[r] Nelson seameth to be of this opinion; the book I sent yo*w* from m:[r] Howard[946] was undouptedly an answer to an Epistle written by doctor weston for he him selfe is now come over and arived hether to Bruxels and acknowledgeth yt to have ben his but sayeth that widdrington hath maliciously falsified yt in 3 or 4. places or rather widdringtons master for he affirmeth in playne tearmes the author of the same as alsoe of the Apologie before not to have ben widdrington but the party[947] of whome yo*w* have heard heretofore suspicious rumors yet because this is soe untastfull unto some wher yo*w* are I desire that yo*w* should not take any further knoledge of any thinge that yo*w* here from me hereof. ther is as yet noe secretarie made in

[939] Richard Broughton reported to More on 26 October 1612 that Peretti, who 'came onelie they say to see th*e* Cuntry', visited the Clink and 'talked with M[r] Pres. [Roland (Thomas) Preston OSB]. I pray God he relate trulie the state of thinges as they stand w*i*th us', AAW A XI, no. 190 (p. 551). Champney said that Peretti 'was w*i*th m[r]. preston att masse in the Clink', AAW A XI, no. 180 (p. 525). As he returned from England through Brussels Peretti was honourably received by the archduke, AAW A XI, no. 208.

[940] Thomas Sackville.

[941] Thomas Worthington.

[942] John (Augustine) Bradshaw OSB.

[943] Bradshaw wrote to More on 4 October 1612 (NS) that he had been away visiting OSB houses in Brittany and Lorraine (St Lawrence's at Dieulouard, where there was bitter conflict among English Benedictines over the ownership of the property, see Lunn, *EB*, 96–8). Now he has been ordered back to Spain. This is the result of whispering by his enemies (particularly Roland (Thomas) Preston), AAW A XI, no. 177. For Bradshaw's deposition on 29 September 1612 (NS) from his posts of vicar general and prior of St Gregory's, Douai, and replacement by John (Leander) Jones OSB, see Lunn, *EB*, 99.

[944] Identity uncertain.

[945] On 31 July 1612 (NS) George Russell reported to William Trumbull from Louvain that news was brought from England that thirty priests imprisoned in Newgate were 'all like to be poisoned in their salades at supper, which grew upon this that the archbishop of Canterb. did solicit the king to rid the land of as many as were in present hold', but James had refused, *Downshire MSS* III, 341. *Cf.* **Letter 30**.

[946] See **Letters 28**, **32**.

[947] Roland (Thomas) Preston OSB.

England nor tresorer and therfore that w*h*ich yo*w* heard of si*r* Tho: Lacke is assueredly false. The mariage of our prince[948] w*i*th the sister of florence is heare held as unprobable[.][949] I have sene theses of the question in utra*mque* partem wherin the difficulty of the Cheefest poynte is not placed in regarde only of the danger of the princes but rather in respect of sacriledge by administeringe the Sacrament to a subiecte incapable of grace both partyes actually and wittingly concurringe therin w*i*thout necessity and this is urged to be intrinsice mal*um* in w*h*ich the pope nether can nor oughte to dispence. The spanishe Embassadore Don Pedro[950] is styll remayninge in England, the post expected out of spayne is retorned more then a weeke past yet noe newes is heard astouchinge the conclusion of his busines.[951] The Palatine is in preparation towardes Englande[952] and the Hollanders prepare in like sorte to receave him w*i*th all royalty. they have appoynted Counte Henry[953] Grave Maurice his brother to accompany him and have geven him two hundred thousand florins for his Iornay and 20^{ti} gentilmen to attend one him unto whome alsoe they have geven honorable stipendes.[954] The marques spinola is sayed to have ben honorably receaved by the Emperour & dimissed w*i*th great contentment[.] he is now agayne dayly here expected. D: weston bringeth me extraordinary newes[.] great perseqution he reporteth to be in England[955] the pursuivantes raginge and rainginge in every corner, great feares at Coudry[956] in soe much that they have sent all ther church stuff secretly by nighte to London, he speaketh much in disprayse of my L:[957] and findeth faulte w*i*th all proceedings of our clergie, yo*w* know him and his humor and therfore I nead not enlarge my self much about him[.][958] M:^r Mush

---

[948] Prince Henry.

[949] The proposal for a match with the sister of the grand duke of Tuscany had in fact already ground to a halt by the end of July 1612, because of opposition at the court in London and at Rome, *CSPV 1610–13*, pp. ix–x, 431, and *passim*; Strong, 'England and Italy: The Marriage of Henry Prince of Wales', 70–3. *Cf. Downshire MSS* III, 338.

[950] Pedro de Zúñiga.

[951] According to the Venetians, Zúñiga's embassy had not been a success, *CSPV 1610–13*, 427, 431, 433. For Robert Pett's very different view, see **Letter 36**.

[952] Frederick V, Elector Palatine deferred his arrival, partly because of the death of Philip Lewis, Count of Hanau, but also to wait until the Spanish ambassador had departed, *CSPV 1610–13*, 433.

[953] Henry, Prince of Nassau.

[954] *CSPV 1610–13*, 392.

[955] See **Letter 31**.

[956] Cowdray.

[957] Anthony Maria Browne, second Viscount Montague.

[958] As early as mid-June 1611 Birkhead had written to More that Edward Weston was planning to leave the country and that 'I feare he is not for us', AAW A X, no. 71 (p. 189). Champney noted in October 1612 'some say he wilbe Iesuit', AAW A XI, no. 180 (p. 525). While Birkhead thought well of Weston's anti-Preston polemical tract, *Iuris Pontificii Sanctuarium*, AAW A XII, no. 110, Robert Pett thought Weston's 'good parts'

he sayeth is departed this world god geve rest unto his soule.[959] I recommend him unto yo*ur* good prayers. yo*w* write that yo*ur* principal suite[960] goeth slowly forwardes and soe I feare yt will doe as alsoe yo*ur* others[.] yo*w* have I thanke yo*w* sent me the copies of many memoriales that yo*w* have exhibited but I could never heare of any one that hath ben effected. that second sonne of Modina[961] is he w*hi*ch heretofore I wrot unto yo*w* of but yo*w* by mistakinge a letter called him Medina[.] yo*w* may yf yo*w* please [p. 512] Change the first letter of his name and call him duke of Nodina for yt seameth that our kinge by gevinge him a horse hath metamorphised him into an ass.[962] all m:*r* Ishames[963] letters I have sent to his sonne who in aunswer of the former retorneth this inclosed. m:*r* Mayney is now here folowinge hard his law matters w*hi*ch I could wish he had ended for he will wery not only his freandes but his lawyers alsoe yf his suites doe longe continew[.] he is soe tedious in his discourses and soe unconstant in his designements[.][964] yf yo*w* heare not from me agayne accordinge to my ordinary course I shall request yo*w* to pardon me for I ame this next week upon some occasion of busines to take my Iornay towardes Colon[965] from whence yt may be

were 'placed in a bad subject that wanteth both witt and iudgment how to use and dispose them', and that the preface of his book was an exercise in flattering Cardinal Borghese. As for the substance, there is 'nether method nor matter of worth in yt but souch as I feare will not only redounde to his one discredite and disgrace' but others of his 'cote and profession' as well, for he had given 'soe great advantages' to Preston, AAW A XII, no. 98 (p. 215). Benjamin Norton did not think much of it either, but noted that the Jesuits thought well of it, AAW A XII, no. 126. See Allison, 'Richard Smith's Gallican Backers', part I, 353–4.

[959] John Mush died on 22 November 1612 (rather than in 1613, Bellenger, *English and Welsh Seminary Priests*, 90; or in 1617, Anstr. I, 241), AAW A XI, no. 225.

[960] For the appointment of a bishop.

[961] Luigi D'Este, the second son of Cesare, Duke of Modena, visited England during the summer, *CSPV 1610–13*, 367, 384.

[962] Antonio Foscarini noted that Princess Elizabeth had presented Luigi D'Este with 'two beautiful mules', *CSPV 1610–13*, 384.

[963] Christopher Isham.

[964] John Mayney was involved in a dispute about money with Thomas Owen SJ, rector of the English College in Rome. In December 1611 Thomas Poulton had reproved Mayney for his hostile letters to Owen and for his 'uniust taxing' of SJ, AAW A X, no. 158 (p. 437). Birkhead reported to More on 9 May 1612 that the quarrel between Mayney and Owen had been resolved, AAW A XI, no. 74. But Mayney was soon involved in another financial dispute with Anthony Hoskins SJ. An attempt at arbitration failed (William Trumbull negotiated for Mayney), AAW A XI, nos 208, 234. Hoskins's evidence against Mayney was judged sufficient, and he obtained 'sentence and execution agaynst m*r* Mayney' who 'was arested and for some tyme committed and soe compelled to pay the mony and this was some 3 dayes before Christmas [1612]', AAW A XI, no. 234 (p. 675). In January 1615 Mayney was rumoured to have renounced Catholicism, AAW A XIV, no. 9.

[965] Pett wrote to More on 6 October 1612 (NS) that he had been sent for by Thomas Sackville to come to Mechlin where they had had 'much conference'. Sackville then gave

that I shall not retorne before some three weekes hence or more[.]
howsoever yf yt please god that I retorne agayne salfly I will make yo*w*
amendes with recountinge yo*w* the newes of thos partes and doe in the
meane tyme recommend yo*w* to the protection of our blessed saviour
and my selfe to yo*ur* good prayers and soe with kindest remembrances
doe take my leave restinge ever
yours most assueredly
    Rob: Pett
Bruxells this 30th of september 1612
send me worde I pray yo*w* what is becum of f: Rob: Grey.^{966}
Addressed: To his very worshipfull and Reverend freand M:^r Tho: more
              priest geve thes   At Rome.
Endorsed: (1) Sept. 30. 1612. R. P.
            (2) Rece. frid. Oct. 19.⎫
                Answ. sat. Oct. 20.⎭ 1612
            (3) herwith one for Mr Isham fro*m* his sonn. an other for f W.
            Thompso*n*.

36 *Robert Pett to Thomas More (10 November 1612 (NS))*   *(AAW A XI,*
        no. 200, pp. 575–6. Holograph)

My very Revere*n*d good s*ir* althought the week past I have geven yo*w*
notice of my retorne from Colon^{967} and have withall answered souch
of yours as expected me here in my absence soe that noe great occation

him some business to transact at Cologne (where Pett had previously studied divinity
and where Sackville acted as patron to the Capuchins), AAW A XI, no. 182 (p. 529);
Belvederi, 288.

    ^{966} Pett had written to More on 21 July 1612 (NS) that Gray, who had just returned
from Rome, AAW A XI, no. 106, was in Brussels to 'procuer permission for the erecting
of a Cloyster of Englishe franciscans haveinge obteyned the graunt of a convent at
dunkirke with two or three Guardians handes for the furtheringe of the affayer, yet thos
here at Bruxells would not subscrib to his petition'; he stayed at 'a publike In and not at
his one Cloister and beinge knowen to carie mony about him contrarie to his rule he
was advertised that the Guardian here would call him to accounte for yt wherupon he
spedily departed the towne', AAW A XI, no. 124 (p. 338). He told More further on 1
September 1612 (NS) that 'father Greyes preferment' was offensive to all English and
Scottish Franciscans, and that Gray had written that More was 'much his enemy as alsoe
the Irishe of his order'. He was claiming that 'he hath great favor with the duches of
florence and that her hyghtnes hath promised him that yf she cannot procuer him a
convent in England she will at the lest procuer yt soe neare England as may be'. Pett
suspected this was all an underhand effort 'to affront' William Stanney OFM the
Franciscan superior in England, AAW A XI, no. 142 (p. 393). For Gray's return to
England, see **Letters 40**, **47**.
    ^{967} See **Letter 35**.

doth rest which should move me this week to write yet to shew my self
willinge to make some satisfaction for my former silence in tyme of my
absence I have ben induced to breake my ordinary coustome of 15
dayes and this weeke alsoe to send yow thes few lines and the rather
to certefie yow of the arrivall of don pedro de suniga from out of
England unto this towne some six dayes past beinge now alsoe yesterday
departed from hense towardes spayne. our kinge is sayed to have very
honorably intreated him in his one [?] particuler and at his departure
to have geven him in plate to the valew of 1500[li] stirlinge and at his
request to have granted liberty unto 7 priestes wherof 3 are of our
bretheren secular the 4th is f: Harington[968] the franciscan frier and the
other 3 are of the society and two of them thos which were taken in
m/rs Vaux her house,[969] yt is alsoe sayed that he hath the grant and
promise for the delivery of f: Baldwin upon condition that one now in
the inquisition at Rome who was sometyme tutor[970] to my lord Rosse[971]
may be alsoe set at liberty, his chaplaine[972] tould me that exception was
taken agaynst the benidictans soe that he could not procuer liberty for
any one of them[973] nether for souch of our seculer as he demanded,
but only for three best pleasinge to them selves. there names as yet I
know not but m:[r] Musket[974] is none of them thought [sic] he was
demanded, 6 are arived to S:[te] Omers as m[r]: cape[975] writeth unto me
but I here nothinge what is become of f: Harington; the busines of the
Embassador with the kinge is sayed to remayne very secret only to his
maiesty two of his counsel and one interpreter as alsoe in spayne yt is
only to the kinge, the duck of Lyrmo,[976] one secretarie and the
Embassador which was sent, from whose chaplaine I had this narration
who although he confesseth great extremity to be in England now
used towards catholicks yet doth he withall indevor to insinuate great
hopes of some speady redress, and for confirmation hereof they now
geve forth that the mach of our prince with florence is broken of and
that our kinge doth rather inclyne for the daughter of savoy and doe
insinuate great hopes for Catholiks hereby. The Palatine is in England
very honorably receaved yet some think that his mariage with the Lady

---

[968] Martin Harrington OFM.

[969] Nicholas Hart SJ and John Percy SJ. See **Letter 19**.

[970] John Mole. See Smith, *Life*, I, 488n, II, 126–7.

[971] William Cecil, Lord Roos.

[972] Presumably the Minim friar Bartholomew Teles.

[973] This may have been a way of protecting Roland (Thomas) Preston OSB, for whom
release might bring the danger of a summons to Rome, Lunn, *EB*, 51–2.

[974] George Fisher. On 5 December 1612 Birkhead thought that Fisher and John Almond
were likely to be executed almost immediately, AAW A XI, no. 220. In the event only
Almond was.

[975] William Cape.

[976] Francisco de Sandoval y Rojas, Duke of Lerma.

Elizabeths grace shall not soe sone be solemnised as he expecteth qua supra nos nihil ad nos god dispose all to his honor. I have written into England to Tho: Heth asconcerninge your busines as yo*w* willed me yet rather to satisfie yo*ur* request then of any hope I have of aunswer for of all yo*ur* letters w*hic*h we have sent unto him by his one direction he never retorned us aunswer of the receipt of any one althought the same hath ben craved and requested particulerly from him; I have heertofore alsoe intreated yo*w* to signifie two or three lynes to m:ʳ Heth as concerninge that 20ᵗⁱ florins w*hic*h I took of him by yo*ur* appoyntment for mʳ Isham.[977] I pray yo*w* remember yt for accordinge to the humor of the person I know yt to be requisite. the vicar generall[978] and m:ʳ Chambers[979] are not yet retorned from ther visite;[980] thus therfore not haveinge further wherwith to troble yo*w* I take my leave and doe ever rest

yours most assueredly
    Robert Pett
Bruxells this 10ᵗʰ of November 1612
(On p. 576)
Addressed: To the worshipfull and very Reverend priest M:ʳ Tho: More
        geve thes   At Rome
Endorsed: (1) Novemb. 10. 1612. R.P.
        (2) Recea. sat. Decemb. 1°. ⎫
            Answ. sat. Decemb. 1°. ⎬ 1612
                      ⎭

37 *John Nelson (Jackson) to Thomas More (9 November 1612)*   *(AAW A*
    XI, no. 197, pp. 565–7. Holograph)

Much reverenced & as much beloved Sir
    In the last I receaved from yo*w* I had newes of mʳ Hairsteins[981] for

---

[977] Presumably William Isham.
[978] Caesar Clement.
[979] Robert Chambers.
[980] TD V, 34f for the visitation of Douai College.
[981] In June 1612 Anthony Champney wrote to More that Jackson was enquiring after news of 'a scotishe youthe called Hairestaynes' [*i.e.* at Rome], AAW A XI, no. 100 (p. 283), perhaps the same as or related to Matthew Haistenes, a page of Anne of Denmark's chamber, *CSPD 1603–10*, 156. In a list of the queen's household in December 1612, this page was a receiver of mourning cloths for Prince Henry's funeral, PRO, LC2/416, fo. 26r, though this does not conclusively establish that he was present. He is not on an accounts list for the household drawn up in 1614, PRO, E 315/107, fo. 17v (for all which information I am very grateful to Helen Payne). John Jackson was at court for some of this period. His letters recite speeches made by James and Anne when he was present. On 1 March 1613 he noted 'our q. did of late speak to the K. in behalfe of Cath. & he answered saucy. why will you speak for them th*a*t neyther love yo*w* nor mee nor myne. but wold doe w*i*th us as they went about to doe in the powder treason', AAW A XII, no. 46 (p. 102). See also **Letter 51**. Helen Payne has suggested to me that Jackson might

the which I hartely thank yow and yow shall hear more thearof hearafter. I suppose the untymely death of owr yong prince[982] wyll be come before thease. he died on the 6th of novembre in the evening. Thowgh the L. Sanchar died with great edification[983] yet if the speech which is thear come abroad it will be very scandalous and much impayre the estimation of that holy sea and give our adversaries greater ground of their slanders of our canonizing of wilfull murderours & wicked men which aspersion they have cast upon us in their writings from tyme to tyme.[984] yow know the state of an heret. cowntry & thearfore may with greater freedome lett them know the harme that ensues such blind zeall.[985] His cheif & I may say soole helper was one of owrs, namely the party that hath written the late large letter to his hol. which I sent yow word of & I suppose yow have ere this receaved.[986] I commend your affection to d. Smith[987] whearin I will be a corrivall with yow, but yet I shold not think fitt that he before soe many shold be named for the place yow mention in yowrs to our superiour.[988] Owr sup: hath of late given yow information of some things which I was willing shold be made known unto him for that end. and I think it not a miss to second

have been in the entourage of Lady Jane Drummond, first lady of Queen Anne's Bedchamber, a committed Catholic. As early as September 1611 Richard Smith reported (somewhat ambiguously) 'there is a speech that our Queene [Anne] is reconciled and that by M[r] Nelson [John Jackson]' who 'is in a good place to get intelligence', AAW A X, no. 117 (p. 339). (The Spanish ambassador Alonso de Velasco noted in September 1611 that Mass was being said for Anne by a Scottish priest who posed as a servant of Jane Drummond, A.J. Loomie, 'King James I's Catholic Consort', *Huntingdon Library Quarterly* 34 (1971), 303–16, at p. 308, for which reference I am grateful to Helen Payne.) In July 1614 Champney noted that in Paris there was a priest 'of the order of S[t]. Iohn of Hierusaleme' who had been in England 'for these two yeares and more and haunted the court knowne to the kinge and sayd mass often before the queene and her mayd ladie Dromon', though he had eventually been imprisoned in the Gatehouse and then exiled, AAW A XIII, no. 146 (p. 412). See H. Payne, 'Aristocratic Women and the Jacobean Court 1603–1625' (forthcoming Ph. D. thesis, London).

[982] Prince Henry.

[983] See **Letters 28, 29, 30**.

[984] Jackson may be referring here to the adverse publicity which greeted the secular priest and martyr Robert Drury's absolution of the murderer Humphrey Lloyd in the courtroom in which they were both convicted, *A True Report of the Araignment, Tryall, Conviction and Condemnation of. . .Robert Drewrie* (1607), sig. B4r–v.

[985] Possibly Jackson's hostility to Sanquhair was coloured by knowledge of the rumours that Sanquhair had once been regarded as on good terms with SJ, *CSPD 1601–3*, 145.

[986] Jackson refers to John Colleton who had recently written a long address to Pope Paul V, a nine-page letter, on the general purposes of the secular clergy's agency in Rome, AAW A XI, no. 137 (16 August 1612). In 1615 Colleton was at loggerheads with other priests in the Clink (where Jackson himself was imprisoned from December 1613) over what he regarded as their lax moral standards, TD V, pp. clxxvi–vii; Anstr. I, 186. See also Folger Shakespeare Library, MS V a 244.

[987] Richard Smith.

[988] George Birkhead.

the same by my *lettres* also. ut in ore duum l. trium stet *omne* verbu*m*, and it may be I shall add something to his relation. thear hath been hear a secretarie[989] of the d. of Savoy all this sumer & of late thear is an other come whom they call an Imbass:[990] but theyr is expected an other greate man from thence who is the cheif Imb.[991] whe*n* he comes. this th*at* is hear did offer co*n*ditions but being talk'd w*i*thall by a freind of myne about those points w*h*ich owr <u>sup</u>: hath written unto yow he doth in part excuse them. thus talking w*i*th th*e* k. he asked him how many co*n*fessariuses she wold have[.] he answered but one, (whearupon th*at* report w*h*ich yo*w* have is grounded), but he sayth th*at* he meant th*at* her howshold shold have 4 or 5.[992] as for her going to th*e* chappell w*i*th th*e* prince[993] he sayth th*at* he did it upon the queens[994] words who told him th*at* she went but did only laugh at them. but now he knoweth his errour he will amend it. upon the death of o*ur* prince the[y] have sent over a post and will expect to know whether a motion shall be made for th*e* yong duke[995] who is 13 years old & somewhat above.[996] and of a ['soft' deleted] milde & gentle disposition but of a very good witt[997] somewhat weak but not sick. before the prince died the Archb.[998] & some th*at* ioyn'd w*i*th him offred the k. th*at* if he wold let

[989] Fulvio Pergamo of Asti.

[990] Battista Gabaleone. See *CSPV 1610–13*, 427.

[991] The Marchese di Villa, who finally arrived in England in April 1613, *CSPV 1610–13*, 531.

[992] *Cf.* McClure, 392, for Chamberlain's account that on 19 November 1612 James told the privy council 'how litle was agreed shold be allowed the daughter of Savoy that way yf the match had gon forward'. Concerning the Savoyard marriage proposals (for Princess Mary to wed Prince Henry), Birkhead wrote to More on 5 November 1612 that 'yf yt be concluded upon such conditions (in regard of religion) as they ['the Agents of that prince'] do tell and utter to some our principall Lords heare, it is like to be basely don by the Savoian, and Little to our edification and Comfort. for they demaund no more preistes but one to be permitted unto her selfe and her retinue. wheras yt is said that his m*aie*stie wold never have offered them so base an offer, but rather that she shold have had foure, 2 for her selfe, and 2 for her familie. insomuch as that our protestantes are much scandalized at such baseness. besides it is also given forth, that she shall both have masse, and goe to the kinges service also. w*h*ich is a point worthie to be exclaymed against. for yt wilbe much to the hurt of poore catholiques that have so longe susteyned so many tribulations for not yeeldinge to such an absurditie', AAW A XI, no. 195 (p. 561). *Cf.* Smith, *Life*, I, 124–5.

[993] Prince Henry.

[994] Anne of Denmark.

[995] Prince Charles, Duke of York.

[996] Birkhead mentioned this proposal in his letter to More of 10 November 1612, and said also that the Savoyard ambassador had now learnt his lesson about too freely discussing the religious terms of prospective dynastic marriage alliances 'and wilbe more cautelouse hearafter', AAW A XI, no. 201 (p. 577).

[997] The words 'milde & gentle' and 'but of a very good witt' are inserted above the line.

[998] George Abbot.

the prince marry with the landsgraves[999] daughter of Hess they wold
make a purse & give the k. as much as any papist prince wold give,
rather then to permitt a papist to entre into the bowells of owr
kingdome, to use the Archbish. his owne words. the palsgrave[1000] hath
been hear about a month and had free access to the La: Elizabeth her
grace. the k. made very much of him & the whole court & citie. I am
this night told he is not well. & some think that the prince his death
will hindre the marriage because thear is none between her grace &
the kingdome but the duke who is but a weakling.[1001] others think it
will forward it because thear is none whom the k. can think soe fitt in
all respects as the palsgrave & his religion is his cheif grace. they say
he is a fyne yong yoth & of good carriage. he is accompenied with
count Henrique (whom I take to be Grave Maurice his brother) &
diverse other counts. [In margin: '8°. novemb. 1612'] the yonge Ladie
takes her brothers death exceeding passionatly, soe that she refuseth
even to eat. [p. 566] The savoyans thinking (belike upon information)
that the spaniard was not gratefull to us gave owt for the furthering of
their own suite, that the k. of spayne had wrong'd there mayster & that
he had not as yet payed the marriage money etc. but they wear told
after that they tooke a wrong course for a lettre was seen in which the
k. had written to the LL of the councell that they shold not entertayn
any speech with them but upon condition that the k. of sp. shold adopt
her for his dawghter and confirme the peace anew. some wicked people
gave owt that the papists had poysoned the prince,[1002] and it is strang
to think how such reports, spreadders, and beleivers to the hurt of
religion [sic]. I did write unto yow within this month[1003] and a litle
before I did write all the newes of this place & send them to m[r] pett
praying him to copie owt all that he thowght wold gratifie yow & send
yow them. I have heartofore when I did not write to yow write to d
champ or some other praying them to write all I related which I
thowght was as good as if I had written my selfe unto yow. All that
owr superiour desired, concerning Imbassadours chapleyns was only to
give them facultie to hear confessions of such Inglish Irish and Scottish
as shold come unto them, they having before facultyes for those of
their owne countryes.[1004] and doe they stand at the graunt heerof? they
have reason. for it wear indeed against their axiome. nihil innovandum
as they doe construe it. but when any thing is to be doone which they

[999] Maurice, Landgrave of Hesse-Cassel. His daughter had been proposed as a bride
for Prince Henry in June 1612, *CSPV 1610–13*, 383.

[1000] Frederick V, Elector Palatine.

[1001] Chamberlain thought the delay was simply a matter of decorum, McClure, 391.

[1002] *Cf.* McClure, 388–9; *cf. Dowsnhire MSS* III, 419.

[1003] AAW A XI, no. 185 (20 October 1612), part printed in TD V, pp. cxvii–ix.

[1004] See **Letter 25**.

wold then wee find & feel innovations enow. The president of dowaye[1005] expecteth a visit (if it be not already) and the visiters are the Iesuits, the provinciall with some others as it is written from thence.[1006] It is thowgh[t] they intend his displacing and what els god knoweth. will not yow enform the p. of thease, and will his hol. being informed delay redress of thease thear usurpations, it is too mean a terme to call them innovations.[1007] verely I am perswaded his hol. will find cause to repent it eyther in this world or in the world to come & and soe perhaps I shall be bold to tell him ere many months pass over. Thowgh Hereticks and schismaticks shall find no excuse at the day of dome to deliver them from eternall paynes yet I think it wyll also appear that the strange dealing of some that have been placed in that Sea, and other officers under them, gave great occasion to their wofull falls. & some stick not to say that which happly is a truth, that the priests and cath. of Ingl: are the most dutifull tryed children that the p. hath because the causes of greif which they have given them partly by neglecting their requests, partly by permission of the Ies. to doe what they please against them (in the the [sic] Breve of doctors in the confessarius of doway & other things belonging to that college) wear able withowt gods speciall grace to break their obedience, as it hath almost even broken their harts, and notwithstanding it may easily be proved that they be the most dutifull children though perhaps the other make fayrer showes to his hol. to have us remayne dutifull, and yet for his hol. to hold us undutifull & thearupon proceed accordingly must needs be a great tryall. mee thinks the pope cold not take it amiss if yow shold collect all thease passages owt of my lettres & others and tell him yow have brought him what wee write that he may understand the state of things hear & how his actions are thowght of. yow are only a faithfull relaytor, if he be offended it must be with us. I will acquaint yow with a secret which is knowne to few and soe close up. The savoyans doe labour underhand for marriage between the La. Elizabeths Grace and our duke whearin they will spayre for noe [word deleted] expence [?] to

---

[1005] Thomas Worthington.

[1006] Robert Pett reported on 3 November 1612 (NS) that the nuncio in Brussels 'favoreth not our affayers' by sending Caesar Clement and Robert Chambers as visitors to Douai, AAW A XI, no. 193 (p. 557).

[1007] On 11 September 1612 (NS), shortly after arriving in Brussels, John Jackson had sent More a long memorandum about SJ's hold on Douai, and that the secular priest Robert Pilkington had said that Anthony Hoskins SJ had procured the nuncio at Brussels, Guido Bentivoglio, to 'write to the doctors of doway forbidding them to dispute' on theological issues 'in controversy between the Ies. & Dominicans, (which they toke not well because he forbad not the Ies. to doe the like)' and the nuncio sent to the college a copy of the papal breve concerning English Catholic clergy proceeding to the degree of doctor. Even Worthington was thrown into turmoil by this, AAW A XI, no. 147 (p. 403).

compass it. I praye recommend my love to m^r Nich: Fitz.[1008] I think
thear is none els thear of my acquaintance but your selfe whom I salute
with my whole hart humbly praying to be remembred in your devotions
at those holy places. 9° 9^{bris} 1612
yours as yow know
      N

(On p. 567, a separate slip of paper)

Addressed: To the worship*full* and my worthy freind m^r Tho: Moore
give thease
Endorsed: (1) Admodum R^{do} viro D. Thomae Moro hae dentur Romam
        (2) Novemb. 8. 9. 1612. N.
(On p. 565)
        Recea. mond. febr. 18.⎫
                              ⎬ 1612
        Answ. twesd. febr. 26. ⎭

38 *Extract from a letter of John Jackson (11 January 1613)*   *(AAW A XII,*
    no. 5, pp. 11–14. Copy. The margins of pp. 11 and 13 are worn away. The
    interpolations in square brackets are the suggestions mainly of Edwin Chadwick)

Out of m^r nelson his letter of ii [= 11] of Ianuarii[1009]

You have heard ere this of m.^{r} Mush his death[.] he would say any
tyme this halfe yere or more that he should assuredly dy upon the next
sicknes if it were not an ague. His frendes having buylt a new house
he went to ly there a fortnight before the rest, which as is verily thought
was cause of his death[.] he went reasonably well to bed on a satterday,
and at mid-night waking a[nd] fynding him self sick called presently for
his man and his frendes alsoe com[ing] to him he told them at the first
that he should dye, and therupon began [to] prepare himself: and
among other preparations gave his bookes to his fre[nd to] doe therwith
what she would upon condition shee should geve 50. poundes for his
[soul ?] and thus he continued till morning and all the fore noone and
till fower [of the] clock after noone when he yielded his soule to god.
when I know mor[e] you shalbe acquainted therwith.

[1008] In a letter of November 1611 Jackson had asked More to remembre my love' to
Nicholas Fitzherbert 'whom I much honor & hold my selfe indebted to particulerly for
his kindnes to me when I was thear [at the English College in Rome between 1592 and
1597]; thowgh perhaps he have now forgot me', AAW A X, no. 145 (p. 409).
[1009] In Anthony Champney's hand.

Mr. Salkild the collapsed Iesuit hath printed a book[1010] the title wherof is The nature essence, place, power, science, will, apparitions, grace, sinne, and all other proprietyes of Angelles etc. by Iohn Salkild lately fellow of the Iesuites Colleges in the university of Conimbria Corduba, and Compl[utum] Assistant in studies to the famous Iesuites Franciscus Suarez and Michael Gabriel Vasquez. In his preface to the king he sayth the king is by office an Angell and to him in particuler hath bin much more: and after he geveth thankes unto his Maiesty ut Angelo liberatori, and sayth he will boldly pronounce with Peetor Nunc scio vere quia misit deus angelum suum et eripu[it] me de manu Haerodis Papae Hispanicae Inquisitionis omnique expectati[one] Iesuitarum and intitleth himselfe the kings Convert page 294. spe[aking] of S. Denyse (he saith this) (if soe be that wee have the true Dyonisius as [some] of our schoole men doe avouch or suppose, though others of more worth doe bo[ldly] deny and disproove it: such like things ther are as this I suppose in other p[arts] of the booke, for I light of this by chaunce but I thinck he hath bin w[rong] in poyntes of fayth especially in mayne poyntes of controversy.

M𝗋 Mullanax alias Almond[1011] being brought to Tiberne upon a sle[dge] after the wonted manner[1012] was ther pulled up into the cart and then look[ing] first upon the gallowse with a smyling countenance he turned him after tow[ards] the sherife and intreated that he might be permitted to speak saying that he would not speak any thing that should be offensive either to the king or the state or any man in particuler and that he would be as briefe as might be which being graunted him he began to make relation how at his first taking he was carryed before a man whom he would not name (because he would [not] geve offence) and the oath which was commonly called of Allegiance [p. 12] being tendered him by the same partie he gave him many reasons which he could not answer when [sic for 'why'] neither himself nor the partie that offered it could take it without manifest periury and therupon refused to take it, and therfor committed to Neugate. upon an escape of certen priestes from thence he with others were put into the dungeoun, the place being most darke full of stench and ill savours being full of the ordure of such condemned men as had bin formerly ther. And for 24. howres he nor his fellowes had neither meat nor drink, and being here interrupted by the Sherife, because that poynt was distastfull, he answered howsoever it was distastfull it was truth, yet because it was distastfull he would speak no more of it.

[1010] John Salkeld, *A Treatise of Angels* (1613), sigs *2r-Ar.

[1011] John Almond.

[1012] Robert Pett noted that Almond was 'exequted...about five or six a clok in the morninge by torch light', AAW A XII, no. 2 (p. 3).

Then he began to speak of what passed at the Sessions, where he was condemned: and sayd ther were two thinges layd there to his charge, first, that he should say, that if a man should kill a king, he would absolve him: which accusation he sayd was most untrue, but being invited by the keeper to dinner (and being amongst other speeches at the table demaunded, he knew not to what end) whether a priest could absolve a man that should kill a king, he answered that if after the fact committed, the partie were truly penitent for it, a priest might geve him absolution, though he had killed a king, or the pope, or his owne father and mother, saying, that Godes mercy exceeded all his other workes.[1013] Here the thing that was layd unto his charge was that he was a priest, to which he answered, that neither did any man ever geve evidence against him, nor did he ever confesse him selfe to be one. And therfor at his arraignment, he refused to put himself to be tryed by the iury, not upon any contempt or disobedience, but only for that he would not have his death lye upon those poore mens consciences, who either for feare or otherwise were like enough to have condemned him for a priest without any witnesse therunto, or any other knowledge or proofe therof only at the Sessions. He desyred all that were there present to beare witnesse that he was a Catholike, and did beleeve whatsoever the Catholike Church did beleeve, then he made a deepe protestation which he sayd did proceed from the bottom of his hart, and as he should answer it before Almighty God, which was, that he never intended any treason against his Maiesty in all his life nor ever heard of any intended, and if he had ever heard of any, he would have revealed it if it had not bin in confession, and if it had bin revealed to him in confession, he would have sought all the meanes he could, that it should not have taken effect, he also protested that he did think that king Iames his maiesty of England, had as much power and authority over his subiectes, as the king of Spayne, or the king of Fraunce had over theirs, and that his Maiestyes subiectes of England doe owe as much allegiance unto him, as any of the kings of Spayne or France doe owe unto them: and though any forrein power, yea even the Pope himselfe should invade the kingdom, yet that we ought to fight in the defence of his Maiesty, and wheras his Maiesty hath now but one heyre male of his body, the which he doth hope will never fayle, he could wish that he had many more, and that the crowne may alwayes continue in his Maiestyes lyne, and being there interrupted by the mynister who sayd, but if the Pope should [p. 13] excommunicate his

[1013] Champney recounted to More on 15 January 1613 (NS) that George Abbot had maliciously asked Almond 'what he would doe to one who should confess unto him that he hadd killed a kinge whether he would absolve him or noe & he answeringe yea supposinge he were penitent this I say ys thought to have bene the occasione of his deathe', AAW A XII, no. 9 (p. 21).

Maiesty, he would think it lawfull to murder him, he answered, that the Catholike doctrine holdes noe such opinion, and that he thought it to execrable and damnable [so] to think, and further he sayd, that he was now come (although unworthy) to loose his life in defence of the Catholike fayth, the which life he sayd if it were 10000. or that every drop of blood of his were a life, he would as willingly loose them all as he would that one and wished that ther were some greater tormentes prepared for him, or that they wou[ld] not hang him first, but rip him up before and quarter him alive as he stood, that [all] might see how willingly he would endure either that or any other torment that [might] be devised, for his saviours sake. some other things he sayd to the sherife which I hea[rd] and being after interrupted by the minister, and having twise or thrise replyed unto hi[m,] at length he desyred him not to trouble him any further, for now was noe tyme of disp[ute] but to have his thoughtes fixed upon an higher obiect, onely this I marked that the mini[ster] speaking against the Papistes attributing much to their workes, which he sayd notwithstan[ding] they could not performe, m^r Almond amongst other answers of his, made a solemne pro[testa]tion, that it was noe tyme to boast, much lesse to lye, but seeing no one vertue was by th[e] Protestantes thought to be soe hardly to be performed, as the strict observation of chastity, h[e] could not but protest, for the clearing of soe important a poynt that himselfe had never knowne woman in all his life. Some doe report that he did take god to witnesse that he dyed as true a mayd as he came out of his mothers wombe. After these, and other such like speeches, having throwne all the mony, and such other things as he had to the standers by, and prepared himselfe to the execution, having a handkerchei[fe] put before his eyes, he desyred the Sherife that he might have notice geven him when the Cart should be taken away, that the last word he should speake might be Iesus for whose sake he lost his life: and when he heard commandment that the Cart should be driven away, he called instantly on the name of Iesus and so continewed to his last breath.

(In Champney's hand:) of m^r molinax m^r Archprest gevethe this singuler testimonie that he died with much constancie and shewe of learninge as anie that ever died befor [him.] he died the 5 or 6 of theyre December[1014]

(On p. 14)

Endorsed: (1) Extract out of m^r nelsons letters ii [= 11] of Ianuarie
(2) Extract out of m^r Nelsons letters ii [= 11] of Ianuarie. [sic]
(3) Of m^r Mullinax, alias Almond the Martyr

[1014] Almond was executed on 5 December 1612.

39 *Benjamin Norton to George West (Thomas More) (31 January 1613)   (AAW A XII, no. 26, pp. 59–62. Holograph)*

Beeloved & muche respected S.^r

your lettres any tyme this halfe yeare have miste theire waye in comminge unto mee. for some I feare mee come not at all, & othersome come with soe stale a date as that theye bee in that respecte the lesse welcome unto mee. for example yours of the laste of Iune came not to mee untill the 9th of December, & those of the 3 of November which are the laste I receaved (none of october beinge yett come) came unto mee the 26 of Ianuarye by which as alsoe by the former of Iune I understande your meaninge concerninge your ringe,[1015] which I coulde have wisht I had understode sooner. for gatheringe (rather then perfectlye knowinge your minde) owte of your lettres of september I thought it to bee to have the 20^s beestowedd in pios usus for the good of your Patronesse[1016] which made mee within 24 howres after the receipte thereof to beestowe it accordinglye uppon such as promised to praye for her & I hope theye have soe donne. In verye deede when I perceaved that ytt was an usuall trike for my lettres (which I make noe doubte but thatt theye weare sente in the same packett with my neighbours) to [s]tagger [?] in theire iorney I thought theire was some falsehoode in fellowshipp (never for all that any whitt mistrustinge your good selfe) & I halfe purposed not to have writtne any moore unto yow untill m^r Godfredo[1017] weare come unto yow & shoulde by his lettres unto mee insinuate & directe mee howe to wright unto him butt notwithstandinge this determination, I have once moore writtne by the other meanes cheefelye thatt yow maye understande my minde & not mistake mee if my lettres comme not as heeretofore owte of order unto yow. yow maye if it please yow continewe your coorse butt I shall bee lothe to sende any more unto yow unlesse it bee by suche a meanes as m.^r Godfrey shall directe mee to whome I praye yow to remember mee uppon whome I assuredlye [word obliterated] thatt hee will doe any thinge that is in his power tendinge to the good of our countrye. & I thinke further thatt hee hathe that good opinion of your sinceritye & wisedome that hee will conferr with yow & saye moore to yow then to any other. His sister Katherine[1018] is soe neere mee thatt I see her everye daye & her carriage is suche thatt she winnethe greate love of all her neighbours[.] for my parte I equalize her to my mistres her sister[1019] & can not saye nor wright to well of her. I thinke for all thatt thatt I shall

[1015] See **Letter 30**.
[1016] Magdalen, dowager Viscountess Montague (d. 1608).
[1017] Geoffrey Pole.
[1018] Katherine Pole, resident in Midhurst.
[1019] Constance Lambe, who was, in fact, Katherine Pole's first cousin.

not longe enioye her good company (not for thatt I thinke nowe as
formerlye I suspected thatt shee was marryed, which shee denyethe soe
constantlye that I beleeve her) but) [sic] for thatt the Ladye Blanche[1020]
desirethe her company this lente (if not longer) & she hathe a determination to goe unto her. of his other sister at London or other 3 sisters
in other places I heere noe one worde.[1021] the laste newes I hearde was
by m.ʳ Doctor Bullaker whoe yow maye tell him to bee returned a
sounde [?] doctor [p. 60] and suche an one as is likelye to doe muche
good.[1022] for for [sic] my parte had I an ague uppon mee the sight of
him withoute any phisicke weare able (soe muche I am affrayed of his
phisicke) to fryght awaye the fever from mee. since whose returne I
thanke god I have had my helthe better then beefore but yett I have
taken noe phisicke of him. & I have halfe covenaunted with him thatt
he shall administer noe phisicke unto mee untill he have gotten some
experience by killinge halfe a dozen att the leaste. Howe ever your
matters goe forewarde in those partes, or in Muscovia or Polonia[1023]
shure I am thatt all thinges goe woorse & woorse with us. The othe (as
it [sic for 'is'] sayed) muste bee offered a freshe to all Recusants, & it
is sayed that theye all shall bee warned to bee att the Assises either to
take it or els to indure the payne of the Lawe. All the Laytye almoste
ether bye frailetye or otherwize have either taken it alreadye, or I feare
mee will take it: for theire is notable dealinge under handes as well by
Nominalls[1024] as Realls[1025] & many of either sorte have strayned a stringe
to save theire goods. m.ʳ Warmington hathe writtne a booke to warrante
them to take the othe as it lyethe notw[ith]standinge Paules[1026] Breves &
it is suche a booke as will drawe many to followe his example.[1027]
Everye one will aske nowe both Paule Bellarmine, & one which Sheldon
caulethe bladeringe Coqueus[1028] whatt thinge there is in the othe
againste Faythe. & they saye thatt neither Paule hathe nor Bellarmine

---

[1020] Blanche Arundell, daughter of Edward Somerset, fourth Earl of Worcester.

[1021] Geoffrey Pole's four other sisters were Jane, Constance, Martha and Mary.

[1022] John Bullaker was a central figure in Sussex recusant Catholicism, and relied from
time to time on Viscount Montague's protection. He had received his degree of Doctor
of Medicine from the University of Caen in October 1612, T.J. McCann, 'The Catholic
Recusancy of Dr. John Bullaker of Chichester, 1574–1627', *RH* 11 (1971–2), 75–85, at pp.
78–9.

[1023] See *CSPV 1610–13*, 538; *Downshire MSS* IV, 16, 19, 34.

[1024] *i.e.* lay people who support Jesuits.

[1025] *i.e.* lay people who support (anti-Jesuit) secular clergy.

[1026] Pope Paul V.

[1027] See **Letter 22**.

[1028] Léonard Coqueau, *Examen Praefationis Monitoriae, Iacobi I. Magnae Britanniae et Hiberniae
Regis, Praemissae Apologiae suae pro Iuramento Fidelitatis* (Fribourg, 1610); Sheldon, *Motives*, sig.
Kv; *cf.* J.P. Sommerville, 'Jacobean Political Thought and the Controversy over the Oath
of Allegiance' (unpubl. Ph. D. thesis, Cambridge, 1981), 63. Coqueau's book against
James I attracted unfavourable attention in France as well, *Downshire MSS* III, 65, 69.

can or will ever bee able to shewe it, & therefore theye take Paules
Breves to bee butt declarations of his private opinion which theye take
not to bee the greateste divine, nor the tendereste harted Father that
ever sate in that chaire over us his poore Children. ytt will shortelye (I
feare mee faule oute) [sic] thatt suche as my selfe am whoe nether
allowe of the othe, nor dare to administer sacraments to suche as after
theye have taken the othe defende the takinge of it & purpose toties
quoties to take it againe, thatt suche I saye maye goe wheare theye will
for anye thatt will harboure or receave them. & wee feare if wee come
to Paule for Releeffe wee shall have butt an Italian shrubbinge or
shrinkinge upp of the shoulders. god Comforte us for the wordle [sic]
affordethe us but smaule comforte. This laste weeke I was a broad
havinge not gone abroad one halfe [word illegible] in some monethes
beefore. & by good lucke I came a daye after the fayer. for the Iustices
of the pease vz 3 Knights e[t]cetera hadd beene att the place thatt I
came unto [word deleted] beeinge sente thither as alsoe to many other
places bothe beefore & after to take from Recusants theire armour &
weapons which made many to thinke thatt theye intended a Massacre[.]
they brought the Councells warrante for it & did accordinglye.[1029] ytt

---

[1029] Birkhead observed on 2 February 1613 that 'the catholiques are falsly thought to
be enemies' to the Palatine match, 'and the common people are persuaded that the
Spaniardes and turke ioyne together to hinder yt', and 'therfor the iustices in everie
shyre repaire to chathol. houses to take there armour from them', AAW A XII, no. 29
(p. 68). Norton wrote again to More on 21 February 1613 that the Palatine match had
sparked anti-Catholic rumours 'namelye that Catholiques woulde burne Chichester
Winchester, and suche Cityes', that the Spaniards with the earl of Tyrone had landed in
Ireland, '& some of our Company together with my selfe have run upp & downe from
place to place for feare of the Iustices which weare to come to all places to take a waye
all armor & weapons from Catholiques, leaste wee might meete with them or they with
us and tender the oathe of alleageance unto us as they have donne in some places when
they seemed to come for armor onelye', AAW A XII, no. 40 (p. 85). For copies of the
privy council letters ordering the disarming of papists, see AAW A XI, no. 27 (28
February 1613) [misdated in AAW A catalogue to 1612] incorporating an earlier letter to
the same effect of 10 January 1613 [printed in TD IV, p. clxxxviii]. AAW A XI, no. 28
(29 February 1613) [misdated in AAW catalogue to 1612] is a privy council letter
explaining who is to be disarmed and exactly what constitutes being 'ill affected' in
religion. Robert Pett reported that 'in [the absent] Sir william Ropers house was found
armor sufficient to furnish 300 men', AAW A XII, no. 41 (p. 87). See also **Letter 42**.
John Chamberlain linked the proclamation issued on 16 January 1613 against the carrying
and possession of 'Pocket-Dags' with the disarming of papists, McClure, 410; Larkin and
Hughes, 284–5; cf. *Downshire MSS* IV, 23; *Salisbury MSS* XXI, 221). Champney informed
More on 18 June 1613 (NS) that Richard Bourke, fourth earl of Clanricard (presented as
a recusant in March 1613, but not proceeded against, Cockburn, *Calendar of Assize Records:
Kent Indictments: James I*, no. 761) was disarmed; and Champney in error claimed that
Clanricard 'died for the disgrace and sorowe', AAW A XII, no. 112 (p. 245). For the
attempt to disarm Catholics in early 1613, see B.W. Quintrell, 'The Practice and Problems
of Recusant Disarming, 1585–1641', *RH* 17 (1985), 208–22, at pp. 208, 210–11.

maye bee that they feared or woulde have the wordle [sic] to thinke
thatt theye feared least some thinge might be attempted by Recusantes
againste the state when theye are in theire cheafeste Ioletye banquetye
iuslyinge & ryotinge at the marriage of our Princes[1030] & the Palgrave
which shall bee solemnized shortlye. for theye are alreadye beetrothed
on St Ihons days[1031] in Christmas which was as tempestious a daye as
happelye [p. 61] hathe beene seene or hearde of in the memorye of
man att that tyme of the yeare. at which tyme (as my sister Sib:[1032]
wrightethe unto mee & hathe it from the minister of the towne wheare
shee dwellethe whoe spake with some that weare then hurte). the Divell
came into the churche of great Charke[1033] in Kente at the tyme of
theire eveninge prayer when theye weare in the Churche with light-
ninge & smell of stinkinge Brimstone, & stroke the booke owte of the
Minsters handes kylled one (to witt a miller) & wounded eight others
some of which wounded men tolde the minster this storrye. I verelye
thinke it to bee true & some saye thatt it is in printe & that the Divell
came in the forme of a hornedd Bull which is butt malum omen. in this
booke theye saye thear is greate speeche of many other misfortunes by
sea & lande and thatt theare are many sayle of shipps caste awaye &
the Carcases of dedd bodyes daylye caste upp on our shore.[1034] Questionlesse ytt hathe beene an extraordinarye wett winter. in all which
winter theare was never as yett either in ower shire or any other thatt
I can learne any snowe. nor scarce soe muche as any Ice. for my parte
I assure yow I can not saye thatt ever I sawe anye & I have [?] talked
with others that saye theye have seene some but it was very seeldome &
verye thin, & that stayed not toe dayes together[.] wee feare therefore
unlesse god sende us a very drye Marche thatt theire will bee a greate
mortalitye. wee feare likewize thatt theire will bee scarcitye of Corne
of which I can saye nothinge butt that if the vale cuintryes bee noe

[1030] Princess Elizabeth.
[1031] McClure, 399.
[1032] Norton's sister, Sybil. See **Letter 1**.
[1033] Great Chart.
[1034] Thomas Dekker (attrib.), *The Windie Yeare* (1613) contains a section (sig. C3r) entitled
'Certaine hurts done at Great Chart in Kent, the Sunday after Christmas-day last [27
December], by the Tempest of Windes', but does not mention the story of the devil.
(Nor did John Thorys's account of 7 January 1613 sent to William Trumbull, *Downshire
MSS* IV, 8, though Thorys said that thirty persons were hurt as well as the one who was
killed. Trumbull was sent a detailed report of the apparition by Sir John Throckmorton,
Downshire MSS IV, 19, who said that the minister of the parish (possibly Adrian Saravia)
had written a narrative of it which he sent to Sir Francis Barnham.) *The Wonders of this
windie winter* (1613), sig. C2v, makes the demon at Great Chart a punishment for the
people's inattentiveness and bad behaviour at service time. John Chamberlain attributed
the injuries and death at Great Chart to lightning, McClure, 412; *DNB*, *sub* Saravia,
Hadrian à. See also *The Last terrible Tempestious windes and weather* (1613); *Lamentable Newes*
(1613).

woorse the*n* the hill cuintryes if drought come [?] in any tyme wee maye yett doe well enoughe. My Nedd[1035] hathe beene sicke ev*er* since Bartholomewtyed & is not able to goe abroad. Howe my neareste neighbours doe I knowe not for I have not beene amongst the*m* almoste this twelvemonethe. I heare some tymes of the*m* & fro*m* them butt I thanke them theye acqua*n*te mee w*i*th noe newes fro*m* yo*w*. Yt Remaynethe in the ende of my lett*r*e thatt y*o*w reme*m*ber mee moste kindelye to m.ʳ Doct Thornell Don Anselme[1036] m.ʳ Poole (if he bee come) and the reste[.] Y*o*w maye p*er*ceive by my scriblinge that I wright in haste and I knowe not howe heereafter to sende unto [yow]. wherefore I praye y*o*w to have mee excused untill suche tymes as god & good fre[n]ds shall provide an other meanes. untill w*h*ich tyme I com*m*itt yo*w* to god in all haste. the 31 of Ianuarye. 1612.

My Dame & Man[1037] desire y*o*w thatt by yo*u*r meanes theye maye heare howe theire sonne Anthony dothe. I praye y*o*w to have a Fatherlye care of him for the boye I hope will doe well if hee bee not croste & iniuried for some of his frendes sake[.][1038]

Adieu B N

(On p. 62)

Addressed: To his approoved good frend m.ʳ George Weste.

Endorsed: (1) Ianuar. 31. 1613. B N
(2) Recea. sat. May. 4. } 1613
Answ. frid. May. 10. }

40 *George Salvin (Birkhead) to Thomas More (1 March 1613)*   (*AAW A XII, no. 45, pp. 97–100. Holograph. Quoted in part in TD V, 56 in note. The manuscript is badly damaged in places*)

my verie good Sʳ, I have receyved yo*u*rs of the 3 and 18 [?] of Ianuarie. I passe not much for there late arrivall when they come safe. my indisposition is such that neither fish nor flesh will goe downe. and yet yo*w* wold iudge me able to live, w*h*ich I f[ea]re verie much. mʳ mush is gon,[1039] and so is m.ʳ Southworth[1040] in lancashyre. be yo*w* assured that yo*u*r course is pleasinge to us, and for my part I do approve it, and lik verie well therof. I am sorie that fra Bartholomeo Telles hath

[1035] See **Letter 1**.
[1036] Robert (Anselm) Beech OSB.
[1037] Constance and Richard Lambe.
[1038] See **Letter 12**.
[1039] See **Letter 35**.
[1040] Christopher Southworth, secular priest, son of Sir John Southworth of Samlesbury, Lancashire. See Harmsen, *John Gee's Foot out of the Snare (1624)*, 130, 179; Anstr. I, 326–8.

served us in such sort. alas poore man, he knoweth full little owr needes and miseries, nor his master also, who doth what lieth in him to please [2 words deleted] and giveth catholiques faire wordes.[1041] I dare not write what is said of his unfittnes [?] for his place: neither do I know whome to gett to enforeme [?] him. for my selfe dare not venture upon it. but be yo*w* full of good couradge, and be ['yo*w*' deleted] sure that in what I can I will assist yo*w*. heare is such sturre for Letters taken of late by my L of Canturberie, that it hath wrought us great trouble.[1042] do not marvell I praie yo*w* that men write of our matters in generall. for in particular they dare not. to get some to regist[er] all particulars wilbe so chargeable, as I shall not be able to beare it out. I can gett little or nothinge, but some faire well. yet yf we were sincerely ioyned, we should be strounge enough[.] m*r* mush before he died com*m*ended D harrison[1043] to his place. he is now accepted, and I have made him my assistant in his roome. I hope he will do well, although but soft in his actions. it is straunge to us that becanus is Censured writinge for the Church a*n*d not others that have written against it.[1044] surely our

---

[1041] Robert Pett wrote to More on 1 February 1613 (NS) that the friar Bartholomew Teles, chaplain-confessor in the Spanish embassy, had been in England for a total of about two and a half years. Teles thought 'that our country cannot morrally be reunited unto the See Apostolique agaynst our princes will and that he beinge brought to any qualification matters would quickly goe far better w*i*th Catholiques' with which Pett and others agreed. But Teles, for this stated reason, was also 'absolutly agaynst the makinge' of bishops, whereas Pett and the other seculars thought that the appointment of an overtly loyal priest as a bishop would not goad James into persecution. Pett wrote scornfully 'he is a religious and therfore noe marvaile yf w*i*th the religious he concur agaynst us in that poynt', AAW A XII, no. 27 (p. 63). See Belvederi, 247–51, for the Brussels nuncio Guido Bentivoglio's report to Rome of Teles's views about England. John Jackson and John Colleton thought Teles had been suborned by SJ, AAW A XII, no. 46. Teles's opinions were taken seriously in Rome. He was a close friend of Cardinal Arrigoni, AAW A XII, no. 29. Colleton noted on 2 March 1613 that Teles 'hath informed his hol: of the stait of o*u*r cuntrie in such sort, as his hol: hath given a plaine deniall to our long sute, and that he will heare no more thereof', AAW A XII, no. 49 (p. 107). For More's memoranda against Teles's advice, see AAW A XI, nos 155, 156, 162.

[1042] John Jackson wrote to More on 1 March 1613 that 'thear was not long since one gentlema*n* stayed in the port. & a bagg taken from him w*i*th above 200 le*tt*rës as it is thowght from the Iesuites & their freinds, whearby they say the Archb. hath. . .advantage given him & great matters are discovered. & the party hath confessed th*a*t he had the le*tt*res from one m*r* Scot. (who is m*r* [Thomas] Laithwayte the Iesuite) & named the place also', AAW A XII, no. 46 (p. 101). *Cf.* AAW A XII, no. 73 (William Bishop's account).

[1043] William Harrison, secular priest, and Birkhead's successor as archpriest. Harrison was accounted by Robert Persons SJ as a moderate, or possibly even an opponent of the anti-Jesuit secular priests, Milton House MSS, Persons to Birkhead, 21 August 1608 (NS) (transcript at ABSI). This was an opinion shared, in 1616, by John Cecil, AAW A XV, no. 65. Birkhead informed More on 2 May 1613 that Geoffrey Pole had advised Birkhead 'once w*i*th verie good reason not to make choice of d harrison for my Assistant', but John Mush and others had changed Birkhead's mind, AAW A XII, no. 86 (p. 187).

[1044] Martinus Becanus SJ had written several works against the Protestant defenders of the oath of allegiance, Milward II, 95–8. But his *Controversia Anglicana* (Mainz, 1612) caused

frendes are deluded with faire wordes. I wished to Card Bell[1045] in some of my letters, that his hol would please to Censure these turbulent bookes, but no other order is taken, then that the Colledge of doway shall given [sic] forth an admonition that there be no more writ[en] and that our writers albeit against heretiques, shall publish no book[e] before it hath ben seen at Rome. which I never had in my minde. I heare D Cecill[1046] commeth to Rome in his quenes behalfe. yow must have an eye unto him. d bagshay hath written a longe letter of late unto me, and obiecteth so many def[e]ctes to me and our frendes that I had rather give 40ˢ then answere it. I gave mʳ Clinch an order full of lenitie, viz to use his faculties still, until his accusation be better examined.[1047] which I take to be the best in these tymes. but if yow saw what a furious and prowde Letter he hath written unto me againe, yow wold blesse your selfe at his furie.[1048] mʳ witherington[1049] and other his frendes were satisfied with my answere, and yet is he now worse then before. mʳ Colleton telleth that fa preston meaneth to addresse another letter unto me in ['his' deleted] mʳ Samuels[1050] behalfe. I never saw religiouse men so farre from beinge satisfied in these molestfull tymes. here is one prise a benedictane[1051] [p. 98] commended unto me by father Leander.[1052] I have not yett seene him, but I am told by them which have had triall, that he is the most peremptorie man that ever

controversy among Catholics. Propositions from this book were condemned by the Sorbonne on 1 February 1613 (NS), ARCR I, no. 1480; *Downshire MSS* IV, 46. Anthony Champney noted on 13 February 1613 (NS) that 'here came by the last ordinarie from the congregatione of the index [in Rome] a sharpe censure' of Becanus, 'which censure hathe freed our facultie frome muche troble which would have ensued aboute the censure of that booke', AAW A XII, no. 34 (p. 76); *cf.* Conway *AH* 23, 43. Robert Pett, however, thought that Becanus 'is a worthy man and hath done great good in Germany and hath been a great scourge to the Calvinists', AAW A XII, no. 41 (p. 87). As J.P. Sommerville explains, Becanus put forward (*Controversia Anglicana*, 120) a 'radical interpretation' of the scriptural case of Queen Athaliah, namely that 'popular consent outweighs hereditary succession' so much so that 'even if the legitimate heir is known to all, the people can ignore his claims and elect another ruler'. The passage in question was omitted from the second edition of the book in 1613, Sommerville, 'Jacobean Political Thought', 301. The appearance of that second edition, 'recognitus et auctus with an epistle to his Holiness', clearly distressed Champney, AAW A XII, no. 93 (p. 203).

[1045] Cardinal Robert Bellarmine SJ.

[1046] John Cecil.

[1047] Birkhead had written to More on 5 December 1612 that 'mʳ Clinch I have appeased, suspendinge the action against him untill it may be better examined. which I think will content him', AAW A XI, no. 220 (p. 625).

[1048] See **Letter 33**.

[1049] Roger Widdrington.

[1050] Samuel (Bartholomew) Kennett OSB.

[1051] William (Benedict) Jones OSB.

[1052] John (Leander) Jones OSB. For John (Leander) Jones's relationship with William (Benedict) Jones, see Lunn, *EB*, 101-2.

came heare.[1053] and yet I meane to give good wordes. they have thrust out f[a]ther whyte,[1054] but upon what tooth I know not.[1055] I am glad your monsignor[1056] had my letter, god reward him for his kyndnes towardes us. yow wold have me acquainted with Cicala[1057] y[et] to tell yow in secret, I dowbt it helpith not our cause to be acquainted with such, how well so ever they b[e] qualified. I thoughte fa grey had ben drowned but now he is alive lately come in, and brought me and my frend Letters from his generall.[1058] how he wilbe accepted in this Land god knoweth.[1059] but he exclaimeth terribly against yow the Archp. Agent, for manifestinge his errors and faultes.[1060] I have not hard this

---

[1053] For William (Benedict) Jones's legendary high-handedness, see Lunn, *EB*, 101.

[1054] John (Augustine) Bradshaw OSB.

[1055] See Lunn, *EB*, 99.

[1056] John Baptist Vives.

[1057] Not identified. In a letter of 19 July 1612 (NS), More had recommended this priest to Birkhead as a useful contact, AAW A XI, no. 146.

[1058] William Stanney OFM, Franciscan Commissary for England, informed More that Robert Gray had left England during the first half of 1612 with letters from Stanney to the general of the Franciscans. (See **Letter 35**.) Now, as he attempted to return from the Continent, he was 'drowned upon the sea I feare in sinn for that he came as an Apostate out of England hearing that I would not send him unto the generall chap[ter]', AAW A XI, no. 237 (p. 681). Gray had narrowly escaped drowning in the recent violent storms, **Letter 39**; AAW A XII, no. 50.

[1059] John Jackson alerted More on 11 September 1612 that Gray had lost all his remaining credit in England by his 'goodfellowship', and, in order to prevent scandal, he should not be allowed to return, at least for some time, AAW A XI, no. 147 (p. 404). Pett noted in December that Gray, who was preparing in Brussels to go to England, 'is since by order from the Card: protector of ther order stayed and called back agayne to Rome without all or any delay upon payne of excommunication to be ipso facto incurred together with the losinge of his office and faculties and this citation was insinuated to him here and delivered by the provinciall of ther order in ther Chapter some 8 dayes past', though clearly Gray did not obey, AAW A XI, no. 234 (p. 675). Stanney was informed by his friends in Sussex that More had told them that Gray was returning to England as the superior of the Franciscans in England, which news 'did much greve' some of More's 'speciall frendes & mine and hath caused others that had given somthing in their wils' to the Franciscans 'now to alter their determination'. Stanney stressed that, if the rumours of Gray's drowning during his passage from the Continent were untrue, 'how great authority soever he bring he must be enforced to returne againe for that every one that heare of him have fully resolved not to recei[ve] him into their houses', AAW A XI, no. 237 (p. 681).

[1060] Broughton told More in March 1613 that Gray was complaining that More had always been opposed 'to his prefermentes', AAW A XII, no. 47 (pp. 103–4). According to Godfrey Anstruther, Gray had been at Cowdray in the late 1580s; Anstr. I, 135. There is, however, some doubt about the identity of the priest called Gray who frequented the Sussex residence of the Browne family in the 1580s, for there was a Marian priest of that name who served Magdalen Browne, Viscountess Montague, PRO, SP12/245/38; F. T. Dollman, *The Priory of St. Mary Overie*, Southwark (1881), 29. The man here is presumably 'Father graye a cordellier ... a Scottche man borne', noted by a correspondent of the earl of Salisbury in August 1610, PRO, SP 78/56. fo. 255ʳ. In March 1613 Birkhead reported that Gray 'hath once pressed to see our frendes, but hath had the repulse, upon

longe tyme of m^r Chamberlaine.[1061] but I can assure yo*w* that the ringe was well accepted.[1062] I loose him and others because I am not able to supply there wauntes: I desyer yo*w* to be temperate in this matter of dowaie. over much importunitie will do us no good. our frendes at paris[1063] are exceedinge hote. I am inclined to approve yo*ur* doinges in my name, so yo*w* use yt with wisdome and moderation. yo*w* offer much for the presidentes[1064] helpe, but it is to late in my opinion. to mainteyne an Agent in spaine is Chargeable and by me not possible to be performed, albeit I like the course verie well.[1065] what so ever yo*ur* Cardinall saith, yf the tyme served, I could have [word obliterated] the testimonie of a hunderd and more for us, I meane for the suit[.] As for the Calumnies yo*w* say are given out against me I must have patience, yf it be for defectes in my behaviour, ['yf' deleted] I hope I live amongst them that will give me a good testimonie: yf it be for any waunt of lerninge or Sufficiencie in the discharge of my office, I yeeld unto my accusers, and shall never sleepe the worse for ther information. it is the thinge that I have alwaies discovered in my selfe. yf they will gett me a discharge I shall thank them for it. And so with my verie hartie com*m*endacions I bid yo*w* fare well. this 1 of march 1613

your loving frend.

Geo. Salv

(On p. 100)

Addressed: To his verie Lovinge frend m^r Thomas moore give this.

Endorsed: (1) Mart. 1°. 1613. Salv.

(2) Recea. sat. May. 4. ⎱
Answ. frid. May. 10 ⎰ 1613

---

iust feares' of danger (*i.e.* for fear that he would betray those who harboured him), AAW A XII, no. 60 (p. 125). William Stanney was now 'Loth to speake with him'. Birkhead understood that Gray 'hath Lost his commission', AAW A XII, no. 68 (p. 145). By April, Gray had become ill because some people 'wold not admitt him to there loginge at an unseasonable tyme of the night', AAW A XII, no. 68 (p. 145). He was arrested with John Varder in January 1614 and sent to Newgate, **Letter 54**. His conformity secured him a pardon late in 1614, *CSPD 1611–18*, 260; PRO, SO 3/6 (November 1614). It was said that he would receive a benefice in the Church of England and preach a recantation sermon, AAW A XIV, no. 139. According to William Rayner, he 'had a queane', AAW A XIV, no. 120 (p. 375). Nevertheless, he left the country in 1615, with the assistance, apparently, of a chaplain in the French embassy, AAW A XIV, no. 129. He returned to Rome and a spell in the Inquisition prison, AAW A XIV, no. 139.

[1061] John Varder.
[1062] See **Letter 23**.
[1063] *i.e.* in the college of writers.
[1064] Thomas Worthington.
[1065] Champney wrote to More on 30 July 1613 (NS) that John (Augustine) Bradshaw OSB 'ys of opinione that a*n* industriouse understandinge ma*n* in spayne would not only procure o*ur* pensione but be a meanes w*i*th a litle directione to procure us a large meanes to entertayne all o*ur* banished prestes', AAW A XII, no. 139 (p. 312).

41 *John Nelson (Jackson) to Thomas More (20 April 1613)*   *(AAW A XII,*
no. 79, pp. 169–70. Holograph)

My very worthy, much reverenced, and asmuch beloved good sir. I
receaved of late yo*wrs* of the 26 of feb. & ['of the [ ] of Ia' deleted] an
other of a [word deleted] later date but I know not the day & I have
sent it to o*ur* super*iour*[1066] to read, in regard of the speciall points
thearof. I acquainted that worthy noble man[1067] w*ith* your desire to
have leave in his name to signifie to his hol. the nature of his greaf &
the triall th*at* his litle regard of o*ur* suites doth put him & others unto.
who answered me th*at* he was very willing th*at* yo*w* shold not only
signifie soe much in his name but also if yo*w* pleased write th*at* or what
els yo*w* shold think good as from him & for th*at* end he gave yow his
seall, w*hich* mee thinks yow might make much good use of. thear is a
bruite & it comes from the Ies. freinds th*at* yo*w* are come from Rome
But I take it as [or 'is'] a dorr. Some say th*at* Salkill the Ies. th*at* is
fallen & lives w*ith* the Bishop of lond.[1068] did make th*at* booke w*hich* I
sent yo*w*,[1069] against his hol. but I can not beleiv th*at* he is able to doe
it. it must be done by some th*at* is better acquainted in Rome
thowgh some say it must be some Ies. or religiouse th*at* have generall
informations of all countryes as that hath of Spayne & Italie.[1070] d.
Hill[1071] is prisoner in the clink and a Ies. one Rand alias Russell alias
lentall[1072] at the same tyme com*m*itted to Newgate. cross the pursuivant

---

[1066] George Birkhead.

[1067] Identity uncertain.

[1068] John King.

[1069] This is a reference to *Supplicatio ad Imperatorem, Reges, Principes, super causis generalis Concilii convocandi. contra Paulum Quintum* (1613) which was known by its soubriquet *Novus Homo*. See N. Malcolm, *De Dominis (1560–1624)* (1984), 41; W.B. Patterson, *King James VI and I and the Reunion of Christendom* (Cambridge, 1997), 119–20. Jackson sent Pett this 'little libell of some five sheets of paper newly published in England agaynst his holynes', but Pett dared not send it on to More because of its dangerous subject matter about 'great persones' in Rome, AAW A XII, no. 87 (p. 189).

[1070] On 12 April 1613 Jackson had written to More that the author might well be Jacopo Marta, but John Salkeld 'or some th*at* have been familiar w*ith* him' were suspected for it, AAW A XII, no. 75 (p. 159). Birkhead believed Salkeld was the author, AAW A XII, no. 68.

[1071] Thomas Hill OSB.

[1072] Thomas Rand SJ. See CRS 75, 274–5. Edward Bennett reported his arrest on 26 April 1613, AAW A XII, no. 85. See Foley IV, 589–92 for Rand's examination (dated by Foley to 1607) concerning his opinion of the oath of allegiance. Rand was evidently soon released for in October 1613 he replaced the objectionable Michael Walpole SJ as confessor in the seminary at Douai. He was removed after six months, allegedly because he was too sympathetic to the anti-SJ line taken by some of the seminarists there, TD V, 69, 71.

told my Lo. of Canter.[1073] that the Ies. did offer him 50[li] & ten pound
per annum from his freinds whear he lived, if he wold let him goe. m[r]
Gray the frier is hear up & downe. Thear was a marques of france
hear who at his returne related to the q.[1074] in the presence of the yong
k.[1075] their execution of prests which he had seen & other persecutions.
the q. gave ordre that she shold be put in mynd thearof when our Ing:
Imbass. legier[1076] shold come for audience. At his next coming they had
speech of other matters & at last the yong k. putt his mother in mynd
of our persecution. who thearupon dealt roundly with the Imb. & also
caused mons[r] villeroy[1077] to send a lettre & messenger to Ing about the
same[.] the k. was moved upon it and when the Bish. of Canter. came
to solicit to have others executed the k. reproved him & said that this
cause mayd him distastfull to all princes abroad. by this wee may see
that if princes abroad did effectually deall & put us in mynd of the
liberty that Hugonots have in france, how much good wold come of it.
the palsgrave & La. Eliz. have been at Canterbury this week expecting
wind. & some say that this day or to morrow which is the 21 of Aprill
they take ship at Marget.[1078] provision was mayd for their keeping of S[t]
Georg his day at Hage with the grave Morrice. thear is now in hand
the motion of a match between the ['k' deleted] q. of france second
dawghter[1079] and owr prince charles.[1080] owr cleargy are building a
college at chelsey for 20. doctors to write only against us & every
doctors [sic] shall have 4. ['roomes' deleted] chambers. the building is
brest high. thear are also lettres sent from the Bish. of Cant. abroad to
make collections for the erecting of an Inglish college in prage. Loe
how industrious they are. what incouragements they give their cleargy
to studie. when will his hol. doe the like to us. nay I wold he (owt of
slownes or carelesnes etcetera) did not hinder us. but sure I am that that
tyme which Ies. preists & others, bestow in informing, suiing, striving,
(they to supplant us, wee to defend our selves they to incroach upon
our colleges we to seek remedy) they in traducing, wee in laboring to
defend our good names, this tyme I say makes us less able to helpe our
country, less learned & oftentymes less devowt. his holines may redress
all [p. 170] & I pray god that at the day of his iudgement our cause be
not heavily layed to his charge. He shold weigh our difficulties & when
our superiour or your selfe makes known our wrongs why doth he not

[1073] George Abbot.
[1074] Marie de Médicis.
[1075] Louis XIII.
[1076] Sir Thomas Edmondes.
[1077] Nicolas de Neufville, Seigneur de Villeroi.
[1078] Margate. See *CSPV 1610–13*, 504, 513, 521, 523–4, 525, 531, 537.
[1079] Princess Christine.
[1080] *CSPV 1610–13*, 459–60.

presently redress the*m*. noe not when he conceyves & understands the*m*. Noe bull against doctors recalld. the confessarius not putt owt. nor any one thing redressed w*h*ich we co*m*playne of. use th*a*t noblemans name th*a*t hath given yow leave, to enforme him of all thease things. for yo*u*r selfe we are all bound to honour yo*w* & to account the whole cleargy more indebted to yo*w* then to any one living. we are ashamed we can not testifie how exceeding kindly & thankfully wee take yo*u*r monsig*nor*[1081] his love & care of owr cause. I wold God th*e* tymes wear such as wee might see him hear w*i*th authoritie of a legate de latere. Is th*a*t not enowgh concerning the oath w*h*ich at severall tymes I have formerly written. all the Ies. freind of any sort take & have taken it, only the L. vaux who nevertheles did not refuse it. noe he stood upo*n* it th*a*t he had not refused it, & offred to take it after the kings booke w*h*ich he had w*i*th him, & they co*n*cluded that his not taking it before the LL. when it was tendred was a refusall.[1082] on th*e* other sides owr freinds suffre for it. agayne those p*r*ests th*a*t are for it doe make noe daintye of their opinio*n* because it is for their temporall good freedome, and thearfore it may easily be thowght that noe p*r*est wold co*n*ceall his opinio*n*. but th*e* religious shold loose their reputatio*n* & hurt their bodie & thearfore they have some cause to deall cloosely. God send us a po: th*a*t will tendre o*u*r cause & shut his ears to all slanders. O*u*r bl. Lord keep yo*w*. my hon. freind takes yo*u*r kind reme*m*brences most thankfully. a 1000 tyme fare yo*w* well my most beloved S.*r*

yours as yo*w* know.   20. apr. 1613.

Addressed: To the right worshipf*u*ll my assured good and much respected Freind m*r* Th. Moore give thease   Rome

Endorsed: (1) April. 20. 1613. N. answ. feb. 26 and an other.

      (2) Recea. sat. Iuly. 6. } 1613
          Answ. sond. Iuly. 7. }

42 *Benjamin Norton to George West (Thomas More) (26 April 1613)*   *(AAW*
    A XII, no. 84, pp. 181–4. Holograph)

What shall I saye to yo*w* Good s.*r* beeinge wearylye co*m*e whome fro*m* nedd & sybbs[1083] howse & findinge a cople of yo*u*rs to bee answered? nothinge good s.*r* butt thatt theye are hartelye welcome unto mee & that I doe thanke yo*w* for them as likewize for yo*u*r Commendacions

[1081] John Baptist Vives.

[1082] For the pardon granted to Vaux and the restitution of his estates, with a condition that the oath would not be tendered to him again and a reservation of any decision about his imprisonment to the king, see PRO, SO 3/5 (October 1612); *cf. CSPD 1611–18*, 181.

[1083] See **Letter 1**.

from m.^{r} Godf:^{1084} to whome I wright not bicause the gapp is not yett opened by which I holped that I shoulde have had meanes to send unto him. I praye yow thearefore to tell him soe muche & withall to thanke him for his kindenes in thatt in thease tymes wheare there is nothinge butt falsehoode in felloweshipp hee sticketh to his welmeaninge frendes & woulde weare it in his power not suffer them to bee oppressed.^{1085} I will not wright to him or yow whatt I thinke of him & howe kindelye I doe take any one thinge thatt hee dothe for any of owers. I hope that his sister Catharine will bee my neighbour againe within this weeke. shee (thowe otherwize in verye deede shee deservethe exceedinge well) shalbee the better used for his sake & soe shoulde his very dogg weare hee heere. His man Rob: was with mee yesterdaye. hee was goinge over to his m^{ris} Radishe^{1086} & havinge spente 3 weekes labour & his moneye to in laboringe to passe the seaes hee coulde not doe it withoute hee woulde take the othe, whearefore returninge to my dames^{1087} howse I forthwith placed him with my Nedd wheare hee livethe & is like to doe [?] as longe as the tyme will suffer it: his man Ihon was wonte to come to mee some tymes butt I have not hearde of him this Easter. Theare hathe beene muche a doe in Sussex this easter laste past. for theare weare fower pursephaunts a searchinge at one Mr Lams,^{1088} and Mr Perceyes^{1089} in Midhurste where theye quicly did leave of bicause theye beeinge craftye fellowes [pp. 182–3] coulde quicklye perceave that theere was noe likeliwhode of any bodyes beeinge theare the howses beinge poore paper walde thinges and standinge in the middeste of a towne. butt at stansteede^{1090} which by reporte is an other manner of howse theare they sought & sought againe yett founde

^{1084} Geoffrey Pole.

^{1085} According to Champney in August 1611 there had been friction between Pole and the promoters of the seculars' causes because of rumours in England that Pole and Cardinal Edward Farnese had fallen out, AAW A X, no. 103. And in October 1612 Champney told More that Pole (who set out for Rome from Paris on 3 October 1612 (NS)) gave Champney a 'verie cowld answer' when Champney asked him to lobby in Rome on their behalf, AAW A XI, no. 180 (p. 525).

^{1086} Jane Redish, sister of Geoffrey Pole.

^{1087} Constance Lambe.

^{1088} This word in the manuscript can be read either as 'Lams' (presumably a reference to Richard, the husband of Constance Lambe) or as 'Lains', i.e. the Lane family of Fishbourne (cousins of the recusant Bullaker family). But the passage implies both of the searched houses were in Midhurst, and therefore indicates the Lambe family. If the reference is to the Lambes, presumably Norton is concealing his residence with the family.

^{1089} Identity uncertain. There was a recusant/occasional conformist family at Midhurst called Percy, CRS 54, 320. Richard and Judith Percy were excommunicated as recusants in November 1610, WSRO, Ep. I/17/13, fos 103r, 105r. On 13 August 1613 (NS) Anthony Champney sent a message to Geoffrey Pole in Rome that 'his acquayntance Richarde percy' had been buried in Paris (on 5 August), AAW A XII, no. 146 (p. 328).

^{1090} Stansted in Westbourne, West Sussex.

nothinge bicause theare scarce bee any suche lefte, of which searche yow shall knowe moore when I talke with the man to whome yow lente moneye, vz 6ˢ [sic for '6ᵇ' ?] ii⁵¹⁰⁹¹ of which I have writtne unto yow beefore. thease knaves did likewize searche Preesteshawes¹⁰⁹² and other places bothe in the easte & weste of sussex. the searche that was at Battell was for one m.ʳ Moore.¹⁰⁹³ Crosse beeinge sente thither by his grace of Canterbberye for that purpose to searche for him. The olde man¹⁰⁹⁴ thatt dyed at Bent¹⁰⁹⁵ was an olde blind preeste. Mʳ Ihon Loane is dedd¹⁰⁹⁶ & shurelye thowh yow wright & wright againe that m.ʳ Ratliffe¹⁰⁹⁷ is alive yett if yow meane by him (as I thinke yow doe) one m.ʳ Ihon mushe then questionlesse hee is dedd or els I have beene oftentymes very ill informed.¹⁰⁹⁸ my Nedd is still a weake man & withoute Phisicke hee can not live scarce this summer & hee is soe trubled with his Sister in Lawe & her Foolishe husbande whoe lyethe in prison for debte & with other matters concerninge his owne & other folks estate beeinge [word illegible: 'sarved' ?] still with wrights to travaile & appeare in propper person that hee distemperethe him selfe muche & can not have tyme to take phisicke. I am moore Ignorante howe matters goe in Englande then yow are & can not tell what to thinke of matters. the Iustices have sought for weapons & taken all armour & weapons from recusants & putt the armour in the custodye of the Puritanes soe that theye maye cutt our throats if they liste, & the protestaunts throates toe:¹⁰⁹⁹ The Nominalls¹¹⁰⁰ in ower partes have

¹⁰⁹¹ The priest Augustine Lee alias Johnson acknowledged in a letter to More in February 1613 that More had lent him £6–11–0, AAW A XII, no. 33.

¹⁰⁹² Priesthawes in Westham parish in East Sussex was the residence of the Thatcher family. James Thatcher had conformed to the Church of England in 1589 (after his recusancy conviction in 1588), PRO, E 368/489, mem. 186a-b; CRS 71, 167. James's elder son, John Thatcher, aged 40 in 1613, had been brought up at Rome and was for a time a page to William Allen, *CSPD 1598–1601*, 380; *Salisbury MSS* IV, 328. James died in 1613 and his younger son William inherited Priesthawes, PRO, C 142/333/36. (Apparently he did not think his elder son John was actually his.) In March 1613 William Thatcher conformed shortly after the family estates were settled on him, PRO, E 368/550, mem. 118a-b; *cf.* M.J. Urquhart, 'A Sussex Recusant Family', *Dublin Review* 512 (1967), 162–70.

¹⁰⁹³ *i.e.* for Thomas More, the clergy agent himself. He and Richard Smith had been chaplains to Magdalen, Viscountess Montague at Battle.

¹⁰⁹⁴ Not identified.

¹⁰⁹⁵ Bentley in Framfield.

¹⁰⁹⁶ His death was certified to the assize judges in mid-1613, Cockburn, *Calendar of Assize Records: Sussex Indictments: James I*, no. 280.

¹⁰⁹⁷ John Mush.

¹⁰⁹⁸ See **Letter 35**.

¹⁰⁹⁹ See **Letter 39**. *Cf.* James Carre's letter to William Trumbull on 20 January 1613 recounting that there had been a 'great terror' among the Catholics 'from a report that the king was determined, in one night, to cut all the Papists' throats in England', *Downshire MSS* IV, 20, *cf.* p. 28.

¹¹⁰⁰ Jesuits.

muche meetings god graunte theye meane not to overthrowe the Realls[.][1101] I understande that your olde acquaintaunce S.[r] George B.[1102] hathe buried his ladye[1103] & morned for her in the verye blackes which hee bought to morne for Prince henry of Wales. for yow muste knowe that hee was the onelye heavie man that bought blacks for him beeyonde the seas. ytt is sayed thatt hee is to come into Inglande againe. lett Bess: Sare[1104] take heede of him if he come & soe will I for feare leaste hee doe I knowe not whatt. m[r] Palmer[1105] is returned & was at my dames[.][1106] I thinke hee & I bee beecome greate straingers. for I hadd not soe muche as a lettre or bare Commendacions from him. neither can I learne thatt hee did soe muche as aske for mee. thus whiles others starte fourthe I am punnished for the sinnes of the people butt tell m.[r] Geffreye[1107] that I waye it not butt will thinke the best untill I feele the woorste. I heare that M.[ris] Dacres[1108] is cloathed god strengthen her. of your Doctor I knowe nothinge wheare hee is or whatt he dothe butt I hope hee bee alive still: of my neighbours I saye nothinge but I thinke enoughe. Remember mee I praye yow to m[r] Doct. Thorkell[1109] whome I wishe in Englande after an other manner then wee bee heere or els I wishe him to keepe awaye & to keepe him selfe in strengthe for wee shall need suche men of Vertue, learninge & govermente as him selfe. in the meanetyme I hope that wee neede not desire him to have a care that our poore cleargie bee not oppressed hee beinge suche an one as wee muche Respecte & Reverence & to whome wee his olde freinds are true[.] with frends suche as wee bee hee is to wize to chainge for those which will give faire woords & nothinge els. nowe is the tyme thatt if ever hee expecte thatt wee shoulde sticke to him thatt wee expecte thatt hee shoulde sticke to us. my Paper is spente wherefore in haste yeat hartelye fare yow well. this 24 of Aprill 1613

    yours B. N

(On p. 184)

Robert m[r] Pooles man is nowe with me & desirethe mee to Remember his all manner of dewtyes to his m.[r] Godfreye P. hee bringethe mee

---

[1101] The secular clergy.

[1102] Sir George Browne, second son of Anthony Browne, first Viscount Montague.

[1103] Mary (Tyrwhit).

[1104] Probably the recently widowed recusant Elizabeth Sayer of Easebourne, WSRO, Ep. I/17/13, fo. 108r, Ep. I/17/14, fo. 40v.

[1105] Identity uncertain.

[1106] Constance Lambe.

[1107] Geoffrey Pole.

[1108] Elizabeth Dacres had entered a Benedictine house in Douai (Florence de Werguignoel's foundation), Lunn, 'English Cassinese', 64. She had written to More on 7 March 1613 (NS) to ask his prayers on her entering religion, AAW A XII, no. 63.

[1109] Edmund Thornell.

newes from my frendes in hamp[s]he that the bayliffs have warrants to apprehende Recusaunts which live theare.

Addressed: To his approoved good frende m.ʳ George Weste.

Endorsed: (1) April 24. 1613. BN. answ. to a coople of myne
                  (2) Recea. mond. Iuly. 1.⎫
                       Answ. sat. Iuly. 6.   ⎬ 1613
                                                    ⎭

43 *John Nelson (Jackson) to Anthony Champney (9 May 1613)*   (*AAW A*
    XII, no. 95, pp. 207–8.[1110] *Contemporary copy*)

I beseech yow remember my best love to Mʳ More, and if yow thinke it will bee a gratefull office [acqu]aint him with such occurrances as I shall sett downe: because the time is soe short that I writ[e] both to yow and him. Upon the 7ᵗʰ of Maii there were certaine convented att the Starchamber for speeches given out against the Earle of North-*ampton*[1111] and upon occasion therof, they did all speake against Religion but especiallie & purposelie against [to]leracion therof: because of a bruite that hee should have made such a motion to the kinge.[1112] The Lo. Cooke[1113] made it noe lesse then treason to speake of anie such matter, or if anie should saie that the kinge had anie such intention, the Archbishopp of Canterbury[1114] inveyhed[1115] bitterly against it, and amonge other wordes, I saie (said hee) & I saie it boldlie that if [the] k. should goe about to give a tolleracion hee shold not bee the defendour of the faith but the betrayer of the faith. The Bishopp of London[1116] made manie imprecacions against it, & amongst the rest, that his eyes should sincke into his head, rather then see such a day, and the like

[1110] Endorsed at top of p. 207, in hand of Anthony Champney, 'Copie of m.ʳ nelsones to me'. AAW A XII no. 94 is an extract from this letter translated into Latin and endorsed by Champney 'the extract of mʳ nelsons letter which I gave to this nuncio' [presumably Robert Ubaldini].

[1111] Henry Howard.

[1112] For Henry Howard's attempt in 1604 to secure concessions for Catholics, see L.L. Peck, *Northampton* (1982), 81; Loomie, *Toleration and Diplomacy*, 55–6. For an account of the Star Chamber case in November 1612 when Howard proceeded against courtiers and others for libelling him (that during his lord wardenry of the Cinque Ports more priests had passed through the ports than before, and that he had written to Cardinal Bellarmine to ask him to ignore his denunciation of Henry Garnet SJ at the Jesuit's trial in 1606), see Peck, *Northampton*, 81–3, 235. Of this earlier case Birkhead noted on 5 December 1612 that Northampton was 'cleared of all suspicion', but 'the contrivers [as opposed to the actual defendants] were thought to be preistes and Iesuites which was much exaggerated by the Lordes', AAW A XI, no. 220 (p. 625).

[1113] Sir Edward Coke.

[1114] George Abbot.

[1115] This word is inserted in Anthony Champney's hand.

[1116] John King.

did the Earle of Shrewesbury,[1117] which I was sorie to here, and should
bee much more, if I thought hee spake it from his hart, and the rest
had every one a vye against it. I am in somme hope to gett yow theire
speeches particulerly but I cannot promise it. The occasion of this Starr
chamber [bu]sines was this. One Bostocke[1118] purser of one of the kinges
Shipps at Rochester, tould one waller[1119] that hee hard S[r] George
Buck[1120] (whoe is brother as I take it to fa: Buck the Iesuit[1121]) saie that
six of the lords of the Councell wherof the Earle of Northampton was
one, had beene on their knees to the kinge, for to obtaine a tolleracion,
and that the Archbishop and the lo: Souche[1122] had hindred it: this
Waller spread abrode & wrote to a frend that the Archbishop (meaninge
Archpapist) your greate Warden (said hee to his frend) goeth about to
doe thus and thus. And what additions they made I knowe not, but
both those twoe are condempned to loose either of them an eare, and
one of them for a fine 10000 markes and the other 5000 markes[1123] and
both perpetuall imprisonment. Yow have hard I suppose of S[r] Tho:
Overbury his committment to the Tower, and S[r] Henry Killigreve[1124]
to the fleet for seekinge to speake with him beinge close prisoner.[1125]
And S[r] William Wade the liefetenaunt[1126] is put out of his office, and
committed to the Lodginges, which hee dwelt in, and one S:[r] Iervis
Elvige[1127] is put in his place. They saie there is a faction of the Puritans
discovered, whoe had agreed to cutt all the papistes throates, to pull
downe all the Howardes, and to bringe the k: to a better goverment,
and by report the preachers have disposed mens affections to such an
exploite, in all theire sermon[s] of late takinge occasion of the powder
plott. S:[r] Tho: Overbury caried the greatest sway with my Lo: of
Rochester, and it was thought that hee with other 5 knightes that were
called his Councellours did almost overrule all buisinesses even, otherwise
then the Lords had sometimes resolved. I am nowe in hast, I therfore
commend my selfe unto yow both, to M:[r] Const:[1128] M[r] H. M.[1129] M[r]

[1117] Gilbert Talbot, tenth Earl of Shrewsbury.
[1118] McClure, 453: John Chamberlain describes him as an 'under customer' of Rochester.
[1119] Sir Thomas Waller, Lieutenant of Dover Castle.
[1120] Sir Henry Wotton and Sir John Throckmorton reported that the accuser's name
was in fact Sir Peter Buck, a naval officer, Smith, *Life*, II, 22–3; *Downshire MSS* IV, 104;
Peck, *Northampton*, 235.
[1121] Robert Buck SJ, Anstr. I, 57; *cf*. CRS 74, 130; Foley IV, 674–5.
[1122] Edward Zouch, eleventh Baron Zouch.
[1123] McClure, 453.
[1124] Sir Robert Killigrew.
[1125] McClure, 451–2.
[1126] Lieutenant of the Tower.
[1127] Sir Gervase Elwes or Helwys.
[1128] Henry Constable.
[1129] Henry Mayler, secular priest, recently appointed to the staff at Douai, Anstr. I,
224.

Midd:[1130] and father [word obscured] & soe take leave this 9th of May
  Yours as yow knowe
(On p. 208)
No address
Endorsed: A letter of m[r] Nelson of newes out of Ingland about the
Tolleration

44 *Benjamin Norton to George West (Thomas More) (31 May
    1613[1131])   (AAW A XII, no. 119, pp. 263–6. Holograph)*

My verye good frende. I can not of late bragg of the favour to receave
many lettres from yow. the reason maye bee either for thatt in this
trublesome tyme theye maye have miscarryed or els bicause yow have
little to wright off either of which excuse maye sarve bicause I shall
never mistake yow what ever faule owte. I praye yow alsoe not to mistake
mee in the like kinde for tymes growe woorse & woorse with mee &
our trubles are soe great that I knowe not wheare to beegin; nor scarce
dare to adventure to wright leaste I add truble to truble: at this present
men daylye expecte the woor[st]e that maye bee & I feare mee that
the indiscretion of some of my neighbours will undoe them selves &
others for company. The gentleman[1132] which borrowed 6[l] xi[s] of yow
takethe what care hee can thatt yow shoulde bee payed & the faulte is
not in him for my Cosin Thomas[1133] hathe receaved as muche moneye
of him & I have spoken to him to sende it unto yow by that good
debter of yours whoe thinkethe that hee can never requite your curtesye
to the full. I understande the manner of that late search at stansteede
which was for many howers together the pursephants havinge beene
kepte oute of doors for 3 howers at which tyme whiles some weare at
the greate gate one of the knaves went unto a backe doore & plucte
owte a box in which hee had tooles to picke locks withall but as it
chaunced the doore was bolted within. well to bee shorte the knaves
enquired for one Buklye alias paye[1134] & an other by the name of
Iohnson or smithe butt they weare not to bee founde then nor heereafter

----

[1130] Identity uncertain.

[1131] See endorsement.

[1132] See **Letter 42**.

[1133] Thomas Heath.

[1134] Not identified. William Pay of Upmarden had married Honor Bickley of Chidham
(half-sister of Ralph Bickley SJ). Both families contained recusants. There had been a
search for Ralph Bickley in the house of Sir John Caryll in Chichester in May 1611,
AAW A X, no. 61. Joan Pay of Westbourne (the parish in which Stansted was) was
presented in January 1607 for attacking a sermon which the vicar William Mattock
delivered on 25 November 1606 and for saying that he 'preached like a foole in a play',
WSRO, Ep. I/17/12, fos 38r, 39r, 42v, 61v, 64v, 172r.

I thinke in thatt place bicause theare bee manifeste presumptions which are as good as proofes that theare bee false bretheren in that howse whoe acquainted the Iustices foorthewith of many things done in that howse which very fewe of the howse knewe of. Mr Shellye[1135] is likewize described. & muche adoe theare is & I feare mee my paper will not sarve to saye thatt which I can not withoute dainger speake of. Theare was in the Rogation weeke a searche[1136] in Hamepeshere at one m.^r Iohn Cottons by vertue of a warrante from the kinge or Counsaile. & 3 knights which dwelte far of weare appointed to doe the feate. vz the deputye liuetennaunte of the shire s.^r Hamden Paulet,[1137] s.^r Robert Oxenbridge s.^r Richard Tytichborne[1138] & s.^r William Udall[1139] whoe was butt a neighbor. the Iustices at one tyme caused not onelye m.^r Ihon Cottons howse whoe dwelt at Subberton to bee beesett but his brothers[1140] to howses of warblington & Bedhampton & one m.^r George Copes[1141] to be beeseett alsoe. and albeeit theye mett not with m^r I Cotton whoe with his wife fledd from his howse halfe an hower beefore theire comminge yett mett they with bookes & churchestuffe which theye carryed awaye. and at a chamber where some tymes m.^r Io: Cotton layed his [word illegible] & trunkes in at warblington theye founde a keye by chaunce which was the keye of a trunke harde bye in which trunke the[y] founde a bagge of bones or as others saye of reliques & abowght everye bone writtne in fayer lettres whose bones theye weare. amongste the reste theare was one of s:^r Ever Digbyes[1142] as the protestants saye, & all saye thatt the name of Dygbye was theare butt foorsoothe theye will have it to bee of some preeste cauled Digbye which I for my parte never hearde of beefore. & a gentleman this daye tolde mee that theare was writtne in the paper or partchemente the daye of his deathe which beeinge examined & compared with the daye

---

[1135] It is not certain which member of the Shelley family (which had important Sussex and Hampshire branches) is indicated here.

[1136] The search was made after the discovery at the court of a politically offensive manuscript tract which was suspected to have been written by John Cotton, *HMC Ancaster MSS*, 354–81; Larkin and Hughes, 291–3.

[1137] Hasler III, 188.

[1138] Hasler III, 508.

[1139] Sir William Uvedale, treasurer of the king's privy chamber and master of the horse to Anne of Denmark. He was a cousin of the recusant families of Uvedale and Brenning. See Mott, fo. 449v.

[1140] *i.e.* Richard Cotton. John, Richard, Sir George and Henry Cotton were all sons of George Cotton of Warblington and Bedhampton, Mott, fos 131r-50r. Henry Cotton was the bearer of one of Birkhead's letters to Richard Smith after Smith's return to Paris in 1610, AAW A IX, no. 58.

[1141] For the closeness of the Cope family of Bedhampton to the Cottons, see J.E. Paul, 'The Hampshire Recusants in the Reign of Elizabeth I' (unpubl. Ph.D. thesis, Southampton, 1958), 343.

[1142] Sir Everard Digby, the gunpowder plotter, executed in 1606.

[pp. 264–5] of s.ʳ Ev: his deathe will make a fowle matter.[1143] whereof when his Maiesty shall knowe (as I thinke hee dothe alreadye) wee looke for greate matters. in the meane tyme the B of Chichester[1144] otherwize heeretofor accownted one of the beste temper beeginnethe to preache of it to the shame & scandall etcetera. ytt weare good yf [?] it might bee that the Iesuits woulde instructe theere disciples better for this mʳ Cotton[1145] is wholye theires & maye chaunce to fare butt hardelye for it if theye can take him as as [sic] yett theye have not done. I woulde to god his holines woulde take order when hee shall knowe whatt inconveniences doe followe of our Iesuited peoples forwardenes that everye one particuler laye man thowgh Iesuited never soe muche maye not bee a Martyrmaker for the sente of the gunpowder is soe stronge in many mens noses that theye will not woorshipp suche saincts. & trulye I feare mee that our enemyes will laughe att it. Theare are warraunts in all Bayliffes handes in hampeshire for the apprehension & takinge & carryinge awaye to prison all convicted Recusaunts. & this daye I am tolde that on thursdaye laste which is not paste 4 or 5 dayes synce the bayliffes broke open 3 doores [?] & came into one m.ʳˢ Edmunds[1146] her howse at Crawlye whose husbande is noe recusaunte & woulde have carryed her away to prison hadd shee not contented them otherwize. In some places I heere ([sic] namelye of one m.ʳˢ Parre [or 'Porre']¹¹⁴⁷ in Oxforde shire that her husbande to have his wife owte of prison payeth xˡ a monethe for her. I tell yow moore thatt I heare that

---

[1143] Here Norton has slightly garbled the story. The dispute turned on whether the relic was one of the bones of the layman John Rigby, executed in 1600. Norton wrote to More a month later on 30 June 1613 that Sir Hampden Paulet claimed 'that the bones which hee founde...had writtne upon' them 'The Ribb of s.ʳ Everad Dygbye. but one the contrarye syde it is affirmed thatt it was a ribb of one Rigbye whoe suffered in the queenes tyme & itt seemeth nowe to mee thatt the latter reporte is the truer', because Cotton was imprisoned in the Gatehouse rather than the Tower of London. Apparently Norton expected that Cotton would be cleared of the authorship of the 'lyebell', i.e. the manuscript tract the discovery of which had led to the searching of the Cottons' houses, *HMC Ancaster MSS*, 354–81; AAW A XII, no. 118 (p. 261). Richard Broughton reported to More on 24 August 1613 that in the tract, which was 'fixed about the kinges Chappell', 'all those places of the Apocalips which were in the K. booke [i.e. James I's *Apologie for the Oath of Allegiance...Together with a Premonition*] for to prove the Pope Antichrist, were applied & expounded; were retorted to prove the king to be the same', AAW A XII, no. 152 (p. 341). A warrant to transfer Cotton from the Gatehouse to the Tower was issued on 5 July 1613, *APC 1613–14*, 116.

[1144] Samuel Harsnett.

[1145] John Copley, the renegade secular priest, had at one time been a household chaplain of the Cottons, his own blood relations, and had been compelled to move in 1610 (a year after George Cotton snr's death) because of friction there, possibly over some of the younger Cottons' political and religious sympathies, Anstr. I, 87; CRS 54, 21. He supplied some of the evidence against John Cotton, *HMC Ancaster MSS*, 367, 381; AAW A XII, no. 152.

[1146] Not identified.

[1147] See **Letter 34**.

M[r] [name illegible][1148] is like to bee pincht yf he looke not toe it, hee
hathe warninge yf hee woulde take it butt hee hathe followed many
coorses (though costelye enough) which pourchase him litle creditt, lett
him goe hee dwellethe (yow knowe) far from mee & I am not like ever
to have any thinge to doe with him. I hea[r]de saye that F. Harrington[1149]
was taken againe & one Townesende[1150] and Yorke[1151] men unknowen
to mee. I am not able to tell any thinge that is woorth the hearinge
even of those which dwell not a mile from mee, I heere scarce of any
thinge, neither doe I meddle with any thinge, & one reason is bicause
I have beene to to muche medled with all. I mett with a Courteouse
[?] nominall[1152] some 3 dayes since which askt mee questions aboughte
Becanus whither hee weare censured or noe & whe[n] I tolde him
somewhatt of that matter concerninge the Parisienses hee knewe thatt
better then I but hee sayed questionles that the Pope had not censured
him e[t]cetera. Then hee wente to Withringtons booke & spake what
hee thought good & yett not muche a wrye & by the waye of kinde
speache I was soe kinde as to tell him that his Company in Fraunce
liked of thatt booke & in particular I tolde him thatt theire Frontanus[1153]
was one that did soe as I heare by suche as I beeeleeve [sic]. hee
seemed not to thinke soe of Frontanus butt yett he was apte enoughe
to beeleeve thatt the Company woulde Condescende as far as theye
coulde rather then to offe[n]de the state theare. in thatt I aggreed with
him, butt had I knowen that then which I doe nowe wee hadd hadd a
longer discourse aboughte bones cauled by them reliques e[t]cetera. At
the wrightinge heereof I knowe not howe to doe to have this lettre
conveyed partlye for thatt I have nothinge almoste to doe with my
neighbours, but cheefelye for that I feare leaste my lettre maye bee
founde in theire fingers, whoe are in apparante dainger or els I heare
an untruthe. butt questionles theye are not free from dainger & I feare
mee some of theire neighbours will fare the woorse for them. Remember
mee to m.[r] Geffry[1154] & tell him that m.[rs]. Catheren[1155] was in my

[1148] This name might be 'Dorme'.
[1149] Martin Harrington OFM had been banished in September 1612, Anstr. II, 372. In
a prison list of 5 June 1618 it is noted that 'he goes to Church and lyes in prison onely
for debt', PRO, SP 14/97/95, fo. 246v. A pardon on the basis of his conformity was
issued in January 1617, Anstr. II, 372.
[1150] This may be the secular priest Thomas Townsend who was listed among the priests
to be released and allowed to go abroad with the Spanish ambassador Alonso de Velasco
in August 1613, APC 1613–14, 179; Anstr. II, 375.
[1151] Identity uncertain. This man could, however, be William York, secular priest, Anstr.
II, 369.
[1152] Jesuit.
[1153] Fronton du Duc SJ.
[1154] Geoffrey Pole.
[1155] Katherine Pole.

Company this daye. I doe not learne thatt hee hathe provided any meanes by which I shoulde wright unto him which makethe mee to staye my handes. I am a meere strainger in my bretherens affayers yett I knowe this muche that his Card*inall*[1156] wrought butt an idle lett*re* to the Archepr*iest*[1157] in which hee insinuated that by v*er*tue of a lett*re* which [word obscured] heertofore hadd writtne hee was not to chuise Assistaunts of him selfe scilicet. A nominall tolde mee that D Wes4on & d singleto*n* had answered Withrington.[1158] I feare mee thatt Withrington will bee to harde for the*m*. doe not expecte many lett*res* fro*m* mee for I have noe meanes to sende. whatt will beecomme of this wordle [sic] I knowe not butt wee feare thatt it will bee woorse & woorse. one tolde mee that the Reformed Recusants (as they caule the*m*) are to bee talkte withall notwithstandinge theire temporizinge[.] sheldon hathe a coople of Parsonages & a nutt browne wenche in signu*m* Ap*osta*tatus.[1159] when the searchinge was at stansteede Bentlye was searched twize one daye after an other & m[r] Thatchers[1160] & s.[r] Thomas Leedes[1161] theire howses. I heare nothing of my [word illegible] bullocke which was like to sett a whole carte of Coales on fyer. I was with him once at his howse & wishe thatt I weare theare againe for I scarse knowe whither els to goe. I am olde [?] & wearye & therefore I take my leeve of y*ow*. not forgettinge my kindest Reme*mbrance*s to M.[r] Geffry and don Anselm*o*[1162] and m.[r] Doct. Thornell to whome I praye y*ow* to remember mee as to one which I have in noe smaule esteeme & Reverence. I will not saye to muche bicause I an not yett Italionated[.] when I am then [I] will wright in a finer fasshio*n* & keape a secretarye for nowe [?] I am ashamed of myne owne lett*res*. Adie*w* good s[r] this 31 [sic] of Iune 1613
     BN
(On p. 266)

[1156] Cardinal Edward Farnese.

[1157] George Birkhead.

[1158] On 9 May 1613 (NS) Champney wrote to More that Edward Weston's book against Preston, *Iuris Pontificii Sanctuarium*, was printed secretly at Douai against his will 'with the permissione of the nuncio' [Guido Bentivoglio], AAW A XII, no. 93 (p. 203); Allison, 'Later Life', 113–15. William Singleton had just published *Discussio Decreti Magni Concilii Lateranensis* (Mainz, 1613). It was answered by Preston in his *Discussio Discussionis* (1618), though he attacked it in his *Appendix* (1616) as well, Allison, 'Later Life', 115; ARCR I, nos 1086, 925.5, 925.4.

[1159] Birkhead wrote to More on 25 March 1613 that 'your frend m[r] [Richard] Sheldon was married upon tewsday the 16 of march to a rich maiden or widdow of hackney', AAW A XII, no. 60 (p. 125).

[1160] William Thatcher of Priesthawes. See **Letter 42**.

[1161] Courtier and conformist son of the recusant and former Catholic exile John Leedes of Steyning, West Sussex. On 23 March 1612 he was present when William Thatcher conformed according to statute in front of Samuel Harsnett, Bishop of Chichester, PRO, E 368/550, mem. 118b. In 1616 Sir Thomas retired with some of his family to Louvain.

[1162] Robert (Anselm) Beech OSB.

Addressed: To his approoved good frende m.ʳ George Weste
Endorsed: (1) Iune. 31. 1613. Ben. perhaps. May.
          Recea. sat. sept. 21.
          Answ. thr. sept. 26.
          1613. 1613.

45 *Anthony Champney to Thomas More (27 August 1613 (NS))*   *(AAW A*
    XII, no. 155, pp. 347–8. Holograph)

wortheley esteemed and beloved sʳ yours of the 1 of August gave us good
contentment in that yt mentioned the arrivall of D Kellisones to the
protectoure[1163] hopeinge that yt with ours unto him also will sett forward
some good resolutione for Doway wherein I feare delay may be
hurtfull[.] Therefore doe we wishe that as you can with anie conveniencie
you should solicit and sett forwarde Doct Kell[i]son his establishement
with all speede for yf there were no feare of other inconvenient [sic] the
only deferringe of sendinge or thinkinge of sendinge some one into
spayne ys cause enoughe to solicit that matter which untill yt be resolved
upon will ever hinder the executione of thother to our great hinderance.
I have writen to Doct Kell and have sent him your owne wordes bothe
aswell in this of the 1 of august as of the 18 of Iuly and have urged
him with all the reasones I cowld to write unto you playnly his mynd, &
his desire, and to entreat you to solicit for him those thinges he
proposethe which what they are in particuler we knowe no more then
that we did by mʳ Harley[1164] his letter. we expect everie day to heare
of his resolutione in this poynt but peradventure you shale heare frome
him by mʳ pett his meanes sooner. I think I wrote to you before howe
earnestly the padry[1165] doe seeke for Doct worthington his returne which
may geve you light enoughe howe to comport your self in his affayres.
I send you heare a great number of stale letters out of Ingland[.]
Amongst which ys one for our protectoure frome Doct Harrison whoe
ys made assistant in mʳ Mushe his place and succidethe him also in his
residence[.] He labourethe for us as m.ʳ Archprest[1166] writethe but ys
cowld for that he seethe our adversaries more potent then we[.] with
these letters come one frome mʳ nelson[1167] unto D. B[1168] and my self
wherein we are muche blamed for mʳ Reyner so harde a thinge yt ys
to please all men or that all showld be of one opinione. for writinge to

[1163] Cardinal Edward Farnese.
[1164] Thomas Harley, Provost of Cambrai.
[1165] Jesuits.
[1166] George Birkhead.
[1167] John Jackson.
[1168] William Bishop.

Doct Smithe use yo*ur* discretione[.] when he was here I towld him that
we understoode certeynly that his will was not to come to us but to
returne into Ingland where the nature of his place beinge so altered
that all his frendes wished him rather to stay where he was he was
willinge to stay rather w*i*th the Bishope[1169] then to come to us upon
hope as he [word deleted] p*er*suaded us that his beinge there would be
more pr*o*fitable for o*ur* countrie the*n* yt could be here w*hi*ch thoughe
we cowld hardly believe and therefore made noe smale difficultie to
geve thereunto o*ur* co*n*sentes yet seeinge his inclinatione and the
bishopes earnestness we were like marchantes that cast theyre wares
into sea in a storme rather forced tha*n* willinge to yeld unto his
returne.[1170] I towld him furdermore that yf m^r Doct Kellison showld
have pleaded the like our pore colledge and co*n*seque*n*tly o*ur* whole
affayres would have beene in badd tearmes. In fewe wordes I cowld
wishe bothe in him and in his cosin[1171] more appearance of affectione
towardes the com*m*one[.] But this beinge a defect almost universall I
see not howe yt showld be mended[.] this I speak unto you as to one
whome I knowe will ether use the knowlege thereof to the comone
good or burie yt w*i*thin him self to avoyd the com*m*one hurt[.] yf you
by yo*ur* frendes there understand anie p*ar*ticuler reason why we showld
be warie in receavenge Doct Carier[1172] supposeinge the matter might
come in deliberatione I pray you certefy yt for we think that he and
suche as he would doe duble good amongst us[.] m^r southcotes[1173] ys
more retyred then he hadd wont to be[.] m^r Thomas Shelley fa
Rectoures[1174] nephewe ys in chamber and diet w*i*th him in a litle colledge
in the universitie[.] yt seemethe he ether triethe o*ur* co*n*versation or
els he hathe hadd some advertiseme*n*t from others not to be over
familier w*i*th us and we are co*n*tent yt be as he please[.] Here came
hither thother day a prest banished from Exciter whoe cominge to see
us we invited to dinner or supper but his leasure or listinge was not to

[1169] Armand-Jean du Plessis, Bishop of Luçon.
[1170] Smith had assured More in early July 1613 that, though many people 'misconstrue'
his 'abode' with the bishop of Luçon, he was not thinking primarily of himself: the
Collège d'Arras would not, for at least two years, have sufficient books for him to exercise
his scholarly talents; Luçon was paying him a pension; and, moreover, the bishop had
sworn that Smith's residing with him would benefit England as well as France, AAW A
XII, no. 125 (p. 277). In 1616, as *grand aumonier* of Anne of Austria, Luçon obtained a
grant of royal patronage for the Collège d'Arras, AAW A XV, no. 114.
[1171] William Rayner.
[1172] Benjamin Carier. See **Letter 49**.
[1173] John Southcote. He had been ordained in April 1612 and had left the English
College in Rome in April 1613, Anstr. II, 305; CRS 1, 97. He joined the Collège d'Arras
in 1617 but left in 1621, Allison, 'Richard Smith's Gallican Backers', part II, 259.
[1174] Thomas Owen SJ. See **Letter 14**; Mott, fo. 364v. Owen's sister Elizabeth married
John Shelley, father of Thomas who entered SJ in November 1619, CRS 75, 293.

accept of ether[.] He callethe him self Fenner[1175] and ys gone for [p. 348] St Omers[.] we shale have here this michelmass two or three youthes come to studie in this universitie which peradventure may make the way for moe in tyme[.] I wrote unto you for a copie of Harpsfeeld his historie which we desire may be copied in a legibile hande[.][1176] you knowe ma[n]y Italiane handes are not so here[.] therefore good s^r take care in that lest the money be bestowed without profitt and see yf you can get wikcliffes historie[1177] out of the vatican[e]. we heare m^r Ihon pittes ys about a historie of Ingland[1178] whome yf we can gett to ioyne with us att least in laboure we will entreate to undertake besides the setting forthe of Harpsfeelde a continuatione of Sanders[1179] which I have longe desired as a thinge verie gratefull to posteritie[.] out of Ingland we have nothinge by these stale letters of worthe [word omitted ?: 'except' ?] a generall want of money and thereupon an expectatione of a parlement[.] A speeche here ys that the Duke of lenox[1180] ys shortly to returne hither Embassadoure to treat upon a matche betwene the 2

[1175] Robert Venner. He had been in prison in Exeter since about November 1609, Anstr. II, 328. He left with the departing Savoyard ambassador, the Marchese di Villa, *APC 1613–14*, 94–6. He entered OSB at Dieulouard in 1614.

[1176] In May 1613 Champney had written to More to procure from Robert (Anselm) Beech OSB 'a copie of m^r Harpesfeeld his historie [*i.e.* the manuscript of Nicholas Harpsfield's book, eventually published at Douai in 1622, *Historia Anglicana Ecclesiastica*] whereof he hathe one exemplare by Doct Smithes meanes whoe as I remember saythe he holpe him unto yt upon conditione he showld have permissione and libertie to copie yt out', AAW A XII, no. 101 (p. 223). (According to William Bishop, Smith had helped Beech make a copy of it while Smith was in Rome in 1609–10, AAW A XII, no. 121.) In June 1613 Bishop advised More to demand from Thomas Worthington 'as president of the Colledg of doway...the ecclesiasticall history of m^r Harpesfild, which my lord Cardinall [William] Allen left unto that Colledg. and if it were lent out to f. persons before his time, let him help to recall it backe agayne [from Rome] to the Colledg', AAW A XII, no. 106 (p. 234). In August 1613 Bishop told More that the Collège d'Arras would pay for copying out Harpsfield's book 'though it cost ten pound as you write'. Either Geoffrey Pole or Tobie Matthew (who, despite his affection for SJ, was regarded as moderate and 'iudicious' by Champney, AAW A XII, no. 230 (p. 667); *cf.* Belvederi, 193) would bring it to Paris, or a French man coming from Rome would carry it, AAW A XII, no. 157 (p. 351). But, in October, Champney was still procrastinating about it, 'seeinge yt will amount to so great a somm', AAW A XII, no. 190 (p. 423). By November 1613 Champney had heard that Richard Gibbons SJ (who finally published the work, ARCR I, no. 639) had a manuscript copy and was planning to print it, while the seculars simply could not afford to, AAW A XII, no. 205.

[1177] For Harpsfield's 'Historia Haeresis Wicleffianae' (incorporated in the published version of Harpsfield's *Historia Anglicana Ecclesiastica*), see ARCR I, no. 639.

[1178] John Pitts, a secular priest, had substantially completed this work by September 1613. It was eventually published in 1619 (seen through the press by William Bishop) as *Ioannis Pitsei...Relationum Historicarum de Rebus Anglicis Tomus Primus* (Paris, 1619); ARCR I, no. 907. Pitts's mother was the historian Nicholas Sander's sister.

[1179] Nicholas Sander, *Doctissimi Viri Nicolai Sanderi, De Origine ac Progressu Schismatis Anglicani* (Rheims, 1585). An enlarged edition in 1586 included substantial additions by Robert Persons SJ, ARCR I, no. 973.

[1180] Ludovic Stuart, second Duke of Lennox.

daughter[1181] here and our prince of wales[.][1182] Cardinall Rochfauco[1183] ys expected here this day[.] we shale be commended to him by the Bishope of lusson[.][1184] remember my love and service to our Honorable frend m[r] Pole to whome I have desired Doct Kell to write as to whome he ys behowldinge[.] noe more but all good wishes to your self with hartie commendaciones to m[r] vahan[1185] reio[i]ceinge muche att his good fortune hopeinge you wilbe able to doe somethinge for the mayntaynance of one whoe may help you and when needes you must remove may succeede you in your charge which ys most necessarie for our countrie August 27 1613

yours ever as you knowe

    Champney

Addressed: To his worshipfull and esteemed freind m[r] Thomas more these

Endorsed: (1) Aug. 27. 1613. A Ch. answ. Aug. 1.

    (2) Recea. sat. Sept. 21.⎫

        Answ. thr. Sept. 26.⎭ 1613

    (3) herwith one to Card. farn. out of Ingland.

46 *Benjamin Norton to George West (Thomas More) (2 October 1613)*   *(AAW A XII, no. 178, pp. 393–4. Holograph)*

Very good s[r]

Yt is even nowe erkesome to mee to wright suche dainger I apprehende in sendinge & receavinge lettres for but yesterdaye a lettre which a brother of myne wrought unto mee beeinge t[ake]n by the purs[evan]tes beefore hee came to my handes muste coste either the wrighter or the receaver xi[li] to free [t]he car[r]ier which was my Cosin

---

[1181] Princess Christine.

[1182] Prince Charles. For the negotiations in July and August, see *CSPV 1613–15*, 4–5, 11–12, 14–15, 18, 22, 23, 28. Champney wrote to More on 10 September 1613 (NS) that Lennox's embassy was not 'of muche moment' since 'he hadd noe comisione to deale for anie matter of marriage unless yt came to him the day before he departed as some think there did for haveinge taken his leave of the kinge and queene he folowed the court beinge out of towne to communicate some thinge which he freshely receaved which some think to have beene the matter of mariage which ys so farr from bringinge us tolleratione that some of our frendes think yt wilbe worse for us then otherwayes howe soever there ys nowe a speeche that the Duke ys to come agayne and to treat thereof in deede which we shale see whether yt be soe or noe', AAW A XII, no. 163 (p. 363).

[1183] Cardinal François de la Rochefoucauld. He had returned to France from Rome only a few weeks before this letter was written. (I am grateful to Joseph Bergin for his help with this point.)

[1184] Luçon had written in late January 1613 to Rochefoucauld (in Rome) on the secular clergy's behalf, AAW A XII, no. 30.

[1185] Lewis Vaughan.

Tho: H.[1186] from dainger. I perceave that yow keepe a fixte order in
sending unto mee yett did not yours of Maye & Iune come to my
handes untill the 17 of september & I verrelye feared that some dainger
might have come by them through the indiscretion of my man Rich:
whoe contrarye to my appointemente sente them upp & downe the
countrye after mee. butt god bee thanked I receeved them & have torne
them & halfe forgotten the contentes of them. I [am] sorye to heere that
my good frende m[r] Godf.[1187] shoulde by reason of his lamenes[1188] leave
the coorte[1189] & come downe into F:[1190] for I knowe thatt if hee live
where & with whome hee desirethe theare will arise an inconvenience.
his sister Cather:[1191] & I live in one howse & I take suche comforte in
her companye thatt I woulde bee lothe to leave her to any butt your
Kitt.[1192] to which purpose I have writtne to yow[1193] & daylye expecte
your answeare. I praye yow to thanke m.[r] Godfreye for his kinde offer
in offeringe mee to live with him. I hope hee will interprett it to bee a
livinge with him to live with his dere Cate. for meethinkes I see him
in her many waies. yow woulde have mee to wright to a Mount[s]g[r] &
an Auditor neither of which I knowe, neither knowe I howe, or vhereof
[sic for 'whereof'] to wright suche a strainger[.] I am in all matters
havinge noe knoledge of any matters butt what I can picke owte of
your lettres. I praye yow to have me therefore excused, butt good s.[r] if
yow can gett any man in these partes to wright suche lettres either nowe
or hereafter to them or any bodye els, I will willinglye beare the name
of th[em] & father any thinge thatt yow shall thinke fitt to bee writtne
to which purpose (if this warrante will not satisfye [y]ow) I will sett my
name at any tyme to any blanke paper & give yow full authority to
wright whatt yow shall thinke fitt therin. my neighbours & I bee
exceedinge straingers & the olde man played mee suche a parte as I
maye sooner forgive then forgett & weare it not for that that I will not
laye upon my Fathers nakednes hee shoulde heare of his doinges
when & where hee woulde. [word obliterated] hee [word obliterated]
in a nett & thinkethe I see him not. but others knowe thatt I see & will
not see for causes & Consideracions. heere [is] noe good newes in the
earthe. & though I heere somethinge some tymes y[et] I he[e]re it in
suche a manner as I can not builde uppon it: for example heere is

[1186] Thomas Heath.

[1187] Geoffrey Pole.

[1188] Benjamin Norton had mentioned in September that an accident had befallen
Geoffrey Pole, AAW A XII, no. 164.

[1189] *i.e.* in Rome.

[1190] France.

[1191] Katherine Pole.

[1192] Christopher Cresacre More, Thomas More's brother.

[1193] The letter is AAW A XII, no. 164 (10 September 1613), in which Norton asked for
'an answere from' Thomas More 'concerninge my Kate & your Kitt' (p. 365).

newes thatt m^r Edw: sackvill the erle of Dorsetts[1194] brother hathe slaine the lord Bruse beeyonde the seas: which I think[e] to bee true.[1195] as alsoe that beesides [?] the lorde cheefe Iustice[1196] whoe died vi weekes since that the Lordes Riche:[1197] Harrington,[1198] Peeter,[1199] & Earles of Kente[1200] Bedforde[1201] & Arundell[1202] bee dedd butt for all thatt I thinke the to latter bee alive. theare is a devorcemente made beetwixte the Earle of Essex[1203], & Suffolks daughter.[1204] ytt is sayed alsoe that s.^{r} Thomas overberye is dedd in the Tower. this knight was a greate enemye to the Howardes & to Catholique Relligion. hee was a greate piller of Puritanisme of a nimble witt, & one thatt holped in tyme to have beene cheefe secretarye butt as yett neither hee nor s.^{r} Harrye Nevill bee which is as ranke a puritane as the tother[.] butt s.^{r} Thomas Lake dothe exercise thee office though hee have not the title. some professores alsoe heere aboughts give owte thatt the lorde cheefe Baron of Ireland[1205] is slaine goinge to administer the newe othe to the Irishe. m^r Warmington is yett (for owght I can learne) with the B. of Winchester.[1206] & a gentleman tolde mee thatt theare was a gatheringe for him in the parishe churches & that the parson of his parrishe gave 5^s.[1207] I heare thatt Withrington hathe writtne a woorse booke then beefore,[1208] howe hee & his will answere it I knowe not. my Dame[1209]

[1194] Richard Sackville, third Earl of Dorset.

[1195] See **Letter 47**.

[1196] Sir Thomas Fleming.

[1197] Robert Rich, third Baron Rich, created earl of Warwick in 1618. (His son had been in Sir Henry Wotton's suite in Turin in June 1612 while Wotton negotiated the Savoyard match. The Venetian ambassador in Savoy described the son as behaving there in an explicitly Catholic fashion, *CSPV 1610–13*, 368.)

[1198] John Harrington, first Baron Harrington of Exton. See McClure, 476.

[1199] John Petre, first Baron Petre. See McClure, 479.

[1200] Henry Grey, fifth Earl of Kent did not die until January 1615.

[1201] Edward Russell, third Earl of Bedford had recently been involved in, but had survived, a riding accident, McClure, 470.

[1202] Thomas Howard, second Earl of Arundel.

[1203] Robert Devereux, third Earl of Essex.

[1204] Frances Howard, daughter of Thomas Howard, first Earl of Suffolk.

[1205] The lord chief baron, appointed in 1612, was Sir William Methold, a strong opponent of Catholic recusancy, F.E. Ball, *The Judges in Ireland* (2 vols, New York, 1927), I, 243, 310. It is not clear what gave rise to this false rumour. Richard Broughton reported (also erroneously) that it was the lord chief justice of Ireland, Sir John Denham, who had been killed, see **Letter 47**.

[1206] Thomas Bilson. Bilson had been ordered in February 1612 to take the priest William Warmington into his household, PRO, SO 3/5 (February 1612).

[1207] On 16 March 1612, an order had been transmitted through the Signet Office to George Abbot that he and other 'Cleargy of the best hability' around London should make a collection for Warmington, PRO, SO 3/5; *Salisbury MSS* XXI, 343.

[1208] Roland (Thomas) Preston OSB, *Disputatio Theologica de Iuramento Fidelitatis Sanctissimo Patri Paolo Papae Quinto Dedicata* (1613). John Colleton wrote to More on 17 October 1613 that the English translation (*A Theologicall Disputation concerning the Oath of Allegiance* (1613))

desirethe thatt her Iewell[1210] shoulde knowe thatt shee will from hen-
cefoorthe sende 4[l] per annum to m[r] Godf: his sisters[1211] in Paris for to
paye for the wrightinge of his dictates soe longe as hee shall neede it.
shee desirethe therefore thatt her Cosin Godfredo will laye owte the
moneye for him & shee will satisfye him by her Cosins his sisters
meanes. & I praye yow to tell m.[r] Godf thatt shee takethe it kindelye
that m[r] Godfreye hathe a care of the boye. for I tolde her thatt yow
wrought soe unto mee. I muste coniure yow never to forgett my kindest
Remembraunce to m[r] Godf with thanks for all [his] favors & kindenesses
to mee or others for my sake. Remember mee alsoe I [pray]e yow to
[m].[r] Doct. Th[orn]ell. & lastelye to D Ansel:[1212] att whome I wonder
thatt I can never perceave by any thatt hee is willinge to doe for the
Clergye. I wonder I saye [thatt] I [c]an heere nothinge takinge the
man to bee wize & sincere & shure if hee hange backe nowe I feare
mee thatt some cause hathe beene given him which I am sorye for. I
ho[pe] thatt whatt wantethe in him m.[r] Doct Thornell will supplye to
whome I praye yow to harken for hee can not butt bee a verye wise
experienced man & I ass[ure] my selfe thatt hee will not bee backe or
slacke in the effectinge of any thinge [word partially obliterated: 'which']
in his wisedome hee shall apprehende to bee to the honor of god &
good of his cuntrye. oh thatt it weare in my power any waye to exalte
that man accordinge to his deserts hee shoulde finde mee moore
forewarde then peradventure hee wi[ll] Imagine & I thinke in suche a
case I shoulde gett others to ioyne with mee. for gods sake thearefore
make accoumpte of him & followe him for hee maye well bee a guide
by this tyme & more then I will saye bicause my paper is full & I am
wearye. which makethe mee to ende in haste this 2.[de] of october 1613
    yours assurdly B N
(On p. 394)
    yow maye perceave by this latter date which is the 19 [of] october
thatt lettres lye longe in my handes beefore I knowe howe to sende
them whereat yow woulde not wonder if yow lived nowe nea[re] us or
amongst us. I heare thatt in lorde cheefe Iustice of Englandes place
Iudge Cooke dothe succede. in Cookes place comes s.[r] Hubberte[1213] the
kings Atturneye and in [th]e Atturneyes place s[r] Frauncis Bacon. the

'is expected to come forth in print som eight or ten daies hence', AAW A XII, no. 186
(p. 411). Colleton was, on and off, a prisoner in the Clink with Preston, and much of the
seculars' information about Preston came from Colleton, Conway *AH* 23, 45.
[1209] Constance Lambe.
[1210] Constance's son, Anthony Lambe.
[1211] Mary and Constance Pole. Champney reported to More on 18 December 1613
(NS) that Mary and Constance were remaining in Paris while the other prospective nuns
for the abortive Cassinese foundation there had gone to Rheims, AAW A XI, no. 230.
[1212] Robert (Anselm) Beech OSB.
[1213] Sir Henry Hobart.

deuek of linnex¹²¹⁴ [word illegible: 'is' ?] created earle of Richemonde &
s.ʳ Robert Car a scott & vicounte of Rochester shall shortelye bee earle
of westmerlande¹²¹⁵ & abought thatt tyme if not beefore hee shall marrye
with the earle of Suffolkes daughter whoe I sayed to bee devorced from
the earle of Essex whereas I shoulde rather have sayed thatt by the
wizer sorte of the Bishopps it was thought & declared thatt theye weare
never man & wife by reason of an impediment ere[c]tans [?]. either of
Frigiditye or Maleficii or I knowe not whatt but sure it is thatt the
kinge woulde have [it ?] to bee as it is like to bee albeeit Canterburye¹²¹⁶ &
London¹²¹⁷ & some of that side had rather it weare other wise but
those to prelates bee overmatched with Bilson of Winchester, Neale of
Litcheffeelde,¹²¹⁸ Edwardes of Elye¹²¹⁹ & Buckeridge of Rochester.¹²²⁰ I
feare thatt some of my frendes have greate truble faulen [?] unto them
butt bicause I knowe not whatt it is I can wright nothinge. of late a
frende of myne havinge some busines att Newegate was putt in a fright
thatt hee shoulde have been stayed theare by reason of a greate thronge
of people thatt came abought the place. butt the matter was this some
4 or 5 prisoners weare to suffer thatt daye & beefore theye weare to
dye a man & a woman which weare to of that companye woulde needes
bee marryed beefore theye wente & soe theye weere & came into the
carte with Rosemarye¹²²¹ in theare handes butt theye needed noe
Rebbondes for hempen haulters did sarve theare turne well enoughe.
[praye] for mee good sʳ for I neade it. of my Nedd & sibb:¹²²² I here
nothinge of late & I thinke it go[o]d newes when I here noe ill. Adiewe
good sʳ this 19 of october. 1613

Addressed: To his approoved good frende m.ʳ George Weste

Endorsed: (1) Oct. 2. and 19. BN. 1613. answ. May & Iune.
  (2) Recea. wed. December 25. 1613
  Answ. mond. Ian. 20. 1614

---

¹²¹⁴ Ludovic Stuart, second Duke of Lennox, created first Earl of Richmond on 6
October 1613.
¹²¹⁵ See McClure, 485. Ker was created baron of Branspeth at the same time as being
made earl of Somerset, though it had been rumoured he would be made earl of
Westmorland, *ibid.*, 480. See also M.J. Tilbrook, 'Aspects of the Government and Society
of County Durham, 1558–1642' (unpubl. Ph. D. thesis, Liverpool, 1981), 188–90, 648, for
Ker's influence in the north of England at this time.
¹²¹⁶ George Abbot.
¹²¹⁷ John King.
¹²¹⁸ Richard Neile.
¹²¹⁹ Norton means Lancelot Andrewes.
¹²²⁰ John Buckeridge.
¹²²¹ See *CSPV 1617–19*, 135.
¹²²² See **Letter 1**.

47 *Robert Clapham (Richard Broughton[1223]) to George West (Thomas More) (22*
       October 1613)   (AAW A XII, no. 191, pp. 425–8. Holograph)

My very wor*ship*full and Rev: S.ʳ

Some few weekes past I receyved a letter of yo*u*rs, wher by I perceive
th*a*t from dyvers of your frends you had receyved letters, myne onelie
you found wantinge, wherat some accidentall cause was to be feared &
some errour com*m*itted by not delivery of o*u*r mutuall *lett*res, or that
w*h*ich is worse might be deemed, (w*h*ich I dare say you never firmelie
app*r*ehended) th*a*t I ungratfullie & unkindlie behaved my selfe, in beinge
unmindfull of my deare frends; but none of thes happened, as I take it
in this defection: for th*e* truth is I know not any certayne time sett
downe when as yo*u*r said frends ioyntlie writt to concurre w*i*th them
but as time & matter do afford I do accordinglie, for when I find small
subiect to make any relation upon I differ it somewhat longer, for about
th*a*t time I wrot unto you,[1224] but some weekes after the date of those
letters as I collect, & you er this may well p*e*rceyve. In thes bad daies
manie thinges do happen to th*e* undoing of many men, as searchinge,
app*r*ehendinge, imprisoninge, losse of goodes, & lyvelihoodes w*h*ich do
continew still as they have done many dayes & in some kind much
worse, for th*e* pursevantes are never quiet nor rest, but they searchinge
or app*r*ehendinge, & no Cath. they will let go w*i*thout he redeeme
himself for a round some of money if he or his frendes be able to make
it. otherwise they would not ech one of them pay every six moneths
threscore pounds for a new licence, as they do, & like gentlemen keepe
men & geldinges, & be worth hundreth in a short time as some are,
iste quaestus est nunc uberrimus. sed melius est modicum iusto, super divitias
peccatorum multas. Mʳ Rouse hath laitlie written a very penitent letter[1225]
to all Cath. in Engl: acknowledginge th*a*t in th*e* said kind he had
receyved many a round som*m*e, but nothinge would thrive w*i*th him
w*h*ich he pr*o*miseth he will hearafter set downe, all th*e* time of his fall
he thought th*e* earth did open to receyve him but sought to drive it
away by keepinge company, & allwayes when th*e* clocke did strike, he
remembred our B. Ladie by sayinge somethinge in her honour, he

---

[1223] Broughton had recently succeeded the deceased John Bavant as assistant to the
archpriest for the South-West, AAW A XII, no. 92.

[1224] The last letter from Broughton to More which More had received was dated 24
August 1613, AAW A XII, no. 152.

[1225] John Gerard SJ (who had reconciled Anthony Rouse to the Church of Rome in
1590) supervised this new change of heart and religion. Rouse's defection had been
caused by his irritation at SJ's cavalier attitude to his own property, Thomas Bell, *The*
Anatomie of Popish Tyrannie (1603), 130; Watson, *Decacordon*, 90; Lambeth Palace Library,
MS 2014, fo. 95ʳ.

confesseth th*a*t fallinge into vice,[1226] he followed th*a*t bad course of life, but he allwaies in his hart loved & honoured those of his function, he humbly of all sorts of people craveth pardon, he remaineth in Lovaine at th*e* Nuncios[1227] ['his' deleted] disposinge. The deputie of Ireland [in margin: 'Chichester'] they say shall be chainged,[1228] & S[r] Charles Cornewallis shall succeed,[1229] a rumour was laitelie th*a*t the cheife Iustice ther was slayne about offeringe th*e* Oath,[1230] a talke allso was th*a*t the kinge had made a pr*o*clamation th*a*t he had no meaning to trouble them for ther religion, some maketh this inferance not untill he hath effected his purpose; M[r] Talbot[1231] who was in th*e* Towre & the rest of his company[1232] are released out of prison, & are gone over into Ireland againe.[1233] my L. Cooke iudge of the com*m*on pleaes is made, is now made [sic] cheif Iustice of Engl. No talke nor speech is of o*u*r noble yonge prince, scarce you shall heare him named of men, nor of any great store of followers I heare he hath, all w*h*ich I impute onelie to his yonge yeares; of his mariage heare is as litle talke, it is thought they most incline to th*e* daughter of th*e* duke of Savoy.[1234] I dare say you have hard or this of th*e* combate w*h*ich was neare to Anwarpe by my L. Bruice[1235] & m[r] Edw. Sackvile wher my L. Bruice was killed, some say he dyed a Cath. & wrot to some of his frends to p*e*rswade

---

[1226] In July 1614 George Abbot wrote to William Trumbull concerning Rouse, now at Zichem, that 'Our Lady' of the miracle-working shrine there would 'have work sufficient to clear him of the pox wherewith he was infected, before his going out of England', *Downshire MSS* IV, 458.

[1227] Guido Bentivoglio.

[1228] Arthur Chichester, first Baron Chichester of Belfast, Lord Deputy of Ireland, was still rumoured to be on the point of dismissal in April 1614 but he continued in office, *Downshire MSS* IV, 362–3.

[1229] Cornwallis came to Ireland in 1613 with a commission to probe into the grievances arising from parliamentary elections there, A. Ford, *The Protestant Reformation in Ireland, 1590–1641* (Dublin, 1997), 60; *Downshire MSS* IV, 193, 269; McClure, 475–6.

[1230] See **Letter 46**.

[1231] William Talbot, at the head of a group of Irish representatives, had come to London concerning the grievances generated by the recent Irish parliament.

[1232] See A. Clarke, *The Old English in Ireland, 1625–42* (1966), 45; *CSP Ireland 1611–14*, p. lii. Chichester had agreed to Irish Catholics' demands that commissioners should be sent to explain their grievances to James, McClure, 462–3. The representatives refused to take the oath of allegiance. William Talbot 'answered th*a*t it belonged not to them nor could extend to any one of ther cuntrye'. At a second interview they refused to state their views on the deposition of princes. Lord Chancellor Ellesmere and Archbishop Abbot secured their imprisonment, AAW A XII, no. 152 (p. 341). On 5 October 1613 (NS) Champney remarked that Abbot's harsh words to them had led them to complain to James, and that James rebuked Abbot for causing him to be labelled 'tyrannicall' and 'bloodie' amongst his 'neighbeure princes', AAW A XII, no. 179 (p. 395).

[1233] Cf. McClure, 509.

[1234] See *CSPV 1613–15*, 2, 19; McClure, 459, 464, 466–7, 468.

[1235] Edward Bruce, second Baron Kinloss.

them:[1236] An other combat ther had like to have bene betwixt my L. of Essex & S[r] Henry Haywoode,[1237] they were gone over, but were recalled, the Earle is commaunded to his owne howse, thother is committed to the fleet.[1238] The dyvorce was proclamed laitlie betwene the Earle & his wife[1239] in Cant. haull, wher ther was assembled the B. of Cant.[1240] & London[1241] & some six doctours opposits, & the B. of winchester[1242] & other six Bish.[1243] for it who brought out the Cannon Law, Casuists, & the Popes wordes, for the divorce of them which were Maleficiati,[1244] as

---

[1236] On 14 September 1613 (NS) Robert Pett relayed to More the now-circulating narrative of the duel: 'the occation of this fray began betwene them in England many monethes past and was composed by the kinge and Counsel yet as is sayed in souch sorte as that the Scotishe Lord conceaved him self to receave therby some disgrace and therfore upon the departure of the Lady Elizabeths grace from England he obteined licence to travaile into france but before his departure m:[r] Sackfeald as is reported found meanes to geve him a blow one the face with his fist and willed him to take that with him, which he did and after his beinge in france sent m[r] Sackfeald a chalenge which he accepted and the place appoynted and agreed upon was neare unto Antwerp and this week past they came thether with ether of them a gentilman Copartener and a surgion and soe concluded to fight ther combatt with single curtelax but the Lord Brus would admitt noe partyes as standers by wherupon m:[r] sackfeald as is sayd towld him that he well perceaved that he came with intent rather of murther then honorable fight and therfore towld him that he accordingly would soe account of him and take him yf he could at all advantages and soe willed him to doe the like which he aunswered he should be assuered of and soe one this accorde they two only with ther two surgions standinge apart far of went to the combate in ther shirtes wher first the L: Bruse wounded m:[r] sackfeald in the upper parte of the [le]ft arme and soe up into his sholder, and then agayne in the right arme with which he heald his sword towards the wreest yet kept he styll his sword and fought valiently and perceavinge that he began to lose much blod determined to make the combate short and soe runninge full at his adversary missed his body and ra[n] his sword betwene his arme and his body and soe closed with him whe[r]upon each toke hould of others sword with ther left hands and soe standinge graplinge together m:[r] sackefeald founde meanes to get his sword lose and soe haveinge the Lord Bruse at the vantage towled [?] him to render his sword or els presently he should dye[.] the other would not render wherupon he presently persed him thoroug[h] the body and drawing his sword back thrust it forward agayn and made a duble wound wherof he dyed in short tyme after', AAW A XII, no. 167 (pp. 371–2). Pett made no mention of the rumour that Bruce had converted to Catholicism. For copies of Sackville's account of the duel, see BL, Harleian MS 4761, no. 47; BL, Lansdowne MS 213, fos 72r-4r.

[1237] Henry Howard, third son of Thomas Howard, first Earl of Suffolk, and brother of Frances Howard, Countess of Essex. Cf. McClure, 474–5; CSPD 1611–18, 200. The quarrel was over statements made by Howard about Essex in the matter of the divorce.

[1238] See McClure, 478–9; AAW A XII, no. 177; Larkin and Hughes, 295. On 10 October 1613 (NS) Sir John Throckmorton wrote from Flushing to Trumbull that 'Essex and Mr. Henry Howard are by H.M. made friends', Downshire MSS IV, 220.

[1239] Frances Howard.

[1240] George Abbot.

[1241] John King.

[1242] Thomas Bilson.

[1243] See McClure, 469.

[1244] Cf. McClure, 456, 458.

he is taken to be, & for the lawfullnes therof, & made Cant: confesse that he was his superior in yeares, learning & iudgment. If mens words could they have maried the Ladie allreadie to the Lord Rochester. Ther are deceased of laite my L. Peters[1245] and Barlow B. of Lincolne.[1246] many of the Lords were said to be dead, besides, but are verie untrue,[1247] savinge my Lord Harrington who died in his iourney comming from my La: Elizab. The new Commissarie,[1248] who surreptiouslie hath obteyned that name, hath remayned some small time about the Court, & hath had some private conference with the cheifest ladie of this land [in margin: q. An[1249]] *sub sigillo secreto*. & for reward had 30ᴸ: put himselfe presentlie in silkes but afterwards was constrayned to pawne them for money, hath now relinquished thes partes & taken his iourney to Scot. besides this & such his domesticall demeanours, it is now commonly abroad dyvulged in what manner he came to the said office, by a maide who was laitlie at Bruxells, & hard ther related to her by his brethren, how the Generall letters were delivered to him who kissinge them & perusinge, they thought he presentlie would have obeyed, but by & by he stoll away into his cuntrye, whensoever he shallbe catched he shall be sent unto the galleyes. this maide was ther for to complaine of his predicessor for detayninge xviᴸ of hers, (beinge her porcion) this sixteine yeares, lent of goodwill, & cannot as yet have it repayed. you have hard I am sure of one m.ʳ Rontree[1250] who was a minister, & had a good reputation for his preachinge and became a pr: & hath bene entringe into the Bened: & Ies: is now become an Apostata as men say, but I cannot learne the certayne, he sheweth not himself as yet, & hath detected many thinges wherfor many stand in feare;[1251] [in margin: 'this was reported but it is not as yet perfectlie knowne but much doubted he should be in Flanders'.] Mʳ Stillington[1252] is committed close prisoner at yorke, his frends cannot surmise the reason therof; I feare it is,

---

[1245] John Petre, first Baron Petre.
[1246] William Barlow died on 7 September 1613.
[1247] See **Letter 46**.
[1248] Robert Gray OFM. See **Letters 35, 40**.
[1249] Anne of Denmark.
[1250] Leonard Rountree, secular priest.
[1251] Rountree had made his submission to George Abbot on 9 September 1613, Questier, *Conversion, Politics and Religion*, 47, 48; **Letters 49, 53**; PRO, SO 3/5 (September 1613). Rountree was used by Abbot to try to entice Benjamin Carier back to the Church of England, AAW, OB I, i, no. 31.
[1252] John Mush had noted in May 1612 that William Stillington of Kelfield was in prison at York and that he was involved in the factional divisions within the gaol. Mush said that Stillington had requested financial aid for the prisoners from Birkhead, and Birkhead's refusal had been badly taken, AAW A XI, no. 70. Stillington had visited Cowdray before travelling to Brussels via St Omer in late December/early January 1611, AAW A X, nos 7, 20. His ecclesiastical links seem to have been with SJ, CRS 54, 261–2, 287–8.

because he hath bene to good a frend to him.[1253] I iudge that m[r] widdrington new booke[1254] in defence of the new Oath & provinge every part therof to be lawfull, is come into your coasts or [*i.e.* 'ere'] this, for that it is dedicated to the Pope, & one I hard was sent to Nun:[1255] at Paris, many marvelled what will become of this man undertaking thes courses, & that his Superiors put up all in scilence[.] an other they say is in the presse against Sculkinnius[1256] & d. weston. some say the king procureth all this to make the P. yeild somewhat, or els the Pope to make him, which some thinketh would be quicklie done, if some couraige were used. I am credible informed of a monstrous huge fishe which laitelie cast it selfe upon the shoore in Holdernes, hurt by some shipe, as men do iudge which caused it approch ['neare' deleted] unto the land. this fish was of such marvelous greatnes, that two talle men one upon the others [p. 426] head might stand betwene the upper and lower iawe; twelve teeth it had in the head six above & six below, & every tooth was ['thre' deleted] one faddome about, a tale man standinge upon the lower teeth could but reach unto the higher, thirtie men were thre dayes in cuttinge in sunder the iawe bone, out of which ther issued out a marvelous deale of oyle, much of which beinge unexpected runne upon the sandes which still increasinge they made a pitt for it to runne into, it was very hott that it would allmost scald ones hand, & puttinge a little therof on your hand or arme it would come forth on the other side, this was some fortnight before Michelmas, whenas he which told it me was in that cuntrie ['that cuntrie' deleted] when two of your acquaintance the one an Assist[1257] was mett returning from seinge it, at which time ther was threscore wayne load of [word deleted] yt caryed away & foortie was behind, besides that was covered with sandes, men thinke it will be worth five hundreth poundes a peece to my L. Admirall[1258] & S[r] Henry Constable,[1259] who are the lords of

---

[1253] *i.e.* to Rountree. Richard Broughton reported on 27 February 1614 that William Harrison had written to Cardinal Edward Farnese that Stillington's own brother had given evidence against him and that he was now condemned in praemunire for refusing the oath, AAW A XIII, no. 38. See PRO, E 178/4864 and PRO, C 231/4, fo. 20v (a commission dated 26 May 1613 for assessing his estate, some of which was protected by trusts); PRO, SO 3/6 (August 1614).

[1254] Preston, *Disputatio Theologica*.

[1255] The nuncio Robert Ubaldini.

[1256] Adolf Schulcken. For the authorship of the recently published *Apologia Adolphi Schulckenii* (Cologne, 1613), see ARCR I, no. 1540; Milward II, 103; Lunn, *EB*, 46. The book answered Preston's *Apologia Cardinalis Bellarmini*.

[1257] *i.e.* an assistant to the archpriest, possibly William Harrison.

[1258] Charles Howard, first Earl of Nottingham.

[1259] The future Viscount Dunbar, son of Sir Henry Constable (d. 1608) and Margaret Dormer. For the arbitration between Sir Henry Constable and the admiralty over this matter, see Bodleian Library, Eng. Misc. c. 855, fo. 125r (Lord Sheffield to Sir Henry Constable, 18 October 1613). I am grateful to Simon Healy for this reference.

such commodities in that territorie; some of the skinne therof I did see, which was no thiker then a good paper, it was alyve sometime after it was a shore, & at the death made such a noyse that it did feare the dwellers by, and presentlie did stinke scarce to be tollerated. A scateringe report ther was that Geneva had receyved the duke of Savoy for ther protector, & had admitted two religious Companies into the towne. Ther are some xxvi prisonners in Newgate thirteine p: the rest Laikes, In the Clinke ther are xiii p: besides the lay people, vi or vii of them are now very earnest & hote in defence of the Oath, onelie M[r] Haynes a B. was left at the gatehouse,[1260] but laitlie one M[r] Kighley[1261] is brought thither, accused by a bad fellow at Dover, that he hard him say Mass at Doway: and I heare that Bracy[1262] the purs. hath brought one m[r] White or Greine[1263] out of Staffordshire. M[ris] P.[1264] is in very good health, and would be glad to heare of her brothers[1265] recoverye of his laime knee, whom all his frends heere greeteth well; Ben.[1266] lyeth wonderfull close, scarce salutations commeth from him; and all our frends of the same sort abroad are studious of all peace & quietnes and retirednesse so much as they may be suffred; no bitter or inveighinge speaches, you shall heare of to be utterred, but are readie to concurre and accord to any thinge, which may be to the helpe & releife of our estate eyther at home or abroad, & live still in indurance, & in a longinge expectation to heare somewhat effected or enterprised for the restauration & consolation of a lamentable & distressed clargie & cuntrie. commonly it is the iudgmentes of all men that it lacketh nothinge but courage & boldnes to deale with the K: which hath bene expected, & without which & some instigation, he will not yeild to ['no' deleted] any mitigation, he would soone inclyne himselfe & had good reasons ['to' deleted] both to force & induce others, if that the cheifest with you & some other estates and christian princes, beinge moved therto by his hol: would but zealouslie & stoutlie seame to engage and conioyne themselves in our miserable estate, & charitable tender our cause & case; He thirstieth after ease, which lyveth in great payne, & supposeth his frends giveth no succourse, when he feeleth no insuinge effect. *In protectione Dei commovabimur, qui factus est refugium pauperi, & adiutor in*

[1260] This unidentified man is to be distinguished from the secular priest Joseph Haynes who went into exile in October 1612, Anstr. II, 153.

[1261] Thomas Kighley, secular priest. George Abbot noted that he had crossed between England and Flanders often, acting as an intelligencer, *Downshire MSS* IV, 240, 291.

[1262] Richard Bray.

[1263] Presumably this is John Green alias White, of Staffordshire, Anstr. I, 137. He had been one of the principal opponents of Christopher Bagshaw and the anti-Jesuits during the 'Wisbech Stirs' in the 1590s and in the Appellant controversy.

[1264] Katherine Pole.

[1265] Geoffrey Pole.

[1266] Benjamin Norton.

tribulationibus. But I need not seame to move you heerin who hath a
fellow fealinge in our miseries, & is made a companion of our calammities
who is not wantinge to your power, both by daylie labours & prayers
to administer to the afflicted some comfort, & wher the one taketh not
effect, thother doth supplie not cooled or diminished by any disasters;
and wheras your charitie is extended zealouslie much in generall make
sometimes I pray application therof to some of yours [sic] frendes in
particular, as to my selfe, who is of such treasurie very indigent, &
layeth up but small stoore who both now doth & I feare me at the last
periode shall stand in great want: And as in this, so in all the rest I do
commend myselfe unto you, most kindly and lovinglie; and remayne.
22ᵗʰ of October. 1613.
yours allwaies to his power
    R. Clapham
In my last[1267] I sent you a letter of Atturney touchinge the money
owinge to d. Peares,[1268] with some small notice of his frendes
(On p. 428)
Addressed: [To] the worshipfull and his most worthie [fr]end Mʳ George
West give thes.
Endorsed: (1) Oct. 22. 1613. answ.
          (2) Recea. wed. December. 25. 1613.
          Answ. sond. Ian. 19. 1614.

48 *George Salvin (Birkhead) to Thomas More (7 November 1613)*   (*AAW A
    XII, no. 199, pp. 443–6. Holograph*)

Rev. sʳ havinge written as much as I am able alredie, yett can I not
hold my hand, but that I must informe yow still how matters do passe
amongst us. att the comminge forth this terme of widd disputation[1269]
in latine for defence of the oath against the reasons of Card bell,[1270]
lessius, Gretzerus,[1271] and becanus, yow will not beleve how the Clinck
is visited with many, and how they seek to wipe the imputation from
fa preston with such excuses as to wise men seame verie weeke. well
such books will certenly worke us much woe. the favorers of that

---

[1267] AAW A XII, no. 152.
[1268] William Percy. Thomas More had informed Anthony Champney of Percy's death
in a letter of 10 May 1613, AAW A XII, no. 108.
[1269] Preston, *Disputatio Theologica.*
[1270] Cardinal Robert Bellarmine SJ.
[1271] Jakob Gretzer SJ had recently published Βασιλικον Δωρον *sive Commentarius Exegeticus
in Serenissimi Magnae Britanniae Regis Iacobi Praefationem Monitoriam* (Ingolstadt, 1610), and
Antitortorbellarminianus Ioannes Gordonius Scotus Pseudodecanus et Capellanus Calvinisticus
(Ingolstadt, 1611).

congregation flock together, and bragge that many both Iesuites and secular preistes are of widderintons opinion, wherin they faile, albeit widderinton nameth 13 seculars[1272] of the best lerned in this Last booke, but vainly and falsly: and now they give out further (as I suppose for the better excuse of fa preston) that Clinch m^r widd ghostly father, and one of the best lerned northerne seculars is the maker of that booke; but as true as the rest.[1273] diverse recusantes had Compounded with the kinge for there livinges,[1274] and strickly enough, but now through the malice of some, officers are sent abroad ad melius inquirendu*m*; so as that they will never cease till poore catholiques be utterly beggered. the spanish Gentlewoma*n* donna aloisia,[1275] who wrote thither against us, was not longe since appr*e*hended in her owne howse[1276] by the maior[1277] and sheriffs[1278] and com*m*itted to the gate howse, where she is much courted with sundrie Embassadors. a Iesuit called m^r laithwait was taken in redcrosse street.[1279] the abetters of m^r widd disputation hold that he speaketh not against the denial of the oath: and yet he confuteth all argumentes against it, and therfor the conclusion must be that he defendeth it, ['argueth' deleted] arguinge against those w*h*ich denie it.[1280] yo*w* have ben I feare to familiar with Anselmo,[1281] I praie yo*w* take heed what yo*w* doe: all that crew[1282] are as vehement against bb as the padri[1283] be: albeit some of the spanish[1284] are temperate,

---

[1272] *i.e.* the thirteen priests who signed the Protestation of Allegiance in 1603. See **Letter 32**.

[1273] In October 1612 John Mush had said that he thought William (Gabriel) Gifford OSB was the author of Preston's previous works *Apologia Cardinalis Bellarmini* and *Rogeri Widdringtoni Catholici Angli Responsio Apologetica*, Lunn, *EB*, 42–3.

[1274] *Cf. CSPD 1611–18*, 165.

[1275] Luisa de Carvajal y Mendoza. She was a patron of SJ, McCoog, 77–8.

[1276] For her arrest in Spitalfields and her imprisonment, see CRS 68, 16–23; *Downshire MSS* IV, 231. The arrest was directed by George Abbot, *Downshire MSS* IV, 239. The charge, not baseless, was that she was establishing a house of religious in London.

[1277] In fact, Sir Henry Montague, Recorder of London, CRS 68, 23.

[1278] Thomas Bennet and Henry Jaye, CRS 68, 23.

[1279] Thomas Laithwait SJ. See **Letter 40** for his previous arrest. He had been banished at the Venetian ambassador's request but did not leave the country, Foley VII, 1046.

[1280] Preston had evolved a variation on the casuistic doctrine of probabilism in connection with the legitimacy of the oath, Sommerville, 'Jacobean Political Thought', 379–85. In Sommerville's words, Preston argued 'that the oath could not be taken until the question [of the papal deposing power] was resolved' but so long as the deposing power 'was controverted the pope could not put it into practice; he also relied on the legal maxim *in causa dubita sive incerta melior est conditio possidentis*', *i.e.* 'as long as the controversy was undecided it was necessary to side with the present possessor of the kingdom', citing Roland (Thomas) Preston OSB, *An Adioynder to the late Catholike New-Yeares Gift* (1620), 10, 17.

[1281] Robert (Anselm) Beech OSB.

[1282] The English Benedictines of the Cassinese congregation.

[1283] Jesuits.

[1284] The English Benedictines of the Spanish congregation.

though one of them the other day stuck not to call fa p[1285] a knave, in regard of his writinges, and another of the seculars termed him a villanous schysmatiane. it is to longe for me to write what I heare of the difference amongst them for the keepinge there rule, some beinge cold and given to pollicie of the tyme, and some more zealous for the observation of there order. I remember yow once told me, that I was to forward in tellinge the faultes of my brethren, which in deed I did, but it was to prevent the ill opinion that might be conceived of all the rest. for better it is that I should do it, then to have it written in bookes to the whole world, as now it is by widderinton, who accuseth many of myne and of the laitie also: wheras in verie deed, some few of all sortes have taken it, but the greater number is of the laitie, who never the lesse did it onely for feare of the lawes, ['reteyninge' deleted] remaininge still with a perturbed [p. 444] conscience for the same. those of m^r widderintons opinion (as I am told) will never suffer him to leave writinge untill his hol give some formal Censure of his doctrine. for they take them selves to be as good catholiques as live, though sculkeynnius be of another opinion, who to say the truth, hath <u>written</u> most excel<u>lently</u>[1286] against widderintons first booke, and giveth such sober, discreet, and lerned answeres, as content all those that read him. but all will not serve. it is said that m^r Charnock translateth the booke for defence of the oath into English this terme.[1287] yow may easily gesse, what harme will come therof. for my selfe I live as warily as I can, and take no notice of m^r preston till I see what is said from thence. I have given most of myne, admonition to stand to his hol breves and therfor what soever [word deleted] yow may heare is blased abroad, do not beleve it. for they say that <u>d kellis.[1288] and diverse other</u> on that side do hold with widderinton,[1289] as likewise all the prisoners in newgate which to my knowledge is false. sculkennius will not beleive it is m^r widderinton that keepeth all this sturre, but saieth he understandeth that he is a good catholique gentleman, and the writer of this booke under his name, is ementiti nominis et religionis <u>a</u> catholique. m^r warmington is yett with the bish of winchester,[1290] all that side giveth out that he is still a catholique, and thinketh he hath ben much iniured that I gave him and the rest no more formall an admonition. yt is thought that

---

[1285] Roland (Thomas) Preston.

[1286] Schulcken, *Apologia Adolphi Schulckenii*.

[1287] The title page of Preston, *Theologicall Disputation* declares that the author is the translator.

[1288] Matthew Kellison had been publicly installed as president of Douai College on 11 November 1613 (NS), TD V, 47.

[1289] These charges against Kellison would be repeated in late 1614, AAW A XIII, no. 230, and again in 1616, TD V, p. ccviii.

[1290] Thomas Bilson.

the b of winchester shalbe of the Counsell. all the bb thinke they are true bb after our fashion, and widderinton seameth to say that no circumstance necessarie waunteth in there creation. Hardinge etc*etera* ['well' deleted] were [?] farre overseene belike in teachinge us the contrarie.[1291] thus much of this matter[.] I write to yo*w* selfe onely to Lett yo*w* see how matters goe. yo*w* may utter it to yo*w*r frendes as yo*w* see cause. but yo*w* may be sure that few will now regard my com*m*ission. I am tediouse in writinge and yett I write not halfe that I wold. we heare nothinge as yett what successe d worthinton hath had.[1292] my fellowes thinke nothinge will goe well unlesse good order be taken for doway, and that bb be granted us. the state careth not much what be don. for they are in case to care no more for bb then they for the Archp.

the earle of Essex and his La are parted by sentence given by the bishope of winchester. for that he is proved to have ben maleficiatus ab initio etiam ante contractu*m*, albeit they have ben maried these v or vi yeares. the L of Canturburie[1293] was utterly against there separation for feare of scandall, because they had ben so longe together, the Church allowinge no more then three yeares for triall of such an impotencie. donna iloisia[1294] after some v or vi daies imprisonment as I thinke [p. 445] is now by the Ambass[1295] means sett at Libertie, and sett out of prison with great triumph to the admiration of the Londoners. one S*r* Pexall Brocas a knight of oxford shire did penaunce of late at paules crosse and els where for gettinge 30 women with child, farre more impiouse then mahomet that used but 14.[1296] when I had written thus much came yo*w*r Longe Letter with thee paternes.[1297] my frend

---

[1291] A reference to the debate between Thomas Harding and John Jewel over Jewel's *Apologia Ecclesiae Anglicanae* (1562). See W.M. Southgate, *John Jewel and the Problem of Doctrinal Authority* (Cambridge, Massachusetts, 1962), 198–9.

[1292] Worthington had been summoned to Rome in April 1613, TD V, 45. He had to some degree sided with the anti-Jesuit secular faction when Douai was subject to the turmoil of the visitation in late 1612. Seculars like William Bishop still hoped in April 1613 that he would break with SJ completely, AAW A XII, no. 73. But they soon began to worry that he was gravitating back to SJ and its views about the running of the seminary, TD V, 46–7. In November 1614 he informed the nuncio in Flanders that Paul V had made him protonotary apostolic and consultor to the Congregation of the Index, and he had decided to return to England. He hinted even that the pope thought of sending him there in episcopal orders, AAW A XIII, no. 236 (p. 607).

[1293] George Abbot.

[1294] Luisa de Carvajal y Mendoza.

[1295] Diego Sarmiento de Acuña.

[1296] *Downshire MSS* IV, 242.

[1297] The 'patterns' sent from Rome for Birkhead were for the design of his new clerical apparel which he might legitimately wear to indicate his status as an apostolic protonotary. Birkhead, however, became anxious and, in a letter to More of 13 December 1613, complained that 'some obiect daunger, for that yt will be given out thereupon that the partie w*h*ich weareth it is a bishope, w*h*ich will offend his m*aies*tie and that yt beinge but

and I do think our selves much beholden to yo*w* for yo*ur* care. the chardge yo*w* have ben at, we are redie to dischardge with thankes when we may have meanes to do it. the Letters that came by Paris I have also received; but havinge not yet tyme to read them, I cannot answeare them as I wold till better opportunitie. yo*w* chide me much in yo*ur* Longe Letter, but because I have many from yo*w* of later date, I hope by this tyme yo*w* are otherwise satisfied. some hote and zealous fellowes are angrie both with yo*w* and me, because we bringe nothinge to effect: but Lett them say what they will, we must do as we may. yo*ur* doinges there, are well Liked of the best of my Companie, proceede in godes name with couradge. And so with my lovinge com*m*endacions I leave yo*w* to god this 7 of november 1613.

yo*ur* assured frend

    Geo. Salvin

(On p. 446)

Addressed: To his verie Lovinge frend m^r Thomas moore give this. Rome.

Endorsed: (1) Nov*ember*. 7. 1613. Salv.

    (2) Recea. sat. febr. 1° ⎫
     Answ. thursd. febr. 13 ⎭ 1614

49 *George Salvin (Birkhead) to Thomas More (20 November 1613)* *(AAW A XII, no. 206, pp. 461–2. Holograph)*

my good S^r, albeit I find my selfe wearied, because of the Little good we doe, yet I thanke god my couradge faileth not to do any thinge w*i*thout pr*e*iudice to the state, that may sett forward our cause. I have said enough in diverse Letters about m^r Pett. I suppose he will to spaine, and I have gotten him leave to prosecute his busines there. yo*w* have no more to do but to helpe him to some good frendes. I am sure yo*w* have hard before this of one Carier a minister of great sufficiencie Lately converted. yf he seeke to yo*w* for acquaintance, I could wish yo*w* to give him the best comfort yo*w* can. lest for waunt of such courtesie he fall againe as diverse have don; and namely now of Late one Rontree a minister,[1298] first offeringe him selfe to the benedictins. and after to the Iesuites, for Lack of kyndnes became discontented and

the habit of a protonotarie, cannot bringe the estimation that a new habit propre for an Archpr*est* wold have don'. He still wanted, however, to know whether 'the cloke and cassock may be lyned or no', AAW A XII, no. 222 (p. 495). John Jackson had previously assured More that it would be worn only when Birkhead was 'private among those th*at* harbour him', AAW A XII, no. 75 (p. 159).

[1298] See **Letter 47**.

is now returned to his vomitt with much offence and scandall to others. one of thes daies I meane to send yow a Letter to the protector and one to his auditor,[1299] who yow say is our frend. my letters come slowly unto yow I confesse, but they come with the best speed that I can use. and yf it will not serve to satisfie my frendes, I shall give them good leave to putt some other in my place. there is no man in my case in all this land, and the katt never watched so greedily for the mouse, as the magistrate, who knoweth where I am, watcheth my cariadge and doinges. the least thinge in the world, will sett him upon me (which I regard not) and upon my frendes whose over throw will touch my hart. yow talke of some to come in from thence. truly I have no meanes to comfort them. the distributers of the common almes[1300] are not our frendes, but think to curbe us by keepinge us short. yet god provideth us somewhat, and when I have it, I have meanes sufficient to employ it. nothing greveth me more then that I cannot helpe these yonge men[1301] at there entrance; and I see no remedie. for so many are in so great extremitie, that all is gon in a trice which commeth to my handes. we must have patience: our opposites will have frendes about our superiors do what we can: and therfor yf the secretarie deal not securely and sincerly for us, we must abide the worst. my desyre in havinge yow to deale with the president,[1302] is alwaies to be understood, so farre as it doth not preiudice our cause. and in that I trust he will have patience, yf yow be not so open as he craveth. yow undo us yf yow think of goinge into spaine; for whome could yow leave in your place that we might trust? there is no great agreement betwene the padri[1303] and the benedictins, but yet I feare that both are opposite to us in our suit: and so it hath ben told me by some of there owne coate. yow do well to use them kyndly, but I wish yow to take heed of both: for be yow sure they take that course with us. I use them [p. 462] all kyndly, and yf I can do them any good without our owne hurt, I will not stick to do it. I praie yow suspend your opinion of m[r] Broughton.[1304] he was the fittest in that circuit, and I did nothinge therein but that m[r] Sara[1305]

[1299] Mozzenega. Birkhead wrote to Mozzenega on 3 December 1613 concerning the urgency of the suit about appointing a bishop and asked him to intercede with Cardinal Edward Farnese, AAW A XIII, no. 73 (pp. 182–3).

[1300] See **Letter 5**.

[1301] Seminary priests.

[1302] Thomas Worthington.

[1303] Jesuits.

[1304] Birkhead had already assured More in July 1613, when he appointed Richard Broughton to replace the recently deceased John Bavant, that Broughton was now 'of another humor, and most willinge to do anythinge for the helpe of the Clergie'. He is 'nothinge the man he was', AAW A XII, no. 132 (p. 291).

[1305] Edward Bennett. In April 1613 Bennett told More that Bavant (a consistent opponent of the suit for a bishop) had recommended Broughton as his successor, which

and m^r D Harrison was acquainted therewith. I trust he will prove another man then yow imagin. Commend me most humbly to my master,[1306] to whome but for feare I wold write more often. In a worde, do as yow and your frendes think good in all thinges. I meane shortly to send a letter to your auditor with the best reasons I can invent for the necessitie of bb, yf he will forward it to our protector, he cannot but do yow and us a singular favour. And so wishinge yow all prosperitie, I beseche god to stoare upp for yow an eternall reward for your paines in our common cause. this 20 of novemb. 1613.

your lovinge frend

    Geo. Salv.

Addressed: To his Lovinge frend m^r Thomas moore give this. Rome.

Endorsed: November. 20. 1613. Salv.

        Recea. twesd. Ian. 21. }
        Answ. thrusd. [sic] Ian. 30. } 1614

50 *[John Jackson] to [Thomas More] (25 November 1613)*   *(AAW A XII,*
no. 211, pp. 471–2. Holograph)

my very Reverend and much reverenced good sir. There be many reasons why I shold (as I doe) much honor and love yow. yowr speciall vertues and worth, yow [sic] great love & labors for the generall cause of our church, wherin thowgh my love and desires may be as great as yours, yet in paynes, and all things els that may further the good therof, I am incomparably behind yow. also your sweet disposition & conversation with the continuance of your love to me soe much above my deserts, your frendly constructions of my negligence in writing, and notwithstanding my faile [sic], the continance of yours. thease and such like did at the first beget and after nourish, continew & increase those respects in mee towards yow which shall not decay godwilling whiles I breath. And I doe faithfully assure yow that if I had the power and liberty to chuse my selfe a freind to live & converse with, I know very few (if I know any one,) whom I wold make choyce of soe sone as of your selfe. Now for my excuse. I may assure my selfe that yow are fully perswaded that my silence hath not been owt of any want of respect to yow, but upon some other cause. and in truth it hath. and thowgh I doe not plead, Not guiltie, in point of negligence yet I assure yow I

---

meant Broughton must be suspect, AAW A XII, no. 85. But by September Bennett was satisfied because it emerged that Broughton had 'fownd owt a great legacy which 6 yeare agoe was left by (in deed) a Iesuited Gentlman to the disposition of m^r Arch [Birkhead]', AAW A XII, no. 169 (p. 375).

[1306] Cardinal Edward Farnese.

had diverse discouragements. first I saw noe thing to write of, in my opinion, worth our labours and your expences for I suppose lettres be chargeable. also I observ'd that all owr writings informations & suites were coldly interteyn'd & as the effect shewed, litle credited by his hol. yea the world tooke notice and wondred that the padri[1307] cold eyther obtayne ['any' deleted] beleif of any report, or grawnt of what suite they wold or stopp any sute of ours, and that all our labors in that kind were but vayne. and thinking upon thease points, I observed three sorts (among others) of pr: here in Ing. one sort being wholly disgusted by his hol. proceedings (who hath lost by his carelesnes of their suites more love then wyll easily be recovered) did not only give over all their expectations of any good to come from R. but also in all <u>things</u> <u>disputable</u> or <u>undefined</u> rather ['to' deleted] did incline to that side which was against his prerogative then the other, for having found soe litle regard of all their labours hazards, affections etcetera they thowght they had noe reason to stand any longer for him more then they held them <u>selves tyed in con</u>science, (and yow know how affection or disaffection may sway the understanding) and finding also that the course they hold was less daungerous to themselves they [word deleted] toke a course to live (as they thinke) upright with god & many wayes beneficiall to themselves thowgh litle favorable to his hol. & as other think nothing beneficiall towards the generall cause & good of owr church. Others ther are that observing how litle his hol. doth for pr. or at their requests notwithstanding their labors etcetera & how ready to beleive countenance & favour the others, thowght it best to live (as much as the persecution will give them leave) at rest & not any waye to labour in the comon cause otherwise then in the use of their function & not to oppose against eyther thease former or any others, but to keep credit withall asmuch as they cold & withowt reprehension of any. the 3ᵈ sort amongst which I rang'd my selfe had a great desire to set forward the comon cause stood strongly for the sea Apost. (even in those points wherein his hol. is perswaded they are opposite to him) & trobled themselves in writing solliciting, informing etcetera & therby became odious to the state, & incurr'd also the disfavour of the first sort & lost freinds freindship & favours & hazarded themselves more then they needed, & notwithstanding did litle good because his hol. made noe shew that he had any good conceyt of them or respect to their requests, thowgh their requests were no whit beneficiall to them selves in private, but only for the good of the church wherof he is head. [p. 472] as for my selfe I did soe litle like of the first sort that I have lost much freindship & favour by opposing against them. as for the last sort though truly I was and am caried to like of them & commend their

---

[1307] Jesuits.

course seing them labour the comon good p*er* infama*m* et bona*m* fama*m* w*i*thout any private respect, nay w*i*th private loss, yea w*i*th much troble to them selfe & sometymes to their freinds (as it hath fallen out w*i*th me) [word deleted] yet the love to the generall cause drown'd all thease) [sic] thowgh (I say I adhered even as I think naturally to thease) yet I find th*a*t the second sort live at much quiet, follow their private studies to their own comforth & to the good of their private acquaintances & freinds w*i*thout any inconvenience, or dislike of any p*a*rty, & can yo*w* blame me if I did begin to affect this course & by litle & litle to let these follow th*e* publick busines th*a*t were more ingaged then my selfe. Even at this tyme I assure you I have lost a whole week in writing to p*a*r:[1308] dow.[1309] & in sending over money, harkning after bookes for them etc*etera*. w*hi*ch week if I had bestowed towards a prep[ar]atio*n* for an exercise for the next sunday I shold have pleas'd god p*er*haps more, done private good to the hearers, contented my freinds, credited my selfe & therby also th*e* bodie I am of, though but in the opin[i]o*n* of those th*a*t shold know therof. w*hi*ch may be thought a private good. yet it is such a private good as redowndeth to the good of the bodye & helpeth to take away <u>an obloquie w*hi*ch</u> some wold father upon us, for there are th*a*t say th*a*t there be none learned but the Ie.[1310] & that others doe nothing neyther preech nor write etc*etera*. I doe acknowledge a man may doe both, yet it must be w*i*th most labour & if it be comendable in us why doth not also his hol. soe much incourage us to take notice by granting our iust & generall demaunds, th*a*t he thinketh well of the cleargy, for as for his good thoughts of any private ma*n*, I think he were ambitious that shold expect, & even in the expectation shold make himselfe unworthy therof. A man th*a*t hath but one eye may see th*a*t it is the com*m*on good th*a*t most of us seek after. de his hacten*us*. yor brother[1311] was yesterday w*i*th me & is ever whe*n* he cometh to towne[.] I am much co*m*forted in his vertuous co*n*versation. your sisters dawghter[1312] at Brux. shold be professed. yet but a lay sister (w*hi*ch I am sory for,) in regard she bringeth not such a portion as they

[1308] Paris.

[1309] Douai.

[1310] Jesuits.

[1311] Christopher Cresacre More.

[1312] Tentatively this person may be identified as Joan/Jane More, professed as a lay sister at the Abbey of the Glorious Assumption of our Lady at Brussels, B. Weldon, *Chronological Notes containing the Rise, Growth, and present State of the English Congregation of the Order of St. Benedict* (Stanbrook, 1881), appendix, 33. She was a daughter of Mary, Thomas More's sister. In February 1616 she wrote to Thomas, her uncle, saying that she had been professed for more than a year, AAW A XV, no. 40. I am grateful to Caroline Bowden for this information.

expect. is your cosen the Ies.[1313] at Brux. of soe litle credit? and for the
portion which she must pay the[y] cold intreat yowr help. I was willed
to signifie soe much unto yow. I suppose yow know he hath been long
widower.[1314] he hath a very fine sonne[1315] & two very pretty daughters.[1316]
I have written to them at par.[1317] what I think is the best way to set
downe owr iustification against widdr.[1318] his alleaging of our names[1319] &
I intreated them after they had drawen a page or 2 to that purpose
that they wold send it up to yow that yow might get it delivered to him
(whosoever he is. Bell[1320] Andreas Eudaemon[1321] Gretserus or any other)
that shall answer the booke that out of it he may as of himselfe excuse
our action. there is come out the same booke of pseudowidd[1322] in Ingl.
with an addition of many sheets, (some say 50) in confutation of Suarez
his booke.[1323] which booke of Suarez was burnt at powles church yeard
at the sermon tyme (which was all against it & us) the last sunday. which
was the 24 post pent.[1324] they give out & mr Leak avowed it to me that

[1313] A reference to Thomas More SJ, first cousin of the clergy agent Thomas More,
CRS 75, 244.
[1314] Christopher Cresacre More's wife, Elizabeth Gage, had in fact, died only in 1610,
D. Shanahan, 'The Family of St. Thomas More in Essex 1581–1640', Essex Recusant 1
(1959), 65.
[1315] Thomas.
[1316] Helen, who was persuaded to enter religion by William (Benedict) Jones OSB,
Lunn, EB, 101, and Bridget, who also entered OSB. Helen's writings were collected and
published by David (Augustine) Baker OSB as The Holy Practises of a Devine Lover (Paris,
1657), and The Spiritual Exercises of...Gertrude More (Paris, 1658).
[1317] i.e. at the Collège d'Arras in Paris.
[1318] Roland (Thomas) Preston OSB.
[1319] See **Letters 32, 48**. Champney wrote to More on 14 January 1614 (NS) that 'I
thought to have sent you a litle thinge in answer' of one of Preston's 'argumentes in his
last booke which is drawne out of that fact' of the priests 'whoe made theyre protestatione
of obedience to the last queene' though it has not yet been copied out. When it arrives
More is to show it to Cardinal Bellarmine and others, AAW A XIII, no. 4 (p. 8). But
this political activity on the Paris college's part irritated the English privy council.
Champney observed in the same letter that Sir Thomas Edmondes, the English
ambassador in France, had persuaded the French council of state to order 'that we must
breake our companie'. Villeroi asked the former ambassador to England, Antoine le Fèvre
de la Boderie, who had been an effective diplomat there, to intervene but de la Boderie
was unsuccessful, AAW A XIII, no. 4 (p. 7). On the same day William Bishop wrote to
Cardinal Farnese that they had been ordered not to live collegially but disperse and live
in two separate houses, a situation which Bishop asked the cardinal to rectify, AAW A
XIII, no. 8 (p. 20).
[1320] Cardinal Robert Bellarmine SJ.
[1321] Andreas Eudaemon Joannes SJ.
[1322] Preston, Theologicall Disputation.
[1323] The appendix of Preston's Theologicall Disputation answers Francisco Suarez SJ
Defensio Fidei Catholicae (Coimbra, 1613), ARCR I, nos 1541–3; ARCR II, no. 660.
[1324] See McClure, 488. Certain passages from Suarez's book were condemned by the
parlement of Paris in June 1614, ARCR I, no. 1544, and the book was burnt there as
well, CSPV 1613–15, 165.

he writeth that the p. may depose & after standing out he may authorize the ['laitye' deleted] cleargy to kill him, they say the cleargy because they be more his subiects then the laytie is. one m̲ʳ Kightly[1325] of our bodie, a gent. well borne as I am told) [sic] hath caried himselfe very constantly & stowtly of late before the LL. of the councell & the Bish. of Cant.[1326] who wold willingly have him acknowledge himselfe to be a pr. but the other answereth very stowtly & wisely. his fath. is an earnest protest. & urgeth against his owne sonne whom he wold disherite if they cold prove any such thing by him. he gave them reasons that without periury he cold not take the oath. & after the B. wold have had him urg'd with the oath of Supremacy. and yet that bodie wherof this man is, is not respected by his hol. as I have often thowght to tell him in a lettre to himselfe. I am now forced in hast to cloose up with my best respect to your selfe my very loving remembrances to mʳ Tho. Ro.[1327] & mʳ Io. Ro.[1328] if he be come thither. Hear was lately an Imbass.[1329] from the Muscovite who told our k. that the k of polonia[1330] is driven owt thence. I my selfe hard the k. say that Suarez held a coercive powre & that the p. was iudge over kings & the cause why they did it not was only ob decentiam which words he diverse tymes repeated ironice. there is a Nullitie declared between the Earle of Essex & the la: Frances Howard to whom he had been maried diverse years. & vicownt Rochester who is Earle of Somerset shall marry her this christenmas. Some say the Bish. of winchester[1331] who was the cheif in declaring the nullitie will set owt a booke in defence of the sentence.[1332] the Arch. of canterb. was against it & in regard therof hath lost some favour as it is sayd.[1333] there is a great persecution towards in all probabilitie. many gentlemen & there wives sent for owt of the north & great charges given in lond to looke after cath. & they are about to bind all cath to good abearance which as some say is forfeyted ipso facto & soe when they wyll they sease on all they have. whether this bee done by the kings particuler appointment or noe I know not. but I think it is not. 25. 9ᵇʳᵉ 1613.

(On p. 471)
No address

[1325] See **Letter 47**.

[1326] George Abbot.

[1327] Thomas Roper.

[1328] John Roper.

[1329] Alexis Zyuzin. See McClure, 482, 485; *CSPV 1613–15*, 65, 67, 81; *Downshire MSS* IV, 242, 246.

[1330] Sigismund III.

[1331] Thomas Bilson.

[1332] *Cf.* D. Lindley, *The Trials of Frances Howard* (1993), 82.

[1333] The secular clergy sent to More in Rome an account of George Abbot's discourse to James on the divorce and of James's reply, AAW A XII, no. 240.

Endorsed: (1) November. 25. 1613. N.
     (2) Recea. twesd. Ian. 21.⎱ 1614
        Answ. wed. Ian. 29. ⎰

51 *John Nelson (Jackson) to George West (Thomas More) (18 December 1613)   (AAW A XII, no. 228, pp. 509–10. Holograph)*

my very R. and much honored good sir. I receaved of late from m^r clapham[1334] 2. lettres of yours to him, which did please me soe well (especially th'one which was very iudiciously written, & to good purpose) that I made a meting and presumed soe much of your allowance as to read it in the hearing of m^r coll. and a knight a freind of myne and an other gentleman that is noe stranger to our affayres. it was noe less liked of them then of mee, and seemed for the present to put life in them, the effects wherof I was in hoope, yow shold have seen, but I doe in part excuse them, for besides the generall difficulties many men are soe puzled with diverse particuler buisinesses sometyme in regard of religion and sometyme for their private state of life as they can hardly (unles greater zeall then usually I finde now a dayes move them) find any tyme to attend to the generall buisines. especially having soe litle incouragement (as they finde wee have) from those that shold yeeld us more comforth then they doe. but I only now towch that point, least yow applye that unto mee. ridiculus citharaedus – chorda qui semper oberrat eadem. I saw a lettre written owt of Ireland, that reported that there bee arrived in waterford 3. Irish Iesuits[1335] of rank & place. who browght with them pardons (as the lettre said) from the beginning of the world to all those that opposed themselves to the parlament, and continued therin, and they have made known that they have comission from their superiours to preach 3. sermons (the party that did write the lettre was promised the texts and a draught of their discourse) and they incouraged that people to continew & assured them of succour in tyme of need. The comissioners whom the k. sent are returned as I am told but as yet their report of the state of things thear is not knowne.[1336] 2. dayes since m^r Fayreclooth the Iesuite was apprehended and is now in

[1334] Richard Broughton.

[1335] See F.M. O'Donoghue, 'The Jesuit Mission in Ireland 1598–1651' (unpubl. Ph. D. thesis, Catholic University of America, 1981), 119.

[1336] See **Letter 47**; Ford, *Protestant Reformation in Ireland*, 60.

the Gatehowse, who not long since was taken & redeemed him selfe.[1337] comissions were sent into every shire to the officers to give up all the names of all the recusants or their favorites, & many have returned up accordingly their relations & countrye cunstables have given up the names of some that are not recusants and such as lived not at their howses in the country thease 7. years.[1338] the pursuivants continew prolling & praying upon all sorts. pseudowiddrington[1339] had put his latin booke of the oath into Inglish with an answer to Swarez booke[1340] with further purpose to answer Suarez in latin at large, but the Inglish booke is stayed thowgh some copies be dispersed at the least for a tyme, because the king doth seem to dislike it much. as thowgh the author played fast & loose. if this be reall (as it is probable) I suspect that some that be adversaries to the author have by one means or other gott this suggested to the k. (and indeed his bookes affoarded matter to ground the suggestion.)[1341] if it be not reall, then hath the nimble head of the authour procured this shew of dislike for a tyme to stopp such courses as might be intended from R. against him & his bookes, but I will hoope that this later is but only my surmise, yet I thought good to acquaint yow even with surmises. whose iudgement can make good use of all things without wronging any. The k. did lately speak of 4. things in a very feeling maner. the first that he cold be glad to know those catholicks from the rest, that wold adhere only to the p. in spirituall matters and not in this point of deposition, for yow must suppose that still hee excepteth against this as not belonging to his spirituall iurisdiction, the 2^d was [p. 510] that the p: shold at least give over this clayme or let it lye in the deck tyll a generall councell, & 3dly he lifted up his hands towards heaven saying O that I might be soe happie as to live to see a generall councell in my dayes to appease thease disagreements, how willingly wold I lend my best help therto.[1342] 4^{ly} he

---

[1337] For Alexander Fairclough SJ, see CRS 74, 184 n. 88. John Blackfan SJ reported from Brussels on 4 January 1614 (NS) that Fairclough had been arrested 'att Christmasse day' coming 'from the Dutch Embassador', ARSI, Anglia 37, fo. 132v. He was regarded as one of the most dangerous of the clerical prisoners who were transferred to Wisbech Castle in April 1615, PRO, SP 14/80/77–84. But Fairclough, when interrogated in March 1615, though guarded in his replies, implied that he was a political moderate in the matter of the oath of allegiance. He would not take it but he said that he was 'unwillinge to censure itt', Foley IV, 592–5.

[1338] On 1 November 1613, Edward Bennett had written to More that agents of the 'hie commission' were sent 'into all cuntries to enquier of papistes Brownistes' and all nonconformists, though they were particularly directed to search out Catholic recusants. He was informed that it was 'after the maner of the Spanish inquisition', AAW A XII, no. 195 (p. 435).

[1339] Roland (Thomas) Preston OSB.

[1340] See **Letter 50**.

[1341] See **Letter 53**.

[1342] See Patterson, *King James VI and I*, ch. 2.

said he wold very gladly know some certeynty whether the p. did approve or consent or thought well of the powder plott, or whether their act was lawfull or not because he cold never here that he disliked therof. m^r Alabaster standeth by with the rest when the k. is at meall and discourseth & telleth any thing he can to please amongst the rest he said that he brake fa. parsons hart. & they say that he telleth strang stories. they may see what it is to give men distast. for though I excuse him not yet I say it is not unprobable but that with good usages he wold have continued on that side the seas in good ordre. there was one m^r Smalman (whom I tooke to be a Ies. & know yet nothing to the contrary) that riding by the high way was intreated by a country man to help him to turne a cowe & as he was riding after her his horse began to fling and kick and therwith cast him and pitch'd him on his head & he never spake word but died therwith.[1343] they say he was holden a good man but sevear, yet perhaps never the worse for that. requiescat anima eius in pace, et liberet nos deus a subitanea et improvisa morte. thowgh perhaps if one of owrs had had such a chance it wold have been thowght a punishment for opposing against them, for soe the seeking of the right of owr owne body is miscalled. therbee a couple of lettres one to the Auditor & the other to your monsignor ready but I can not send to m^r coll. for them at this tyme. our bl. lord prosper your good endevors & make me partaker of your prayers & merits. 18. of decembre. 1613

yours as yow know.

N.

Addressed: To the right worship*full* my very assured good Freind m^r George west give thease

Endorsed: (1) December 18. 1613. N.
          (2) Recea. twesd. febr. 11. } 1614
              Answ. frid. febr. 14.

52 *John Nelson (Jackson) to George West (Thomas More) (26 December 1613)*   *(AAW A XII, no. 234, pp. 521–2. Holograph)*

My very Reverend good s.^r upon occasion of some of yours I did scrible over a lettre of thankgiving to your monsignor.[1344] but afterwards it was cast by for a long tyme, and finding it by chance of late among other papers, I read it over, and resolved to send it, for thowgh there be

---

[1343] 'Smalman' was the secular priest Emmanuel Johnson, Anstr. II, 173. He was the first priest recorded as living at Harvington Hall in Worcestershire. He was buried at Chaddesley Corbett, M. Hodgetts, *Secret Hiding Places* (Dublin, 1989), 83–4.

[1344] John Baptist Vives.

errours in it, yet owr difficulties, the distance between yo*w* & us, the want of pa*r*ticuler information and such life [sic for 'like'] may excuse them. at the least he will see th*a*t wee take notice of his worth & favours to us. yow may doe well hereafter both to send us a copie of ther titles & stile w*h*ich wee must use in o*u*r let*t*res to those to whom we write as also to enforme us of their states in pa*r*ticuler for m^r coll. & I did differ in owr opinions about this monsig*n*or yo*u*r freind. because he thinketh that he is noe cleargy ma*n*, I mean noe p. and he alleaged his reasons for it, by w*h*ich yow may see how ignorant wee are. I have touched in the later end therof owr requests made to the po: & have leaft th*e* relation of the*m* to yo*w*. I mean th*a*t of Ecclesiasticall government, of the cancelling of th*a*t Breve[1345] w*h*ich is soe preiudiciall to such of owr breethre*n* beyond the seas as shold take degree as m^r pet and others & hath noe president in th*e* church of god. of the reforming of o*u*r colleges & the like abuses, w*h*ich we have soe long & earnestly sued for. there are abuses here w*h*ich wee can never looke to have redressed tyll wee have th*e* ordinary iurisdiction w*h*ich is in gods church. I was told by a preist who hath been very great w*i*th the Ie:[1346] & to this day keepeth good quartre w*i*th them, that beeing at a widdow gentlewomans howse, she was resolved to receyve the sacraments of him the next morning; in the evening after this thear came 2. gentlewome*n* who brought w*i*th the*m* a Ies. th*a*t had never been there before, & it is a fashion to have such sisters to comend the*m* & bring them acquainted where there is noe need of the*m*. the pr. & the Ie. lodg'd togither. In the morning the mistres of th*e* howse came to the pr. & prayed him th*a*t he wold not take it offensively for sayd she I wold gladly have the sacraments of this R*e*verend ma*n*, who as I understand by my cosens (soe she called the gentlewome*n*) ['he' deleted] hath very many extraordinary graces & privileges & yo*w* know it is good to take all the benefitt we can of the church. the pr. gave her such an answer as he though[t] was fitt rebus sic stantibus. and therupon she went to the Ies. since w*h*ich tyme they have made her howse a kind of residence for them & yo*w* know how welcome preis[ts] bee where they gett hold. I suppose that the graces et*cetera* w*h*ich gott the Ie. this favour are plenary pa*r*dons to every one the first tyme he or she cometh to them, to co*n*fession. w*h*ich I see not how the pope can graunt, especially as they practise it to gett the preists ghostly children from the*m*. the pope & Italians who understand not well the maner how preists live here in Ing. can hardly conceyve the daungerous event of this practise. I suppose yow are myndfull of the removing of the Ies. co*n*f. fro*m*. d.[1347] & of procuring

---

[1345] Concerning English clergy proceeding to higher degrees in foreign universities.
[1346] Jesuits.
[1347] Douai.

that the pres.[1348] may make choyce of the seniors & of having readers
of owr owne etc*etera*. the Arch.[1349] hath writte*n* a *lettre* to the po. for th*e*
same w*hi*ch he sent me to see & hath it now returnd, and I expect it
shortly agayne to send. w*i*th thease yo*w* shall receave those th*a*t I told
yo*w* of to th*e* Auditor[1350] & yo*ur* monsign*or* fro*m* m*r* Coll. d. Carier did
write a booke[1351] to th*e* k. of the causes of his going owt of Ingland
w*hi*ch doth good to the cause and if wee can have him gott to paris[1352]
hee will credit owr howse very much. The Irish have offred for liber[t]ie
of co*n*science 5000[li] p*er* an. for 4. years. m*r* Alabaster hath gott 300[li]
p*er*. annu*m* w*hi*ch was the dean of powles[1353] before he was chosen
Bishop. they are co*n*sulting whether to have a parliame*n*t or noe, the
great lords th*a*t is the Howards are against it, fearing th*a*t the lower
howse will give the k. noe more co*n*tentme*n*t the*n* he had in th*e* last, &
yet work their owne ends w*hi*ch owt of parlame*n*t they cannot doe.
even the puritanes the*m*selves doe speak broadly of the meannes (not
to tearme it basenes) of the ladie Elizabeths marriage w*i*th the palsgrave,
w*hi*ch is thought to be one cause th*a*t hath lessned the B. of cant:[1354]
[two words deleted] th*a*t supereminent credit w*hi*ch once he had w*i*th
o*ur* k. there bee midwives sent over to her of late, to bring her in bed.
The great marriage between the Earle of somerset & the La. frances
Howard who was once married to the Earle of Essex, is now this day
celebrated. there bee twoe bookes owt against it from calvenests beyond
see & the one fro*m* Geneva as it is sayed. whe*n* I said th*a*t the bookes
wear against it, I meane against the Nullitie w*hi*ch was declared to be
between her & Essex wherein the B. of winches:[1355] gave sentence &
the Archb. of cant. & the B. of london[1356] was against it. & some think
th*a*t the puritanes have procured thease boakes. The L. Tho. Howard
of Suff. L. chancelor her father is one of the most powerfull in Ingl. at
this tyme. But thease be things th*a*t yo*w* care not for & I suppose yo*w*
will now say manu*m* de tabula. and be as weary of my *lettr*es as before

[1348] Thomas Worthington.

[1349] George Birkhead.

[1350] Mozzenega.

[1351] See Questier, 'Crypto-Catholicism', 47, for speculation about the writing and
publication of Benjamin Carier's motives for his conversion, *A Treatise Written by Mr.
Doctour Carier* (Brussels, 1614).

[1352] *i.e.* to the Collège d'Arras.

[1353] John Overall, formally elected to the see of Coventry and Lichfield on 14 March
1614. (His election was thought likely by John Chamberlain on 11 November 1613,
McClure, 486.) In March 1614 Alabaster was granted a benefice of Overall in Lincolnshire
diocese, void because of Overall's promotion, PRO, SO 3/6 (June 1614).

[1354] George Abbot.

[1355] Thomas Bilson.

[1356] John King.

yo*w* desired them. yo*u*r brother[1357] is well w*i*th his litle ones[.] he was
w*i*th me this day & is to come againe in the morning for he lyeth in
towne thease holidayes. thus praying hartely to be remembred in yo*u*r
good devotions I rest
yours ever most lovingly and faithfully
   N
s. steevens day.

The persecution is greivous to many & most followed by the L.
cooke. cheif iustice of Ingl. & privie councello*u*r & who expecteth
shortly to be Baron.
   [In margin on p. 521] The spanish ladie[1358] died 2. dayes before
christmas. m[r] Hurlston[1359] also is departed. I suppose I have heretofore
writte*n* of the death of m[r] Dolma*n*[1360], & m[r] Mumforth.[1361]
[p. 522]
   I can not but acquaint yow w*i*th the freshest newes w*h*ich is at th*e*
court. vz. that Suarez his booke is ce*n*sured and co*n*dem*n*'d in spayne
and an answer therunto sent over to th*e* spanish Imbass.[1362] here to
deliver to owr k. this was brought yesternight fro*m* the court. there is
also speech in towne of a le*tt*re of the Nu*n*cio of flanders[1363] who saith
th*a*t the pope refuseth the dedicatio*n* of widdr.[1364] because he holdeth
not the author to be ecclesiae filiu*m* aut catholicu*m* & forbiddeth the
same & hath referred the ce*n*suring therof to th*e* Inquisitio*n*.[1365] There
is now at th*e* court one Shamburg[1366] who came hither first w*i*th the
count palatine whe*n* he maried the La. Eliz. he was once a captayne,
and is now come as Imb. fro*m* the princes calvenist & palatine to the
k. upo*n* this occasion as I am told. the Calvenists of Germanie have a
league among the*m*selves defensive and offensive & owr k. is ioyn'd
w*i*th the*m* in the defensive part only. now they labour (by this Shamburg)
to win him to ioyne also w*i*th the*m* in the offensive p*a*rt likewise.
Addressed: To the right worship*full* my ever assured good Freind m[r]
      George west give thease R.
Endorsed: (1) Dece*m*ber 26. 1613. N.

[1357] Christopher Cresacre More.
[1358] Luisa de Carvajal y Mendoza.
[1359] Identity uncertain.
[1360] Presumably Alban Dolman.
[1361] Identity uncertain. If a priest this may be either Francis or Thomas Montford. See Anstr. I, 232–3.
[1362] Diego Sarmiento de Acuña.
[1363] Guido Bentivoglio.
[1364] *i.e.* Preston's *Disputatio Theologica*.
[1365] Preston's *Apologia Cardinalis Bellarmini* and *Disputatio Theologica* were put on the Roman Index on 16 March 1614 (NS), ARCR I, no. 925. 1.
[1366] Hans Meinhard von Schomberg. See McClure, 493.

(2) Recea. twesd. febr. 18.⎫
    Answ. frid. febr. 28. ⎬ 1614
    with one to my monsignor⎭

53 *Robert Clapham (Richard Broughton) to George West (Thomas More) (31
December 1613)   (AAW A XII, no. 235, pp. 523–4. Holograph)*

my most kind and worthy S.^{r}

Your last which I received was that wherin you gave us to understand
of the establishinge of d K.[1367] in the Coll. to whom I have addressed &
I hope they are receaved by this some few lynnes, as speedilie &
effectuallie as I could, accordinge to your desire; and the matter which
was entreated of, since which time I am credible infomed that the place
which is imposed upon him is a thinge forced contrary to his minde &
will, but he is willinge to concurre & conioyne with us in all thinges in
what he can, but he seameth somewhat to timorous, (as I have he [sic]
obiected it unto him as his fault) to enterprise any thinge not practised
before because of the censure given in such affaires by P.[1368] *Quod nihil
est innovandum* & therfor dares not as yet make you his Agent[1369] untill
it be motioned by some meanes unto the cheifest. I have moved M^r
Nel.[1370] to writt unto the d^r as touchinge this busines, as allso unto you
concerning all other our affaires, which I doubt not but he hath
performed. The Bened. say heare that your cheife suite[1371] was opposed &
resisted for that it was propounded that the Bis. might be their superiours
for so hath Mr Beach written to them, & that f. Owen[1372] gave him the
first knowledge therof, & so they conioyned together in opposition: they
frame dyvers reasons & argumentes that it is thinge most inconvenient
that they should be subiected or commaunded by any such superior
who is ignorant of ther rule, life, discipline, & other affaires belonginge
to ther company; and that ther Superior should be commaunded by an
other not proportionated to them as they say, a thing most unagreable[.]
But it seameth they are not willinge to any at all, upon any fashion
whatsoever. for beinge asked whether they thought them necessarie &
convenient for thes times all thinges being well considered answere was
made that they could not tell it was a thing disputable, & they had not
weighed the reasons. that of ther willingnes heerto you may easelie take

[1367] Matthew Kellison, president of Douai College since 11 November 1613 (NS).
[1368] Pope Paul V.
[1369] *i.e.* agent for Douai College. Thomas Fitzherbert was still the agent for Douai in
Rome.
[1370] John Jackson.
[1371] For the appointment of a bishop.
[1372] Thomas Owen SJ.

a scantlinge. But if it were propounded as they say, (which I denyed firmelie) & not simplie without any other connexion, in my iudgment it was not well, for it might have bene easelie foreseene, that so they would resist it with all strenght [sic] & meanes they could, & so spoile the whole procedance, the substance of the suite once graunted many thinges by consequence would have followed, & what remayned further necessarie & requisite might afterwardes be obteyned by petition. A straite proclamation was set forth for observinge fastinge dayes, as friday, Lent, & other fastinge day [sic] commaunded by the Englishe Church, but it is but slowlie prosecuted by the magistrate, for experience findeth it to be neglected allreadie. A hundreth poundes worth of bookes was reported to have bene laitlie burnt, as of Miss: Brev. Bi. e[t]cetera [in margin: 'some of [sic for 'or'] all of thos were burnt'] but since I heare (as I iudge more trulie) that ther [corrected from 'they'] were allso some few of Suares his bookes touchinge the Oath.¹³⁷³ dyvers of the Nunnes of Gravelinge are dead, as the Abbas,¹³⁷⁴ the sister Brookes¹³⁷⁵ & sister dorrell,¹³⁷⁶ through lodginge to sone in ther new howse, & allmost twentie of them hath bene sicke.¹³⁷⁷ Sister Lyne¹³⁷⁸ at Sᵗ Omers is chosen to be ther Abbas. My L. Cooke now cheife iustice & councellour breatheth forth many bitter & cruell threates against Catholiques, he sent for some Cath. by warrant for to take the Oath,¹³⁷⁹ & some under Sherifes, returninge the Commission with *Non inventi* he put them in prison [in margin: 'the Kinge they say is the cause heerof']; since he hath sent dyvers warrantes into the North partes, & allso into most parts of England, & saith he will have all of them in generall to be bound to good behaviour those which take the Oath shall not therby be freed from it; Sʳ George Cotton¹³⁸⁰ was laitlie convented before him at the last Session at Newgate after the tearme, havinge denyed the oath twice, the third tyme he tooke it. at which time the L. cheife Iust. said he was sory at his improvidence, & backwardnes in shewinge himselfe a good subiect for that the iurie had given ther verdit of him allreadie, but he would stay sentance, & in love towards him deale with the kinge to use all clemencie towardes

¹³⁷³ See **Letter 50**.

¹³⁷⁴ The abbess of the Poor Clares of Gravelines was Mary Gough, daughter of Thomas Gough and Mary Lloyd (for which information I am grateful to Caroline Bowden, as also for the information in the next two notes).

¹³⁷⁵ Anne Brooke, daughter of John Brooke and Anne Shirley of Madeley, Shropshire.

¹³⁷⁶ Lucy Darell, daughter of Thomas Darell of Scotney Castle, Kent.

¹³⁷⁷ In a letter to More of 7 December 1613 (NS) Robert Pett had claimed that they were poisoned by a barrel of beer sent from England, AAW A XII, no. 219.

¹³⁷⁸ Not identified.

¹³⁷⁹ See McClure, 491.

¹³⁸⁰ The third son of George Cotton of Warblington, see Mott, fo. 146r; *HMC Ancaster MSS*, 377–80.

him. he remayneth still in prison they say sorowfull & penitent. in his speach at this Session this L. Iudge said that he had found out what persons they were which most perturbed the common wealth, to witt, Rogges & Recusantes: of malefactors he condemned at this time, six and thirtie, & xxx^tie of them were hanged; allbeit at the same instant they did Robbe & breake howses about London as nothing fearing death either temporall or eternall. *Ut non erat timor Dei ante oculos Anglorum.* Some doth make this coniecture & construction of this vehement persecution that it is for to infringe the authoritie of the High commission,[1381] but if this coniectures [sic] were truthes, which is not likelie, neverthelesse it will bringe many soules & bodyes to ruyne & perdition[.] Ther was a preist banished from Excester who they say was called Mr Fennell.[1382] the French Embassadour[1383] looketh shortlie to depart & another to supplie his roome who will be willinge to begge some preistes to be banished but few I thinke will give ther names, for that they find so coold entertaynment in forreyne cuntryes, that they had rather lyve in prison at home & suffer all endurance for Gods cause. M^r heborne[1384] dyed in the Clincke the 4. of december. Mr Musket[1385] prisoner in Newgate they say is become a Ies: Mr Rontree[1386] hath preached at yorke often, the Bis.[1387] called him before him & reprehended him for preachinge Cath. doctrine, wherof they say his sermons wholie consisted, he answered his doctrine was sound & good, & that it was confirmed by authoritie, doctors & all good learninge. the B. replied that he smelt of them from whence he came of the dreggs of poperye, & that if he preached not other doctrine, & give [sic for 'gave'] better testomie [sic for 'testimonie' ?] of his sinceritie of his faith & conformitie,: [sic] he should have no pension, which was L^l by yeare,: to whom he made answere it was for money he onlie came to them, & wild them to take it for that he was a Cath. preist & so would lyve & dye; and was sorie

---

[1381] Cf. Fincham, *Prelate as Pastor*, 40–1.

[1382] Robert Venner. See Anstr. II, 328; **Letter 45**. (The priest Simon Fennell had left the country in mid-1613 in discontent after Birkhead had dismissed him from his assistantship and replaced him with John Bennett, though Bennett said Fennell had been allowed to choose Bennett as his successor, AAW A XII, nos 110, 149, 255.)

[1383] Samuel Spifame.

[1384] John Jackson had reported to More on 6 December 1613 that Anthony Hebburn died on 2 December, and that John Colleton 'was with him to reclayme him from his opinion & he told him that he submitted him selfe to the church & if any thing he did were offensive to god he was sory for it. yet he added withall. as yow said he to m^r coll. deall with me to change my opinion soe I prayee give me leave to perswade yow to it, and I wold loose a finger upon condition yow wold alter yours', AAW A XII, no. 218 (p. 486).

[1385] George Fisher.

[1386] See **Letter 47**.

[1387] Tobias Matthew, Archbishop of York. Cf. J.C.H. Aveling, *Northern Catholics* (1966), 208.

for th*a*t he had done. [in margin: 'he remaineth in yorke prison.']¹³⁸⁸
The booke w*hi*ch Widd: made in behalfe of th*e* Oath was translated
into English,¹³⁸⁹ & an addition was put therto as they say against Swares,
wher he did allow his opinion as pr*o*bable, wherfor it is restrayned &
called in;¹³⁹⁰ and th*e* deane of Paules¹³⁹¹ is inioyned to writ against
Suares. you have hard I dare say or this of one dʳ Caryer who was the
K. chaplyne & of great fame for preaching & learninge, is now w*i*th
Card. Peron, he hath bene sent for backe againe, w*i*th great offer of
pr*e*ferment.¹³⁹² One dʳ Bull¹³⁹³ is become a musitian to th*e* Archduke,
but it was for debt more then for devotion.¹³⁹⁴ The Irerishe [sic]
speaker¹³⁹⁵ was sent for out of the towre unto th*e* counsell as if he
should have bene dismissed, but the L. cheif Iustice did much inveigh
against him, & so was sent backe againe. he onely of th*a*t companie
remayneth. The Ladie Elizabeth they say is w*i*th child & w*i*thin two
monethes of her account, two Ladies are sent to her,¹³⁹⁶ they w*hi*ch
come from her say that she is but in poore estate, supplie must be
made yearlie from hence. Two mariages is celebrated this Christenmas
as th*e* one betwene Mʳⁱˢ drummer¹³⁹⁷ th*e* Q. cheife & best beloved
woman, & the L. Rockesbury,¹³⁹⁸ and th*e* Earle of Somersett, & th*e* L.
Francis hawert,¹³⁹⁹ th*e* laitleie dyvorced L: of th*e* Earle of Essex w*hi*ch
is p*e*rformed w*i*th great solemnitie.¹⁴⁰⁰ It was a report th*a*t the B. of
Cant.¹⁴⁰¹ & of London¹⁴⁰² were cited to appeare before the counsell to
give ther reasons why they did not give ther voyces to th*e* dyvorce, but
I heare not what was done[.] it is thought they are not in so great
favour w*i*th the King as they have bene. Allso th*e* L. Sᵗ Iohns th*e* Marques
his sonne¹⁴⁰³ hath maried the L. Mountagues eldest daughter,¹⁴⁰⁴ & one

¹³⁸⁸ Rountree's pardon was renewed in February 1618, Anstr. II, 273.
¹³⁸⁹ Preston, *Theologicall Disputation*.
¹³⁹⁰ See **Letter 51**.
¹³⁹¹ John Overall.
¹³⁹² Questier, 'Crypto-Catholicism', 51.
¹³⁹³ John Bull, composer and organist of the Chapel Royal.
¹³⁹⁴ George Abbot claimed in mid-December 1613 that Bull had gone abroad because
of an adultery charge laid against him before the ecclesiastical commissioners, *Downshire
MSS* IV, 270.
¹³⁹⁵ William Talbot. See **Letter 47**.
¹³⁹⁶ McClure, 489.
¹³⁹⁷ Jane, daughter of Patrick, third Baron Drummond. See McClure, 504, 507.
¹³⁹⁸ Robert Ker, first Baron Roxburgh.
¹³⁹⁹ Frances Howard.
¹⁴⁰⁰ McClure, 485, 495–7, 498–9.
¹⁴⁰¹ George Abbot.
¹⁴⁰² John King.
¹⁴⁰³ William Paulet, Lord St John, son of William Paulet, fourth Marquis of Winchester.
¹⁴⁰⁴ Mary Browne.

M[1405] Tirwhit[1405] of Lincolnesh. the second.[1406] but to litle comfort or content.[1407] one M[r] Reasbye S[r] Thomas Reas. soonne of yorkesh. who was brought up a paige to the Archduke havinge lyved badlie about the Court & the cittie, havinge spent riotously his fortunes, cut laitly his owne throat & so withall made shipwracke of his owne soule:[1408] It is a report from the Low cuntryes that widdr: last booke is condemned & reiected by P.[1409] And that the Ies. are settinge up schooles at Leades;[1410] & that the Archd:[1411] hath prohibited them by edict for that it would be hindrance unto Lovaine, gyvinge them in choise eyther to forgoe them, or ther teaching at doway.[1412] Thus commendinge me most hartelie unto you hopinge you remember me daylie in your prayers who day by day standeth in more & more need, which you earnestlie you [sic] would do if you saw the bad disposition & daylie decay in all thinges & estates. 31. december 1613.

(On p. 524)

The Bishope of Winchester his sonne[1413] is made knight, for his fathers good service about the laite dyvorce, & some in iest & scoffinge manner call him Nullatie Billson, of the nullatie of the mariaige.[1414] S[r] Henry Iames for denyinge the Oath hath lost all his landes & goodes, at the

[1405] William Tyrwhit of Kettleby, Lincolnshire.

[1406] Katherine Browne.

[1407] Robert Pett had reported to More on 29 September 1613 (NS) that a letter from Birkhead via William Cape at St Omer informed him that the second Viscount Montague's daughter, Mary, was being pushed into marrying Lord St John whereas her own inclination was to marry Sir Thomas Somerset, second son of Edward Somerset, fourth Earl of Worcester (though he was not worth above £500 a year), AAW A XII, no. 177. However, in March/April 1615 it was being said by Francis Hore and Robert Pett that the two were 'good frendes' and living 'lovingly and peaceably' with each other, AAW A XIV, nos 71 (p. 239), 75 (p. 253). (Her second husband was William, second son of Thomas Arundell, first Baron Arundell of Wardour.)

[1408] This seems to be a false rumour about Gilbert Reresby, son of Sir Thomas Reresby of Thribergh and Mary, daughter of Sir John Monson of Carleton, Leicestershire. See Sir William Dugdale, ed. J. Clay, *Dugdale's Visitation of Yorkshire* (3 vols, Exeter, 1899), I, 330 (noting that Gilbert, who died in Paris in 1641, had been brought up with the Archduchess Isabella, infanta of Spain, in the Low Countries). His sister Jane married Sir John Shelley of Michelgrove, Sussex. The Reresbies and the Brownes of Cowdray both married into the Tyrwhit family of Kettleby in Lincolnshire, W.C. Metcalfe (ed.), *The Visitation of the County of Lincolnshire* (1882), 69; W.B. Bannerman (ed.), *The Visitations of the County of Sussex* (1905), 84. It was alleged in January 1616 that Sir William Monson, Gilbert Reresby's uncle, had recommended that Gilbert go abroad to be a page to the archduke, PRO, SP 14/86/7, fo. 14r.

[1409] Pope Paul V.

[1410] Liège.

[1411] Archduke Albert of Austria.

[1412] See Guilday, *English Catholic Refugees*, 151–2.

[1413] Thomas Bilson jnr.

[1414] McClure, 484.

first he might have compounded for two thousand poundes but now the K. will not suffer it to be taken, but that he shall forfeit all, & since he hath laitlie befallen him allmost some 18. hundred Acres of marsh grownd about Rumney which allso is seized upon.[1415] Adeu, god send you a good new yeare, and all your frends a better then the last. This 31. of december. 1613.

yours, yours for ever

    Ro. Cl.

Addressed: To my wellbeloved and very worthy [fr]eind Mr George West thes

DD

Endorsed: (1) December. 31. 1613. Claph.

        (2) Receaved: wed Mart. 19⎤

            Answ: good fr Mart. 28.⎦ 1614

54 *Robert Clapham (Richard Broughton) to George West (Thomas More) (1 February 1614)   (AAW A XIII, no. 17, pp. 39–40. Holograph)*

My very deare & true frend.

    It doth much trouble me that since St Barnabas day wherof my letter[1416] was dated which you last receyved you have not receyved any more, so many moneth now expired; in August I wrot as I take it,[1417] wherin somethinge did particularly concerne a frend of myne, sendinge you therwith a bill of Atturney for the recovery of a certayne debt,[1418] wherof I stood in hope neare this time to have received an answere, since which time I have together with this writen five times,[1419] as you may gather by some of my former lettres, according to my true account, though of the dates I do but make coniecture, reservinge no notes therof; I should be sorie that any of them should miscarrye for I did my endevour to satisfie your expectation,: [sic] in a whole yeare I

[1415] See **Letter 28**; Bowler, 'Sir Henry James'. For grants upon this forfeiture (to David Ramsay, William Ramsay, John Sandilands, Sir Thomas Cornwallis and Sir Richard Wigmore), see PRO, SO 3/5 (August 1613).

[1416] AAW A XII, no. 105 (11 June 1613).

[1417] AAW A XII, no. 152 (24 August 1613).

[1418] In his letter to More of 24 August, AAW A XII, no. 152 (p. 341), Broughton said that he was enclosing a letter of attorney from the unidentified friend for the recovery of the debt. The friend 'hath a brother yet lyvinge (I mean the d^r) who by right is his heire, his wife is a Cath. & he in mind, though some esteeme him perverse in manners & neighberhood, his name is Henry'.

[1419] Broughton's letters to More since August 1613 were written on 24 August 1613, AAW A XII, no. 152, 22 October 1613, **Letter 47**, 21 November 1613, AAW A XII, no. 209, and 31 December 1613, **Letter 53**. The reason for the late arrival of these letters is not clear.

have not written more oftener then within this halfe: and now I cannot
tunne my pipes unto a more ioyfull note, then heertofore, but day by
day more lamentable. The pursevantes rageth fare & neare with seaven
sometimes in a company onelie <u>one havinge a commission</u>, with two
men to attend him in his lyverye as they say, no shire is a moneth free,
my neighbors have bene of lait very much molested, more then ever
heertofor; men are so fearefull that they <u>will scarce give a nights</u>
<u>lodginge, never lesse comfort & charitie found</u>. thes courses of impov-
erishing men, & takinge from them <u>ther</u> lyvelihoodes, hath bene more
hurtfull then if they had taken ther lyves. New writes *ad melius inquirendum*
hath bene sent into every <u>shire yea for those w</u>hich had the kinges
broad seale:[1420] a widowe one M^ris Banister[1421] havinge the broad seale
havinge made a composition for a sume of money, & paying yearlie a
Rent into the Excheker, her landes is found at a higher rate then ever
they were let for, & she must compound againe, & soe it hapneth to
many moe;[1422] Mr Abington[1423] havinge lost all through that wicked &
unhappie pouder plott, baught his landes againe, wherfor he standes
thousandes in debt, now they have taken halfe of his landes quite from
him, & left onelie the other halfe for his heire. The counsell hath [been]
sitting very hard upon Irish affaires.[1424] One Sr Iames Goffe[1425] they
say, being to returne into Ireland went unto the King to know if he

---

[1420] See **Letter 48**.

[1421] Mary Banester, widow of Edward Banester snr. She was a sister of Robert Southwell
SJ. She appears to have been assessed for her recusancy after her husband's death on 9
September 1606, PRO, C 142/292/177; PRO, E 368/533, mem. 153a. The inquisition,
on 11 October 1608, was carried out under the direction of Sir George Gunter and
Adrian Stoughton. The sums levied on her estate (in Compton, Stoughton, Trotton,
Chithurst, Southampton and the Isle of Wight) were indeed trivial, perhaps not unrelated
to the fact that she had Gunter relatives. Benjamin Norton reported to More on 19
November 1613, however, that her residence in Sussex had been searched on 1 November
(as had her conformist son (Edward jnr)'s house in Hampshire), AAW A XII, no. 204.
(The Banester family had links with the secular priests' patrons – Viscount Montague
and the Dormers. Mary Banester's daughter had married into the Dormer family, PRO,
PROB 11/131, fo. 32r-v. Edward Banester snr had sat in the Commons early in Elizabeth's
reign for Midhurst, effectively in the gift of the Browne family, Hasler I, 390–1.)

[1422] From the records of receipts of recusancy fines in PRO, E 401 there appears to
have been no increase in payments which Mary Banester made between this date and
her death in 1617. Other recusants within the group of families regularly mentioned by
the secular newsletter writers, for example Edward Wyborne, were subject to sharp
increases in payments for their recusancy at this time, PRO, E 401/2303–5.

[1423] Thomas Habington of Hindlip, Worcestershire.

[1424] For the political situation in Ireland, see A. Clarke with R. Dudley Edwards,
'Pacification, plantation and the catholic question, 1603–23', in T.W. Moody, F.X. Martin,
and F.J. Byrne, *A New History of Ireland*, vol. 3, *Early Modern Ireland 1534–1691* (Oxford,
1976), 213–17.

[1425] Sir James Gough. See Clarke and Dudley Edwards, 'Plantation', 216–17; *CSP Ireland
1611–14*, p. lv.

would commaund him any service into Ireland amongst other thinges
wherof his Maiestie spooke he told him he would not trouble them for
ther religion; as this Goffe saith. He goinge into Ireland reported thes
speaches confidentlie, wherupon [th]e deputie[1426] sent for him to know
if he would stand to such reportes, for which he put him in prison,
afterwardes they s[a]y a proclamation was sent thither that the kinge
mente not vi et armis to compell them, but by good & whole some
lawes to drawe them to conformitie & due obedience for betwene
religion & loyaltie he maketh no differance; he is thaught to be very
much adverse to all papist & against P.[1427] It is said that they pay
weeklie money for not cominge to church, dyverse of the Irishe is sent
for & are comming over. Hundred of writes were sent into the Cuntreys
for gentlemen to come to be bound to good abearance to the Kings
Maiestie a thing intollerable, which cannot be so stricklie observed, but
that they shall be found transgressinge in somethinge; the execution
was untill Candlemas transferred, god knoweth what will afterwardes
ensue, & be the conclusion. Ther are xx p. againe in Newgate, Mr
Grey[1428] the great Commis. is committed thither & one Mr Chamberlaine[1429] of laite, Mr Samson Faircloth[1430] is prisoner in the gatehouse.
one Mr Smallman who came from your partes & from Ierusalem was
cast of his horse upon his head & never after spake word,[1431] many such
mischaunces have hapned this yeare. Sr Tho: posthumus Hobbie
persecuteth in the North.[1432] Ther is some speaches that a parlament
shall be in England shortlie & another in Ireland. The kinge being told
that many of the nobilitie was given to papistycallie [sic], he sent for
the younge L. Mordan,[1433] to be delivered to be brought up by a
Bishope, his mother pretended that he was sicke, [t]he K. sent his
phisition who found him in bed, who feeling his pulse said that [he]
must returne a true answere, (for he was sworne,) that he found him
not sicke. Don Luysa the Spanishe Ladie died on St Tho.[1434] even before

---

[1426] Arthur Chichester, first Baron Chichester of Belfast.

[1427] *i.e.* priests.

[1428] According to Richard Broughton, writing to More on 27 February 1614, 'Grey the
Comis of fran: [Franciscans]...giveth no good edification for the keeper hath complayned
that he is drunke allmost every day, & hath bad women comminge to him'. Gray had
not been with the other priests 'at any good exercise since Candl.', AAW A XIII, no. 38
(p. 89).

[1429] John Varder.

[1430] Alexander Fairclough SJ.

[1431] See **Letter 51**.

[1432] For Hoby's activities as a JP and a recusancy commissioner, see Questier, *Conversion,
Politics and Religion*, 107, 140, 166.

[1433] John Mordaunt, fifth Baron Mordaunt and future Earl of Peterborough was
removed to the custody of Archbishop Abbot, Cokayne X, 496.

[1434] 20 December. *Cf.* **Letter 52**.

Christenmas. her bodie is to be caryed into Spaine.[1435] the Ies. had all her goodes. M[ris] Dakers is dead the xth of Ian. according to ther account.[1436] The Ladie Eliz. the Palsgraves Ladie is delivered of a sonne, great reioysing ther was neare the Court with bonefyres, & the Prince[1437] with his Court plaid at foote ball with ther hates. My L. of Somersetes mariage was accounted the greatest mariage that was of a subiect in England thes many yeares, some reportes that the giftes which were given him were worth a hundred thousand poundes. the Sp. Emb. was invited therto, & was ther at dynner. he is esteemed the greatest subiect in Engl. he hath obteyned as the rumour is thirteine Mannors of the Earle of westmerlandes,[1438] one of the kinges sonnes titles, and a noble Ladie. My L. of Northampton is not in that favour & grace that he hath bene. Widdring:[1439] is writinge (they say), books very hard.[1440] Ther is a light report that M[r] Ed. Walp.[1441] is now made Superiour of the Ies. Some are to be sent over to move a mariage for the prince with France & some sayth it will be with spaine.[1442] My grandfather[1443] is very feeble & weake, men iudgeth that he cannot endure very longe by reason of his infirme constitution, he wisheth his children[1444] to provide as well as they can in the meane space for ther estates heareafter, for that he lingreth but the time. I do not doubt but you consider the estate of thinges, & will provide therfor as much as you can, to prevent what daungers may befall. my iudgment is he doth dailie decay, looketh very weeklie, eateth but litle, but lyveth more by drinke, troubled with thinges as much at home as abroad, & often times with small matters; but he is of that mind that he shall continue longer yet one yeare[.] M[r] Ben:[1445] hath refused to be one of the number of twelve[1446]. your letter

[1435] CRS 68, 26.

[1436] Matthew Kellison noted that she died on 'Friday in the octaves of the Epiphanie', i.e. 11 January 1614 (NS), AAW A XIII, no. 9 (p. 22).

[1437] Prince Charles.

[1438] Cf. Tilbrook, 'Aspects of the Government and Society of County Durham', 188–90.

[1439] Roland (Thomas) Preston OSB.

[1440] According to Richard Broughton, in February 1614, 'Widdrington of the South is up every day be foure of the cloocke & is gone abroad. Men iudge that he is printinge of bookes', AAW A XIII, no. 38 (p. 89).

[1441] See CRS 75, 323.

[1442] John Chamberlain noted on 10 February 1614 the appointment of twelve commissioners to negotiate for a match with France, McClure, 506.

[1443] i.e. George Birkhead.

[1444] The secular priests.

[1445] Benjamin Norton.

[1446] Birkhead noted on 31 January 1614 that he had urged Norton to become an assistant 'but he refuseth it utterly, and giveth me leave to compleine against him'. Birkhead also said that another priest 'm[r] vaughan' [identity uncertain] in Staffordshire likewise would not accept the charge 'though willinge of him selfe', 'because his patrone threatneth him to putt him out of the doores', AAW A XIII, no. 15 (p. 34).

of November 24. I have receyved. we heare that Count Buckoy[1447] in Fl. is to go with fyve thousand horse to helpe the Emperor against the Turke, & that the Archduke is dead[.][1448] Ther is no doubt but d[r]. K.[1449] w[ill] conioyne in all thinges in what he can, for so hath he written, onelie he is fearfull to displease his Sup: & to ordayne hastilie any new matters, I did write to him & caused some of our frendes to do the like. It is a marvelouse thinge that men should be made beleeve abrod by some false & forged taile caryers, that ther is no persecution, whenas never the Cath. cause was moore shaken therby, & the times more hard & daungerous. every one searchinge, as a wolfe for his prey, to find out some wayes and pretences, that wrongfullie he may possesse a Cath. lyvinge. Accept in good part (my deare frend) my scribled, abrupt, false & bad englishe lynes, I seeke more for brevitie, & matter, then for to attend to wordes & methode: And helpe us with all christian pittie & continuall prayers that you eyther have or can begg for us, that we may constantlie & stoutlie abide the furious fyre & heate of the day, & to the end possesse our soules with patience. And so I rest. yours for ever.
    R. C.
[In margin: 'The first of Feb: 1613'.]
(On p. 40)
Addressed: [To] the worshipfull his very lovinge Frend George West Esquier give thes.
Endorsed: (1) febr. 1. 1614. Claph.
    (2) Recea. wed. Mart. 1 ⎫
        Answ. good fr. Mart. 28.⎭ 1614

55 *John Nelson (Jackson) to George West (Thomas More) (1 March 1614)   (AAW A XIII, no. 39, pp. 91–2. Holograph. [p. 92 is obscured in places.])*

My v.r. & b. sir
    Being at this present in a pathmos[1450] yow cannot expect the certayne report of any fresh occurrences, yet because I did not lately write I thowght my lettres wold be welcome how meanly soever they were fraught. I receyved a comission of procuration for yow from our

[1447] Charles Bonaventure de Longueval, Count of Bucquoi. *Cf. Downshire MSS* IV, 258, 262, 264, 296, 301–2, 319.
[1448] *CSPV 1613–15*, 84, for Archduke Albert's illness (but not death) at this time.
[1449] Matthew Kellison.
[1450] Presumably a reference to the island at the northern end of the Dodecanese group, where St John the Divine was exiled under Domitian, Cross (ed.), *Oxford Dictionary of the Christian Church*, 1024.

superior[1451] & at my coming from london which was 6. dayes agoe I
sent it. I did also in my last to m[r] pet,[1452] intreat him to signifie unto
yow that I had dealt about the money and that I found yowr cosen[1453]
ready to pay it at easter tearme at the furthest, thowgh he wold presently
have disbursed some part therof. but I now fear me, that it cometh too
late for m[r] Mayny as I perceave, is arrived and hath made it over to
my la. R.[1454] for m[r] Th. & m[r] Io: R.[1455] who are there with yow. and
upon occasion of this I hold it fit to enforme yow, that pseudowiddr.[1456]
is great with their mother and yow know how easy a matter it is for a
man of sufficiency to sway with his freinds & consequently yow must
think that she will incline to think favorably of what he doth. which
disposition is soothed from thence. for she told me that she had lettres
from thence (but wold not graunt that they were from her s.) that widdr.
his boke was not censured and that they there did hold it a learned
work & that much was not spoken against it etcetera. I wold not have
yow take notice of this for it wi[ll] be knowne to come from mee but
yow may make use of the knowledge. it is also written to her that Fitzh.
is answering the booke,[1457] but that he hath not the ground of learning
and therfore must in such points have others to set him downe what
he must say. verely if theyr come not some one substantiall & theologicall
answer to such points as he is thowght to have the advantage in against
Bell[1458] Gretz.[1459] Less.[1460] etcetera, they will never have that credit they
formerly had, for some of his obiections are plausible and they are
holden to have been much overseen in those points which he excepteth
against. Fitzsimons[1461] an Irish Ies. as I am told for a certayne, hath
written an answer,[1462] in tearmes, against Rolandum prestonum but as
yet it is not come owt, and I fear me it is not soe substantiall as is
requisite. there is dayly expected an other booke in aunswer to skul-
kenius, weston, & soarez in latin. Io. Harsenet[1463] Bishop of Rochester

[1451] George Birkhead.
[1452] Robert Pett.
[1453] Sir William Roper.
[1454] Anne (daughter of Sir John Cotton jnr of Lanwade), wife of Sir William Roper.
[1455] Thomas and John Roper, sons of Sir William and Lady Roper.
[1456] Roland (Thomas) Preston OSB.
[1457] Thomas Fitzherbert published *The Reply of T.F. in defence of the two first Chapters of his Supplement to the Discussion &c. impugned by one falsely naming himself Roger Widdrington, in a Latin Booke intituled, Disputatio Theologica de Iuramento Fidelitatis* (St Omer, 1614). See ARCR II, 58–9; Milward II, 112–13.
[1458] Cardinal Robert Bellarmine SJ.
[1459] Jakob Gretzer SJ.
[1460] Leonardus Lessius SJ.
[1461] Henry FitzSimon SJ.
[1462] If published, this work has not survived. FitzSimon briefly noticed Preston in his *Brittannomachia Ministrorum* (Douai, 1614), 173, 179.
[1463] Jackson means John Buckeridge.

(who was if yet he be not, very well affected to cath. rel.) hath written a great booke[1464] as bigg as stow his large chronicle[1465] against the p. his power in temporalls in answer to all that Bellar hath written therof & in defence of Berclay.[1466] there is a litle booke under D. singletons name,[1467] done as they say by lessius which hath handled some things more substantially & very breifly then any that I have seen. yow may doe well to get m^r fitz. to shift of that of the 13 preists[1468] soe as their reputations may be saved & their persons not indaungered as v.g. Noe mervayle if he seek to wrest their action to his purpose how undeservedly soever who was not ashamed to wrest owt of Bellar. his works an Apollogy for kings against Bellarmine. but yow have this point & much more in that paper which d. champ. hath sent yow. Is it not strang that all this while the po. will not graunt us that the Ies confessarius may be removed from the colledge of doway. Is their any society in the world that hath one of an other body appointed over them. How litle love doth he shew unto us that suffer soe much for him. thowgh he will answer that it is for God & the good of owr owne soules that we suffer. yet considering that wee incurr many daungers ['wyll' deleted] which (happly) wee need not & that he is to have a respect to the bodie wherof he is head one wold think that he shold grawnt us such easy requests as wee make, being things that weere to be graunded [sic] thowgh wee deserved nothing at all. Is there any colledge or monastery in christendome forbid to have private lessons among themselves? wee are. Is any cleargy prohibited to take degree when they shall be thowght fitt by any university? wee are. Is any Body forced to have a conf. of an other bodie? wee are. Are the clergy of any nation forbid to live collegiatly togither? owrs is at paris. and as it is more then probably thowght by the popes officers. for m^r sackvile[1469] told me that the Nuncio[1470] his Auditor did threaten as much to him when wee were there. [p. 92]

I fear mee our superior wyll not continew long[.] his stomack is quite gone[.] his leggs doe swell & the swelling goeth to his bodie also himselfe not able to go owt of his chambre, yet he taketh great paynes & care

[1464] John Buckeridge, *De Potestate Papae in Rebus Temporalibus* (1614).

[1465] For John Stow's chronicle, see STC 23319–40.

[1466] Barclay, *De Potestate Papae*.

[1467] William Singleton, *Discussio Decreti Magni Concilii Lateranensis* (Mainz, 1613); ARCR I, no. 1086.

[1468] See **Letter 48**.

[1469] Thomas Sackville had appointed John Jackson as sole trustee of the fund which Sackville had set up to sustain the writers' college, Allison, 'Richard Smith's Gallican Backers', part II, 261.

[1470] Robert Ubaldini. Anthony Champney thought that Ubaldini had been less than energetic in opposing the French council of state's order that the priests should not live collegially in Paris, AAW A XII, no. 239.

in the common buisines. I cold willing [sic] intreat yow to procure me a dispensation thowg[h] perhaps I shall not much use it, yet it will be a great quietnes to my mynd. I as others noe dowbt also, doe live sometymes amongst Heret. or protest. such as I wold not have know me for a cath as when I am forced to hire a lodging etcetera for a tyme. Now, it is soe unusuall to refuse flesh they ordinarily dressing noething els, or at least having litle fish an[d] [word illegible] of flesh with it, and often tymes they use their [word deleted] fish on fleshedayes[.] herof groweth diverse inconveniences. first a troble to them for me v.g. to dresse a speciall diet, wherby I may be the lesse gratefull thowgh I pay for what I take[.] next, an [word illegible] token that I am a cath and they not knowing from whence I come and of what place I am, as they do of other cath. gentlemen, they presently coniecture that I am more. mᵣ coll. doth dispense with me when I am dowbtfull wherfor I may or noe, but because that is but an occasion of much scruple & disquietnes, for I shall be dowbfull whether it be a reall doubt or noe, or whether I flatter my selfe, or whether he may dispense if I shold be at any such place, at such tyme as I might be at an other where I need not be put to that diet, for indeed sometymes I might be at some other place without [three words illegible] make choice [(] at the least for the contentment of my mynd etcetera) to be at a lodging with expense. theise I say & the like make mee [word obliterated] yow to get me [word illegible] of him who can in this point etiamsine causae dispense, which an other [can] not. & the like I intreat for 2 meales, it being as notorious to abstayne from supper as from flesh. it may be added also that they here take noe notice of vigills as yow know & a man shall in his travayle or [?] at other place be wondred at if he refuse the ordinary diet[.] I did write to your monsignor[1471] & also subscribe to 2 others one to hym, the other to the Auditer[1472] but I hear not of your receipt of them. God ever keep yow & prosper your indevours. In hast. 1 martii.

yours ever N.

Addressed: To the worshipfull my most assured good Freind Mᵣ George West give thease
Endorsed: (1) Mart. 1. 1614 N. [word deleted]
    (2) Recea. twesd. April. 15.⎫
        Answ. sate. May. 10.   ⎬ 1614.
                                ⎭

[1471] John Baptist Vives.
[1472] Mozzenega.

56 *Anthony Champney to Thomas More (25 March 1614 (NS)* [1473]*)   (AAW A XIII, no. 56, pp. 141–2. Holograph. [p. 142 is obscured in places.])*

Ever honored s[r]

to yours of the last of Februarie I say I will not forgett to signify your mynd to Thomas Heathe att the first commoditie. The matche with France goethe still forward and ys sayd to be accorded also in England[.] think with your self howe you may doe anie good and soe shale we for others doe not sleepe therein. Doct. Kellison dothe alwayes continue his good desire to bringe althinges into good order but he differethe in way of proceedinge from us. He hathe geven a procuratione to Father Anthonie[1474] in spayne for his business there[1475] which I doe not knowe what effect yt may have[.] m[r] pett will goe thither yf he be advised by other his frendes[.] And for my [word deleted] part I think well of his iorney thoughe he have not yet procuratione to deale for the colledge[.][1476] For he may have yt in tyme and his presence will further the matter as I suppose and he may folowe in the meane while his owne affayre[.][1477] I feare yf nothinge be resolved there to Doct Kell contentment in competent tyme he will leave his place to whome will take yt:[1478] therefore as you can yt would doe well to solicit the graunt of his iust demandes lest all be brought to former despeyre. of m[r] maine[1479] I have writen long since. and also of your frendes dispositione to content you. we will endevoure to put m[r] Griffithe[1480] in credit

[1473] Wrongly assigned in AAW A catalogue to 26 March.

[1474] Anthony Hoskins SJ.

[1475] Hoskins had arrived in Spain in mid-1613 to succeed Joseph Creswell SJ as vice-prefect of the English SJ mission, *Downshire MSS* IV, 149; Allison, 'Later Life', 79–80.

[1476] *i.e.* for Douai. See **Letter 40**.

[1477] *i.e.* the suit against Gabriel Colford. See **Letter 35**.

[1478] In September 1613 Kellison had complained to More how he had come 'to this troublesome place, from a place [Rheims] where I was so well beloved, and am still desired importunately, where I had a quiet and honest condition, and was promised, under the bishop's hand and seal, the prebend and dignity of the great church, after the decease of one who is almost fourscore years old', TD V, p. cxci.

[1479] See AAW A XIII, nos 4, 23. It is not clear whether this indicates John Mayney.

[1480] Griffin Floyd. See **Letter 26**. In mid-December 1612 Birkhead had notified More that Floyd was 'most redie to helpe us, and I have in part alredie begonne to employ him. he hath the languages and is much addicted to serve us in our cause', AAW A XI, no. 228 (p. 657). It seems this was partly to make up for the loss of Thomas Heath, see **Letter 17**, and partly for the purpose of communicating safely with foreign ambassadors in London. See AAW A XI, no. 252 (p. 737), a memorandum specifying among other things the need for someone 'to reside at london bothe practicall & skilfull in langwages to moove the Imbassadores to affecte us & our cause'. But Birkhead informed More in April 1613 that Floyd, 'not being able to shew his face, is not fitt for me to use', AAW A XII, no. 78 (p. 168), and shortly after, that since Floyd had 'disgusted a frend of ours' it was better to have no more to do with him, AAW A XII, no. 86 (p. 187). Floyd later offered his services to the regime in England, PRO, SP 14/81/59. ii, 60, 61, 70. There are several letters from Floyd to More in AAW A.

agayne. Here ys with us a good honest man one of those which were
banished by the Spanishe Embassadores meanes[1481] whome I would
commend unto you to putt In Lygorno[1482] yf your camerado[1483] doe not
stay. He would discharge anie thinge well with the Inglishe and wantethe
not latin but he hathe not anie other language[.] God rewarde you for
the generall care you shewe of all. I hope in tyme your example will
breed emulatione in others to folowe your steppes: Doct Bishop hathe
writen unto you the calumnie geven out there agaynst our Reverend
superioure[1484] and enquired after here by the nuncio to whome m^r
Grifithe hath geven satisfactione in writinge as understandinge the
matter and this ordinarie yt ys sent upp as they say[.] This which I
send you of m^r nelsons[1485] I doubt not acquaintethe you with the
declininge state of our superiores healthe beinge suche as ys not expected
can continue till Easter there. And therefore necessarie to be insinuated
before hand. And after the matter commended to god and to his
Holiness to omitt noe occasiones wherein we may benefit the comone[.]

   In Ingland ys a parlement to begin the fift of theyre aprill where
some hope of a dispositione to more moderatione[.] I sawe yesterday
cardinall perron and towld him yt was wished that he would present
the kinge with some part at least of his traveyles agaynst that tyme as

---

[1481] For the priests released in August 1613 to go abroad with the Spanish ambassador
Alonso de Velasco, see *APC 1613–14*, 179. They included Richard Cooper alias Henry
Cooper alias Palmer.

[1482] Livorno.

[1483] Lewis Vaughan. See **Letters 15**, **16**. Birkhead reported on 20 May 1612 that
'about michaelmas' Vaughan would come to Rome 'for devotion', and intended to stay
for three or four years, AAW A XI, no. 83 (p. 237). See AAW A XII, no. 245, a draft
petition from Vaughan, who had already spent six months studying in Rome, asking for
an augmentation of his papal pension of twenty-five ducats. By April 1614 Vaughan was
writing to More asking for financial help, though he had not surrendered his place at
Livorno, AAW A XIII, no. 81. The anti-Jesuit Vaughan was clearly intended to strengthen
the seculars' number and influence in Italy, AAW A XIII, no. 78. On 12 May 1614 (NS)
Vaughan wrote to More that one 'mr palmer hath bene heare of late and staied heare
14 daies[.] I used him kindly and for his sake did his brother some good turnes' but now,
according to English Catholics at Livorno, Palmer 'hath sought to supplant me and to
geat my place frome me. it is saide that hee hath prevailed and that he is to come downe
shortly', AAW A XIII, no. 100 (pp. 255–6). It is not clear whether 'Palmer' is the priest
Richard Cooper alias Henry Cooper alias Palmer who was listed for banishment in
August 1613.

[1484] Birkhead had reported to More on 26 July 1613 that, in England as much as in
Rome, some people were giving out 'false rumors against us', including the slanders that
More had returned to England and 'offered your selfe to the magistrate', and that
Birkhead was 'in great favour with the state because' Archbishop Abbot, 'gessinge where
I am, causeth me not to be apprehended'. Birkhead did, however, inform More that
Birkhead's 'greatest frend' (*i.e.* Viscount Montague) was summoned by Abbot who
questioned him about the archpriest, but unaggressively, and so, clearly, 'they have no
great tooth' against the archpriest, AAW A XII, no. 132 (pp. 291, 293).

[1485] **Letter 55**.

beinge a meane to dispose him further. He answered me that he would
hasten yt for that consideratione[.] m^r Ireland^{1486} and I went to him
cheefly to deliver [p. 142] him a letter frome Doct Carrier who hathe
made the spirituall exercise with the Iesuits att [word obscured: 'liege'
?] and as he writethe, thinkethe to goe [to] lovayne^{1487} A course litle
sortinge [?] with his cheef desire which ys to worke some good with the
kinge for catholique Religione. And in this he hathe beene ether craftely
or forcibly overrought[.] ['The' deleted] He saythe yt ys writen him
that the kinge hathe read his motives and nether compleynethe of the
maner of his writinge nor of the thinge yt selfe yet [?] spake openly in
approbatione of prayer to saintes of confessione, of worshipinge Images
and adoratione of the b sacramente[.] The cardinall tooke his letter
verie kindly and will answer yt. He hathe procured him all [word
illegible] the pensione which was geven by the clergie to m^r Constable^{1488}
which ys 200^{li} [?] and promisethe more. The Doct [word deleted]
writethe that he ys profered good conditio[n]s where he ys but will
entertayne none till the kinge hathe dispossessed him of his benefices[.]
The cardinall added further that he knewe well that his cominge to
him would be well taken by the kinge so that I think we shale see him
here in tyme[.] I wonder m^r Fixer^{1489} ys so backwarde or slow in his
owne affayre[.] I hope you are wise enoughe for advanceinge anie
money before you see good assurance of his deliverie and also of his
employment ether there with you or with us here[.] The noyse of these
troubles here ys not altogether layd downe thoughe yt be generally
hoped that all wilbe pacifyed[.] you say noe more of Father creswell.
nor ever write ye anithinge of the affayres of Hungarie or of the
proceedinges of the Turk[.] I ame not my selfe muche desirouse of this
latter newes but here ys a frend that often enquirethe of me what
newes theare of those matters knowinge I have letters often tymes[.]
Father Austin^{1490} passed this way this last weeke and towld me that he
expected answer of a letter frome you this ordinarie[.] Here I have one
for Father Gabriell^{1491} but that canot be yt[.] Comend me to your

^{1486} Richard Ireland, formerly of Christ Church, Oxford, and headmaster of Westminster school since 1598. In 1610 he had left the country for France where he was
subsequently reconciled to the Church of Rome and was ordained a Catholic priest,
Anstr. II, 167; Questier, 'Crypto-Catholicism', 60.

^{1487} Foley VII, p. xlvi.

^{1488} Champney informed More in a letter of 22 October 1613 (NS) that Henry
Constable, 'departinge...long since towardes the Spawe [Spa] to meete there therle of
Southampton and cominge short of him' went to Liège 'to meete with Doct Carrier' but
'was seased with a hot feaver and dissenterie and dispatched in 7 or 8 dayes', AAW A
XII, no. 190 (p. 421).

^{1489} John Fixer. See Anstr. I, 118.

^{1490} John (Augustine) Bradshaw OSB.

^{1491} William (Gabriel) Gifford OSB.

cosines[.]¹⁴⁹² These letters which I send you here for card Burgheses and your montsignor¹⁴⁹³ are not so well writen as we wishe but we have not [?] a better scribe for the present[.] God ever keepe you this 25 of marche the feast of the most glorious v¹⁴⁹⁴ 1614

yours ever Champney.

all our companie desire to be remembred in best manner to our Honorable frend Pole and my self in particular[.] Mr Griffin¹⁴⁹⁵ returnethe his to you. I must entreat you to endorse this letter.

No address

Endorsed: (1) Mart. 26. 1614; A Ch. answ. febr. 28°.

(2) Receaved. twesd. April. 15 [?].⎫
   Answ. frid. April. 25.   ⎬ 1614
   ⎭
   with one for burgh. one for my Monsignor.

---

¹⁴⁹² Thomas and John Roper.
¹⁴⁹³ John Baptist Vives.
¹⁴⁹⁴ Virgin.
¹⁴⁹⁵ Griffin Floyd.

INDEX

Names are given in the form in which they are most commonly written. Where an individual/topic appears in the text and in a related footnote, I have separately indexed the footnote citation only when it contains significant additional information about the cited individual/topic.